ACTS 6:1–8:4
THE AUTHOR'S METHOD OF COMPOSITION

SOCIETY
OF BIBLICAL
LITERATURE

DISSERTATION SERIES

edited by
Howard C. Kee
and
Douglas A. Knight

Number 41

ACTS 6:1–8:4: THE AUTHOR'S METHOD OF COMPOSITION
by
Earl Richard

Earl Richard

ACTS 6:1–8:4 THE AUTHOR'S METHOD OF COMPOSITION

Scholars Press

Distributed by
Scholars Press
PO Box 5207
Missoula, Montana 59806

ACTS 6:1–8:4
THE AUTHOR'S METHOD OF COMPOSITION
Earl Richard

Ph. D., 1976
Catholic University

Adviser:
James P. Clifton

Library of Congress Cataloging in Publication Data

Richard, Earl.
Acts 6:1–8:4.

(Dissertation series ; 41 ISSN 0145–2770)
Thesis—Catholic University.
Bibliography: p.
1. Bible. N.T. Acts VI, 1–VIII, 4—Criticism, interpretation, etc. I. Society of Biblical Literature. II. Title. III. Series: Society of Biblical Literature. Dissertation series ; 41.
BS2595.2.R48 226'.6'06 78–12926
ISBN 0–89130–261–1

Printed in the United States of America
1 2 3 4 5
Edwards Brothers, Inc.
Ann Arbor, Michigan 48104

TABLE OF CONTENTS

For Suzanne

ACKNOWLEDGEMENTS

This study finds its origin in a course taught by Professor James P. Clifton on the Acts of the Apostles. It is to a great extent due to his interest, encouragement, and assistance from that time on that I am now presenting the results of my research. Thus I would like to acknowledge my gratitude not only for help in pursuing this endeavor, but also for the graciousness with which this assistance was forthcoming.

I would also like to thank Peter Kearney both for his valuable criticisms and for his unfailing support as my academic adviser. My second reader, Frank Gignac, was most gracious with his assistance, particularly in philology. To all three this study is greatly indebted. However, the writer bears responsibility for any deficiencies therein.

In the long pursuit of this particular goal, a number of scholars have contributed generously of their time and effort in providing me with the background required for this study. I wish to thank Professors Martin Roberge (University of Ottawa: my introduction to Old and New Testament literature and languages); Samuel Iwry, Delbert Hillers, and Hans Goedicke (Johns Hopkins: Aramaic, Hebrew, and Coptic); Joseph Zalotay (Catholic University: New Testament Studies) and Paulinus Bellet (Catholic University: Coptic and especially for allowing me to use the as yet unpublished Coptic manuscript, G67). Special thanks is also due to Père Pierre Benoit of the École biblique de Jérusalem for giving generously of his time to discuss this subject with me. Finally a host of librarians should be mentioned here: from the École biblique for unlimited privileges in the summers of 1972-73; Johns Hopkins University; Catholic University of America; Lexington Theological Seminary; University of Kentucky; Hebrew Union College in Cincinnati; and the inter-library loan department of Berea College.

Thanks are also due to Berea College for providing me with

research and publication funds during the course of this project. Among the many people who have lent me their assistance, I should mention especially the following: Dr. William J. Schafer (for reading the manuscript), Mark Mueller (proofreading), Julia Weatherford (calligraphy), and my ever patient and conscientious typist, Janice Hensley.

To Suzanne, my wife, I wish to dedicate this research since she was a full partner in this endeavor from beginning to end. I am indebted to her many valuable suggestions, particularly in organizing the linguistic data into a typological corpus. Her help in methodology, research, and the tedious mechanics involved in the preparation of this project brought this dissertation to a successful conclusion.

ABBREVIATIONS

Abr.	Philo, On Abraham
Acts	Acts of the Apostles
Am	Amos
Ant.	Josephus, Antiquities of the Jews
Assump. Mos.	Assumption of Moses
BA	Biblical Archaeologist
Barn	Epistle of Barnabas
BASOR	Bulletin of the American Schools of Oriental Research
Beginnings	Foakes Jackson and Lake, eds., The Acts of the Apostles, The Beginnings of Christianity 5 vols.
Bib	Biblica
BL	Bibel und Leben
BT	The Bible Today
BTB	Biblical Theology Bulletin
BVC	Bible et vie chrétienne
BZ	Biblische Zeitschrift
CD	Damascus Document
Ch. Hist.	Eusebius, Church History
1/2 Chr	1/2 Chronicles
1/2 Cor	1/2 Corinthians
Dn	Daniel
Dt	Deuteronomy
Eph	Ephesians
1 Esd	1 Esdras
Est	Esther
EstBib	Estudios biblicos
ETL	Ephemerides Theologicae Loveniensis
Ex	Exodus
ExpT	Expository Times
Ez	Ezekiel
Gal	Galatians

Gn	Genesis
Heb	Hebrews
Hos	Hosea
HTR	*Harvard Theological Review*
Int	*Interpretation*
Is	Isaiah
Jb	Job
JBC	*Jerome Biblical Commentary*, eds. Brown, et al.
JBL	*Journal of Biblical Literature*
Jdg	Judges
Jdt	Judith
Jer	Jeremiah
JETS	*Journal of the Evangelical Theological Society*
Jn	John
Jos	Joshua
JQR	*Jewish Quarterly Review*
JTS	*Journal of Theological Studies*
Jub	*Book of Jubilees*
JW	Josephus, *Jewish War*
1/2 K	1/2 Kings
Lk	Luke
LL	*Living Light*
Lv	Leviticus
LXX	Septuagint
1/2/3/4 Mc	1/2/3/4 Maccabees
Migr. Abr.	Philo, *On the Migration of Abraham*
Mk	Mark
Moses	Philo, *On the Life of Moses*
MT	Masoretic Text
Mt	Matthew
Nb	Numbers
Neh	Nehemiah
NT	New Testament
NT	*Novum Testamentum*
NTS	*New Testament Studies*
OT	Old Testament
1/2 P	1/2 Peter

Ps	Psalms
1QapGn	*Genesis Apocryphon*
4QFlor	Florilegium
1QH	*Thanksgiving Psalms*
1QIsa	Isaiah Scroll
1QpHab	*Pesher on Habakkuk*
1QS	*Manual of Discipline*
4QTest	Testimonia
RB	*Revue biblique*
RE	*Review and Expositor*
Rev.	Revelation
Rm	Romans
RSR	*Recherches de science religieuse*
1/2 S	1/2 Samuel
Sir	Sirach (Ecclesiasticus)
Spec. Laws	Philo, *On Special Laws*
ST	*Studia Theologica*
TDNT	*Theological Dictionary of the New Testament*, ed. Kittel
TS	*Theological Studies*
TZ	*Theologische Zeitschrift*
VC	*Vigiliae Christianae*
Wis	Wisdom
Zech	Zechariah
Zeph	Zephaniah
ZNW	*Zeitschrift für die neutestamentliche Wissenschaft*
ZTK	*Zeitschrift für Theologie und Kirche*

CHAPTER I

BIBLIOGRAPHICAL INTRODUCTION

While this study proposes to limit itself to an examination of the Stephen material (Acts 6-8), it seems necessary, nevertheless, to situate it within the broader concerns of contemporary scholarship. In recent years, Luke-Acts has claimed much attention, and these works have become a veritable center of controversy.[1] That the situation has not always been thus will be demonstrated by a brief survey of critical scholarship devoted to the Acts of the Apostles.

The nature of this research seems to demand the following threefold plan. First, a survey of the principal stages of Acts research will summarize the important turning points of scholarly work, and will offer critical bibliography for these stages. Secondly, a short history of research relating to the speeches of Acts will be presented. Again, the principal objective will be an examination of the main concerns of scholarship, insofar as they shed light upon the purpose of this study. Thirdly, there will follow a discussion of scholarly opinion as it pertains to the Stephen material. This section will call for the greatest attention.

A. Principal Stages of Acts Research

From the outset the gospel of Luke and the Acts have enjoyed a separate existence, since they apparently entered the canon in their present condition, and have until recently received independent attention. The controversy concerning their relationship before their canonical acceptance need not

---

[1]William C. van Unnik, "Luke-Acts, a Storm Center in Contemporary Scholarship," in Studies in Luke-Acts: Essays Presented in Honor of Paul Schubert, eds. Leander E. Keck and J. Louis Martyn (Nashville: Abingdon Press, 1966), p. 15. See also Charles K. Barrett, Luke the Historian in Recent Study, Facet Books (Philadelphia: Fortress Press, 1970), p. 7.

detain us.[2] We need only glance at patristic literature to see that Acts fared poorly in comparison with the gospel. Commentaries devoted to the former are few in number, relatively late (Ephraim, Didymus the Blind, Theodore of Mopsuestia, Chrysostom, and a few later and minor ecclesiastical writers such as Isho'dad of Merv, Oecumenius, etc.), and have survived mainly in catenae. However, numerous quotations of Acts are found throughout patristic literature, the study of which has contributed greatly to our understanding of the early Church's use of the scriptures and has shed considerable light upon the history of textual transmission.

The period from the fourth century to the late eighteenth freely accepted the complete veracity both of the book and of tradition which ascribed this work to the physician Luke, the companion of Paul. The work does not seem to have enjoyed any special popularity, and its history can be briefly summarized as a series of translations and editions, along with the other books of the NT.[3]

> The traditional view remained unchanged until the close of the eighteenth century, when the Acts began to come under the same scrutiny that was given to the gospels and other writings of the New Testament by the awakening historical criticism of the day. It was evident at once to the critical eye that the book fulfilled in a very imperfect way the historical purpose which had been ascribed to it by tradition.[4]

---

[2]Ernst Haenchen, The Acts of the Apostles: A Commentary, trans. Robert McL. Wilson (Philadelphia: Westminster Press, 1971), p. 99, n. 1, states the problem in the following way: "Many (e.g., Torrey, Sahlin, Menoud, Trocmé) have surmised that Luke's work was once a single book, which was only divided 'when it was taken into the canon,' on which occasion the conclusion of Luke (24.50-3) and the beginning of Acts (1.1-5) were added"; confer also p. 139, n. 1. See the treatment of Werner G. Kümmel, Introduction to the New Testament, rev. ed., trans. Howard C. Kee (Nashville: Abingdon Press, 1975), pp. 157-59, for a more lengthy and detailed analysis of the variety of scholarly opinion on this subject.

[3]For a rather extensive list of ancient editions as well as early critical commentaries see Eugène Jacquier, Les Actes des Apôtres, Etudes bibliques (Paris: J. Gabalda, 1926), pp. viii-xiv. Furthermore, the early period is well summarized by Werner Bieder, Die Apostelgeschichte in der Historie: Ein Beitrag zur Auslegungsgeschichte des Missionsbuches des Kirche (Zurich: EVZ-Verlag, 1960), pp. 4-23.

[4]Arthur C. McGiffert, "The Historical Criticism of Acts

With the work of Michaelis, Griesbach, Eickhorn, Meyerhoff, and others, the study of Acts began to acquire more urgency.

After the initial stage of uncertainty, Acts research came to emphasize one of two approaches. In the words of Schwanbeck, scholars believed that either ". . . the author would not tell more or he could not."[5] Characteristic of the first approach was the Tendenzkritik of the Tübingen school at the beginning of the nineteenth century. The long, drawn-out battle[6] between the principal proponents of Tendency-criticism (Bauer, Zeller, J. Weiss, etc.) and its opponents (Schneckenburger, Bauer, Renan, Overbeck, etc.) has been sufficiently commented upon by McGiffert, Haenchen, and Wilson.[7] The demise of the Tübingen point of view did not prevent later scholars from gaining a number of lasting insights. From that time on, it has become necessary to view the Acts ". . . par le milieu et le temps qui les avaient produits."[8] Furthermore, it is com-

---

in Germany," in The Acts of the Apostles, The Beginnings of Christianity, part 1, gen. eds. Frederick J. Foakes Jackson and Kirsopp Lake, vol. 1: Prolegomena I: The Jewish, Gentile, and Christian Background, gen. eds. (1920); vol. 2: Prolegomena II: Criticism, gen. eds. (1922); vol. 3: The Text of Acts, by James H. Ropes (1926); vol. 4: English Translation and Commentary, by Kirsopp Lake and Henry J. Cadbury (1933); vol. 5: Additional Notes to the Commentary, eds. Kirsopp Lake and Henry J. Cadbury (1933); 5 vols. (London: Macmillan & Co., 1920-33), 2:363.

[5]Über die Quellen der Schriften des Lukas, 1847, p. 74 cited by McGiffert, "Criticism," p. 364, n. 1.

[6]A number of scholars in England participated in this polemic; see Joseph W. Hunkin, "British Work on the Acts," in Beginnings, 2:418ff.

[7]McGiffert, "Criticism," pp. 368ff., Haenchen, Acts, pp. 14-24, and Jack H. Wilson, "Luke's Role as a Theologian and Historian in Acts 6:1-8:3" (Ph.D. dissertation, Emory University, 1962), pp. 2-3. Note Haenchen's statement on p. 15, n. 7, that in his opinion the three following works provide the best survey of Acts research: McGiffert's article referred to above, the introduction to Loisy's great commentary, and finally Jacquier's introduction. See also Kümmel's rather lengthy treatment of Baur and his influence in The New Testament: The History of the Investigation of Its Problems, trans. Samuel McL. Gilmour and Howard C. Kee (Nashville: Abingdon Press, 1972), pp. 127-84.

[8]Alfred Loisy, Les Actes des Apôtres (Paris: Emile Nourry, 1920), p. 21.

monplace today to view Acts as the work of a theologian, of an author with a very distinct point of view. The recognition of this fact owes largely to the labors of Tendency-critics.

The second approach to Acts emphasized the author's inability to say more; in other words, the author had limited sources at his disposal when he composed his work. This restriction, scholars pointed out, would explain his less than accurate historical schema. Characteristic of this point of view is the method called source criticism. Haenchen describes the movement this way:

> This idea played a big part at the beginning of the nineteenth century. One hundred years later the question of sources again became a burning topic. On both occasions a spate of writings promptly poured forth. But soon the flow dwindled and at length it ceased altogether.[9]

Only the last sentence of the German scholar's statement, I believe, calls for modification, and this will be done later in the chapter. For a few excellent treatments of this long quest for sources, I would refer to the following authors: McGiffert[10] (Haenchen's work is admittedly derivative[11]), Loisy,[12] and Dupont.[13] The contributions of this new science are still contested. Dupont states: "Malgré les recherches les plus soigneuses et les plus minutieuses, aucune des sources utilisées par l'auteur des Actes n'a put être définie d'une manière qui rencontre un large accord parmi les critiques." However, the same author adds: "Ils ont mis en valeur les particularités

---

[9]Acts, p. 24.

[10]"Criticism," pp. 385ff. The author is particularly good in reviewing the earlier period of the movement, but is less successful in treating the later period, except for the role played by Harnack.

[11]Acts, p. 24. For the period he states: ". . . we shall make grateful use of his [McGiffert's] information." In the second period, however, Haenchen provides much new and pertinent bibliography, pp. 27-34 (here he seems to have drawn generously upon Loisy; see p. 15, n.7).

[12]Actes, pp. 17ff. His work is especially good for the evaluation of source criticism.

[13]Les sources du Livre des Actes: état de la question ([Bruges]: Desclée de Brouwer, 1960). Dupont's entire work, even though he divides the book into two sections, "La critique des sources" and "La critique des formes," is devoted to an evaluation of the entire range of source theories.

de la composition du livre et ces particularités autorisent à penser que l'auteur ne l'a pas écrit d'un seul jet."[14]

Following the period of source criticism in the last decades, dominated by the powerful figure of Harnack,[15] the study of Acts took a decidedly new turn. Authors such as Haenchen, Trocmé, Dupont, and Wilson[16] have called this the period of Form-criticism, and have particularly linked the name of M. Dibelius with this new phase (Trocmé less so).

> The year 1923 may be said to mark a turning point in the study of Acts. It had been the achievement of the liberal scholars, notably of Harnack and Johannes Weiss, to have finally overthrown the Tendenzkritik of F. C. Baur and the Tübingen school. But the study of Acts in the age of Harnack had been preoccupied with the question of literary sources and with the corresponding treatment of Acts itself as source material for the beginnings of Christianity.[17]

Historical reliability and the quest for sources receded into the background. Instead, greater attention was given to smaller, independent units and their structure. The work of Dibelius, though begun in the early twenties,[18] had little effect upon the scholarship of Acts until after his death and the advent of redaction criticism.

In certain academic circles, the work of the form critics and of Dibelius and Cadbury, in regards to Acts, was either ignored or summarily dismissed. The works of many French, English, and American authors until recently have been of just

---

[14]Ibid., p. 159.

[15]Etienne Trocmé, Le "Livre des Actes" et l'histoire, Etudes d'histoire et de philosophie religieuses, no. 45 (Paris: P.U.F., 1957), pp. 9-13, is tempted to call the research from 1905-30 "l'âge de Harnack," and reviews a long list of scholars such as Wellhausen, Norden, Loisy, Cadbury, and the authors of Beginnings in relation to the numerous concerns of the period.

[16]Haenchen, Acts, pp. 34-41; Trocmé, Livre des Actes, pp. 14-17; Dupont, Sources, pp. 9-14; and Wilson, "Theologian and Historian," pp. 4-5 and 11-14.

[17]Reginald H. Fuller, The New Testament in Current Study (London: CSM Press, 1962 and New York: Scribner's, 1962), pp. 104 and 92 respectively.

[18]See Haenchen, Acts, pp. 34-37 and 39-41 for an evaluation of the work of Dibelius; also Fuller, Current Study, pp. 104-7.

such a conservative nature, especially the commentaries.[19]

However, in the wake of the influence of Dibelius, Acts research has been most prolific. The works of Vielhauer, Conzelmann, and Haenchen are especially important in this regard.

> In these studies Luke appeared no longer as a somewhat shadowy figure who assembled stray pieces of more or less reliable information but as a theologian of no mean stature who very consciously and deliberately planned and executed his work. . . . Luke was not primarily a historian who wanted to give a record of the past for its own sake, but a theologian who, by way of historical writing wanted to serve the church of his own day amid the questions and perils that beset her. This "discovery" of Luke the theologian seems to me the great gain of the present phase of Luke-Acts study, whatever may be the final judgment about the character and importance of that theology.[20]

Another important characteristic of redaction criticism, both in regards to the gospels and to Acts, is the tendency to attribute greater and greater freedom and creativity to the author. Haenchen, in particular, holds for a remarkable degree of free composition by the author of Acts.[21] While he does not dismiss the idea of sources entirely, he tends to downplay the use of earlier traditions and would rather see a greater measure of creation by the author. It is precisely in the light of these presuppositions that we must understand his statement, quoted earlier, that source criticism has ceased to be of great concern.[22] C. K. Barrett has done a great service, in his

---

[19]The works of Clark, Easton, Knox, Torrey, Goguel, Jacquier, Bruce, Charles S. C. Williams, Dix, and others are briefly commented upon in Haenchen, Acts, pp. 37-39 and 41-43. He then concludes his study of the literature by discussing more recent scholars, such as Cadbury, Trocmé, Simon, Morgenthaler, and Conzelmann (pp. 43-49).

[20]Van Unnik, "Luke-Acts," pp. 23-24. See Bieder, Historie, pp. 45-55 for a good review of the works of the authors mentioned above, also confer p. 11, n. 40 below.

[21]He has expressed this conviction rather consistently throughout his commentary, has dealt with the problem more systematically in the long and valuable introduction especially from pp. 72-110, and, finally, has conveniently summarized his overall position in an article, "The Book of Acts as Source-Material for the History of Early Christianity," in Studies, eds. Keck and Martyn, pp. 258-78.

[22]Haenchen, nevertheless, considers the recent revival of source criticism at some length in later editions of his com-

evaluation of contemporary Acts scholarship, by contrasting Bultmann as the champion of sources and Haenchen as that of free composition. In his evaluation of Haenchen, he concludes:

> The moral of the dispute between the champion of written sources and the composition analyst seems, however, to be clear: the one fundamental error in this kind of study, not least as applied to Acts, is to neglect any possible relevant method. None may be excluded a priori. In each passage one must consider the possibility that Luke may have used a written source or sources, and interpolated his own redactional glosses; equally in each passage one must consider the possibility that oral traditions have been worked over, or that Luke has constructed a narrative on the basis of his general view of the situation and course of development.[23]

Haenchen's great contribution, as well as his methodological weakness, is the desire to see the author not so much as "a historian in our sense of the word," but as "a fascinating narrator" and, I might add, one who wishes to edify.[24]

The influence of Dibelius, however, has been felt in a completely opposite direction. Since it is precisely under his impetus that the author of Acts has been granted greater artistry and creativity in recent scholarship, it is only fitting that one of the strongest and most able advocates of source criticism in contemporary research, Trocmé, should have chosen the work of Dibelius for special consideration.[25] The French scholar is far from alone in seeing in the book of Acts numerous problems (contradictions, obvious sutures, doublets, constants, Semitisms,[26] etc.), which can only be dealt with in

---

mentary, "The Work Continues," Acts, pp. 116-32.

[23]"The Acts and the Origins of Christianity," in New Testament Essays (London: S.P.C.K., 1972), p. 107.

[24]Haenchen, "Source-Material," pp. 260, 258, and 278 respectively.

[25]See Haenchen's statement, Acts, p. 44, regarding Trocmé's work: "As indicated by the fifty-three references in the index, a running controversy is sustained against Dibelius . . ."

[26]The problem of Semitisms must be related to the attempt by Charles C. Torrey to find an Aramaic document for the first part of Acts. The work particularly of Max Wilcox, The Semitisms of Acts (Oxford: Clarendon Press, 1965) has brought this problem to the fore. Matthew Black's An Aramaic Approach to the Gospels and Acts, 3d ed. (Oxford: Clarendon Press, 1967),

light of source criticism.[27]

The study of Acts continues, at present, to investigate a wide range of problems.[28] A few recent and, doubtless, promising areas could be mentioned, such as the analysis of structure,[29] theological themes,[30] and authorship/historical setting;[31] however, only the research which has more direct interest for the present study has been considered. This has been done to provide the precise context within which our investigation of the Stephen material must be placed.

---

should also be mentioned in this connection.

[27]French scholars, in particular (Cerfaux, Dupont, Menoud, Benoit), as well as a number of American and British scholars, continue to emphasize the role which sources and traditions have played in the redaction of Acts.

[28]Two short but excellent bibliographical studies of recent work on Acts are I. Howard Marshall's "Recent Study of the Acts of the Apostles," ExpT 80 (1969): 292-96, and Barrett, Luke the Historian. The latter not only evaluates recent scholarly contributions, but also surveys avenues of future research. [It should be noted that Ward Gasque's book, A History of the Criticism of the Acts of the Apostles, Beiträge zur Geschichte der biblischen Exegese, no. 17 (Tübingin: Mohr, 1975), was not yet available when the above was terminated.]

[29]Pursuing the important work of Henry J. Cadbury [The Making of Luke-Acts (New York: Macmillan Co., 1927; reprint, London: S.P.C.K., 1961) and "Four Features of Lucan Style," in Studies, eds. Keck and Martyn, pp. 87-102, among other works] and Robert Morgenthaler [Die lukanische Geschichtsschreibung als Zeugnis: Gestalt und Gehalt der Kunst des Lukas, 2 vols. (Zurich: Zwingli-Verlag, 1949], Helmut Flender [St. Luke: Theologian of Redemptive History, trans. Reginald H. and Ilse Fuller (Philadelphia: Fortress Press, 1967)] and Charles H. Talbert [Literary Patterns, Theological Themes and the Genre of Luke-Acts, Society of Biblical Literature Monograph Series, no. 20 (Missoula, Montana: Society of Biblical Literature and Scholars Press, 1974)], among others, have directed their attention to the important problems of style and structure; see the survey of the literature in Talbert, ibid., pp. 1-5; 11-12 and Barrett, Luke the Historian, pp. 36-40, on Morgenthaler.

[30]Among the many studies devoted to significant themes of Luke-Acts, I note particularly: Charles F. D. Moule, "The Christology of Acts," in Studies, eds. Keck and Martyn, pp. 159-85; Schuyler Brown, Apostasy and Perseverance in the Theology of Luke, Analecta Biblica, no. 36 (Rome: Pontifical Institute, 1969), and Stephen G. Wilson, The Gentiles and the Gentile Mission in Luke-Acts, Society for New Testament Studies, Monograph Series, no. 23 (Cambridge: Cambridge University Press, 1973).

[31]In attempting to situate the Acts of the Apostles more firmly into its historical setting, scholars have reexamined

B. The Speeches of Acts

It would be possible to study the views of early critics concerning the speeches in Acts, their sources, nature, and role;[32] however, it is far more crucial for our purpose to examine the work done by three recent scholars: Dibelius and Cadbury on the one hand, and Dodd on the other.[33] As a result of the research of these scholars, considerable attention was paid to the speeches of Acts as distinct entities; but, also as a result of their work, two diverse trends became evident in the approach to the speeches. Dibelius and Cadbury[34] were perceptive enough to see that the speeches in Acts served a very similar function to speeches in the works of ancient historians, both in composition and situation (Cadbury further emphasized that this was also true to some extent in Jewish histori-

---

this question in a manner similar to Cadbury's *The Book of Acts in History* (New York: Harper and London: Adam & Charles Black, 1955). For example, J. C. O'Neill, *The Theology of Acts in Its Historical Setting*, 2d rev. ed. (London: S.P.C.K., 1970), compares Acts not to its Greek, Roman, Jewish, and Christian background but more specifically to early Christian writers, especially Justin. Aubrey W. Argyle, "The Greek of Luke and Acts," *NTS* 20 (1974): 441-45, also in quest of a more precise understanding of Acts and its historical setting, has reinvestigated on linguistic grounds the common authorship of Luke and Acts, reviving the work of Albert C. Clark, *The Acts of the Apostles: A Critical Edition with Introduction and Notes on Selected Passages* (Oxford: Clarendon Press, 1933; reprint, 1970).

[32]This has been done to some degree by Ulrich Wilckens, *Die Missionsreden der Apostelgeschichte form-und traditionsgeschichtliche Untersuchungen*, Wissenschaftliche Monographien zum Alten und Neuen Testament, no. 5, 3d rev. ed. (Neukirchen-Vluyn: Neukirchener Verlag des Erziehungsvereins GMBH, 1974), pp. 7-12.

[33]Richard F. Zehnle, *Peter's Pentecost Discourse: Tradition and Lukan Reinterpretation in Peter's Speeches of Acts 2 and 3*, Society of Biblical Literature Monograph Series, no. 15 (Nashville: Abingdon Press, 1971), pp. 13-14, gives a brief, but well-balanced survey of the research. Wilckens, *Missionsreden*, pp. 12-13, gives a longer, but less well-balanced historical view of the research. Like Haenchen, he does less than justice to the important research of Cadbury.

[34]The most important article of Martin Dibelius on the subject is "The Speeches in Acts and Ancient Historiography," in *Studies in the Acts of the Apostles*, ed. Heinrich Greeven, trans. Mary Ling (New York: Scribner's, 1956 & London: SCM Press, 1966), pp. 138-85. Cadbury has treated this problem in a number of works (e.g., "Speeches, Letters and Canticles," in

cal works).[35] Once the conclusion was reached that the speeches were not simply reproductions of ancient sources, but rather, to a large extent, the product of the author, later scholars no longer hesitated to examine the purpose and plan of these orations.

This movement did not take place until the late fifties and early sixties, due primarily to a very different trend in Acts research.[36] The influence of Dodd is hardly to be underestimated in this regard, despite the early research of Cadbury. In his classic work, The Apostolic Preaching and Its Developments,[37] Dodd advanced two very important conclusions. First, he maintained that the speeches of Acts had a similar schema and, secondly, that this outline was, in effect, the kerygma of the primitive Christian community. The former conclusion has spurred recent research into the structure of the speeches,[38] but the latter has fostered an historicist approach to the speeches which was adopted by numerous scholars. The important article of Charles F. Evans in 1956 succeeded in demonstrating

---

Making of Luke-Acts, pp. 184-93); however, his two major contributions are both to be found in Beginnings: the first in vol. 2 "The Greek and Jewish Traditions of Writing History," 1922, pp. 7-29 and the second in vol. 5 "The Speeches in Acts," 1935, pp. 402-27.

[35]For a very good recent discussion of historiography, both for the Hellenistic and Jewish elements, see Barrett, Luke the Historian, pp. 9-19. As might be expected, Barrett gives credit later in his work (pp. 26-30) to Dibelius for emphasizing the importance of classical models, but no mention is made of Cadbury for his lasting contribution in studying Jewish history in this regard--the same criticism can be made of Wilson, "Theologian and Historian," pp. 11-14. Instead, Barrett discusses at great length the work of Bertil Gärtner (1955) in this area (pp. 30-32).

[36]In Germany, no doubt, the delay was due in large measure to war conditions of the thirties and forties, but it must be remembered that Dibelius' major article on the subject (referred to above) did not appear until 1949. It is only a few years later that redaction criticism came to the fore.

[37](London: Hodder and Stoughton, 1936). For an evaluation of Dodd, see especially Wilson, "Theologian and Historian," pp. 7-11.

[38]The two most important studies are those of Eduard Schweiser, "Concerning the Speeches" in Studies, eds. Keck and Martyn, pp. 186-93, and Wilckens, Missionsreden.

the weakness of Dodd's historical conclusions.[39]

With the advent of redaction criticism and in the light of the early work of scholars such as Käsemann, Vielhauer, Conzelmann, and Haenchen,[40] the speeches of Acts became the center of attention. It became evident that these, more than any other part of the work, could contribute to the understanding of its author. Continuing in the direction indicated by Dibelius and Cadbury, biblical critics began seriously to study the speeches as the product of the author of Acts. While the vast majority of scholars hold that the author enjoyed great freedom in composing these sections of his work, the range of scholarly opinion varies considerably. Although Dibelius still maintained that these texts were reliable witnesses of the earliest theology of the church,[41] he believed that the speeches were interpolated by the author into a received narrative tradition. Recent scholars have adopted a more skeptical attitude in this regard. John A. T. Robinson, for example, argues that the theology and, therefore, the source of chapter three predates the writing of Acts, but that chapter two is a creation of the author.[42] Other scholars admit of few reliable traditions as a

---

39"The Kerygma," JTS 7 (1956): 25-41.

40The overall influence of these four authors is considerable, primarily in the effect their works have had on the direction and concerns of contemporary Luke-Acts research. While Ernst Käsemann has not written any major work on Acts, his theory that Luke-Acts is responsible for the introduction into the New Testament of "Early Catholicism" has been very influential [see especially his article: "Paul and Early Catholicism," in Essays on New Testament Themes, Studies in Biblical Theology, no. 41, trans. W. J. Montague (Naperville, Ill.: Allenson, [1964]) pp. 236-51]. Philipp Vielhauer has been particularly effective in establishing the fundamental differences between the Paul of the epistles and that of Acts (see his "On the 'Paulinism' of Acts" in Studies, eds. Keck and Martyn, pp. 33-50). It is primarily to the credit of Hans Conzelmann, The Theology of St. Luke, trans. Geoffrey Buswell (New York: Harper and Row, 1961), that redaction criticism was applied both to Luke and to Acts. Finally, the work and influence of Ernst Haenchen will be seen throughout this chapter and as a matter of fact the whole dissertation. For an evaluation of the contribution made by these authors to the study of Acts, see Barrett, Luke the Historian, pp. 40-50; Wilson, "Theologian and Historian," pp. 14-18; and Fuller, Current Study, pp. 86-100.

41"Speeches in Acts," p. 165.

42"The Most Primitive Christology of All?" JTS (1956): 177-89, also in Twelve New Testament Studies, Studies in Bib-

basis for the creation of Acts. Haenchen, for one, believes that the writer "made free with tradition"[43] both in the narratives and the speeches. Other exegetes argue for the generous use of sources or ancient traditions by the author in his work of composition. Advocates of source criticism obviously defend this position,[44] while numerous scholars seek many and sundry sources for the theology of the speeches.[45]

By far the most extreme position is advanced by U. Wilckens who, after examining the framework of the speeches, concludes against Dibelius that, not only are they not secondary interpolations into the narratives, but that they are perfectly suited to their context, so much so that it is necessary to see both the speeches and narratives as the work of the one author.[46] The German scholar's conclusions, however, are seriously contested:

> Nevertheless, the matter is far from being settled. Wilckens has to allow that the speech of Stephen is not amenable to his method of investigation. Further, he has to concede that the

---

lical Theology, no. 34 (London: SCM Press, 1962), pp. 139-53.

[43]Acts, p. 110.

[44]Trocmé, Livre des Actes, pp. 111, 152-53, 207f.; Pierre Benoit, "La deuxième visite de saint Paul à Jérusalem," Bib 40 (1959); 778-92, see especially p. 790; Dupont consistently in his Sources; see also his long critique of Wilckens' work in "Les Discours missionaires des Actes d'après un ouvrage récent," RB 69 (1962): 37-60.

[45]Too numerous to mention are the works seeking to find Aramaic or Hebrew sources or influences in Acts, since the work of Torrey [Hedley F. D. Sparks, "The Semitisms of the Acts," JTS 1 (1950): 16-28; Wilcox, Semitisms; John W. Bowker, "Speeches in Acts: A Study in Proem and Yallammedenu Form," NTS 14 (1967-68): 96-111; E. Earle Ellis, "Midrashic Features in the Speeches of Acts," in Mélanges bibliques en hommage au R. P. Béda Rigaux, eds. Albert Descamps and André de Halleux ([Gembloux]: Duculot, 1970), pp. 303-12; D. F. Payne, "Semitisms in the Book of Acts," in Apostolic History and the Gospel: Biblical and Historical Essays Presented to F. F. Bruce on His 60th Birthday, eds. W. Ward Gasque and Ralph P. Martin (Exeter Devon: Paternoster Press, 1970), pp. 134-50] or in reaction to Vielhauer attempting to seek in Paul the necessary background for a proper comprehension of Acts [Bertil Gärtner, The Areopagus Speech and Natural Revelation, Acta Seminarii Neotestamentici Upsaliensis, no. 21 (Uppsala: C.W.K. Gleerup, 1955); Peder Borgen, "Von Paulus zu Lukas," ST 20 (1966): 140-57].

[46]Missionsreden, p. 71.

> speeches addressed to the Gentiles in Acts 14 and 17 do show affinities with the pattern of preaching to Gentiles found in our other sources. Wilckens' claim that Luke constructed the pattern for the speeches to Jews in the first part of Acts on the analogy of the pattern for Gentiles probably falls short of proof. Nor has it been satisfactorily shown why Luke should have been so diligent in framing speeches for Jewish audiences if the Chruch of his day had given up evangelizing the Jews.[47]

Finally, Eduard Schweizer, fully in the tradition of Dibelius, has subjected the speeches ("which contain the missionary proclamation of the apostles to Jews and Gentiles") to a detailed structural analysis. He concludes that these speeches present ". . . a far-reaching identity of structure . . ." sufficient ". . . to show that one and the same author is decisively involved in the composition of all the speeches . . . investigated."[48] Schweizer's structural argument is decisive. But, he readily admits that the extent and identification of traditional material utilized by the author of Acts is another matter.[49]

The interest of contemporary scholars in the speeches of Acts goes beyond the limits of this present study, and this subject is intimately related to problems of the canon, the position of Luke-Acts theologically and historically within the early Church, etc. The subjects touched upon serve as needed background for the study of the Stephen story.

C. The Stephen Material in the History of Scholarship

The story of Stephen (his speech, trial, and death) marks a turning point in the systematic expansion of the Church,

---

47 Marshall, "Recent Study," p. 295. The above citation is a critique of the second edition (1963) of Wilckens' book. In fact, the author includes an analysis of Stephen's speech in the third edition (1974). However, it is my opinion that Marshall's observations remain valid for methodological reasons even for the latest edition. I will return to this subject in chapter four.

48 "Speeches," pp. 208, 210 and 212 respectively.

49 Ibid., pp. 210-11, 212, and 214. For a similar point of view see James P. Clifton, "Shaping the Kerygma: A Study of Acts," LL 10 (1973): 522-30, where the element of traditional content, in a fully structural context, is examined at length.

according to Acts, from Jerusalem, to Judaea and Samaria, and, finally, to the ends of the earth (1:8). This episode has received its share of scholarly attention; it is the goal of this part of the study to examine these contributions. To accomplish this objective I will proceed chronologically until the time of Harnack in the survey, then, owing to the diversity of scholarly opinion from that point on, adopt a topical approach.

1. Acts 6-8 as a Historical Document

From the earliest stages in the critical study of Acts, even the most liberal scholars (Gfrörer, Zeller, Harnack,[50] etc.) have been tempted to see in the Stephen story a privileged piece of authentic history. As a matter of fact, this section played an important part in the source schemes of the early nineteenth century and has, until the present, figured prominently in the reconstruction of early Christian history.

After the tentative beginnings of early source critics,[51] the scene was easily dominated by E. Schwanbeck's work, Über die Quellen der Apostelgeschichte of 1847. It is to this scholar's credit that he was able to perceive clearly enough the two directions in which Acts studies were heading, namely, the quest for sources and the examination of the author's purpose.[52] At the same time, it was Schwanbeck who gave definite form to the suggestions of earlier scholars. For him the author of Acts was a compiler who made use basically of four categories

---

[50]The editors [Foakes Jackson and Lake], "The Internal Evidence of Acts," Beginnings, 2:123, state: "Gfrörer thought that the compiler of Acts . . . used a collection of unhistorical legends arranged by a zealous Petrinist; this source covers Acts i-xii, and only the speech is of first-rate historical value." Of this same episode, Edward Zeller, The Contents and Origin of the Acts of the Apostles Critically Investigated, 2 vols., trans. Joseph Dare (London: Williams and Norgate, 1875-76), 1:237, writes: "The death of Stephen is incontestably the clearest point in the history of Christianity prior to Paul." With the Stephen story (Acts 6-8), in Adolf von Harnack's scheme of things, begins the trustworthy Antiochene source, see New Testament Studies, Part 3: The Acts of the Apostles (London: Williams and Norgate, 1909), pp. 162-202.

[51]The works of such scholars as Königsmann, Riehm, Gfrörer, Schleiermacher, etc., have been amply studied: Zeller, Contents, 2: 291-7; Foakes Jackson and Lake, "Internal Evidence," pp. 122-24; McGiffert, "Criticism," pp. 385f.; Dupont, Sources, pp. 52f.; Haenchen, Acts, pp. 24-26.

[52]See p. 3 above.

of sources. He had a biography of Peter (1:1-6:7; 8; 9:31-11:18), a biography of Barnabas (4:36f.; 9:1-30; 11:19-30; 12:25-14:28; 15:2-4), a memoir of Silas (15:14 to the end of Acts), and special sources (the martyrdom of Stephen: 6:8-7:59 and 8:2 and the council: 15:3-13).[53] With this hypothetical reconstruction, source criticism reached a high point both in theoretical complexity and in analytical skills.

There set in, however, a reaction to such research. The Tübingen school, under the inspiration of Ferdinand C. Baur, began in earnest the quest for the author's purpose.[54] E. Zeller, the great Tübingen scholar and disciple of Baur, studied at great length this new approach to Acts in a chapter entitled, "The Acts: A Tendency-Writing," and expressed succinctly the position of the school: ". . . the investigations already made have shown how much of the narratives before us must be laid to the score of the author, and how little of the episodes, additions, and alterations essential to the parallel between Paul and the original Apostles, can be the work of history or even of legend." Owing to the school's philosophy of history, the Acts of the Apostles became an excellent candidate to illustrate the dialectical process which occurred in early Christian history. Speaking for the Tübingen school, Zeller states: "According to all this, we can have no scruple in describing the tendency of the Acts as conciliatory, and itself as an attempt at mediation between Judaists and Paulinists."[55] Within this philosophical scheme the Stephen material played an important part.[56] Even though Zeller concedes that ". . . with

---

[53]This material was taken from Zeller, Contents, 2: 297-98, with the correction made by Dupont, Sources, p. 53, n. 1, namely, instead of "9:11-13:18" (misconstrued and falsely corrected by later scholars), we should read "9:31-11:18."

[54]See McGiffert, "Criticism," p. 124: "To them it appeared that any minute criticism of sources was unprofitable and unnecessary, and they passed on to develop their famous series of inquiries into the reason why Acts was written rather than into the method of its composition."

[55]Zeller, Contents, 2:139 and 154.

[56]It will be noted that Baur devoted an early work to the Stephen material: De oratione habita a Stephano consilio, Tübingen 1829. This book is entirely neglected and inaccessible.

this event we find ourselves for the first time on undeniably historical ground," he concludes: "Nevertheless, we must acquiesce in Baur's doubt as to its authenticity." The material, while it might depend upon earlier documents, fits so well into the work's tendency, and the style is so much in accord with that of the entire book, that Zeller feels that he must ascribe the work, in its present form, to the author alone.[57]

Beginning with the work of B. Weiss in 1886, the theory of sources once more came into prominence. The list of authors is too long[58] and, according to the editors of Beginnings, their research too unimportant to merit considerable attention.[59] Nevertheless, it will be noted that the new source critics concentrate their efforts upon the first part of Acts, and generally argue for parallel documents at the disposal of the author. Precisely in light of these new developments the doublets of the Stephen material acquired added importance, even to the extent of implying two sources for the speech.

> The least unreasonable analysis is that of Feine. He postulates a Jewish-Christian source containing vi.9-11, vii.22-28, 35-43, 51-56, 59-60, vii.1b, 2, and a Hellenistic source containing vi.12-14, vii.2-21, 29-34, 44-50, 57-58, viii.1a, 3.[60]

The renewed interest in source criticism reached its climax and classic formulation in the work of Adolf Harnack, whose theories dominated the study of Acts in the early twentieth century. He postulated parallel Jerusalem sources for most early chapters of Acts (A-source being of great historical value, B-primarily legendary) and a very reliable Antiochene source to which belonged, among other materials, the entire Stephen story.[61]

---

[57]Contents, 1:237, 241, and 315-16.

[58]For a critique of the views of Weiss, Sorof, Feine, Spitta, Clemen and others, see Haenchen, Acts, pp. 27-30.

[59]"Internal Evidence," pp. 124-25; confer also Bieder, Historie, pp. 36-37.

[60]Foakes Jackson and Lake, "Internal Evidence," p. 149, n. 1. Paul Feine's analysis is to be found in Eine vorkanonische Überlieferung des Lukas (Gotha: Friedrich Andreas Perthes, 1891), pp. 184-95.

[61]For a brief analysis of source studies as they relate to the Stephen story, see Rudolf Schumacher, Der Diakon Stephanus (Münster: Verlag der Aschendorffschen Buchbandlung, 1910),

2. Post-Harnack Scholarship

The influence of Harnack, although it continued to inspire a quest for sources of early Christian history and thought, began to diminish as a result of the stylistic and literary studies of Cadbury and the form and redaction insights of Dibelius. Because of these developments, the opinions regarding the Stephen material have become extremely diversified. To attempt a chronological survey of these theories would serve no purpose. Thus, it seems best to group recent views under four main categories, as they relate a) to the quest for sources; b) to composition; c) to the purpose, theology, place, and function of the speech; and d) to the identification of Stephen and the Hellenists.

a. Quest for Sources

The study of Acts in terms of source criticism has continued to the present. While the debate regarding the source or sources of the second part of the work can hardly be said to have abated,[62] that over the first half has been pursued with more satisfactory, though varied, results. For some scholars the anomalies of this work are explained by the theory of successive redactions: either revision by a later author of an older "Acts"[63] or translation and edition of an original "Aramaic Acts"[64] or even "successive rewritings" by the author him-

---

pp. 3-9.

[62]Dupont, Sources, has devoted the entire second part of his work, pp. 73f. to this problem; see also Haenchen, Acts, pp. 81-90 and Kümmel, Introduction, pp. 176-85.

[63]Eduard Norden, Agnostos Theos: Untersuchungen zur Formengeschichte religiöser Rede, 4th ed. (Stuttgart: Teubner, 1956), appendix 1: "Zur Komposition der Acte Apostolorum," pp. 311-32; and, in a much more systematic way, Loisy, Actes, proposes a complete revision of an earlier work by a later unknown author; so in reality the various inconsistencies, doublets, etc., are to be explained in terms of a second edition.

[64]It is the work of Charles C. Torrey, The Composition and Date of Acts, Harvard Theological Studies, no. 1 (Cambridge: Harvard University Press, 1916; New York: Kraus Reprint, 1969), proposing a single Aramaic source for the first half of Acts, which has brought this theory into prominence. Particularly through the study of mistranslation, the author sought to establish this thesis. In recent years this hypothesis has not won considerable approval, although it has stimulated the research into the problem of Semitisms in Acts (supra, nn. 26 and 45). Finally, and most recently, Harold Sahlin, Der Messias und das

self of his own work.[65] Other scholars still prefer to see parallel sources for chapters two-five of Acts,[66] and to defend some form of the Antiochene source for a large portion of the following chapters, to which source the Stephen story is assigned.[67] Finally, a number of scholars discard the concept of a continuous source or sources[68] and speak instead of a variety of fragments, whether oral or written, which the author used

---

Gottesvolk: Studien zur protolukanischen Theologie, Acta seminarii neotestamentici upsaliensis, no. 12 (Uppsala: Almquist & Wiksells, 1945), succeeded in combining the theory of a Semitic original and that of successive redactions. According to him, an earlier Judaeo-Christian text (Hebrew for Lk 1:5-3:7a and Aramaic for Lk 3:7b and following), consisting principally of Luke 1:5 to the end of Acts 15, was translated (agreeing with Torrey) and revised by a later Hellenistic Christian (p. 9). As regards the Stephen story, Sahlin holds the following as the work of Luke (i.e., the Hellenistic redactor): 7:2-50 and 7:58-8:5 in part (pp. 351-57). Finally, the author postulates a third edition at the time when the two works became part of the canon, namely, the addition of the introduction to Acts (1:1-5) as well as the ending of the gospel 24:50-3 (see especially pp. 9f.).

65 Benoit, "La deuxième visite," pp. 778-92, maintains, in his study of Acts 11, that Luke does in fact use numerous short documents, but that these are his own composition. In other words, he has reedited his own first draft, adding and expanding his work as he discovered new material. In a private conversation, Benoit indicated that the Stephen speech would have been added by Luke precisely during such a revision. Recently, Udo Borse, "Der Rahmentext im Umkreis der Stephanusgeschichte (Apg 6,6-11, 26)," BL 14 (1973): 187-204, has proposed a similar theory of redaction; see my comments on his methodology, infra, p. 304.

66 See Bo I. Reicke, Glaube und Leben der Urgemeinde: Bemerkungen zu Apg. 1-7, Abhandlungen zur Theologie des Alten und Neuen Testaments, no. 32 (Zurich: Zwingli-Verlag, 1957), especially pp. 55-108 for Acts 2-5.

67 Following upon the work of Harnack, both Joachim Jeremias, "Untersuchungen zum Quellenproblem der Apostelgeschichte," ZNW 36 (1937): 205-21, and Rudolf Bultmann, "Zur Frage nach den Quellen der Apostelgeschichte," in New Testament Essays: Studies in Memory of T. W. Manson 1893-1938, ed. Angus J. B. Higgins (Manchester: University Press, 1959), pp. 68-80, defend the traditional Antiochene source, bringing few changes to the position formerly held by Harnack. Bultmann, however, points out that the following texts within the Stephen story are interpolations: 6:12b-15 and 7:1-53 (p. 78).

68 Haenchen, Acts, p. 83, after discussing the Stephen story concludes: "We see, then, that here Luke had no continuous source at his disposal (the same holds for chapters 1 to 5)" and adds in a footnote: "This is now fairly generally admitted."

with lesser or greater literary freedom.[69]

b. Composition

Since theories regarding the composition of the Stephen story cover the entire range of possibilities, it is deemed necessary to consider separately both parts of the episode. I will direct my attention first to the narrative element, then to the speech, relating to each the conclusions of contemporary research.

1) Narratives

At a very early date, scholars noted the composite nature of the narrative material. Both the introductory (6:8-7:2a) and concluding (7:54-8:4) narratives were recognized as being composite in nature. While earlier source critics were content to assign these doublets to one or the other of the major sources of Acts,[70] later scholars, commenting solely upon the accusations (6:11-14), prefer to see the influence of the Synoptic trial narrative upon the composition of that of Stephen,[71] to understand the omission of certain elements from the trial of Jesus and their inclusion within the Stephen story as the work

---

[69]Trocmé, Livre des Actes, particularly pp. 183-91 and 191-207, renounces the theory of a continuous source, except for chapters 3-5, and prefers instead to see a variety of traditions which the author has used with considerable freedom. Haenchen, Acts, pp. 81-90 but especially p. 86, proposes the theory that the author had before him "a collection of reports" which he himself no doubt obtained from a variety of sources. On the one hand, Trocmé tends to multiply sources and to rely upon the author's fidelity to these; on the other, Haenchen is generally reluctant to admit of sources and lends the author a considerable amount of freedom. In regard to the Stephen material in particular, we would add that, to varying degrees, this is also the position of Johannes Bihler, Die Stephanusgeschichte im zusammenhang der Apostelgeschichte, Münchener theologische Studien, 1. Historische Abteilhung, no. 30 (Munich: M. Hueber, 1963) and Wilson, "Theologian and Historian."

[70]See p. 15 above.

[71]Trocmé, Livre des Actes, pp. 186-87; Marcel Simon, St. Stephen and the Hellenists in the Primitive Church, The Haskell Lectures, 1956 (London: Longmans, Green, [1958]), pp. 20-26; Haenchen, Acts, p. 274. At an earlier date Wilhelm Soltau, "Die Herkunft der Reden in der Apostelgeschichte," ZNW 4 (1903): 143, had proposed a rather elaborate process of influences: Jesus' trial had served Luke as a model for Stephen's martyrdom; however, he had then used the Stephen story to reedit his gospel account, thus bringing it into closer conformity with Mark.

of Luke,[72] or, expanding the investigation to the entire narrative, to regard the present composition as being fashioned upon the Synoptic materials about Jesus and traditional sources concerning Paul.[73]

Nevertheless, the death scene rather than the accusations has received the greater attention. In attempting to reconcile the composite nature of 7:54-60, scholarly opinion has been consistent in postulating a lynching scene (7:54-58a) and a trial scene (7:58b-60). Some source critics opted for one as historical over against the other,[74] but the majority concluded

---

[72]See Bihler, Stephanusgeschichte, pp. 11-16, but especially p. 16, where it is proposed that the modification of the temple saying into a two-fold statement of "eine destruktive Tendenz" on the part of Jesus and Stephen is deliberate. Loisy, Actes, p. 312, also admits of willful omission of certain elements from the gospel; however, his explanation is in terms of a later redaction: ". . . on peut soupçonner cette omission d'être le fait du rédacteur, Luc ayant coordonné implicitement à la parole attribuée à Jésus l'accusation portée contre Etienne, et le rédacteur, après avoir supprimé la parole dans l'evangile, n'ayant pas vu d'inconvénient à laisser subsister dans le présent récit une allusion qui devait échapper à ses lecteurs." Flender, St. Luke, pp. 128-29, also sees the parallelism between the death of Jesus and that of Stephen as being due to the author. See the discussion of this problem in chapter four (p.281--references to Trocmé, Foakes Jackson, and Talbert).

[73]Wilson, "Theologian and Historian," pp. 41-100, in a consistent way lends great freedom and creative imagination to the author in his use of tradition, and concludes his long analysis of the narratives: "The cumulative effect of the parallels in language and content is to lead one to suspect that Luke has fashioned much of his narrative by turning to characterizations of other important figures in his two-part work, particularly Jesus and Paul" (p. 100).

[74]The study of the Stephen material has not been free of historicizing tendencies. While it is not possible to survey the large number of works of this nature, two recent examples will suffice. Martin H. Scharlemann, Stephen: A Singular Saint, Analecta Biblica, no. 34 (Rome: Pontifical Institute, 1968), after conceding the possibility of a double tradition regarding the death of Stephen nevertheless concludes: "It is conceivable, to be sure, that these doublets only appear to be such. It may well be that Stephen was tried by the Sanhedrin, but that this official body lost control of the situation to a mob which intervened and rushed Stephen to his death" (p. 13). Such a statement reveals a lack of critical judgment in attempting to gloss over obvious textual difficulties (see Hans D. Betz's short but incisive review of this work in Int 23 (1969): 252). Even more recently, S. Dockx, "Date de la mort d'Etienne le Protomartyr," Bib 55 (1974):73, after opting for a trial

that the present text of Acts was the result of the conflation by a compiler of different sources.[75] In recent years it is the lynching scene theory which has received the strongest support,[76] even though a large number of scholars has come to the defense of the trial hypothesis.[77] Haenchen's statement can be

---

scene nevertheless adds: "Cette exécution attire une foule tumultueuse, hostile à Etienne." In this way, he is able to maintain the historicity of both the trial and mob elements of the text; but this he has done at the expense of critical textual analysis and by means of, in my opinion, arbitrary deletion of problem texts; see pp. 66 and 72. For similar attitudes see also the analyses of Arnold Ehrhardt, The Acts of the Apostles: Ten Lectures (Manchester: Manchester University Press, 1969), p. 32; Reicke, Glaube und Leben, pp. 171-74; and Wilson, Gentiles, p. 137.

[75]Dockx, "Date," p. 65, summarizes the status of scholarly opinion: "Au sujet de la mort d'Etienne la critique des sources avait soutenu trois position: 1°--la source de Luc rapportait une émeute populaire contre Etienne qui aurait finalement été lapidé par la populace; Luc aurait ajouté tous les détails concernant le porcès devant le Sanhédrin (ainsi B. B. Weiss, 1889; H. H. Wendt, 1913; J. Bihler [sic!], 1957; E. Haenchen, 1959); 2°--la source de Luc rapportait l'historie du procès intenté contre Etienne par les autorités juives; Luc serait responsable de la mise en scène de la populace (ainsi A. Loisy, 1920); 3°--Luc aurait eu à sa disposition deux sources: l'une faisant mention d'un procès devant le Sanhédrin, l'autre d'une émeute populaire dont Etienne aurait été la victime (ainsi P. Feine, 1891; F. Spitta, 1891; J. Jungst, 1895; J. Weiss, 1897; A. Harnack, 1906; O. Bauerfeind, 1939; G. Stahlin, 1966)." See an almost identical statement in Haenchen, Acts, p. 273.

[76]Trocmé, Livre des Actes, p. 186, opts for the author's modification of a mob scene which he received from tradition into a trial. O'Neill, Theology, also concludes that "Stephen's prophetic denunciation of God's people . . . is probably formalized by being made part of a trial scene . . ." (p. 95) and in discussing the doublets of the death scene states: "The stoning is mentioned again to show that this is a judicial execution, in which the witnesses rolled stones down on the man they had first thrown over the cliff" (p. 92).

[77]The attempts of numerous scholars to defend the trial hypothesis by reference especially to the Mishnaic tract "Sanhedrin" [Theodor von Zahn, Die Apostelgeschichte des Lucas, Kommentar zum Neuen Testament, no. 5 (Leipzig: A. Deichert, 1919), pp. 264f.; Karl B. Bornhäuser, Studien zur Apostelgeschichte (Gütersloh: Bertelsmann, 1934), pp. 71-88; Joachim Jeremias, "Zur Geschichlichkeit des Verhörs Jesu vor dem Hohen Rat," ZNW 43 (1950-53):145-50] or to historical considerations [for example Dockx, "Date"] have done this with little attention paid to textual problems. Bo Reicke, to cite but one example, in The New Testament Era: The World of the Bible from 500 B.C. to A.D. 100, trans. David E. Green (Philadelphia: Fortress Press, 1968), particularly pp. 145 and 191, combines

quoted as typifying present opinion:

> In chaps. 6-8:3 two accounts are clearly mingled: the stoning of Stephen by an unruly crowd and his execution by the High Council. This second item was probably introduced by Luke himself; in his eyes the Sanhedrin was always the real enemy of the Christians and at the same time this detail furnishes him the needed audience for the extended speech of Stephen.[78]

2) Speech

Opinions regarding the lengthy discourse also vary greatly. In terms of its composition, scholars have proposed a wide range of possibilities. For some the speech is pre-Lukan without any doubt. It is taken over from Alexandrian Hellenism[79] or the Hellenism of the Diaspora.[80] However, few modern scholars would insist that the speech was a copy of Stephen's defense. Instead, owing to difficulties raised by the apparent lack of relationship between the accusations and the alleged response, authors began to subject the speech to closer scru-

---

Mishnaic with historical reasons to defend a rather over-simplified and historicist view of the Stephen episode (see p. 20, n. 74 above). It is obvious that such attempts have won little acceptance. In recent years, considerable attention has been given to various problems relating to the trial of Jesus, and, as a consequence, numerous statements have been made regarding the trial of Stephen, see Joseph Blinzler, Der Prozess Jesu, 3d ed. (Regensburg: Verlag Friedrich Pustet, 1960), particularly appendices 7, 8, and 10, none of which is in the 1959 English edition; Paul Winter, On the Trial of Jesus, Studia Judaica, no. 1 (Berlin: Walter de Gruyter & Co., 1961); and most recently, The Trial of Jesus: Cambridge Studies in Honour of C.F.D. Moule, ed. Ernst Bammel (London: SCM Press, 1970). Finally, I would note that Bihler, first in his 1957 dissertation, then in the reproduction of part of this work in BZ 31 (1959):252-70, and then in 1963, Stephanusgeschichte, opts for an original trial scene after referring to the works of Jeremias and Blinzler (Dockx to the contrary, see p. 21, n. 75 above).

78"Source-Material," p. 264. Note a very similar conclusion in Hans Conzelmann, Die Apostelgeschichte, Handbuch zum Neuen Testament, no. 7, 2d ed. (Tübingen: Mohr, 1972), p. 59.

79Leslie W. Barnard, "Saint Stephen and Early Alexandrian Christianity," NTS 7 (1960-61):31-45, especially pp. 31 and 44-45, where it is stated: "Possibly Stephen originally belonged to the more liberal wing of the hellenistic synagogue in the Egyptian metropolis."

80Simon, Stephen, p. 40, affirms: ". . . we are, I think, entitled to admit that it expresses what can be called the Hellenist tradition of thought."

tiny.[81] Still retaining the theme of the accusations as central to the problem, some have proposed that only part of the speech is pertinent to the defense and, therefore, from the source. The remainder of the material would have been introduced by the author.[82] Others, however, have given up the idea that the speech is a defense[83] and instead attribute to the author either the total composition of the speech or the revision of an older document. These scholars variously describe chapter seven as a typical martyr's apologia,[84] a synagogue

---

[81]Haenchen, Acts, pp. 286-88, for a treatment of this topic.

[82]Hans H. Wendt, Die Apostelgeschichte, Kritisch-exegetischer Kommentar, Part 3 (Göttingen: Vandenhoeck & Ruprecht, 1899), pp. 149f., and again "Die Hauptquelle der Apostelgeschichte," ZNW 24 (1925):296, notes that the Moses-Jesus parallel (7:23-29 and 35-43) is a later addition to the original source. Werner Foerster, "Stephanus und die Urgemeinde," in Dienst unter dem Wort: Festgabe für H. Schreiner (Gütersloh: Bertelsmann, 1953), p. 27, however, insists that only the section dealing with Moses is from Stephen while the rest is a Lukan composition based on material received from Philip. Burton S. Easton, in Early Christianity: The Purpose of Acts and Other Papers, ed. Frederick C. Grant (London: S.P.C.K., 1955), particularly "A Note on Stephen's Speech," pp. 115-18 (the article "The Purpose of Acts" was delivered as a lecture in 1935 and published by S.P.C.K. in 1936), argues that there were two charges made against Stephen, one concerning the law and the other about the temple, the second of which seems secondary, vv.44-50. This last piece could be omitted entirely from the speech.

[83]Frederick F. Bruce in The Speeches in the Acts of the Apostles (London: Tyndale Press, [1943]), pp. 21f., and again The Acts of the Apostles (London: Tyndale Press, 1953), pp. 160-61, recognizes that the speech is not "a forensic defence"; however, he stoutly maintains that this speech and the others as well, are faithful renderings of the original speeches. Bruce concludes his analysis of the speeches with the following implausible statement: "Taken all in all, each speech suits the speaker, the audience, and the circumstances of delivery; and this, along with other points we have considered, gives good ground, in my judgment, for believing these speeches to be, not inventions of the historians, but condensed accounts of speeches actually made, and therefore valuable and independent sources for the history and theology of the primitive Church," Speeches, p. 27.

[84]Luke, according to Wilhelm Mundle, "Die Stephanusrede Apg. 7: eine Märtyrerapologie," ZNW 20 (1921):133-47, has composed and strategically situated a typical martyr's apology to comment upon a problem faced by the Church of his generation.

sermon,[85] or more precisely the revision of an older text: an earlier Ebionite Acts,[86] a neutral synagogue sermon,[87] (even

---

[85]Hans W. Surkau, Martyrien in jüdischer und frühchristlicher Zeit, Forschungen zur Religion und Literatur des Alten und Neuen Testaments, Neue Folge, no. 36 (Göttingen: Vandenhoeck & Ruprecht, 1938), pp. 105-10.

[86]Already (German edition 1854) Zeller [Contents, 2:176, n. 1] in a footnote had drawn attention to Ebionite parallels to the Stephen story: "Our narrative has likewise a striking resemblance to the Ebionite legend of the death of James the Just," and had concluded: "The coincidence, which is scarcely likely to be accidental, proves at any rate how much our narrative is according to Ebionite taste." However, Hans-Joachim Schoeps, Theologie und Geschichte des Judenchristentums (Tübingen: Mohr, 1949), has posited an Ebionite origin for the Stephen story and speech. According to him, the figure of Stephen has been invented by Luke as a substitute for James, whose ideas, in modified form, he has incorporated into the speech (pp. 440f.). The introduction of Stephen is an attempt, according to Schoeps, to minimize, by means of a middle position, the tension between James and Paul. His source for this material, both martyrdom and speech, is an Ebionite Acts of the apostles which he has attempted to reconstruct from pseudo-Clementine writings (pp. 381f.). Schoeps has returned to this subject numerous times: Urgemeinde Judenschristentum Gnosis (Tübingen: Mohr, 1956), pp. 12f.; "Die ebionitioche Wahrheit des Christentums," in The Background of the New Testament and Its Eschatology: In Honour of C. H. Dodd, eds. William D. Davies and David Daube (Cambridge: Cambridge University Press, 1956), pp. 115-23; Das Judenchristentum (Bern: A. Francke, 1964), pp. 40f.; and "Das Judenchristentum in den Parteienkämpfen der alten Kirche," in Aspects du Judéo-Christianisme, Colloque de Strasbourg, 23-25 avril 1964 (Paris: P.U.F., 1965), pp. 62f.

[87]Dibelius, "The Speeches in Acts," pp. 167-70, proposes the thesis that Luke draws from a Hellenistic synagogue source a recital of the history of Israel, and that the polemic passages: 7:35-43, 44-50, and, of course, the diatribe 51-53, are to be ascribed to him. Thus, he ". . . introduces the conflict between Christianity and Judaism by means of Stephen's speech in a characteristic manner appropriate to the circumstances," p. 170. In his monumental commentary, Haenchen (Acts, pp. 288-89) proposes an almost identical analysis: verses 35, 37, 39-43, and 48-53 are additions by Luke to "a history-sermon" or "a neutral presentation of sacred history which he has taken over en bloc." (See chapter four of this study for a detailed examination of this theory.) In full agreement, see Conzelmann, Apostelgeschichte, pp. 57-58; Traugott Holtz, Untersuchungen über die alttestamentlichen Zitate bei Lukas, Texte und Untersuchungen zur Geschichte der altchristlichen Literatur, no. 104 (Berlin: Akademie-Verlag, 1968), pp. 86ff. (who sees editorial activity also at 7:6-7, confer pp. 98-99) and Wilckens, Missionsreden, p. 217, n. 1 (see also p. 210 where he insists upon the editorial nature of 7:17a--dependent upon the Göttingen dissertation of R. Storch, Die Stephanusrede Acta

the homily of an Alexandrian synagogue[88] or a document reporting the martyrdom of a Jewish prophet),[89] or ". . . a long fragment of a Christian retelling of Israelite history," product of the mission to Samaria.[90] Still others insist that the speech is a creation of the author of Acts, who, much in the style of the classical authors,[91] has drawn heavily upon the Synoptic tradition and the LXX version of Israel's history.[92]

7.2-52, 1967, which work I have not been able to consult).

[88]For Soltau, "Herkunft," pp. 144f. and especially pp. 152-53, the Stephen speech as well as those of Peter (chapters 2 to 4) and Paul (chapter 13) was drawn by Luke from an Alexandrian homily.

[89]O'Neill, Theology, pp. 89-94, after noting that there are but four references to Jesus in the entire Stephen story, namely, 6:14, 7:52, 7:55b, 7:59, and after eliminating these as later interpolations, concludes that Stephen was in fact a non-Christian Jewish prophet. The account of his martyrdom and speech were used by Luke in composing Acts simply by identifying Stephen the prophet with Stephen the Hellenist (pp. 93-94).

[90]Robin Scroggs, "The Earliest Hellenistic Christianity," in Religions in Antiquity: Essays in Memory of Erwin Ramsdall Goodenough, ed. Jacob Neusner (Leiden: Brill, 1968), pp. 176-206, holds that the entire speech except vv. 50-53 was taken over by Luke from a Hellenistic missionary source, product of the mission to the Samaritans, and was situated within the Stephen story, ". . . although he reworked the language to conform to his own style" (p. 183); see especially pp. 182, no. 3 and 183-84.

[91]Confer p. 9, n. 34 above on Cadbury and Dibelius.

[92]Bihler, Stephanusgeschichte, p. 86 (see also pp. 19 and 28); see Wilson, "Theologian and Historian," pp. 165ff. and p. 244, where he presents, in cautious terms, the following conclusions: "It has already been shown that Luke has touched almost every aspect of the speech, and one can assume that there are no parts of it which conflict with his own standpoint. Thus, whether he actually compiled this particular set of facts or found them already collected by someone else is inconsequential in view of what he does with them." I would also note that Georges Duterme ["Le Vocabulaire du Discours d'Etienne AA. VII.2-53" (Licence en Théologie thesis, University of Louvain, [1950]), who concludes from his detailed study of the vocabulary of the speech that Luke is the author and, on p. 28, further asserts: "Chaque section du discours, aussi bien les citations que les parties narratives, trahissent la main de Luc pour qui s'attache à les lire attentivement. Une comparaison d'ensemble avec le vocabulaire de l'oeuvre de Luc confirme cette impression."] and Mundle ["Stephanusrede," who surmised as early as 1921 that the discourse was a composition of Luke and, on p. 135, presented an impressive list of lexical and stylistic parallels between ch. 7 and Acts primarily] defend similar points of view.

In light of the above survey, we can only conclude that there exists very little agreement among scholars concerning the origin and nature of the Stephen speech. In fact, the above-listed theories, with considerable variations, represent the entire spectrum of possibilities: the discourse a) is borrowed wholly from tradition, b) is the result of slight/considerable editing, or c) is a total creation of the author.[93]

At this point it is necessary to treat of a recurring problem related to the speech, that is, the question of interpolation. Initially, the observations made in this regard concerned primarily the continuity of the narrative. Scholars observed that, were the speech to be eliminated, the narrative would regain its cohesiveness.[94] However, the works of Cadbury and Dibelius inspired a new approach to interpolation, namely, that the speech, far from being an intrusion, was placed in its position by the author himself. Either the author introduced the long discourse[95] secondarily into the narrative which he had received from tradition,[96] or else he composed a narrative to serve as the context of the speech.[97]

---

[93]I will return to this subject at greater length in chapter four.

[94]Foakes Jackson and Lake, "Internal Evidence," p. 150; Foakes Jackson "Stephen's Speech in Acts," JBL 49 (1930):284-85, and idem, The Acts of the Apostles, The Moffatt New Testament Commentary (London: Hodder and Stoughton, 1931), p. 58.

[95]Loisy, Actes, pp. 318-19, naturally attributes the interpolation of the speech into the narrative to his redactor. Bultmann, "Zur Frage," p. 78, simply states that the speech, along with 6:12b-15, are added by the author to his Antiochene source. See also Wilckens, Missionsreden, p. 209.

[96]Dibelius, "Speeches In Acts," p. 168. For Benoit also (private conversation, see p. 18, n. 65 above), the speech is a later addition by the author. An interesting statement of Barrett, "Acts and Origins," p. 110, should be cited in this context: "The origin of the speech is a special problem. . . . Possibly it belongs to the debates which took place between Christian and non-Christian Jews; in this case it would interestingly enough, belong to the historical, though not to the Lucan origin of the Seven. But in no case does it belong to the trial scene." Note a very similar position in Cadbury, Book of Acts, p. 106.

[97]Trocmé, Livre des Actes, pp. 186-87, insists that the narrative, dependent primarily upon synoptic materials, is the work of Luke, who made this serve as the context for the Stephen speech. Simon, Stephen, also agrees that the narrative is a Lukan composition (p. 4) while the speech is pre-Lukan (p.39).

c. Purpose, Theology, Place, and Function of the Speech

Since the above considerations have been limited to the sources and composition of the Stephen story, I have been forced to delay discussion of the motivating impetus behind this continuous research. As authors began to examine more closely the theology or purpose of Acts,[98] opinions regarding the Stephen material showed a decided change. No longer were authors willing to see in the speech a verbatim report of Stephen's defense. Instead, they began to examine the purpose or theme of the text. As the themes began to multiply and the dissatisfaction regarding the relation of the speech to the surrounding narrative became more manifest, scholars began to investigate more seriously the place and function of the speech, as well as the story of Stephen, within the book of Acts and to relate these to the purpose and theology of the author. The speech, as well as the entire Stephen episode, has been variously represented as an attempt by the author to comment upon the relation of Christianity to Judaism,[99] to reverse the accusations and thereby launch an attack upon Judaism,[100] to describe in a graphic way a new stage in the development of

---

[98]Kümmel, Introduction, pp. 160-73, devotes a considerable amount of attention to what he calls the "literary distinctiveness and theological character of Acts." He presents a convenient collection of the variety of scholarly views in this regard; but since the opinions are not viewed in their historical context, the work proves less than satisfactory for our purpose.

[99]Benjamin W. Bacon, "Stephen's Speech: Its Argument and Doctrinal Content," in Biblical and Semitic Studies (New York: Scribner's, 1901), p. 227; Bruce, Acts, p. 160; Richard B. Rackham, The Acts of the Apostles: An Exposition (London: Methuen, 1957), p. 87; Dibelius, "Speeches in Acts," pp. 169-70. Note also Barrett's statement above, p. 26, n. 96.

[100]Wilfred L. Knox, The Acts of the Apostles (Cambridge: Cambridge University Press, 1948), p. 23 concludes: "The speech of Stephen . . . is concerned to point out that from the beginning the Jews have misunderstood their religion. . . ." Cadbury, Book of Acts, p. 102 states: "Although it is reported as delivered as a defence from Jewish charges against Stephen it is in fact Stephen's charges against the Jews." Haenchen, Acts, p. 289: "His speech must therefore deal with this history [of Israel] and show that the Jews have 'always resisted the Holy Spirit' (7.51)." See also Hanechen, "Source-Material," p. 264.

Christian history, namely, the mission to Samaria,[101] or to present Stephen in a typological way.[102] Other scholars, addressing themselves to more structural considerations, view the discourse as a companion piece to Paul's speech either in Antioch[103] or in Athens,[104] or regard 6:8-8:4 as architecturally equivalent to 14:19-23.[105]

d. Identification of Stephen and the Hellenists

The final area of scholarly research to be considered here is that of the identity of Stephen, and the much-discussed problem of the meaning of "Hellenists." Within the context of the purpose and theology of Acts, some older scholars saw in Ste-

---

[101]William Manson, The Epistle to the Hebrews: An Historical and Theological Reconsideration, The Baird Lecture, 1949 (London: Hodder and Stoughton, 1951), p. 27; Maurice Goguel, The Birth of Christianity, trans. H. C. Snape (London: Allen & Unwin, 1933 and New York: Macmillan Co., 1954), pp. 172-76; Trocmé, Livre des Actes, p. 183; O'Neill, Theology, pp. 94-95. It should be noted that the work of Manson on the Epistle to the Hebrews has stimulated further research on the relation between the Stephen story and that work [e.g., C. P. M. Jones, "The Epistle to the Hebrews and the Lucan Writings," in Studies in the Gospels: Essays in Memory of R. H. Lightfoot, ed. Dennis E. Nineham (Oxford: Basil Blackwell, 1955); see especially pp. 123f. and 141; and Clayton K. Harrop, "The Influence of the Thought of Stephen upon the Epistle to the Hebrews" (Ph.D. dissertation, Southern Baptist Seminary, Louisville, Kentucky, 1955)].

[102]Bacon, "Stephen's Speech," pp. 248f.; Richard P. C. Hanson, "Studies in Texts (Acts 6.12-14)," Theology 50 (1947): 142f.; The Acts in the Revised Standard Version with Introduction and Commentary (Oxford: Clarendon Press, 1967), pp. 96f.; Charles S. C. Williams, A Commentary on the Acts of the Apostles, Black's New Testament Commentaries (London: Adam & Charles Black, 1957), pp. 104f.; Foerster, "Stephanus," pp. 22f.

[103]Soltau, "Herkunft," pp. 139-40.

[104]Bihler, Stephanusgeschichte, p. 185. Albertus F. J. Klijn, "Stephen's Speech-Acts VII.2-53," NTS 4 (1957-58):25, gives a list of theories relating to the meaning of the speech with ample bibliography in the notes.

[105]Talbert, Patterns, pp. 23-24. Furthermore, the parallelism is to be situated within the author's overall plan of Acts: "The correspondences between Acts 1-12 and 13-28 include a loose parallelism of content and sequence along with certain similarities which do not occur in any specific order," p. 23. As an example of the latter, Talbert indicates the similarities between the accusations of 6:13-14 (against Stephen) and 21:20-21; 25:8 (against Paul), p. 24.

phen a forerunner of Pauline Christianity.[106] Others, arguing from the account of Stephen's ideas as given in the speech, variously identify him as a Hellenist, stressing his Greek culture,[107] or as a Palestinian Jew, stressing instead his Hebrew background.[108] However, it is around the term Ἑλληνισταί that the greatest controversy has centered. The history of the problem in modern research is approximately as follows. In 1933 Cadbury began his now classic article, "The Hellenists," by noting that ". . . Ἑλληνιστής is not a common word in the Greek of the age that we call Hellenistic, and its first occurrences do not testify without ambiguity to the generally accepted definition: 'a Hellenist is a Greek-speaking foreigner, specifically a Greek-speaking Jew,'"[109] Instead, he proposed that the term referred to Gentile Christians. While it is not the purpose of this brief survey to evaluate the merits of either position, suffice it to say that Cadbury's conclusion has not been well received, since the evidence from Acts seems to demand that these Hellenists be Jews. The generally ac-

---

[106]Charles Guignebert, Le Christ: L'évolution de l'humanité, Synthèse collective, no. 29 bis (Paris: Albin Michel, 1943), pp. 75f. and 126; Rackham's statement (Acts, p. 88) is interesting in this regard: "S. Stephen then is the connecting link between S. Peter and S. Paul--a link indispensable to the chain. Stephen, and not Gamaliel, was the real master of Paul. . . . For 'the work' of Stephen lasts on till chapter xii (see xi.9), and then it is taken up by his greater pupil and successor--Paul."

[107]Barnard, "St. Stephen," pp. 31-45 (culture of Alexandria); Loisy, Actes (the redactor is a Hellenist writing for the Community of Rome, see especially pp. 104f.); Goguel, Birth (the distinction between Hebrews and Hellenists is one of language, p. 190); Simon, Stephen (". . . the term Hellenists, as used by Luke, includes all Greek-speaking Jews, whether already converted, as in the case of the Seven, or still opposing the Christian message," p. 15).

[108]Gerhard Friedrich, "Die Gegner des Paulus im 2. Korintherbrief," in Abraham unser Vater: Juden und Christen im Gespräch über die Bibel: Festschrift für Otto Michel zum 60. Geburtstag, ed. Otto Betz, Martin Hengel and Peter Schmidt (Leiden: Brill, 1963), pp. 181-215, finds a close relation between Paul's Jewish opponents of 2 Corinthians and the Hellenists of Acts 6-7 (pp. 196f.). The scholars who identify the Hellenists with the Essenes insist also upon their Jewish background, confer p. 30, n. 112 below.

[109]In Beginnings, 5:59.

cepted position today is that stated by C. F. D. Moule in 1959 (basically a reformulation of the old definition), i.e., that ". . . 'Greek-speaking' [be understood] as 'speaking-(only) Greek', in contrast to Jews who also spoke a Semitic language."[110]

In more recent years a number of scholars have pursued the notion--which forms the basic objection to Cadbury's position stated above--that the Hellenists in Acts, as demanded by the context, must be Jewish. One line of thought, reviving the suggestions of E. Zeller,[111] has attempted to identify Stephen and the Hellenists with the covenanters of Qumran.[112] A second

---

[110]"Once More, Who Were the Hellenists?" ExpT 70 (1958): 102; Note also Jan N. Sevenster, Do you Know Greek? How Much Greek Could the First Jewish Christians Have Known?, Supplements to Novum Testamentum, no. 19 (Leiden: Brill, 1969), pp. 32-33. Bo Reicke, Glaube und Leben, pp. 116-17, adopts a compromising solution: the Helenists are proselytes. For a brief survey of the scholarship, see "Ἕλλην" by Hans Windisch, especially pp. 511-12 in TDNT, 2 (1964). Confer also the lengthy discussion of the identity of the Hellenists and of the theological-political problem which caused the difficulties in the Jerusalem community, Walter Schmithals, Paul and James, Studies in Biblical Theology, no. 46, trans. Dorothea M. Barton (Naperville, Ill.: Allenson, 1965), especially chapter 1: "Stephen," pp. 16-37 and most recently an article by Martin Hengel, "Zwischen Jesus und Paulus: Die 'Hellenisten,' die 'Sieben' und Stephanus (Apg 6,1-15; 7,58-8,3)," ZTK 72 (1975):157-72), who, in surveying at length the opinions regarding this problem, ends with Moule's article noted above.

[111]Confer Pierre Géoltrain, "Esséniens et Hellénistes," TZ 16 (1959):241-54 for the history of this problem in scholarship.

[112]Oscar Cullmann, in a number of studies, but particularly in "L'opposition contre le temple de Jérusalem, motif commun de la théologie johannique et du monde ambiant," NTS 5 (1959): 157-73, wishes to make Stephen a convert from Essenism and the Hellenists, Jewish sectarians related to Qumran. Klijn, "Stephen's Speech," pp. 25-31, after a comparison between the speech and the Manual of Discipline and relying heavily upon the use by the former of "our-your fathers," concludes that Stephen belonged to a Jewish Christian group, separate from the temple but nevertheless still remaining within the Jewish community. So in Acts 7, according to Klijn, we are dealing with two groups, those holding for the temple, and those for ". . . a house within the house of Israel as a substitute for the Temple" (p. 30), the latter being quite possibly ". . . related to the Dead Sea Covenanters" (p. 31). Géoltrain, "Esséniens," p. 254, concludes his study: "Le christianisme primitif dans son ensemble a été marqué par ce vaste mouvement spéculatif, apocalyptique, et mystique que fut l'essénisme. Les différents courants qui traversèrent l'un agitèrent l'autre et les Hel-

line of thought, also drawing its inspiration from earlier scholars,[113] has either identified Stephen as a Samaritan,[114] or argued for considerable Samaritan influence upon Stephen, his speech, and the story of his martyrdom.[115]

In view of the variety of scholarly opinions regarding every part of Acts 6:1-8:4, it will be necessary to reevaluate many basic assumptions. To this end the following approach will be adopted: First, an examination of Stephen's discourse, 7:2-53, and its relation to the OT text (chapter 2); second, an evaluation of the stylistic data perceived throughout the speech and, by extension, the narratives, 6:1-7:2a and 7:54-8:4 (chapter 3); and third, a reassessment of the composition of the entire episode (chapter 4).

---

lénistes des Actes nous apparaissent comme les héritiers de l'aile la plus hellénisante de l'essénisme, celle, sans doute, qui permit à Philon de voir dans les Esséniens le Judaïsme idéal."

[113]Most recently Charles H. H. Scobie, "The Origins and Development of Samaritan Christianity," _NTS_ 19 (1972-73):390-400, has traced the history of scholarly statements regarding the relation of Samaritan tradition and the Stephen story.

[114]Abraham Spiro, "Stephen's Samaritan Background" (summary of his lecture by the general editors) in Johannes Munck, _The Acts of the Apostles: Introduction, Translation, and Notes_, The Anchor Bible, no. 31, rev. William F. Albright and Charles S. Mann (Garden City, N.Y.: Doubleday, 1967), pp. 285-300, maintains simply that Stephen was a Samaritan (pp. 285f.), while Lloyd Gaston, _No Stone on Another: Studies in the Significance of the Fall of Jerusalem in the Synoptic Gospels_, Supplements to Novum Testamentum, no. 23 (Leiden: Brill, 1970), pp. 154-61, suggests that he was from the pre-Christian Samaritan sect, the Nazarenes: "If there was a pre-Christian 'sect of the Nazarenes' and if as we surmised this was a Samaritan baptist-sect, then surely Stephen must have belonged to it," p. 159.

[115]Scharlemann, _Stephen_, p. 186, sees in Stephen a Jew from Ephraim who came into contact with Samaritan thought and became convinced of the importance of the mission to Samaria. Scroggs, "Earliest," pp. 197f., argues instead that the speech or its source is a product of the mission to Samaria and that it was inserted into the Stephen story by Luke. [Since the completion of this work I have addressed myself to this subject in "Acts 7: An Investigation of the Samaritain Evidence," _CBQ_ 39 (1977):190-208].

CHAPTER II

The Speech and the Use of OT Quotations

Acts 7:2-53 is a unique portion of the Acts of the Apostles, and because of its unusual character it has generally been overlooked or neglected in scholarly studies of the speeches. Instead, attention has been directed, in source and redaction essays, to the narrative portion of the Stephen story. It is, however, precisely the uniqueness of the speech which merits special study, namely, its use of OT quotations. In reality the text is a history of Israel told by a Christian,[1] and it would seem logical that a detailed examination of the OT sources would contribute in no small way to the vexing problem of the meaning and purpose of this speech, its composition, and, finally, the role it plays in the book of Acts.

A. Introduction of the Data

No text in the Acts of the Apostles is as replete with OT quotations as the Stephen speech. The number is overwhelming and the passage could justly be described as a mosaic of fragments pieced together from biblical history. A precise total is not given here because the categories for enumeration would not do justice to the material. In some cases a word or a short phrase is borrowed from the OT source; in others an expression is used which can be found in several biblical passages; in still other instances several verses are quoted *en bloc*. Actually, in speaking of a number of passages, we would do well to speak of biblical reminiscences rather than quotations. Nevertheless, the citations abound in this text.

---

[1]Contrary to the views of J. C. O'Neill, *Theology*, p. 94, who makes of the Stephen material a Jewish text edited and Christianized by the author of Acts, and the views of Holtz, *Untersuchungen*, p. 109, who says of the historical part of the speech: "Da es christlich nicht wohl denkbar ist . . ."

In light of the preponderance of OT materials in the speech, a study from that point of view is necessary. Surprisingly, few scholars have analyzed the speech from what would have to be considered one of its unique characteristics. Even when scholars do give serious attention to this aspect, it is to discuss the historicity of the speech[2] or the sources or documents used by the author[3] or to illustrate the totally Lukan character of the text.[4] The goal of this particular investigation is to analyze the redactional activity, i.e., the choice, modification, and presentation of the OT data required of the author to produce the Stephen speech.

A serious study of this text must make a critical analysis of the quotations from a number of points of view. First, the ever perplexing problem of textual criticism, especially as regards the Acts of the Apostles, must be seriously considered. Furthermore, this must be done in view of recent advances in LXX studies. In this context, the classification by Clarke[5] of OT quotations into "passages agreeing with the LXX" (exact or substantial agreement) and "free versions of the LXX in Acts" is very outmoded and unscientific.[6] The same judgment applies to his list of the six causes for the "variations from the standard text of the LXX."[7] Nevertheless, these are the only

---

[2]Bruce, Acts, pp. 161-78.

[3]Haenchen, Acts, pp. 288-89 and 278-79; Conzelmann, Apostelgeschichte, pp. 50-51; Holtz, Untersuchungen, pp. 100-9.

[4]Duterme, "Vocabulaire," pp. 8-27; Wilson, "Theologian and Historian," pp. 166-89; and Bihler, Stephanusgeschichte, pp. 38-81.

[5]William K. L. Clarke, "The Use of the Septuagint in Acts," in Beginnings, 2:66-105.

[6]Duterme, "Vocabulaire," p. 6, presents the following classification as the basis for his analysis of the speech: 1) "deux citations explicites" (Acts 7:42c-43 = Am 5:25-27 and vv. 49-50 = Is 66:1-2); 2) "réminiscences littérales ou quasi littérales de l'A.T."; and 3) "réminiscences plus libres qui reprennent au lieu correspondant de l'A.T. quelques, parfois un seul mot." He is obviously dependent on Clarke's work.

[7]Clarke, "Septaugint," p. 93, quotes Swete's study (An Introduction to the Old Testament in Greek, 1900, p. 394): "It may be due to (i.) loose citation, or to (ii.) the substitution of a gloss for the precise words which the writer professes to quote, or to (iii.) a desire to adapt a prophetic context to the circumstances under which it was thought to have been fulfilled, or to (iv.) the fusing together of passages drawn from

noteworthy statements we have on this problem.[8] Owing to the date of the study (1922), no allowance is made for textual variants either within the NT manuscript tradition or that of the LXX. Some recent scholars have made occasional statements concerning particular passages and their text types,[9] but no consistent and thorough study takes into consideration discoveries in the history of textual transmission. Not only the classification "variations from the standard text of the LXX," but also attempts at finding "historical clues" for the identification of Stephen and his milieu will often appear futile in the light of textual history.

A second area needing attention is that of determining actual sources of the quotations. In many cases the author had a variety of texts from which to draw his material. Analysis is required to establish what, in effect, is a quotation and where it comes from, to gain insights into the author's preferences and method of selection. Most commentators tend to be very arbitrary in their listing of OT sources, providing citations without reference to linguistic factors but merely through affinity of idea. Bruce, Bihler, Haenchen, and Conzelmann--to mention a few--speak of the influence of Psalm 104[10]

---

different contexts. Of the variations which cannot be ascribed to one or other of these causes, some are (v.) recensional, whilst others are (vi.) translational, and imply an independent use of the original, whether by the Evangelist, or by the author of some collection of excerpts which he employed."

[8]The recent monograph of Traugott Holtz (Untersuchungen) on OT quotations in Luke is not very helpful for this study of the Stephen material since, not considering the long historical section of the speech as being by the author of Acts, he does not examine its relation to the OT; for further comments see below, pp. 249-53.

[9]Among others: "Citations scripturaires et tradition textuelle dans le Livre des Acts," in Lucien Cerfaux, ed. Recueil Lucien Cerfaux: études d'exégèse et d'histoire religieuse, 2 vols. (Gembloux: Duculot, 1954), 2:93-103; Jean Daniélou, "L'Etoile de Jacob et la mission chrétienne à Damas," VC 11 (1957):121-38; Wilcox, Semitisms, 1965; Eldon J. Epp, The Theological Tendency of Codex Bezae Cantabrigiensis in Acts, Society for New Testament Studies, Monograph Series, no. 3 (Cambridge: Cambridge University Press, 1966).

[10]Chapter and verse references throughout this study will be to the LXX unless otherwise indicated, but citation of titles will follow usual nomenclature, e.g., 1 and 2 Samuel: 1 and 2 Kings, etc.

on the Stephen speech.[11] It is obvious that both the psalm and the first half of the speech can be considered surveys of Israel's history; however, from a linguistic point of view there is no basis for positing any influence of the psalm upon Acts 7:2f.[12] Without a more precise notion of the author's sources and, following this, of his redactional method, the speech will remain for scholars no more than a mechanically contrived mosaic of LXX passages, expressions, and terms. As a result, commentaries of this text continue to be catalogues of OT parallels.

Thirdly, once the author's sources have been investigated at length, it will be possible to examine his redactional activity. The choice of events and traditions, as well as the modifications of the text of the OT, reveals to a surprising degree the intention and theology of the writer. This concern is similar to that of scholars examining the changes imposed upon the Markan and Q sources by the later evangelists. The Stephen speech offers a unique opportunity to apply this method to the book of Acts.

In light of the above observations, it is necessary to present in a detailed fashion the OT data. The list of texts is long, but the chart which follows represents the commonly accepted references of commentators.[13] The complexity and

---

[11]Bruce, Acts, p. 164; Haenchen, Acts, p. 279 (also n. 4); Conzelmann, Apostelgeschichte, pp. 53-54; and Bihler, Stephanusgeschichte, pp. 46, 50, and 52. See p. 50 where, after insisting upon the primary role of Gn 50, Bihler states: "Daneben wird auch die Geschichtsdarstellung in Ps 105 auf Apr 7.9-16 eingewirkt haben."

[12]The style of writing (poetry and historical prose), the thematic concerns, the goals, etc., of the two authors are entirely different. These are clearly reflected in the type of "histories of Israel" found in Acts 7 and Ps 104. See pp. 140-45 below for further discussion of this point.

[13]The OT references are from: Erwin Preuschen, Die Apostelgeschichte, Handbuch zum neuen Testament (Tűbingen: Mohr, 1912); Jacquier, Actes (1926); Beginnings, 4 (1933); Duterme, "Vocabulaire" (1950); Bruce, Acts (1951); J. Renié, Actes des Apôtres traduits et commentés, La Sainte Bible, 11/1 (Paris: Letouzey et Ané, 1951); Lucien Cerfaux and Jacques Dupont, Les Actes des Apôtres, La Sainte Bible, traduite en français sous le direction de l'Ecole biblique de Jérusalem (Paris: Editions du Cerf, 1953). Additional philological references are also taken from Wilson, "Theologian and Historian" (1962); Bihler, Stephanusgeschichte (1963); Haenchen, Acts (1971); Conzelmann,

v.2 Ps 28:3
Gn 11:28-12:7
v.3 Gn 12:1
v.4 Gn 11:26-12:5
v.5 Dt 2:5
Gn 12:7
Gn 13:15
Gn 17:8
Gn 48:4
Gn 15:2
v.6 Gn 15:13
Ex 2:22
v.7 Gn 15:14
Ex 3:12
v.8 Gn 17:10-12
Gn 21:4
v.9 Gn 37:11,28
Gn 39:2,3
Gn 39:21,23
Gn 45:4
Ps 104:17
v.10 Gn 39:21
Gn 41:37f.
Gn 41:40-43
Gn 45:8
Ps 104:21
v.11 Gn 41:54-42:5
Ps 36:19
v.12 Gn 42:1-2
v.13 Gn 45:1,16
v.14 Gn 46:26-27
Ex 1:5
Dt 10:22
v.15 Gn 46:6,27
Gn 49:33
Ex 1:6
v.16 Gn 23:16f.
Gn 33:19
Gn 49:29f.
Gn 50:13
Jos 24:32
v.17 Ex 1:7,20
v.18 Ex 1:8
v.19 Ex 1:10-11,15
Ex 1:17-18,22
v.20 Ex 2:2,3-10
v.21 Ex 2:3f.,5,10
v.22 Ex 7:10
Sir 45:3
v.23 Ex 2:11f.
Dt 34:7
v.24 Ex 2:12
v.25 ________
v.26 Ex 2:13
v.27-28 Ex 2:13
v.29 Ex 2:15,22
Ex 18:3f.
v.30 Ex 3:1-2
v.31 Ex 3:3f.
v.32 Ex 3:6,13
v.33 Ex 3:5
v.34 Ex 3:7-8,10
Ex 2:24
v.35 Ex 2:14
v.36 Ex 7:3
Ps 104:27
Nb 14:33
(Am 5:25)
v.37 Dt 18:15
v.38 Dt 4:10
Dt 9:10
Dt 18:16
Dt 32:45-57
Dt 33:2
v.39 Ez 20:8,13,16,24
Nb 14:3f.
v.30 Ex 32:1,23
v.41 Ex 32:4,6
Ps 113:12
v.42a Jer 7:18
Jer 19:13
Dt 4:19
Dt 17:3
Zeph 1:5
2 Chr 33:3,5
2 K 23:5
Ps 104:41
v.42b-43 Am 5:25-27
v.44 Ex 25:8-9,40
v.45 Jos 3:14
Jos 18:1
Jer 24:9
v.46 Ps 131:5
2 S 7:1f.,26
(1 Chr 17:1f.)
v.47 1 K 5:1f.
1 K 6:2,6
1 K 8:20
v.48 1 K 8:27
v.49-50 Is 66:1-2

v.51* Ex 33:3
Ex 33:5
Ex 34:9
Dt 9:6,13 etc.
Lv 26:41
Dt 10:16
Jer 4:4
Jer 6:10
Jer 9:25
Ez 44:7
Jer 6:10
Nb 27:14
Is 63:10

*For more complete references see the list of scholars given in the previous note (13).

ambiguous nature of this inventory indicates the status of the question. The chart is long, disconcerting, and, in reality, says little about the author's redactional activity. In fact, a large number of references given are certainly not sources of the writer.

It is my contention that no serious attempt has been made to distinguish between OT texts which bear some resemblance, stylistic or thematic, to the passages in question, and those which were actually employed by the author of Acts. Since criticism thus far has been directed at the work of commentators,

---

Apostelgeschichte (1972).

attention must now be directed to the considerably more detailed analyses of J. Bihler and J. H. Wilson. In the case of the former, a too great concern for the ideas expressed and the interpretation of these has led him generally to neglect all textual comparison between Acts and its alleged sources. The result, of course, is an unnecessary proliferation of OT parallels which on closer observation have little in common with the passage being studied, beyond providing added support for the scholar's interpretation.[14] Wilson, on the other hand, more concerned with vocabulary and stylistic matters, reduces source questions to cursory observations such as the following: "These straightforward phrases [7.15] are based on information in Genesis 46:6 (Jacob comes to Egypt), 47:33 (Jacob dies), and Exodus 1:6 (his sons die)" or "Acts 7:24 is largely editorial addenda, . . ."[15] Wilson is admittedly more interested in the OT text which served as the basis for the composition of Acts 7. His failure to analyze these sources leaves without any precision the question of quoting, borrowing, modifying, editing, etc. Thus, the study of the author's originality, as well as the interpretation of the speech, is conjectural at best.

B. The Speech and the OT

Acts 7:2-53 is no less than a lengthy account of Hebrew history, recounted in a style closely related to the LXX. Since the author of this text borrows generously from the Greek version of the Israelite scriptures, this study will analyze this process and note the writer's techniques of choosing, borrowing, modifying, supplementing, and, finally, creating.

With this purpose in mind, attention will be focused upon the relation of each part of Stephen's discourse with the OT text. The whole discourse can be divided, in terms of OT quotations, into four sections. Each of these sections will bear a slightly different relation to the OT source:

---

[14] Stephanusgeschichte, pp. 38ff. See the author's references to Ps 104, Ps 33 or on pp. 56-57 to a considerable number of OT passages. For further observations on Bihler's methodology, see pp. 253-54 and 306.

[15] "Theologian and Historian," pp. 166ff. The quotations are from pp. 173 and 176 respectively. This scholar's approach is treated at greater length in chapter four.

1. Verses 2-16: the history of the patriarchs
2. Verses 17-34: the history of Moses
3. Verses 35-50: thematic section
4. Verses 51-53: invective against audience

1. History of the Patriarchs 7:2-16

From the point of view both of content and of structure, this part of the history of Israel falls into two sections: the story of Abraham 2-8, and that of Joseph 9-16. For that reason, the OT data of these texts will be considered separately.

a. Acts 7:2-8: Story of Abraham

1) Vv. 2-8: Textual Relation to OT

V.2. After the opening address to the audience, the author begins his historical survey by drawing a very peculiar phrase from Ps 28:3, ὁ θεὸς τῆς δόξης. These are the only occurrences of the expression in the Greek Old or New Testaments.[16] Owing to this fact, no doubt, scholars have been led to point out the relation between the two; conversely, owing to the same circumstance, they have pursued the problem no further.[17] A closer examination of this text leads to the conclusion that Acts 7:2 is, in fact a quotation from Ps 28. This conclusion is clearly indicated by the use of a cognate expression in 7:55, εἶδεν δόξαν θεοῦ,[18] and will be further elucida-

---

[16]The analogous phrase of Paul in 1 Cor 2:8, τὸν κύριον τῆς δόξης ἐσταύρωσαν, should be noted here. On the one hand, the starkness of Acts 7:2 might not seem so extreme in view of Paul's statement, and could be explained, on admittedly little evidence, as due to contemporary terminology. On the other hand, the use of ὁ θεός in Acts is consistent with the author's preference for this term rather than κύριος throughout the speech (see p. 39 below for the first source evidence of such a tendency). Further, considering the model utilized, note that κύριος is utilized no less than 19 times in the short psalm and θεός only twice, one occurrence of which is here quoted.

[17]Haenchen, Acts, p. 278; Beginnings, 4:71--the editors refer to the psalm and conclude: ". . . but there seems to be no special reference to it in this passage." See also Wilson, "Theologian and Historian," p. 166 and Bihler, Stephanusgeschichte, p. 41. Foakes Jackson, Acts, p. 58, however, takes the quotation more seriously and proposes that ". . . perhaps the opening words may be paraphrased 'God revealed His glory to Abraham.'"

[18]No author, to my knowledge, recognizes this fact. Foakes Jackson's treatment of the narrative and speech as separate entities, Acts, p. 58, stresses this even further.

ted when the relation of the speech to the narrative is examined. The function of ὁ θεὸς τῆς δόξης will be developed at length in relation to the vision of Stephen and the role it plays in Acts 6:1-8:4.

The following part of v.2 launches directly into the Abraham story. The author draws his material from Gn 12:7, where the first mention of an appearance to Abraham occurs. He is anticipating this incident, since in v.3 he will return to the beginning of the chapter to quote the speech recorded there. This modification of the biblical tradition will be examined later, along with other such peculiarities.

The relation of the two texts is as follows:[19]

7:2-3	Gn 12:7[20]
Ὁ θεός . . . ὤφθη	καὶ ὤφθη κύριος
τῷ πατρὶ ἡμῶν Ἀβραάμ...	τῷ Αβραμ
καὶ εἶπεν πρὸς αὐτόν.	καὶ εἶπεν αὐτῷ.

For the use of ὁ θεός instead of κύριος, one could refer to Gn 18:1 (ὤφθη δὲ αὐτῷ ὁ θεός), although conscious elimination of κύριος or the substitution of ὁ θεός is a constant feature of the speech.[21] The addition of the expression τῷ πατρὶ ἡμῶν. . . is to be understood in relation to the prominent theme of "our/ your fathers." The speech formula of Gn 12:7 serves both as a quotation and as a redactional link, leading the author to Gn 12:1 (see v.3 below).

Finally, one more element of the verse should be considered a quotation: πρὶν ἢ κατοικῆσαι αὐτὸν ἐν Χαρράν. The author draws upon Gn 11:31-32, καὶ ἦλθεν ἕως Χαρραν καὶ κατῴκησεν ἐκεῖ . . . ἐν Χαρραν, to construct his own text. This is the only text which provides him with the necessary elements.

19The Greek text of the OT is taken from Septuaginta, id est Vetus Testamentum Graece iuxta LXX Interpretes, edited by Alfred Rahlfs, 3d ed., 2 vols. (Stuttgart: Privilegierte Württembergische Bibelanstatt, 1949), and that of the NT from Novum Testamentum Graece, edited by Erwin Nestle and Kurt Aland, 25ed., (Stuttgart: Württembergische Bibelanstatt for the American Bible Society, 1963). The orthography of these two works as well as their textual sigla are adopted throughout this study.

20An identical text is found at Gn 17:1.

21See vv.3, 6, 7, 9c, 17, etc.

V.3 For this verse the writer returns to the beginning of Gn 12, following the lead of 12:7, to quote God's command to Abraham:

7:3	Gn 12:1
καὶ εἶπεν πρὸς αὐτόν·	καὶ ἔιπεν κύροις τῷ Αβραμ
ἔξελθε ἐκ τῆς γῆς σου	Ἔξελθε ἐκ τῆς γῆς σου
καὶ ἐκ τῆς συγγενείας σου	καὶ ἐκ τῆς συγγενείας σου
	καὶ ἐκ τοῦ οἴκου τοῦ πατρός σου
καὶ δεῦρο εἰς τὴν γῆν	εἰς την γῆν,
ἣν ἄν σοι δείξω.	ἣν ἄν σοι δείξω·

The above synopsis clearly demonstrates that the author employs the LXX text, a conclusion reiterated throughout this study. Indeed, the verbal similarity leaves no doubt in this regard. By the same token, the differences between the two texts gain in importance. The reasons for these variations are found in a number of areas and thus are treated in different parts of this survey of the material. Already in this short quotation, the reader is confronted by at least three types of modifications: 1) alteration (τῷ Αβραμ becomes πρὸς αὐτόν); 2) elimination (ἐκ τοῦ πατρός σου is omitted); and 3) addition (δεῦρο is inserted within the quotation). The first involves a speech formula and will be treated in the following chapter; the second is related to aberrant biblical traditions and will be analyzed below.

The third modification calls for immediate attention: the insertion within the quotation of the adverb δεῦρο. One might seek textual support for such a reading among the versions, and, in fact, Wilcox proposes just such a solution. The added element would then find "an exact parallel" in the targum *Pseudo-Jonathan*: זיל = δεῦρο.[22] I am inclined to reject Wilcox's "Semitic" solution for several reasons. In the first place, the evidence from the targum is considerably weaker than the author thinks. This is due to the very nature of the text:[23]

---

[22] *Semitisms*, pp. 26-27.

[23] Moses Ginsburger, *Pseudo-Jonathan (Thargum Jonathan ben Usiel zum Pentateuch) nach der Londoner Handschrift* (Berlin: Calvary, 1903), p. 20.

ואמר ה׳ לאברם
איזל לך מארעך
אתפרש מן ילדותך
פוק מבית אבוך
זיל לארעא

The Aramaic translation in this particular case surely does not witness to a different textual tradition (neither the MT nor the ancient versions lend support to this), but rather points to stylistic paraphrase of the Hebrew Vorlage. The addition of a verb for each phrase is clearly due to rhetorical considerations on the part of this particular translator. A better solution is forthcoming in examining the Greek evidence. The following read καὶ δεῦρο: LXX manuscripts E, M (and some cursives), Ethiopic codex C, Acts 7:3, Hippolytus, Origen (Latin), Eusebius, Chrysostom, Cyril of Alexandria, Theodoret (one half of his citations), Cyprian, and the ancient text *Speculum*. To these we might add the corroborating evidence of several cursive manuscripts: c m (καὶ πορεύου), h^b (καὶ ὕπαγε), and a^b (καὶ ἐλθέ).[24] There is, therefore, a strong likelihood that the author of Acts had such a reading at his disposal and that he chose the form which best suited his purpose, a contrast by means of parallelism: ἔξελθε ἐκ ... καὶ δεῦρο εἰς . . . .[25]

Finally, a point of textual criticism should be noted. The text (*supra*, p. 41) agrees with the LXX and most manuscripts against B D sa in reading a second ἐκ for Acts 7:3.[26]

---

[24]Alan E. Brooke and Norman McLean, *The Old Testament in Greek*, vol. 1: *The Octateuch* (Cambridge: Cambridge University Press, 1906), p. 29. Note that the Bohairic adds ⲁⲙⲟⲩ for δεῦρο; however, the Bohairic translation of Acts 7:3 (ⲁⲙⲟⲩ ⲉⲃⲟⲗ ... ⲁⲙⲟⲩ ⲉⲡⲓ...), in contrast to the Sahidic and G67, argues for an idiomatic rather than textual solution. While it might be argued that Hippolytus and Chrysostum (three out of seven quotations) were influenced by Acts (omission of καὶ ἐκ τοῦ οἴκου τοῦ πατρός σου), the rest of the evidence is unassailable. See also John W. Wevers, ed., *Genesis*, vol. 1 of *Septauginta Vetus Testamentum Graecum Auctoritate Academiae Scientiarum Gottingensis* (Göttingen: Vandenhoeck & Ruprecht, 1974), who adds the variant: καὶ ἀπελθέ (Or IV 346) as well as a considerably longer list of LXX manuscripts in support of the reading found in Acts (p. 149).

[25]The writer's love of parallelism, doublets, contrasts of various kinds, etc., will be developed at great length in the following chapter.

[26]Nestle and Aland, *NT Graece*, p. 315, opt for the omis-

While assimilation to the LXX Vorlage cannot be dismissed as a possible explanation, the manuscript evidence for the omission of the preposition is not very compelling.[27] Furthermore, the author's fidelity in quoting from his OT source--a recurring theme throughout this study--argues in favor of conformity to the LXX in the present case. This subject will be considered at greater length at the end of the present chapter.

V.4. This text is particularly difficult to analyze in relation to OT elements, since each phrase betrays some link to its source but still owes much to the redaction of the author. While stylistic features will be examined more particularly in the following chapter, it will be necessary to anticipate several factors to understand the role played here by the OT text.

The first phrase, τότε ἐξελθὼν ἐκ γῆς Χαλδαίων, while it is clearly related to Gn 11:31, καὶ ἐξήγαγεν αὐτοὺς ἐκ τῆς χώρας τῶν Χαλδαίων,[28] and possibly influenced by Gn 12:4, ὅτε ἐξῆλθεν ἐκ Χαρραν (owing to the shift in the locale of the

---

sion of ἐκ along with B D sa, while Kurt Aland, et al., eds. *The Greek New Testament* (New York: American Bible Society, 1966), p. 439, choose to follow the LXX and the majority of manuscripts. The latter is also the position taken by Augustin Merk, ed. *Novum Testamentum Graece et Latine*, 7th ed. (Rome: Biblical Pontifical Institute, 1951), p. 415.

[27]At this point a few observations should be made regarding the manuscript evidence, which on closer examination is considerably less persuasive than one might think. Of the Coptic versions the Sahidic is certainly closer to the Bezan text (to this I might add that the as yet unpublished manuscript G67 also supports the omission of the second ἐκ; this text is unmistakenly related to a text like D) and should carry less weight especially since the Bohairic text follows the majority of manuscripts in reading a second preposition. The evidence of D is also lessened when one considers that the Latin column supports the LXX reading (*a cognatione tua*). Vaticanus will be discussed below.

[28]See the similar text of Gn 15:7; ὁ ἐξαγαγών σε ἐκ χώρας Χαλδαίων. Incidentally, "the country of the Chaldeans" (translated in Greek by ἡ χώρα and representing אור כשדים) is mentioned only three times in Genesis, the third being Gn 11:28. Instead of this rare expression--the only one used in the Abraham story (the same is employed also in the "historical" prayer of Neh 9:7)--the author utilizes the term current in his day; ἡ γῆ Χαλδαίων. This is also the expression employed by Josephus, *Ant*. 1.159, in his version of the Abraham story.

revelation to Abraham), should no doubt be seen more simply as the use of a resumptive technique to express command (v.3) and fulfillment (v.4). This stylistic feature will be examined in the following chapter.[29] In this particular case, the information is taken from the OT source, but the form is dictated by the process of redaction.

The next part of the verse, κατῴκησεν ἐν Χαρράν, is obviously a parallel statement to πρὶν ἢ κατοικῆσαι αὐτὸν ἐν Χαρράν.[30] The structural elements of the verse are most prominent.

While its chronology will be discussed elsewhere, the content of the third part of v.4, κἀκεῖθεν μετὰ τὸ ἀποθανεῖν τὸν πατέρα αὐτοῦ, seems to come from several sources. In composing this passage, the author utilizes Gn 11:32: καὶ ἀπέθανεν Θαρα ἐν Χαρραν. Note, however, that he uses an element, ἐκ τοῦ οἴκου τοῦ πατρός σου, intentionally omitted earlier in v.3 (quoting Gn 12:1). Furthermore, the clause seems to be built on the same pattern: a temporal parallel to 7:2, πρὶν ἢ κατοικῆσαι αὐτὸν ἐν Χαρράν. While κἀκεῖθεν is a favorite expression of the author (of ten NT occurrences, eight are to be found in Acts), I might point to Gn 12:8, καὶ ἀπέστη ἐκεῖθεν εἰς. . . ., where he would have readily found the terminology to his liking.[31]

The last two sections of the verse owe more to the redactional activity of the writer than to the OT, but a few contacts between the two exist.

κἀκεῖθεν ...
μετῴκισεν αὐτὸν εἰς τὴν γῆν ταύτην
εἰς ἣν ὑμεῖς νῦν κατοικεῖτε.

The verb μετοικίζω is particularly interesting in this context. It appears twice in the entire NT: Acts 7:4 and 43, the second of which forms part of a quotation from Am 5:27.[32] Since the verb

---

[29]See pp. 182-85.

[30]The author uses the exact form of the original quotation in Gn 11:31 (κατῴκησεν).

[31]Gn 12:7 is used in 7:2-3, served as an important redactional link for 7:5, and finally will be referred to in relation to the fourth part of v.4.

[32]See William F. Arndt and F. Wilbur Gingrich, eds., *A Greek-English Lexicon of the New Testament and Other Early*

is never employed in relation to Abraham, and in light of the author's tendency to repeat key terms for a given effect, I see a close connection between the two. The remaining part of v.4 is greatly elucidated by its relation to Gn 12:7 and 17:8. In the former (the event occurs in Canaan), God promises Abraham: δώσω τὴν γῆν ταύτην. The latter, which the author quotes in the next verse of his composition, reads as follows: . . . τὴν γῆν ἣν παροικεῖς, πᾶσαν τὴν γῆν Χανααν εἰς. . . (the very part which he omits from his quotation in 7:5). He transforms the verb παροικέω to κατοικέω just as he will transform ᾤκησεν to ἐγένετο πάροικος in Acts 7:29 (=Ex 2:15). This change is motivated by his thematic intentions.[33]

V.5. This particular verse offers unique problems which have plagued commentators. Since there exist so many differences between alleged OT sources and Acts 7:5, scholars have recourse to expressions such as: "the wording reflects Dt. ii. 5";[34] "Gn 17.8 is pressed into service";[35] "Die Verheissung ist nach Gen 12.7, 13, 15, 17.8, 48.4 frei komponiert";[36] or else they readily speak of quotations without considering the important dissimilarities of ideas, style, and word order.[37]

Christian Literature, 4th rev. and aug. ed., 1952 (Chicago: University of Chicago Press, 1974), s.v. "μετοικίζω;" confer also James H. Moulton and George Milligan, eds., The Vocabulary of the Greek Testament Illustrated from the Papyri and Other Non-Literary Sources (Grand Rapids, Michigan: Eerdmans, 1930; reprint ed., 1974), s.v. "μετοικίζω;" also Henry G. Liddell and Robert Scott, eds., A Greek-English Lexicon, revised and augmented by Henry S. Jones and Roderick McKenzie (Oxford: Clarendon Press, 1940; reprint ed., 1966), s.v. "μετοικίζω."

[33]The theme of "place" is central to the author's view of Jewish history and will be treated at length in chapter four.

[34]Bruce, Acts, p. 152 or Beginnings, 4:71: "The phrase appears to be a reminiscence of Deut. ii.5."

[35]Haenchen, Acts, p. 279, also p. 278: "Verse 5 makes use of God's words in Deut. 2.5 as a suitable 'biblical' expression."

[36]Preuschen, Apostelgeschichte, p. 279; see also Jacquier, Actes, p. 207 and Renié, Actes, p. 112.

[37]Lake and Cadbury, Beginnings, 4:71, have noted the problem of word order in regard to v.5: "The Greek text seems to have an impossible order, δοῦναι αὐτῷ εἰς κατάσχεσιν αὐτὴν καὶ κτλ., but all the variants appear to be merely emendations." Since the editors suggest no OT source, their observation concerns not the problem of translation but that of composition. This point will be taken up later.

In view of the above statements, it is essential to determine whether, in fact, one is dealing with biblical reminiscences, and, if so, to examine more closely the author's method of composition. Or, if it is determined that v.5 is indeed a composite of several quotations, then it is necessary to analyze the modifications imposed upon the OT sources by the writer. Without precise information the study of redaction remains tenuous at best.

It is my contention that the author has utilized several biblical texts to compose v.5. Since the procedure and method which he followed will be further elaborated below, it will suffice at this point to present the textual relation between the two.

a	7:5	Dt 2:5
		μὴ συνάψητε πρὸς αὐτοὺς πόλεμον·
	καὶ οὐκ ἔδωκεν αὐτῷ	οὐ γὰρ μὴ δῶ ὑμῖν
	κληρονομίαν	[κληρονομίαν]
	ἐν αὐτῇ	ἀπὸ τῆς γῆς αὐτῶν
	οὐδὲ βῆμα ποδός,	οὐδὲ βῆμα ποδός ...

b	7:5	Gn 17:8	Gn 48:4
	καὶ ἐπηγγείλατο	καὶ	καὶ
	δοῦναι αὐτῷ	δώσω σοι	δώσω σοι
	εἰς κατάσχεσιν		
	αὐτὴν		τὴν γῆν ταύτην
	καὶ τῷ σπέρματι αὐτοῦ	καὶ τῷ σπέρματί σου	καὶ τῷ σπέρματί σου
	μετ' αὐτόν,	μετὰ σὲ	μετὰ σὲ
		τὴν γῆν,	
		ἣν παροικεῖς,	
		πᾶσαν τὴν γῆν Χανααν,	
		εἰς κατάσχεσιν αἰώνιον ...	εἰς κατάσχεσιν αἰώνιον.

c	7:5	Gn 15:2
		τί μοι δώσεις;
	οὐκ ὄντος αὐτῷ τέκνου.	ἐγὼ δὲ ἀπολύομαι ἄτεκνος.

Part a presents several important features. It is obvious that οὐδὲ βῆμα ποδός, an expression which is unique to Dt 2:5, is borrowed from the LXX version. Commentators universally accept this. The synopsis given above illustrates an even closer relationship between the texts.[38] Several grammatical changes are imposed upon the source (γάρ > καί; οὐ . . . μὴ δῶ > οὐκ ἔδωκεν; ὑμῖν > αὐτῷ);[39] but still the structure remains that of the Deuteronomic source. Finally, the relation of κληρονομίαν ἐν αὐτῇ to the LXX text, as found in critical editions, calls for some comment. Even though the Hebrew text, as preserved by the Masoretes, has no corresponding term to the κληρονομίαν of Acts, it seems safe to postulate on the basis of the Syriac, the Samaritan Hebrew and Aramaic textual tradition, as well as the Old Latin and Ethiopic versions, that the author of Acts had at his disposal a Greek Vorlage with such a reading.[40]

The second part of v.5 presents a very different problem, one not easily defined, but, nevertheless, reflected by the variety of scholarly opinion. Some deny that the author is

---

[38]This has also been perceived in part by J. H. Wilson, "Theologian and Historian," pp. 169-70.

[39]The second and third modifications mentioned are easily understood in light of the new setting acquired by the passage in question, while the first corresponds to the author's fondness for the καί-style in v.5a and b (see the commentary of vv. 6, 7, 8, 9, 10, etc.).

[40]All these texts present a term for "inheritance" (Syriac: ܝܘܪܬܢܐ, Samaritan targum: ירתה, and Samaritan Hebrew: ירשה, Old Latin: <u>in sorte</u>, and Ethiopic: <u>hereditatem</u>--for the last two see Brooke and McLean, <u>Old Testament</u>, 1:553) just as Acts 7:5 does. Furthermore, it is clear that the LXX consistently translates the root ירש either by κλῆρος or κληρονομία. Wilcox, <u>Semitisms</u>, p. 27, has noted the Samaritan evidence for such a conclusion and listed this example as one of many "traces of targumic textual tradition" in Acts. The evidence from the Syriac, Old Latin, and Ethiopic versions call for an entirely different conclusion, namely, the existence of a Palestinian LXX tradition with a variety of readings not preserved in our present manuscripts. See pp. 152-54 below for a more detailed discussion of this problem. Another explanation of the appearance of κληρονομία in Acts 7:5 would see the author employing the ending of the very same verse of Dt 2:5: οὐδὲ βῆμα ποδός, ὅτι ἐν κλήρῳ (ירשה) δέδωκα τοῖς υἱοῖς Ησαυ. He would have been responsible for the word order, while the form κλῆρος (the LXX form) could be explained as due to the inconsistency of the translators or the author's own use of the terms as synonyms (see Acts 20:32, τὴν κληρονομίαν ἐν τοῖς ἡγιασμένοις πᾶσιν, and 26:18, κλῆρον ἐν τοῖς ἡγιασμένοις). I am led to choose the first solution, however, because of the textual evidence and especially because of the author's quoting techniques. [Now see Richard, "Acts 7: An Investigation of the Samaritan Evi-

quoting an OT source; others maintain the free composition of the text on the basis of several biblical passages; still others see this part of v.5 as a quotation of Gn 17:8. In each case there are important objections. If the passage from Acts is a quotation, why the dissimilarities, particularly of word order? At the same time, the synopsis given earlier suggests not free composition on the basis of a number of texts, but rather a definite borrowing from one or both passages given, since only in these two verses of Genesis does one find all elements required for the redaction of Acts 7:5b. In effect, the peculiar combination in the three passages (Acts 7:5b; Gn 17:8 and 48:4) of five elements, though admittedly not the order, can hardly be accidental: δίδωμι, two indirect objects (Abraham and his seed after him), the direct object (the land), and εἰς κατάσχεσιν. Therefore, Acts 7:5b is in fact a quotation, even though the word order owes to the redactional activity of the author.[41] Since the necessary background for such an assertion will be studied in the following chapter, it will suffice presently to point out that the word order of the beginning of the verse served as a pattern for the composition of this section of the text:

καὶ οὐκ ἔδωκεν / αὐτῷ / κληρονομίαν / ἐν αὐτῇ
καὶ ἐπηγγείλατο δοῦναι / αὐτῷ / εἰς κατάσχεσιν / αὐτὴν
\+ καὶ τῷ ...

The strange word order then of the passage, noted by the editors of *Beginnings*,[42] owes to the writer's concern for parallelism.[43] Finally, part *c* is readily seen as being a free quotation of Gn 15:2, and with the rest of v.5 forms an interesting parallelismus membrorum.[44]

---

dence," pp. 197-99.]

[41]One could reject the above reading (B C 𝔐 D *al* Ir^{lat}) for δοῦναι αὐτὴν εἰς κατάσχεσιν αὐτῷ ... (P^{74} א A E *pm*). Indeed, the decision is a difficult one owing to the manuscript evidence; however, the *lectio difficilior* should probably be followed. This is further indicated by the redactional considerations given below. Note that the sigla are taken from Nestle and Aland, *NT Graece*.

[42]See n. 37 above where the opinion of the editors is given in quotation.

[43]See the list of parallelismi membrorum, pp. 173-74.

[44]*Infra*, pp. 183-84.

V.6. With this verse the author once again has recourse to the LXX for direct speech:

7:6	Gn 15:13	
ἐλάλησεν δὲ οὕτως ὁ θεός	καὶ ἐρρέθη πρὸς Αβραμ	
	Γινώσκων γνώσῃ	
ὅτι ἔσται τὸ σπέρμα αὐτοῦ	ὅτι πάροικον ἔσται τὸ σπέρμα σου	
		Ex 2:22
		...Γηρσαμ λέγων
πάροικον ἐν γῇ ἀλλοτρίᾳ	ἐν γῇ οὐκ ἰδίᾳ,	ὅτι πάροικός εἰμι
		ἐν γῇ ἀλλοτρίᾳ.
καὶ δουλώσουσιν αὐτὸ	καὶ δουλώσουσιν αὐτοὺς	
καὶ κακώσουσιν	καὶ κακώσουσιν αὐτοὺς	
	καὶ ταπεινώσουσιν αὐτοὺς	
ἔτη τετρακόσια·	τετρακόσια ἔτη.[45]	

While the quotation is readily seen as having been taken from the LXX, several observations should be made. The introductory formula has no relation to the OT source and will be examined later.[46] The modifications which the author imposes upon his citation are of several kinds.[47]

45The variant ἔτη τετρακόσια, as found in Acts, is well attested in the LXX manuscript tradition: "M b d f g h l n p r s v w d_2 Acta Or-gr½ Chr Cyr-ed Thdt Tyc" (Brooke and McLean, Old Testament, 1:36; see also Wevers, Genesis, p. 170, for an even longer list of witnesses).

46A consistent feature throughout the speech is the relative independence of the discourse formulae in relation to the LXX model. The difference between the formulae in Acts 7:6 and Gn 15:13 is obvious, particularly the verbs, ἐλάλησεν and ἐρρέθη. The LXX in this instance diverges from the MT (the other versions do not, including the Syro-Hexaplar) in reading an aorist passive for ויאמר. While it might be possible to see behind the text of Acts 7:6 a variant LXX tradition (i.e., with the aorist active of λαλέω), the evidence speaks against it. In the first place, the LXX translators generally render אמר by some form of λέγω or εἶπον (including ἐρέω) and only occasionally by λαλέω (which usually represents דבר). Secondly, the remainder of the formula has no relation to the alleged model. Also, the author of the Stephen speech usually disregards such formulae or at best borrows a term or the concept from his model and presents his own introduction.

47Most commentators give OT parallels without noting differences: (Beginnings, 4; Bruce, Acts; Haenchen, Acts). Further, Bihler, Stephanusgeschichte, p. 43, and Wilson, "Theologian and Historian," p. 170, dismiss these as unimportant; the

The change from direct to indirect address will be treated in relation to v.7 below, but the transformation of αὐτούς to αὐτό requires some attention at this point. While the alteration of the OT model from the plural to the singular could be explained in terms of grammatical improvement (αὐτό agrees with τὸ σπέρμα) on the part of the author, it should be noted that this modification does not occur in 7:34 where, in quoting Ex 3:7-10 he is confronted with an almost identical situation. The change, it seems, is more thematically than grammatically motivated. The writer is interested in underscoring the posterity of Abraham (note the singular terms of vv.5 and 6: κληρονομίαν, κατάσχεσιν, σπέρματι, τέκνου, σπέρμα, πάροικον), a posterity which history will present as a series of individuals (e.g., Joseph, Moses, Joshua, David), culminating in the coming of the Just One (Acts 7:52).[48] In v.7 the author returns more directly to his source and retains, as in 7:34, the plural of his model (see the discussion of v.7 below). The omission of the second αὐτούς probably owes to stylistic considerations (note 6:12; 7:24, 57-58; 8:3).

Finally, two important points deserve special attention: the conflation of Gn 15:13 with Ex 2:22, and the omission of part of the OT passage. The combination of two biblical passages, a rather frequent phenomenon in the speech, belongs more properly to an examination of quotation techniques and will be examined further (<u>infra</u> pp. 56-58). Still, it should be noted that Gn 15:13 is the primary source of the text of Acts. Both the change in word order (brought about by the simple insertion of the fixed phrase from Ex 2:22, πάροικος ... ἐν γῇ ἀλλοτρίᾳ,

---

former labels them as <u>geringfügig</u> and the latter states: "Acts 7:6-7 contain a quotation from Genesis 15:13-14 LXX, somewhat altered in word order and vocabulary but adding nothing new to the Old Testament passage." The two last scholars mentioned note that the author of Acts agrees with the MT in citing two verbs of "oppression" against the three of the LXX text, but pursue the problem no further.

[48]See chapter four for further discussion of this theme. There is no substantial evidence to support a textual solution here. Acts follows the common LXX tradition in δουλώσουσιν ... κακώσουσιν (against A: κακώσουσιν αὐτὸ καὶ δουλώσουσιν αὐτούς). The change from αὐτούς to αὐτό is attested only by Chrysostom and Theodoret; see Brooke and McLean, <u>Old Testament</u>, 1:36 and Wevers, <u>Genesis</u>, p. 170.

in place of ἐν γῇ οὐκ ἰδίᾳ,[49] and the elimination of the first πάροικος),[50] and the final structure of the text of Acts are to be understood in relation to the original quotation.

The omission by the writer of a phrase from the OT passage would hardly require comment in terms of quotation (any such activity is germane to redaction), and, in fact, this was the case in 7:3. However, this particular instance points to a very different problem. The standard LXX text uses three verbal expressions to correspond to the two terms of the Hebrew version. Other translations follow the Hebrew and, here too, it is reasonable to suppose that the LXX being quoted by the author of Acts did not have this particular phrase.[51]

V.7. The speech continues to draw upon the same OT passage:

7:7	Gn 15:14	
καὶ τὸ ἔθνος	τὸ δὲ ἔθνος,	
ᾧ ἐὰν δουλεύσωσιν	ᾧ ἐὰν δουλεύσωσιν,	
κρινῶ ἐγώ,	κρινῶ ἐγώ·	
ὁ θεὸς εἶπεν,		
καὶ μετὰ ταῦτα	μετὰ δὲ ταῦτα	Ex 3:12
ἐξελεύσονται	ἐξελεύσονται ὧδε	ἐν τῷ ἐξαγαγεῖν σε
	μετὰ ἀποσκευῆς πολλῆς.	τὸν λαόν μου ἐξ
		Αἰγύπτου
καὶ λατρεύσουσιν		καὶ λατρεύσετε
μοι		τῷ θεῷ
ἐν τῷ τόπῳ τούτῳ.		ἐν τῷ ὄρει τούτῳ.

It is clear from this synopsis that Acts 7:7 is a literal quotation. Nevertheless, several modifications and problems related to this verse require careful attention. The change on two occasions of δέ to καί is stylistically significant and

---

[49]The substitution of ἐν γῇ ἀλλοτρίᾳ for ἐν γῇ οὐκ ἰδίᾳ is consistent with the author's tendency to transform particular events, concepts etc., into more generalized statements of the same (infra n. 132 for other examples).

[50]This is further indicated by the fact that all versions, including the LXX, follow the MT in word order.

[51]For evidence of the mission of this last phrase, see Brooke and McLean, Old Testament, 1:36 ("h o* q u x Acta Chr$\frac{2}{4}$ Thdt½ Tyc"); Wevers, Genesis, p. 170, lists only "82* (c pr m)." This subject is developed at greater length below (pp. 152-55).

occurs frequently throughout the speech.[52] The author's fondness for the καί-style is further indicated by the threefold use of that conjunction to unite the three parts of v.7. The modification of ὄρει to τόπῳ is obviously of a thematic nature and is relegated to chapter four, where the interpretation of the Stephen story will be considered. Once again the introductory formula (ὁ θεὸς εἶπεν) is unrelated to the OT quotation, while the addition of Ex 3:12 has necessitated no structural change.

There remain, however, two important problems. The first concerns the question of direct and indirect discourse. Indeed, the transformation from second to third person is a common phenomenon in the speech (already noted in v.5 above), but the transition--as claimed by Cadbury--from indirect to direct speech would be peculiar. It would be odd, not because it is a rarity among Greek writers,[53] but because it involves an explicit OT quotation. A closer examination of Acts 7:6-7 in relation to its OT source shows that Cadbury is only partially correct when he maintains that the author uses indirect discourse in v.6 and then reverts to oratio recta by following his model too closely. In v.6 it is clear that Abraham is no longer spoken to but spoken about. At the same time, there is nothing to imply that God is not the speaker in Acts just as he is in Genesis. In fact, all indications support direct speech throughout vv.6-7. Both verses speak about the Hebrews and both follow the LXX. But, in v.7, while conflating Ex 3:12 with Gn 15:14, the author modifies λατρεύσετε to λατρεύσουσιν.

---

[52]LXX manuscripts b e j n w read καὶ ὁ θ̄ς. as does Acts 2:7 (Brooke and McLean, Old Testament, 1:36) but significantly follow the standard LXX tradition against Acts later in the verse (μετὰ δὲ ταῦτα).

[53]See Henry J. Cadbury, "Lexical Notes on Luke-Acts IV. On Direct Quotation, with Some Uses of ὅτι and εἰ," JBL 48 (1929):412-25, particularly pp. 415-17 and nn. 10 and 12. He has further indicated that such a transition ". . . is more gently made with the help of an inserted expression . . ." (p. 416) and proceeds to speak of Acts 7:6 (addition of ὁ θεὸς εἶπεν) and 25:4 (φησίν) as the two examples of this phenomenon. This structural characteristic of the author to add a variety of formulae within texts of discourse confirms in part the present analysis of Acts 7:7 and 48-50, but, such an observation does not do full justice to the architectural features of this text. See the discussion of this on p. 184 below.

And, as if to further underscore the continuity of direct discourse, the author modifies τῷ θεῷ to μοι. While in 7:5 there is a change in the type of discourse (direct to indirect), a change of addressee also ensues. In vv.6-7 only the latter occurs. In good rhetorical fashion, both the one delivering the discourse, and God himself, address the audience.[54]

The second problem which requires special attention is of a textual nature. In spite of the Aland reading,[55] δουλεύσουσιν (supported by P^{74} A C D <u>pc</u> sa), the majority of manuscripts (B ℵ 𝔄 E <u>pl</u>) present the reading δουλεύσωσιν, which agrees with the LXX. Once again the possibility of conflation exists; but if it is granted that the author quotes faithfully his OT model, then the evidence can be viewed from a different perspective. Indeed, δουλεύσωσιν has the greater number of manuscript witnesses and versions (conflation is unlikely in all cases), while the use of the future indicative by a few codices can be explained in terms of the tendency in Koine Greek to replace the subjunctive by the indicative in such expressions.[56] For these reasons the reading δουλεύσωσιν, in conformity with the

---

[54]This aspect of the speech will be examined in chapter four.

[55]Nestle and Aland, <u>NT Graece</u>, p. 315. The same reading is given in Aland et al., <u>Gk NT</u>, p. 439 and Merk, <u>NT</u>, p. 415.

[56]The versions (Vulgate, Bohairic, and the Latin column of Bezae) represent the LXX reading. The last mentioned (<u>servierint</u>, which could conceivably be future perfect active, is in clear contrast with <u>xibunt</u> and <u>desevient</u> later in the verse) certainly lessens the weight of the D reading and calls into question the claim of recent scholars that the Latin text exerted considerable influence upon the Greek text (see in particular Haenchen, <u>Acts</u>, pp. 53-55). Also contrary to general opinion, Bezae does not have a pronounced tendency to assimilate to LXX readings. In regard to manuscript C, it should be noted that its variant reading λατρεύσωσιν for λατρεύσουσιν (all manuscripts) later in the verse points to inadvertent changes on the part of the scribe. It must be said of P^{74} that, according to the editor, its relation to other manuscript families, is still a matter to be studied [Rudolf Kasser, ed. <u>Papyrus Bodmer XVII: Actes des Apôtres, Epitres de Jacques, Pierre, Jean et Jude</u> (Cologny-Genève: Bibliotheca Bodmeriana, 1961), introduction]. Finally, it should be pointed out that since the Sahidic Coptic is certainly a translation based on an A manuscript, the joint evidence of these witnesses is thereby lessened [see Bruce M. Metzger "The Early Versions of the New Testament," in <u>Peake's Commentary on the Bible</u>, eds. Matthew Black and Harold H. Rowley (London: Nelson and Sons, 1963), p. 673].

LXX model, is retained.[57]

V.8. The author now turns to the theme of circumcision. The double use of the term in this verse both reflects a stylistic tendency of the writer and indicates his two sources. The book of Genesis treats this subject in three different chapters (17,21, and 34). The first introduces the concept and relates it to that of covenant. From Gn 17:10-11 the author of Acts chooses the required terms. The combination, however, is his own (καὶ ἔδωκεν αὐτῷ διαθήκην περιτομῆς), since it is found nowhere else, to my knowledge, either in biblical or intertestamental literature.[58] Furthermore, the expression ἔδωκεν . . . διαθήκην in place of the more usual ἵστημι / διατίθημι διαθήκην is rare. It is not employed elsewhere in the NT and only three times in the LXX: Nb 25:12-13 (God speaks to Moses regarding Phineas); Mal 2:5 (about the messenger of the Lord);[59] Sir 47:11 (about David).[60] It is the first text which should be given particular attention.

Nb 25:12 οὕτως εἰπόν Ἰδοὺ ἐγὼ δίδωμι αὐτῷ διαθήκην εἰρήνης,

13 καὶ ἔσται αὐτῷ καὶ τῷ σπέρματι αὐτοῦ μετ' αὐτὸν διαθήκη ἱερατείας αἰωνία,
ἀνθ' ὧν ἐζήλωσεν τῷ θεῷ αὐτοῦ.

To what extent the author would have been influenced by such a text is difficult to say. Nevertheless, a few observations are in order. Οὕτως is not a common word in the Stephen story and

---

[57]I will deal with the problem of "textual criticism and LXX quotations" later in this chapter. It will be noted that only the Ethiopic and Arabic traditions support a future rather than a subjunctive form for Gn 15:14; see Wevers, Genesis, p. 170.

[58]No doubt the "covenant of circumcision" of Acts 7:8 should be related to the rabinic ברית מילה, see Hermann L. Strack and Paul Billerbeck, Kommentar zum Neuen Testament aus Talmud und Midrash, vol. 2: Das Evangelium nach Markus, Lukas und Johannes und die Apostelgeschichte erläutert aus Talmud und Midrash (Munich: Beck, 1924), p. 671. Compare also Nils A. Dahl, "The Story of Abraham in Luke-Acts," in Studies, eds. Keck and Martyn, p. 143.

[59]Ἡ διαθήκη μου ἦν μετ' αὐτοῦ τῆς ζωῆς καὶ τῆς εἰρήνης, καὶ ἔδωκα αὐτῷ.

[60]Καὶ ἔδωκεν αὐτῷ διαθήκην βασιλέων καὶ θρόνον δόξης ἐν τῷ Ισραηλ.

is, coincidentally, found only in the first verses of Acts 7 (1, 6, and 8). The similarity of Nb 25:12-13 to Acts 7:5 should be noted: αὐτῷ . . . καὶ τῷ σπέρματι αὐτοῦ μετ' αὐτόν. And, finally, the verb ζηλόω will be used in 7.9. True, it will be employed in a negative context (and related to Gn 37: 11); but this too is a favorite technique of the author both in composing and in quoting OT texts.[61]

The second passage of Genesis, which speaks of circumcision (21:4), is also commandeered. Indeed, the text deals with the birth and circumcision of Isaac.

7:8	Gn 21:3-4
	καὶ ἐκάλεσεν Αβρααμ τὸ ὄνομα τοῦ υἱοῦ αὐτοῦ
καὶ οὕτως ἐγέννησεν τὸν Ἰσαὰκ	τοῦ γενομένου αὐτῷ ... Ισαακ.
καὶ περιέτεμεν αὐτὸν	περιέτεμεν δὲ Αβρααμ τὸν Ισαακ
τῇ ἡμέρᾳ τῇ ὀγδόῃ	τῇ ὀγδόῃ ἡμέρᾳ.

Once more we can see that the structure of Acts, despite modifications (δέ > καί; τὸν Ισαακ > αὐτόν, omission of the name of Abraham), is that of the OT source. One last modification needs comment: τῇ ὀγδόῃ ἡμέρᾳ becomes τῇ ἡμέρᾳ τῇ ὀγδόῃ. Several reasons could be given: 1) the only other occurrence of the expression in the NT (Lk 1:59) is identical with that of Acts 7:8; 2) the author had already encountered in Gn 17:14 the version he himself uses (note that he utilizes 17:10-11 at the beginning of 7:8); 3) both Acts 7:8 and Lk 1:59 are probably dependent upon the legal precept of Lv 12:3, concerning a woman who has given birth to a son:

καὶ τῇ ἡμέρᾳ τῇ ὀγδόῃ
περιτεμεῖ τὴν σάρκα τῆς ἀκροβυστίας αὐτοῦ.

4) most decisively, I believe, is the LXX evidence for the reading found in Acts.[62]

Finally, it will be noted that the circumcision of Jacob and his sons (here called: τοὺς δώδεκα πατριάρχας) is nowhere

---

[61] See pp. 57, 120, 136 for examples of this technique and pp. 163-64 as well as chapter three for the discussion of positive/negative contrasts.

[62] See Brooke and McLean, _Old Testament_, 1:50: "D (+D^{sil}) b h t w y d_2 Chr: <εν τη ημ. τη ογ. 32>" and also Wevers, _Genesis_, p. 206, for added evidence.

referred to in the OT.[63]

2) Vv.2-8: Quoting Process

Within the first part of the speech the author of Acts has presented the story of Abraham, spanning from Gn 11 through 21. He has been most selective in his choice of episodes and speeches but remains very faithful to the structure of his model. As we have seen repeatedly, he borrows both ideas and sentence structure from the OT. The modifications are generally made within the framework of the biblical text. The reasons for the changes are not always apparent, but this owes, no doubt, to the overall purpose of the speech and its context. An attempt will be made later to elucidate some of these transformations.

While it will become clearer, in an exegetical analysis, that themes and historical personalities (i.e., their role) play a preponderant part in the redactional process, it suffices here to point out that the author is concerned to present a biblical, but at the same time, a very particular history of Abraham. He chooses the episodes and themes which interest him,[64] but he does this by relying greatly upon the OT text for quotations, ideas, style, and quoting process.

A survey of quotations, allusions, and reminiscences found within 7:2-8 reveals the following relationships (see diagram on next page). This chart shows, even with thematic and stylistic considerations kept to a minimum, that the Genesis account has played a substantial role, not only in furnishing the author with narrative material, but also in aiding his selection of idea and quotation. This process could be described--in what might be considered anachronistic terminology--as stream-of-consciousness: one idea, text or term has led him from the beginning of the Abraham story, through the book of Genesis, to the birth and circumcision of his descendants. This, however, does not suggest that the writer did not direct his inquiry, allowing the biblical text to freely speak for

---

[63]For "aberrant traditions found in the Stephen speech" see pp. 145-49.

[64]See Dahl, "Abraham," pp. 143-44, for a discussion of the author's choice and omission of episodes and themes relating to the Abraham story.

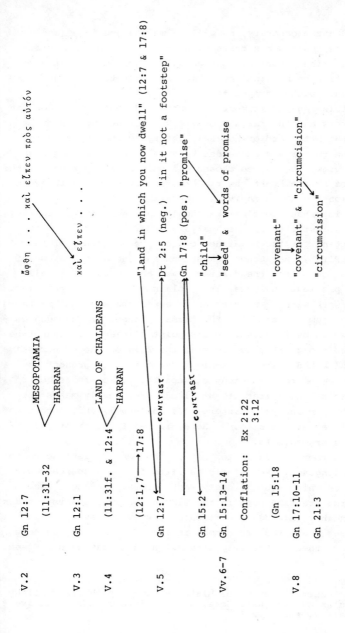

V.2	Gn 12:7		ὤφθη . . . καὶ εἶπεν πρὸς αὐτόν
	(11:31-32	MESOPOTAMIA / HARRAN	
V.3	Gn 12:1		καὶ εἶπεν . . .
V.4	(11:31f. & 12:4	LAND OF CHALDEANS / HARRAN	
	(12:1,7 → 17:8		"land in which you now dwell" (12:7 & 17:8)
V.5	Gn 12:7	← contrast →	Dt 2:5 (neg.) "in it not a footstep"
		→	Gn 17:8 (pos.) "promise"
	Gn 15:2	← contrast →	"child"
Vv.6-7	Gn 15:13-14		"seed" & words of promise
	Conflation: Ex 2:22 3:12		
	(Gn 15:18		"covenant"
V.8	Gn 17:10-11		"covenant" & "circumcision"
	Gn 21:3		"circumcision"

itself. On the contrary, as will be maintained in a later chapter, he chooses his texts with great care to demonstrate his ideas. The important consideration for him is that his demonstration be biblical and that his concepts have the stamp of approval of the scriptures.

In this regard, it must be emphasized that, while both an overall view and an analysis of 7:2-8 give the impression of being straightforward or neutral history,[65] the opposite is true. The author has succeeded very well in presenting his point of view. He has so chosen and edited the episodes of the history of Abraham that the reader does not hesitate to accept his version of the narrative as normative.

Two important conclusions should be drawn now, since they are well illustrated by the analysis of 7:2-8, and since they are important for the remainder of the present study of the speech. First, the author makes abundant and detailed use of his OT source. From the diagram given above, and especially from the previous analysis, it is plain to see that the principal framework within which he operates is the biblical narrative. He seems to seek out the terms, phrases or extended quotations which best illustrate his point of view. It cannot be emphasized too greatly how central the role of the OT narrative is to his method. The above diagram attempts to present an overall view of the relations between the various passages of Genesis which the writer has utilized. He clearly makes great use of three principal chapters, 12, 15, and 17 and, because of various ideas or terms found there, is led to other supplementary texts or concepts.

Furthermore, related to this conclusion is his concern for biblical language. Repeatedly he lifts from his source terms and phrases which are obviously Septuagintal. In some cases these terms are rare both in the Old and New Testaments but are understandably related to particular historical events. In other cases the terms are common in the LXX, but also in Acts. The author, then, is greatly interested in imitating his Greek source.

---

[65]A "neutral" sermon or history-sermon is the terminology made popular by Haenchen, Acts, pp. 288-89 and said to derive from Dibelius, see p. 288.

In relation to the above conclusion, an important corollary should be noted. Because the writer is so concerned with preserving the tone of his OT model, what may often appear a modification of the source is in reality a borrowed term or quotation from a partially lost LXX tradition. This subject will be treated in a more systematic fashion later in the chapter. However, it is necessary to point out that while divergence from the received LXX text does not necessarily indicate a variant textual tradition, such a possibility may often be suggested, especially if the Greek OT is less than faithful to the Hebrew or if there is reason to suspect the existence of a non-Masoretic textual variant. This presumption in favor of a variant LXX tradition is clearly supported by the author's great fidelity to his biblical source in his quoting method.

The second conclusion to be noted is the writer's great freedom in restructuring, conflating, and modifying his material to conform to his purpose, style or what is apparently contemporary usage. This independence, nevertheless, should be classified as relative, since the changes are seldom radical. Owing to the author's readiness to adapt his source to his needs and tendencies, it can be concluded that modifications of the biblical text or tradition are usually motivated, and that careful analysis of these leads to a better understanding of his style and point of view. The possibility of comprehending the writer's goal is greatly enhanced by the fact that he works, modifies, and creates within a very discernible framework: in the present case, Gn 11 through 21 to compose Acts 7:2-8.

One major redactional conclusion should be anticipated at this point, crucial to an understanding of the author's quoting process. A careful examination of the biblical references indicates that Gn 15 is both the focal point of the entire section and the point of departure for the redactional process. Since a discussion of this assertion would involve structural and thematic considerations, the subject will be discussed in chapter four.

b. Vv.9-16: Story of Joseph

1) Vv.9-16: Textual Relation to OT

The author now directs his attention to another part of the biblical story. After having stated the fundamental promise, in his opinion, of God to his people (vv.3-7), he proceeds to the historical precedents of the sojourn in Egypt. He loses no time in introducing his audience to the Joseph story. From the outset it will be observed that the redactional and structural elements gain in importance. This will become even more evident, once the role of the OT is better understood.

V.9. The key word ζηλόω leads the audience immediately to Gn 37:11, ἐζήλωσαν δὲ αὐτὸν οἱ ἀδελφοὶ αὐτοῦ, the source which the author used for the composition of the verse, καὶ οἱ πατριάρχαι ζηλώσαντες τὸν Ἰωσὴφ ἀπέδοντο εἰς Αἴγυπτον. The changes imposed upon the LXX text are both familiar (δέ > καί) and easily understood, in light of the writer's tendencies (οἱ ἀδελφοὶ αὐτοῦ > οἱ πατριάρχαι; see v.8 above). Finally, the word order will be examined later in relation to style and structure.

The following part of v.9, though related to Gn 37:28 and 36,[66] is more properly drawn from Gn 45:4: Ἐγώ εἰμι Ιωσηφ ὁ ἀδελφὸς ὑμῶν, ὃν ἀπέδοσθε εἰς Αἴγυπτον. The peculiar phrase, ἀποδίδωμι εἰς Αἴγυπτον, is found only in Gn 37:36 and 45.4. Furthermore, in the two passages from Gn 37 we read that Joseph is sold (ἀπέδοντο) by the Midianites. Only the text quoted above actually attributes this to the brothers.[67]

Vv.9c-10. The four short phrases that follow--each intro-

---

[66]Gn 37:28 . . . οἱ Μαδιηναῖοι . . . καὶ ἀνεβίβασεν τὸν Ιωσηφ ἐκ τοῦ λάκκου καὶ ἀπέδοντο τὸν Ιωσηφ τοῖς Ισμαηλίταις εἴκοσι χρυσῶν, καὶ κατήγαγον τὸν Ιωσηφ εἰς Αἴγυπτον.... 36 οἱ δὲ Μαδιηναῖοι ἀπέδοντο τὸν Ιωσηφ εἰς Αἴγυπτον τῷ Πετεφρη τῷ σπάδοντι Φαραω, ἀρχιμαγείρῳ.

[67]By way of illustration, I might point out a methodological principle of this study. It is plausible to credit the author with having modified the biblical tradition by transferring the act of selling Joseph from the Midianites (Gn 37) to his own brothers. After all, he seems to intend such attribution. Instead, it seems that the first text (Gn 37) has led him to a similar concept in Gn 45 and that his individual preference, a thematic consideration in this particular case, has led him to opt for the latter. This appears to be a recurring factor in his quoting as well as redactional method throughout.

duced by καί and each having ὁ θεός as subject[68]--are related to the LXX text, but in a variety of ways.

9c καὶ ἦν ὁ θεὸς μετ' αὐτοῦ,

10a καὶ ἐξείλατο αὐτὸν ἐκ πασῶν τῶν θλίψεων αὐτοῦ,

10b καὶ ἔδωκεν αὐτῷ χάριν
καὶ σοφίαν ἐναντίον Φαραὼ
βασιλέως Αἰγύπτου,

10c καὶ κατέστησεν αὐτὸν ἡγούμενον ἐπ' Αἴγυπτον
καὶ ἐφ' ὅλον τὸν οἶκον αὐτοῦ.

V.9c is of particular interest, since it introduces us both to the author's intention with regard to the Joseph episode, and to one of his theological tendencies. In Gn 39 the writer encountered the following texts which bear some resemblance to his own:

2 καὶ ἦν κύριος μετὰ Ιωσηφ

3 ὅτι κύριος μετ' αὐτοῦ

21 καὶ ἦν κύριος μετὰ Ιωσηφ

23 διὰ τὸ τὸν κύριον μετ' αὐτοῦ εἶναι.

In effect, commentators refer to one[69] or more[70] of these texts as being the source used. Since vv.2 and 21 are identical, other arguments should be considered. Gn 39:21 might be favored since it will again be utilized in Acts 7:10. Gn 39:2, however, would follow more closely the Joseph story: v.1 states that he has been brought into Egypt and sold there; immediately thereafter v.2 introduces the key expression for Joseph's sojourn along the Nile, vis., the Lord was with him. In any event, a very serious objection can be made to these and other attempts to find a source for v.9c in this chapter of Genesis: Why the change from κύριος to ὁ θεός? No commentator, to my knowledge, discusses this.

There are two possible solutions. Either the author uses one of the texts mentioned and intentionally substitutes ὁ θεός for κύριος (this would greatly help to understand the editorial process and the writer's point of view), or else the source is

---

68See pp. 330-32 for a discussion of this point.

69Preuschen, Apostelgeschichte, p. 39 (Gn 39:21); Beginnings, 4:72 (Gn 39:2); Haenchen, Acts, p. 279 (Gn 39:21).

70Jacquier, Actes, p. 209 ("expression empruntée à Gen. xxxix.2,21,23"); Bruce, Acts, p. 164 (Gn 39.2,3,21); J. H. Wilto be sought elsewhere. In Gn 48:21 the dying Jacob tells Joseph his son, καὶ ἔσται ὁ θεὸς μεθ' ὑμῶν (this verse as well as the following one will be considered below in relation to Acts 7:16).[71] The author would have found there all the required elements, even the proper word order.[72]

V.7:10a. The structural similarity between the two following texts can hardly be coincidental.

Acts 7:10a καὶ ἐξείλατο αὐτὸν ἐκ πασῶν τῶν θλίψεων αὐτοῦ

Gn 37:21 ἀκούσας δὲ Ρουβην ἐξείλατο αὐτὸν ἐκ τῶν χειρῶν αὐτῶν.

The modifications (δέ > καί, elimination of subject) are typical of the author, who has made repeated use of this chapter also in the previous verse. Later it will be argued that the contrast between Reuben, who was unable to save his brother, and God who did, is intentional.[73] Thus, it is obvious that both the concept and the structure of the verse are borrowed from the LXX.

V.7:10b. The author returns once more to Gn 39 where he finds the required phrase,

Acts 7:10b καὶ ἔδωκεν αὐτῷ χάριν καὶ σοφίαν ἐναντίον Φαραὼ βασιλέως Αἰγύπτου

Gn 39:21 καὶ ἔδωκεν αὐτῷ χάριν ἐναντίον τοῦ ἀρχιδεσμοφύλακος,

and in typical fashion--through the intermediary of a key word (ἐναντίον)[74] --fuses this text with Gn 41:46, . . . ὅτε ἔστη

---

son, "Theologian and Historian," p. 171 (Gn 39:2-3, 21).

[71]At the same time the influence of Gn 21:20 (καὶ ἦν ὁ θεὸς μετὰ τοῦ παιδίου--about Ishmael) should not be discounted, especially since the author drew various elements from 21:3-4 to compose Acts 7:8.

[72]In this regard it should be pointed out that in one instance where one is led to posit the free creation of the author (there is no apparent OT source), Acts 10:38, ὅτι ὁ θεὸς ἦν μετ' αὐτοῦ, the word order does not correspond to that of the LXX as does 7:9. Note also that two minor LXX manuscripts provide the reading ὁ θεὸς ἦν; see Wevers, Genesis, p. 369 (107 and 125--confer also Brooke and McLean, Old Testament, 1:112).

[73]See pp. 333-34 and nn. 195, 198 for my interpretation of this particular section of the speech.

[74]The term occurs only twice in Acts: the text quoted above and 8:32, which is an extended quotation of Is 53:7. Note too the stylistic similarities: ἐπί + accusative and ἐναντίον + genitive in Acts 7:10 (order reversed), 8:32 and Is 53:7.

ἐναντίον Φαραω βασιλέως Αἰγύπτου. The passage, then, is taken directly from the Greek OT with the addition of καὶ σοφίαν, which insert will be studied later.[75]

V.7.10c. This text is particularly difficult to analyze in relation to its OT source. Owing to its composite nature, scholars have proposed a variety of parallels to explain the peculiar terminology of the passage. In spite of the difficulties encountered, I propose the following texts,

Gn 41:40 σὺ ἔσῃ ἐπὶ τῷ οἴκῳ μου

43 καὶ κατέστησεν αὐτὸν ἐφ' ὅλης γῆς Αἰγύπτου,

as the sources employed for the composition of Acts 7:10c: καὶ κατέστησεν αὐτὸν ἡγούμενον ἐπ' Αἴγυπτον καὶ ἐφ' ὅλον τὸν οἶκον αὐτοῦ.[76] Leaving aside the term ἡγούμενος for the moment, it is possible to see that Gn 41:43 is the primary source being used since the peculiar combination of elements, καί + καθίστημι + αὐτόν [ ] + ἐπί . . . ὅλ[ος] . . . , is to be found only here in the book of Genesis.[77] Also, the author's penchant for doublets has led him to utilize Gn 41:40,[78] though the combination is his own. The word order of the text, as well as the use of the accusative after ἐπί, must be seen in light of v.11a below. This passage will receive further study in the next chapter (<u>infra</u> p. 187).

Finally, the expression ἡγούμενος deserves special atten-

---

[75]The matter will be dealt with in regard to style (in the next chapter) and to the writer's purpose (in the redactional study of chapter 4). See the interesting parallel in Tobit 1:13 (καὶ ἔδωκέν μοι ὁ ὕψιστος χάριν καὶ μορφὴν ἐνώπιον Ενεμεσσαρου. . .).

[76]The reading ἐφ' ὅλον τὸν οἶκον αὐτοῦ is supported by P^{74} 𝔖 E <u>pm</u>, while B 𝔄 D <u>al</u> omit the preposition. The latter is the choice of Nestle and Aland, <u>NT Graece</u>, p. 316 and Merk, <u>NT</u>, p. 415; however, Aland et al., <u>Gk NT</u>, p. 440, propose the former, but enclose the term in brackets. While it is possible to explain the addition of the second ἐπί as assimilation to the LXX (a process which is highly improbable due to the complexity of the textual relationship between Acts 7:10 and Gn 41:40-43--besides, the elimination of the second preposition for stylistic reasons is a likely explanation), it is more likely, in my opinion, that LXX phraseology is retained by the author, who is certainly not adverse to the double use of ἐπί in a similar situation, e.g., Acts 5:11 (see p. 66 below).

[77]Ὅλος is employed three times, Gn 41:19, 30, and 43 (with ἐπί only in the last-mentioned passage).

[78]Gn 39:4 and 5 were also at his disposal.

tion. Various scholars have referred to Ps 104:21,

κατέστησεν αὐτὸν κύριον τοῦ οἴκου αὐτοῦ

καὶ ἄρχοντα πάσης τῆς κτήσεως αὐτοῦ,

as the source for Acts 7:10c, presumably to account for the term ἡγούμενος.[79] It seems clear that this OT passage has little or no philological resemblance to the text under consideration. It is, rather, the phraseology of 7:10c which requires explanation since the concept is already present in the primary source. The solution should be sought in another direction. While neither the present LXX nor the MT presents a term to correspond to the ἡγούμενος of Acts 7.10c, I propose that the author utilized a Greek OT with a reading similar to that of the Syriac text and the targums _Pseudo-Jonathan_ and _Neofiti_ I.[80]

V.11. Commentators have seen few problems in analyzing this text. In terms of concepts, the essentials are found in the final verses of Gn 41 and the initial verses of chapter 42, which also contribute the elements for 7:12. The two principal verses involved in the composition of v.11 would be the following:[81]

41:54 καὶ ἐγένετο λιμὸς ἐν πάσῃ τῇ γῇ

42:5 ἦν γὰρ ὁ λιμὸς ἐν γῇ Χανααν.

A comparison between v.11a, ἦλθεν δὲ λιμὸς ἐφ' ὅλην τὴν Αἴγυπτον καὶ Χανάαν, and the alleged sources reveals several problems. Since scholars do not consider the question of redac-

---

[79]Bruce, _Acts_, p. 164, cites Ps 104:21 as the primary source along with Gn 41:40, 43, and 45:8, while Haenchen, _Acts_, p. 279, refers to the former as secondary. I have already spoken of the alleged influence of Ps 104 upon the author (_supra_ pp. 35-36 and n. 11) and will return to this subject later in the present chapter in relation to "histories of Israel" and the Stephen speech (pp. 140-45).

[80]The Syriac version of Gn 41:43 reads as follows: [ܐܒܐ ܘܫܠܝܛܐ] ܘܐܩܝܡܗ ܥܠ ܟܠܗ ܐܪܥܐ ܕܡܨܪܝܢ, (note the use of ܫܠܝܛܐ also in 41:41); _Pseudo-Jonathan_: ומני יתה סרכן על כל ארעא דמצרים (סרכן is employed in 41:41 as well. Note further that Joseph is called in v.43: רב בחכמתא; see below p. 350); and _Neofiti_: ומני יתה רב ושליט על כל ארעא דמצרים. Wilcox, _Semitism_, pp. 27-28, has pointed out the evidence from _Pseudo-Jonathan_ and has concluded that this constitutes a case of "traces of targumic textual tradition." The data, however, extend beyond the targums.

[81]Bruce, _Acts_, p. 164; Haenchen, _Acts_, p. 279; the editors of _Beginnings_, 4:73, refer more generally to Gn 41:54-42:5. Other commentators such as Preuschen, Jacquier, Renié do not

tion, none of these is dealt with. The change from καὶ ἐγένετο λιμός to ἦλθεν δὲ λιμός is peculiar, to say the least, for an author who transformed τὸ δὲ ἔθνος to καὶ τὸ ἔθνος and μετὰ δὲ ταῦτα to καὶ μετὰ ταῦτα.[82] Why should the author of Acts, who certainly employs the expression καὶ ἐγένετο in a way similar to Gn 41:54 (confer 2:2; 5:5, 11; 10:13; 21:30; and see also 7:29 and the paraphrastic constructions of 1:19 and 7:13), reject the expression when to all appearances he is quoting the LXX text? It might be noted that the author could easily have transformed the LXX expression to his more frequent phrase ἐγένετο δέ.[83] Instead he has chosen a rare expression, since ἔρχομαι is used with time expressions only twice in Acts (3:19 and 18:21) and only once of things (7:11--of a natural phenomenon).[84] Certainly ἐφ' ὅλην τὴν Αἴγυπτον is not accounted for by referring to ἐν πάσῃ τῇ γῇ (ἐν δὲ πάσῃ γῇ Αἰγύπτου).

With these observations in mind it seems best to conclude that the writer draws several ideas and stylistic features from his LXX model, but that he imposes a new structure on the whole, all the while betraying his activity by leaving clear redactional traces. The concept of ἦλθεν . . . λιμός . . . καὶ θλῖψις μεγάλη[85] he has obtained from Gn 41:54, καὶ ἤρξαντο τὰ ἑπτὰ ἔτη τοῦ λιμοῦ ἔρχεσθαι and 42:21, ἐπῆλθεν ἐφ' ἡμᾶς ἡ θλῖψις αὕτη. This is especially indicated since the verb ἔρχομαι is not usually employed in this fashion (see also Gn

---

even submit OT references.

[82]Acts 7:7 (both within an explicit quotation). The author of the speech seems to eliminate δέ particles rather systematically, 7:18 = Ex 1:8; 7:27b = Ex 2:14; etc. However, δέ is retained in a poetic quotation, 7:49 = Is 66:1.

[83]At the writer's disposal were two other famine accounts: Gn 12:10, καὶ ἐγένετο λιμὸς ἐπὶ τῆς γῆς, καὶ κατέβη Αβραμ εἰς Αἴγυπτον and Gn 26:1, Ἐγένετο δὲ λιμὸς ἐπὶ τῆς γῆς.

[84]Arndt-Gingrich, Lexicon, s.v. "ἔρχομαι." Note that Lk 4:25, ὡς ἐγένετο λιμὸς μέγας ἐπὶ πᾶσαν τὴν γῆν (see also 15:14) is considerably closer to the Genesis account than Acts 7:11a. See pp. 282-84 below for a discussion of Lk 4:28-29 and its relation to the Stephen story.

[85]The verb does double duty in the same way as does ἐτελεύτησεν in 7:15.

41:50). Furthermore, the second text is fundamental to the author's point of view and style, particularly the introduction of θλῖψις (see also 10a), its association with λιμός, and the use of ἐπί followed by the accusative. Knowing the author's consistent tendency to conflate texts and structures, possibly the frequent famine accounts of Genesis, utilizing λιμὸς ἐν or ἐπί with the genitive,[86] would have suggested an equally frequent idiom, λιμὸς ἐπι followed by the accusative.[87] In this regard the terminology of 2 K 8:1, ὅτι κέκληκεν κύριος λιμὸν ἐπὶ τὴν γῆν, καί γε ἦλθεν ἐπὶ τὴν γῆν ἑπτὰ ἔτη, is noteworthy. The composition, therefore, of Acts 7:11a is the work of the author, who has borrowed from the LXX both concept and idiom. The expression resembles other constructions of Acts: 5:11 (καὶ ἐγένετο φόβος μέγας ἐφ' ὅλην τὴν ἐκκλησίαν καὶ ἐπὶ πάντας τοὺς ἀκούοντας ταῦτα) and 11:28 (λιμὸν μεγάλην μέλλειν ἔσεσθαι ἐφ' ὅλην τὴν οἰκουμένην). The writer has formed an interesting parallel between vv.10c and 11a (note the use in both texts of ὅλος and ἐπί followed by the accusative).

The final part of v.11 cannot be considered a quotation, although it is clear that the concept is related to the biblical account, namely, Gn 42:1-2. In spite of this relationship, however, only χόρτασμα need be examined in reference to the OT. Jacob, in v.2, tells his sons to go down to Egypt, καὶ πρίασθε ἡμῖν μικρὰ βρώματα (see also 43:2). What bearing, if any, does the OT text have upon v.11c? Further, what is the meaning of the NT text? The following opinions have been defended. 1) χόρτασμα in Acts (a _hapax legomenon_ in the NT), as in other literature, means "fodder or provender."[88] 2) The word which

---

[86]The LXX employs both expressions, λιμὸς ἐπί (Gn 12:10 twice; 26:6; 41:56; 43:1; 45:6) and λιμὸς ἐν (Gn 41:54 and 57; 42:5; 47:4).

[87]See 2 K 8:1; 2 Chr 20:9; Ps 104:16; Ez 5:16-17; 14:13; 36:29.

[88]Foakes Jackson, _Acts_, p. 59 translates the term by "provender" and does not indicate that this might be a quotation. Both Wilson, "Theologian and Historian," p. 172 and Bihler, _Stephanusgeschichte_, p. 49, n. 1, refer to the term's occurrence in Gn 42 and 43, where it obviously refers to _fodder_. Jacquier, _Actes_, p. 210, sees the possibility of two meanings: food for humans and fodder.

originally meant "fodder" acquired in late Greek the sense of "food for humans." Important for this conclusion is the relation of Acts 7:11 to βρῶμα of Gn 42:2.[89] 3) The expression under the influence of Ps 36:19 is to be understood as "sustenance."[90]

Before stating my position in regard to the options listed above, a few observations are in order: 1) The eight occurrences of the term in the LXX obviously refer to some type of animal food,[91] even within the Joseph story. 2) The context, as well as the parallelism between vv.11c (χόρτασμα) and 12b (σιτία), seems to demand another meaning besides "fodder." 3) Even if a change in meaning be granted--"food for humans"--why the substitution of terms when βρώματα occurs 17 times in the NT corpus, twice in Luke, though not in Acts? 4) Contemporary papyri indicate that the term had in fact acquired the sense of "sustenance" or "supplies."[92]

From this evidence, and in light of structural analysis, I conclude that χόρτασμα means "sustenance" or "satiation."[93]

---

[89]This is the position adopted by Liddell-Scott-Jones, Lexicon, s.v. "χόρτασμα"; Arndt-Gingrich, Lexicon, s.v. "χόρτασμα"; Beginnings, 4:73; Renié, Actes, p. 113; Bruce, Acts, p. 164.

[90]Preuschen, Apostelgeschichte, p. 39 (followed by Haenchen, Acts, p. 279) states rather laconically: "Der auffallende Ausdruck χορτάσματα 'Nahrungsmittel' 11 erklärt sich aus der Einwirkung von Ps 36.19: καὶ ἐν ἡμέραις λιμοῦ χορτασθήσονται."

[91]Gn 24:25, 32; 42:27; 43:24; Dt 11:15; Jdg 19:19; Sir 30:35; 38:26.

[92]Moulton-Milligan, Vocabulary, s.v. "χόρτασμα."

[93]The nonpopularity of the first option mentioned above, and the implicit reason for adopting the second one, attest to the same fact. Further, the ambivalence of early translators of the NT in rendering χόρτασμα also supports this contention, namely, that the author of Acts was not speaking of "fodder." "La Vulgate a traduit par cibos, e p par frumentum, d par utensilia, mais Gigas par pabula," Jacquier, Actes, p. 210. The variety and ambiguity are sympotomatic. Cibus, which literally means "food for man and beast, nourishment, fodder," even acquired the sense of "sustenance" in writers of the Ciceronian period. The other terms are too interpretative (utensilia = necessities, frumentum = grain, corn) or all inclusive (pabula = food, nutriment, fodder) to indicate anything but the difficulties of the early translators. To Jacquier's list I would add the Coptic versions--Boharic: ⲥⲟⲩⲟ = wheat; Sahidic and G67 ⲟⲉⲓⲕ and ⲁⲉⲓⲕ = bread. The Syriac, however, approaches what I believe is the intended meaning of the author, ܠܣܝܒܪܐ,

For polemical purposes (a positive/negative contrast in which χόρτασμα plays a central role, see pp. 185-88) the author modifies his LXX source, a modification sanctioned by contemporary idiom (papyri).

V.12. With this verse the author returns more properly to the biblical account, after having expounded an important thesis. While he had drawn freely from Gn 41 and 42 for vv.10 and 11, he now focuses more directly upon his OT source to select the required data. The textual relation is as follows:

Acts 7:12		Gn 42
ἀκούσας δὲ Ἰακὼβ	1	ἰδὼν δὲ Ιακωβ ὅτι ἔστιν πρᾶσις ἐν Αἰγύπτῳ, ...
ὄντα σιτία εἰς Αἴγυπτον	2	ἰδοὺ ἀκήκοα ὅτι ἔστιν σῖτος ἐν Αἰγύπτῳ· κατάβητε ἐκεῖ ...
	3	κατέβησαν δὲ οἱ ἀδελφοὶ Ιωσηφ οἱ δέκα πρίασθαι σῖτον ἐξ Αἰγύπτου
ἐξαπέστειλεν τοὺς πατέρας ἡμῶν πρῶτον.	4	τὸν δὲ Βενιαμιν τὸν ἀδελφὸν Ιωσηφ οὐκ ἀπέστειλεν μετὰ τῶν ἀδελφῶν αὐτοῦ.

From this text one can easily see several redactional tendencies in the use of LXX material. In a mosaic-like technique the writer selects elements from his source for his composite picture. Some borrowed pieces he employs unaltered (. . . δὲ Ιακωβ); others he modifies for structural reasons (ἀκήκοα)[94] or stylistic/redactional reasons (ὅτι ἔστιν,[95] σῖτος,[96] ἐν

---

namely, the infinitive of the verb "to satiate or be satisfied." This, incidentally, is the identical term and form of the translation of Ps 36:19, but see the treatment of this in chapters three and four.

[94]Since questions of text and sentence structure are treated in chapter three, it suffices to point out the almost identical pattern of 7:14, which significantly is a free creation of the author.

[95]See 7:2 and 5 and also the author's use of participles as a consistent stylistic feature.

[96]The modification of σῖτος to σιτία and the substitution of χορτάσματα for μικρὰ βρώματα in 7:11 are intimately related to the author's purpose. But presently, it suffices to point out with Liddell-Scott-Jones, Lexicon, s.v. "σῖτος": "In the general sense of food, Prose writers prefer the dim. form σιτία, τά." Further, the term appears once in the LXX, Pr 24:57 (=30:22) where it renders the Hebrew לחם. See Moulton-

Αἰγύπτῳ[97]); still others furnish him the inspiration for his own creation (42:2b, 3, and 4). From the OT narrative the writer concludes that Jacob has dispatched his sons to make purchases of food-stuffs; however, nowhere is it said that the father has "sent" them. In typical fashion he lifts from the historical narrative a verb which he wishes (v.4, ἀποστέλλω)[98] and pursues his own goal (again οἱ ἀδελφοί . . . cedes to a more appropriate, favorite term, see 7:9).

Finally the πρῶτον of v.12 and the ἐν τῷ δευτέρῳ of v.13 are deductions based on the biblical narrative story (Gn 42-43). The construction is due to the writer's redactional activity (<u>infra</u>, pp. 186-87).

V.13. The main part of v.13 is borrowed from the LXX:

v. 13 ἀνεγνωρίσθη 'Ιωσὴφ τοῖς ἀδελφοῖς αὐτοῦ

Gn 45:1 ἡνίκα ἀνεγνωρίζετο τοῖς ἀδελφοῖς αὐτοῦ.

The relationship between the two texts is remarkably close, expecially if one follows the reading of the vast majority of manuscripts instead of the non-LXX reading (ἐγνωρίσθη) of B A p t vg. Once again one is confronted by the problem of pos-

---

Milligan, <u>Vocabulary</u>, s.v. "σιτίον," who present papyri evidence from the 2nd and 3rd centuries A.D. for the use of σιτίον meaning "food or provisions." Note also their references to Musonius (1st cent. A.D.) and Aelianus (2nd-3rd cent. A.D.). For a discussion of the minor variant σῖτα (Ψ 𝔐 1611 <u>pm</u>), see Bruce M. Metzger, <u>A Textual Commentary on the Greek New Testament</u>, A Companion Volume to the United Bible Societies' Greek New Testament (London: United Bible Societies, 1971), pp. 343-44.

[97]The change of ἐν Αἰγύπτῳ of the source to εἰς Αἴγυπτον in Acts 7:12 could be explained as Koine usage, i.e., εἰς for local ἐν [see James H. Moulton, gen. ed., <u>A Grammar of New Testament Greek</u>, vol. 1: <u>Prolegomena</u>, by James H. Moulton (1908, 1957 reprint); vol. 2: <u>Accidence and Word-Formation</u>, <u>idem</u> (1929); vol. 3: <u>Syntax</u>, by Nigel Turner (1963); 3 vols. (Edinburgh: T & T Clark, 1908-63), 3:254]; however, I prefer to see the transformation in stylistic terms, i.e., εἰς Αἴγυπτον should be related primarily to the following verb of "sending." We say <u>primarily</u> advisedly since this local expression, like the name 'Ιωσήφ in 7:9 (. . . ζηλώσαντες τὸν 'Ιωσὴφ ἀπέδοντο εἰς Αἴγυπτον) does double duty.

[98]The author utilizes this particular verb in contrast to ἀπέδοντο of v.9. The two also serve as complementary elements of the theme of mission, especially 7:14, 34, 35; see pp. 330-38 for a discussion of these elements. Finally, the use of verbal roots with or without prepositional prefixes is a characteristic feature of the writer and in the present instance should be seen in relation to v.14: ἀποστείλας.

sible assimilation to the LXX on the one hand, and that of fidelity to an OT model on the other. It is the textual evidence which is the most crucial however. Besides, the opinion of Metzger is very apropos in this regard:

> It is probable that scribes changed the verb ἀνεγνωρίσθη (P74 א C D E H P most minuscules) to the simple form ἐγνωρίσθη (A B it^p vg) because the compound form seems to imply that Joseph had also made himself known to his brothers on their first visit to Egypt.[99]

Two modifications should be noted: the change from a middle to a passive form, and the possible addition of a subject. The former demonstrates the author's predilection for such constructions (see vv.16, 17, 19, etc.), and the latter could be explained grammatically or textually.[100] The rest of the verse is not an actual quotation, even though the idea is unmistakably borrowed from the OT narrative, Gn 45:16.[101]

V.14. Again the source for the NT text, ἀποστείλας δὲ Ἰωσὴφ μετεκαλέσατο Ἰακὼβ τὸν πατέρα αὐτοῦ, is the biblical account, Gn 45:9f., where Joseph instructs his brothers to go and get his father and relatives. Neither the terminology nor the sentence structure of the texts is related though. Instead, as in v.10a above, the author borrows a ready-made construction from the LXX and applies it to a new context. Two examples[102]

---

[99]Commentary, p. 344. Aland et al., Gk NT, p. 440 and Merk, NT, p. 416, support this reading, while Nestle and Aland, NT Graece, p. 316, omit the prepositional suffix, following B A p t vg. See the Statement of Haenchen, Acts, p. 279: "Verse: 13: ἐγνωρίσθη (B A)=Gen. 45.1." In a footnote, he continues: "Most MSS of Acts, influenced by the ἀνεγνωρίζετο of LXX, have ἀνεγνωρίσθη." For further discussion of the textual problem, see below, pp. 150-52.

[100]Both Rahlfs, Septauginta, 1:75 and Wevers, Genesis, p. 423, choose to eliminate Ιωσηφ from the reading of Gn 45:1 (given above); however, Brooke and McLean, Old Testament, 1: 133, add the proper name on the basis of the following witnesses: "A a c m o x a_2 b_2 c_2𝕾."

[101]V.13 constitutes a parallelismus membrorum, the construction of which is paradigmatic. The writer has borrowed the first member from the LXX, structure as well as idea; but the second part he has constructed himself, taking only the idea from his model. The resulting structure is clearly his own. Nevertheless, the influence of the OT text is evident. See chapter three for a detailed discussion of this subject.

[102]The books of Genesis and Exodus furnish two other examples of the construction: Gn 31:4 and Ex 9:27.

from a much-quoted chapter are Gn 41:8, καὶ ἀποστείλας ἐκάλεσεν πάντας τοὺς ἐξηγητὰς Αἰγύπτου καὶ πάντας τοὺς σοφοὺς αὐτῆς, and Gn 41:14, Ἀποστείλας δὲ Φαραω ἐκάλεσεν τὸν Ιωσηφ. The use of the compound[103] instead of the simple verb is not new for the author (see v.12, 24, 29, etc.). The expression Ἰακὼβ τὸν πατέρα αὐτοῦ of v.14 is easily understood as an imitation of biblical Greek (see especially Gn 42:29, 36; 45:25, 27). Finally, the number of Joseph's kindred is drawn from Gn 46:27: πᾶσαι ψυχαὶ οἴκου Ιακωβ αἱ εἰσελθοῦσαι εἰς Αἴγυπτον ἑβδομήκοντα πέντε.[104] However, the peculiar construction of Acts, ἐν ψυχαῖς ἑβδομήκοντα πέντε, needs further attention. Following the suggestion of the editors of Beginnings, I believe that Acts 7:14 is best understood by positing the influence here of Dt 10:22.[105] In effect, following the narrative continuity of his source, the author borrows the "number of souls" from Gn 46:27 (even the word order is indicated, ἑβδομήκοντα πέντε) and, succumbing to his stream-of-conscious tendencies, is led

---

[103]The verb μετακαλέω is rare in the LXX: 1 Esd 1:50; Hos 11:1, 2 (once also in Symmachus: Jb 33:30). Furthermore, its occurrence in the middle voice seems to be a late development (Liddell-Scott-Jones, Lexicon, s.v. "μετακαλέω") and its appearance in the NT (all in the middle) is limited to the book of Acts: 7:14; 10:32; 20:17; and 24:25. Further confirmation of this late development (". . . the mid. of this verb . . . in the sense 'summon to myself,' 'send for' . . .") is to be found in the late 2nd cent. A.D. P Oxy I.33, verso ii.2, iv.7, and the 288-95 A.D. P Oxy X.1252, recto 26; see Moulton-Milligan, Vocabulary, s.v. "μετακαλέω."

[104]See also Ex 1:5 where the same figures are given. While the MT gives a total of 70 persons, the LXX, following a Vorlage similar to the one found at Qumran for Ex 1:5 (4QEx[a]) [Frank M. Cross, The Ancient Library of Qumran and Modern Biblical Studies, The Haskell Lectures, 1956-57 (Garden City, N. Y.: Doubleday, 1958), pp. 137-38; see also Jósef T. Milik, Ten Years of Discovery in the Wilderness of Judaea, Studies in Biblical Theology, no. 26, trans. John Strugnell (Naperville, Ill.: Alec R. Allenson, 1959 and London: SCM Press, 1959), p. 24] provides the same reading as Acts 7:14. This fact tends to confirm a constant preoccupation of this study, namely, that the author of Acts follows one of the textual traditions of his time, admittedly a tradition which is close to that underlying our present LXX, but not totally identical to it, and therefore responsible for many of the variants found in the Stephen speech. See further in this chapter for a discussion of the LXX utilized by the author of the discourse.

[105]Beginnings, 4:73.

by similarity of idea to Dt 10:22, ἐν ἑβδομήκοντα[106] ψυχαῖς κατέβησαν οἱ πατέρες σου εἰς Αἴγυπτον,[107] where he finds the terminology to his liking.[108] Furthermore, papyrus evidence suggests that this particular construction was consistent with contemporary idiom.[109]

V.15. The author finds the idea required for the next step in his historical narrative in Gn 46:6: εἰσῆλθον εἰς Αἴγυπτον, Ιακωβ καὶ πᾶν τὸ σπέρμα αὐτοῦ μετ' αὐτοῦ.[110] However, due to the intervening influence of 45:9 and 46:3, both of which employ the verb καταβαίνω and the latter of which adds εἰς Αἴγυπτον,[111] he modifies his source and imposes upon it a new pattern. It is a pattern which he had encountered earlier

---

[106]The LXX codex Alexandrinus adds πέντε to its Deuteronomic passage. It would be possible to see here only the influence of the LXX, as represented by A; however, knowing the conflating tendency of this manuscript and having observed closely the author's quoting techniques, I prefer the above solution. See the discussion below of the LXX utilized by the author of the speech.

[107]The editors of Beginnings, 4:73, are probably right when they state concerning the reading of D: "It probably should be punctuated ἐν ο̅ καὶ ε̅ ψυχαῖς κατέβη 'Ιακώβ." But to their query ". . . whether the Western text of Acts in this verse is due to the influence of Deuteronomy or is original . . . ," I can only insist that the former is the case, since the word order and grammatical structure is unmistakably that of Deuteronomy and does not conform to the author's quoting process, as I understand it.

[108]See Acts 27:37: ἤμεθα δὲ αἱ πᾶσαι ψυχαὶ ἐν τῷ πλοίῳ διακόσιαι ἑβδομήκοντα ἕξ.

[109]See Moulton, NT Greek, 1:103, where three examples are given (one from the first and two from the second centuries A. D.) of ". . .ἐν = 'amounting to' . . ." and also Moulton-Milligan, Vocabulary, s.v. "ἐν."

[110]The variant reading of Codex Alexandrinus (along with y a_2* --Brooke and McLean, Old Testament, 1:136) is interesting in this connection: καὶ εἰσῆλθεν Ιακωβ εἰς Αἴγυπτον . . . ; but see the discussion below regarding this manuscript.

[111]Gn 45:9: 'Εποίησέν με ὁ θεὸς κύριον πάσης γῆς Αἰγύπτου· κατάβηθι οὖν πρός με; 46:3: λέγων 'Εγώ εἰμι ὁ θεὸς τῶν πατέρων σου· μὴ φοβοῦ καταβῆναι εἰς Αἴγυπτον. That the author has read Gn 45 very carefully can be seen from the abundant use he makes of it (see 7:9 [45:5]; 7:13 [v.1]; 7:14 [vv.9f.]). At the same time the influence of Gn 46:3-4 will be readily seen upon the structure of the speech: Gn 46:3--the God of the Fathers (7:32) orders Jacob to go down to Egypt (7:15) and v.4--he promises to go down with them into Egypt (7:34) to deliver them. Important in this regard is the double use of καταβαίνω both in the speech and in Gn 46:3-4.

in the Abraham story:

Acts 7:15 καὶ κατέβη Ἰακὼβ εἰς Αἴγυπτον

Gn 12:10 καὶ ἐγένετο λιμὸς ἐπὶ τῆς γῆς,
καὶ κατέβη Αβραμ εἰς Αἴγυπτον.[112]

The second part of v.15 again betrays the influence of several LXX texts. The death of Jacob is related in Gn 49:33 (ἐξέλιπεν) and that of Joseph in 50:26 (ἐτελεύτησεν). From these the writer is led to Ex 1:6, ἐτελεύτησεν δὲ Ιωσηφ καὶ πάντες οἱ ἀδελφοὶ αὐτοῦ καὶ πᾶσα ἡ γενεὰ ἐκείνη, and, in his accustomed manner, transforms δέ to καί. He consequently applies the text to Jacob, employing his favorite term for the early Hebrews: οἱ πατέρες ἡμῶν. The structure of v.15b, then, is easily understood in light both of LXX influence[113] and especially of the author's creative tendencies.[114]

V.16. This verse is replete with problems of various kinds, and is probably the most troublesome part of the Stephen material. Grammatically and stylistically there is little or no connection between the LXX rendering of the burial texts and Acts 7:16. Instead, the episodes are recounted employing totally different terminology. While the following texts, Gn 23:16; 33:19; 50:13; and Jos 24:32, furnish most--divergencies of tradition aside--of the narrative detail, none of the vocabulary can be traced to the LXX source (an unusual fact for this author).

2) Vv.9-16: Quoting Process

The second part of the patriarchal story is centered on the role of Joseph and, in relation to him, that of his father. Beginning at Gn 37:11, the writer surveys Hebrew history as it

---

[112]See the discussion above of the expression λιμὸς ἐπί, pp. 62-66, and the relation of Gn 12:10 to Acts 7:10. Furthermore, the author has made ample use of Gn 12 for the initial verses of his history of Israel.

[113]The use of compound subjects is very common in the LXX with both plural (see Gn 46:6) or singular (Ex 1:6) verbs. Examples of both are common enough in Gn 45-50. Furthermore, the particular model found in our text: singular verb followed by αὐτὸς καί + a second subject is also found several times in Genesis: 13:1; 14:15; and 50:22.

[114]The same construction is also employed in Acts 16:33, so that of five such patterns in the NT two are in Acts, one in Jn 4:53 and the final two are in Mk 2:25 and Lk 6:3, the latter being identical to Mark (note that Mt 12:3 has eliminated the

deals with the entrance into Egypt and chooses events and themes relating to this momentous episode.

The redactional process will be examined at length in a later chapter; however, it is essential to note that the quoting process is increasingly directed by the author's purpose. The sojourn in Egypt and its precedents are uppermost in his mind, greatly influencing his choice of texts and the modifications he imposes upon them. Because of his increasingly limited scope, viz., how the fathers got into Egypt, he becomes less open to the variety of the biblical narrative and submits it to more frequent changes.

None the less, the author continues to follow his model in regard both to the sequence of events and to elements of style and structure. Once more one is impressed by the important, though slightly transformed, role of the LXX text, which continues to furnish him with ideas, terms, and structural models. The following sketch illustrates the manifold relations between the Greek OT and the Joseph episode of the Stephen speech. (See diagram on next page.)

In examining the writer's biblical references in this chart, a number of familiar quoting techniques again emerge. As before, a particular passage within the narrative leads him to adopt a similar, but more appealing, text or idea for structural (vv.9c, 10a, 14, 15a) or thematic (vv.9b, 9c, 10b, 10c, etc.) reasons. In his concern for biblical language, he consistently borrows terms or phrases from his LXX source even when he imposes major structural modifications upon his model (v.11, 12, etc.).

An overall view also indicates fidelity to the order of events found in Genesis. Acts 7:9-16 systematically draws from chapters 37 through 50 and ends with Ex 1:5-6, where the pre-Moses story is terminated. Numerous ideas, terms, and passages are drawn from different parts of Genesis. However, the chronological sequence is clearly that of the Genesis account.

Just as in the examination of the quoting process for 7:2-8, where the conclusion was reached that one chapter (15) was central both to the writer's redaction and method of ap-

---

αὐτός from his Markan source).

V.9a	Gn 37:11	ζηλόω	Gn 45:4	sold by brothers
b	28	ἀποδίδωμι		
	36			
c	Gn 39:2,3,23			
	21	Lord with him	Gn 48:21	God with him Shechem portion of Joseph (see 7:16)
V.10a	Gn 37:21	(structure)		(Gn 37:21 & 42:21)
b	Gn 39:21	χάρις ἐναντίον		
	conflation 41:46	ἐναντίον Φαραω		Gn 45:5-9
c	Gn 41:40	(39:4; 41:33)		
	43	καθίστημι	Gn 45:8	
		ἡγούμενον ἐπί		
V.11	Gn 41:54	λιμός		Gn 45:6
	42:5 & 21	θλῖψις		(Gn 37:21 & 42:21)
V.12	Gn 42:1-2	food in Egypt		Gn 45:7
V.13a	Gn 45:1	Joseph reveals himself		
b	16	made known to Pharaoh		
V.14	Gn 45:9f.	sending for Jacob		
	Gn 46:27	75 souls		(Ex 1:5) — Dt 10:22 (structure)
V.15a	Gn 46:6	going down to Egypt	Gn 45:9	
	12:10	(structure)	46:3	[Moses story 7:17f. & 32f.]
b	Ex 1:6	death	Gn 49:33 & 50:26	
V.16		burial	Gn 23:16; 33:19; 50:13 & Jos 24:22	
		at Shechem	Gn 48:22	

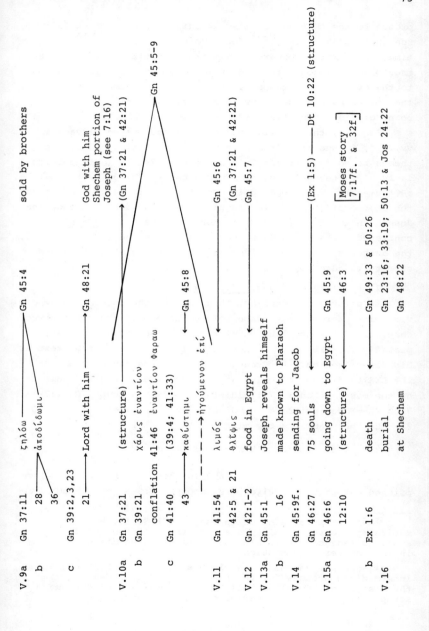

proach to the OT text, so also in this case one cannot fail to see that Gn 45:2-10 is the focal point of 7:9-16. At the same time, as thematic concerns are increasingly evident in the author's composition, it would be well to note that in relation to the overall importance of Gn 45, and in a complementary way, the following passages provide significant elements for his point of view: Gn 37:21; 42:21; 46:2-4; 48:21-22.[115]

Finally, the familiar procedure (encountered already in vv.2, 4, 5, and 8) of summarizing or capsulizing episodes or themes becomes increasingly prominent in 7:9-16 (note particularly v.9, "the selling into Egypt" and vv.12-13, πρῶτον καὶ ἐν τῷ δευτέρῳ). This apparently owes to, and is in proportion to, the degree of manipulation required in the didactic use of the Joseph incident. By means of short phrases, mots justes or conflated texts, usually strung together by the paratactic καί, the author synthesizes a long period of biblical history and submits it adroitly to his purpose.

2. History of Moses: 7:17-34

As pointed out earlier, this part of the speech can be divided into three parts, each related to one of the first three chapters of Exodus. This confirms a conclusion advanced repeatedly in this study: the author is employing the OT text as his direct source.[116] Because of this close dependence upon the LXX text, the following apportionment of the data seems to be the most logical: 7:17-19--the Hebrews in Egypt (Ex 1:7-11); 7:20-29--Moses prior to the Sinai event (Ex 2:1-15); and 7:30-34--the theophany and the mission (Ex 3:1-10).

a. Acts 7:17-34: Textual Relation to OT

1) Vv.17-19

In the analysis of vv.14 and 15 above, it has already been pointed out that the writer drew upon Ex 1:5-6 for his own com-

---

[115]A number of biblical passages (Dt 31:17; Ps 36:19) and motifs (jealousy, God is present to the good and absent to the evil, sustenance, etc.) will be examined in relation to 7:9-16 in the chapter on redaction.

[116]See pp. 141-45 for a discussion of theories suggesting intermediate sources for the part of the speech dealing with the history of Israel as well as an examination of various scriptural and other summaries of those events.

position or was led to these verses by very similar passages.[117] Thus, presently, it is hardly surprising to see that he begins the next part of his narrative at the very point he had reached in the use of his source.

V.17. The first part of the verse bears no relation to the OT text. The second, however, after a very solemn time formula, borrows directly from Ex 1:7. The textual relationship is as follows:

Acts 7:17	Ex 1:7
... ηὔξησεν ὁ λαὸς	οἱ δὲ υἱοὶ Ισραηλ ηὐξήθησαν
καὶ ἐπληθύνθη	καὶ ἐπληθύνθησαν
	καὶ χυδαῖοι ἐγένοντο
	καὶ κατίσχυον σφόδρα σφόδρα,
ἐν Αἰγυπτῳ.	ἐπλήθυνεν δὲ ἡ γῆ αὐτούς.

The changes brought to bear upon the source may appear minimal: a singular subject replaces a plural one--with consequent grammatical adjustment; the first verb assumes an active form; and ἐν Αἰγύπτῳ is added. But a closer look reveals a slightly more complicated situation. The first modification mentioned above (the elimination of the expression οἱ υἱοὶ Ισραηλ) is surely related to the role this and related terms play within the speech. The phrase is omitted or overlooked in several instances (Acts 7:17, 19, 34 twice), and yet is retained once in a quotation (7:23 = Ex 2:11). The result of such redactional activity is very characteristic of the writer. The expression οἱ υἱοὶ 'Ισραήλ appears only twice in the entire speech (v.23, a quotation and v.37, not a quotation), while the term introduced at 7:17, ὁ λαός, is also used only twice within the speech (v.17, which ostensibly is not part of a quotation and v.34, which is drawn from Ex 3:7).[118]

Beyond stylistic/redactional reasons, the following considerations are in order regarding the modification of οἱ υἱοὶ Ισραηλ to ὁ λαός. Throughout the speech the author employs the name "Jacob" for the patriarch, never "Israel." To have

---

[117]For Acts 7:14, note the relation between Gn 46:25, Ex 1:5, and Dt 10:22; and for 7:15, see Gn 49:33, 50:26, and Ex 1:6.

[118]The phenomenon of doublets, their role and relationship to the OT text is examined in the following chapter, pp. 181f. and 206f.

followed his source too closely at this point and to have retained the expression "sons of Israel," especially following the Jacob/Joseph episode, would have introduced unnecessary ambiguity into his narrative. Finally, the influence upon Acts 7:17 of a very similar OT text, Ex 1:20 καὶ ἐπλήθυνεν ὁ λαὸς καὶ ἴσχυεν σφόδρα,[119] should not be discounted, especially in light of the writer's quoting techniques.

That the passive form of αὐξάνω should be transformed to an active form with an intransitive meaning is understandable both as a development of later Greek[120] and as a regular feature of Acts.[121] Furthermore, the combination of αὐξάνω and πληθύνω, utilized only by the author of Acts (6:7; 7:17; and 12:24) in the NT[122] always bears the same peculiarities: both verbs are intransitive, the first being active, the second passive in form.

The addition of ἐν Αἰγύπτῳ is consistent with the author's purpose. And, his tendency to follow numerous clues furnished by his source indicates that Ex 1:5, Ιωσηφ δὲ ἦν ἐν Αἰγύπτῳ, a verse he has already utilized (7:14), is such a clue.

V.18. After having chosen what he desired from Ex 1:7 for the previous verse, the author now makes full use of the next part of his source:

ἄχρι οὗ ἀνέστη βασιλεὺς ἕτερος ἐπ' Αἴγυπτον,
ὃς οὐκ ᾔδει τὸν 'Ιωσήφ.

Ex 1:8 'Ανέστη δὲ βασιλεὺς ἕτερος ἐπ' Αἴγυπτον,
ὃς οὐκ ᾔδει τὸν Ιωσηφ.

---

[119]The penchant to conflate texts or to combine stylistic and thematic elements from similar passages is a constant feature throughout the speech.

[120]'Αυξάνω appears both as a transitive and as an intransitive (active and passive) verb in the LXX, but ". . . the use of the act. in the same intrans. sense belongs to later Gk . . .," Arndt-Gingrich, Lexicon, s.v. "αὐξάνω" (in fact most NT examples); see also Friedrich W. Blass and Albert Debrunner, A Greek Grammar of the New Testament and Other Early Christian Literature, trans. and rev. Robert W. Funk (Chicago: University of Chicago Press, 1961), p. 50; Liddell-Scott-Jones, Lexicon, s.v. "αὐξάνω."

[121]The verb is employed four times in Acts (6:7; 7:17; 12:24; and 19:20) and in each case it is active and intransitive.

[122]2 Cor 9:10 employs the two verbs, in reverse order, in an active, transitive construction.

The writer utilizes the conjunction ἄχρι in lieu of a temporal connective. But, the use of the less frequent ἄχρι οὗ is noteworthy and, doubly so followed by the indicative past, since there are only two such examples in the NT: Acts 7:18 and 27:33.[123]

V.19. Since this verse bears no structural resemblance to its source, it will suffice at this point only to indicate the textual relationship between the two. In effect, the author has simply chosen four terms from the OT text and has used them in mosaic-like fashion to construct an entirely new narrative. (See the two texts, Acts 7:19 and Ex 1:9-22 juxtaposed on the next page.) The four terms borrowed from the LXX provide interesting data in analyzing the redactional process. The relative nonfrequency either in the Old or New Testament of the words involved (κατασοφίζομαι[124] and ζωογονέω[125]), clearly indicates the source being used; while the author's stylistic preferences (his fondness for the terms γένος[126] and κακόω[127]) demonstrate the constant tendency of taking from the LXX many

---

[123]See Moulton-Milligan, Vocabulary, p. 100, for two examples in the papyri of ἄχρι οὗ, both followed by the subjunctive.

[124]The word occurs only three times in the OT and once in the NT. Three of these deal with the same event (Ex 1:10; Jdt 5:11--a history-speech; and Acts 7:19), while the last (Jdt 10:19) involves a more general usage.

[125]The term is found eleven times in the LXX (never in Genesis, but in Exodus only in the following: 1:17, 18, and 22) and three times in the NT corpus (Lk 17:33; Acts 7:19; and I Tm 6:13). Only the present text utilizes a passive construction.

[126]Γένος, which appears only in Ex 1:9 among the texts utilized by the author, is a favorite word of his (nine occurrences in Acts with the meaning of "race/descendant/ancestry"). In the gospels, on the contrary, it is rare (only Mk and Mt) and generally means "kind" (except Mk 7:26). Further, γένος occurs twice in the Stephen speech, once being a quotation (7:19) and once the modification of the LXX text (Gn 45:16 οἱ ἀδελφοὶ Ισραηλ > 7:13 τὸ γένος Ιωσήφ).

[127]Within the LXX passages used by the writer, only Gn 15:13 (quoted 7:6) and Ex 1:11 (quoted 7:19) employ the verb κακόω; however, the term appears six times in the NT, five of which occur in Acts. From this we can see that all occurrences of a favorite term in his source, i.e., the texts used in composing his history, were utilized (note too that τὴν κάκωσιν of 7:34 = Ex 3:7).

Acts 7:19		Ex 1:9-22
οὗτος	9	εἶπεν δὲ τῷ ἔθνει αὐτοῦ
κατασοφισάμενος		Ἰδου τὸ γένος τῶν υἱῶν Ισραηλ
		μέγα πλῆθος καὶ ἰσχύει ὑπὲρ ἡμᾶς·
τὸ γένος ἡμῶν	10	δεῦτε οὖν κατασοφισώμεθα αὐτούς,
		μήποτε πληθυνθῇ καί, ἡνίκα ἂν συμβῇ
		ἡμῖν πόλεμος, προστεθήσονται καὶ οὗτοι
		πρὸς τοὺς ὑπεναντίους καὶ ἐκπολεμήσαντες
		ἡμᾶς ἐξελεύσονται ἐκ τῆς γῆς.
	11	καὶ ἐπέστησεν αὐτοῖς ἐπιστάτας τῶν ἔργων,
ἐκάκωσεν		ἵνα κακώσωσιν αὐτοὺς ἐν τοῖς ἔργοις·
τοὺς πατέρας		καὶ ᾠκοδόμησαν πόλεις ὀχυρὰς τῷ Φαραω,
		τήν τε Πιθωμ καὶ Ραμεσση καὶ Ων,
		ἥ ἐστιν Ἡλίου πόλις. 12-17a
	17	... καὶ ἐζωογόνουν τὰ ἄρσενα.
	18	... καὶ ἐζωογονεῖτε τὰ ἄρσενα;
	20	... καὶ ἐπλήθυνεν ὁ λαὸς καὶ ἴσχυεν σφόδρα.
τοῦ ποιεῖν	22	... Πᾶν ἄρσεν, ὃ ἐὰν τεχθῇ τοῖς Εβραίοις,
τὰ βρέφη ἔκθετα αὐτῶν		εἰς τὸν ποταμὸν ῥίψατε· καὶ πᾶν θῆλυ,
εἰς τὸ μὴ ζωογονεῖσθαι.		ζωογονεῖτε αὐτό.

of his favorite idioms and stylistic patterns. Finally, it should be pointed out that τοῦ ποιεῖν τὰ βρέφη ἔκθετα αὐτῶν, though very dissimilar structurally from Ex 1:16-22, is none the less related in concept. Since the modifications imposed upon the OT narrative relate primarily to the author's plan, purpose, and style, these will be examined later.

2) Vv.20-29

With V.19 the author has brought another part of his history to a close and now proceeds to the story of Moses. For this portion of his narrative, he draws upon the following chapter of the book of Exodus. He selects scattered words and phrases to relate the birth:

	Acts 7		Ex 2
20	... ἐγεννήθη Μωϋσῆς,	2	καὶ ἐν γαστρὶ ἔλαβεν
			καὶ ἔτεκεν ἄρσεν·
	καὶ ἦν ἀστεῖος τῷ θεῷ		ἰδόντες δὲ αὐτὸ ἀστεῖον
	and the rearing of Moses		
	ὃς ἀνετράφω μῆνας τρεῖς		ἐσκέπασαν αὐτὸ μῆνας τρεῖς.
	ἐν τῷ οἴκῳ τοῦ πατρός·		
21	ἐκτεθέντος δὲ αὐτοῦ	5	κατέβη δὲ ἡ θυγάτηρ Φαραω
	ἀνείλατο αὐτὸν		λούσασθαι ἐπὶ τὸν ποταμόν,
	ἡ θυγάτηρ Φαραὼ		... ἀποστείλασα τὴν ἅβραν
			ἀνείλατο αὐτήν.
		10	ἁδρυνθέντος δὲ τοῦ παιδίου
			εἰσήγαγεν αὐτὸ πρὸς τὴν
			θυγατέρα Φαραω,
	καὶ ἀνεθρέψατο αὐτὸν		καὶ ἐγενήθη
	ἑαυτῇ εἰς υἱόν.		αὐτῇ εἰς υἱόν.

While the elements borrowed from the LXX form an important part of the new narrative, furnishing authentic echoes of sacred history in biblical Greek, they are subordinate to the author's purpose. In this regard the analysis of the redaction remains incomplete until the structure of the text, the components added by the writer, the modifications imposed upon the source, and the editing of the same are studied in an attempt to ascertain his main purpose. In the case of vv.20-21, the principal verbs (γεννάω, ἀνατρέφω--twice, and ἐκτίθημι--see also v.19) are not taken from the OT source and, as will be argued below, even ἀναιρέω, borrowed from Ex 2:5, is given an entirely new context and meaning. Nevertheless, the LXX furnishes the author with a few building blocks and with the main episodes of his narrative. As a result of this, the relation between Acts and its LXX source is that of ideas rather than quotations.

Since v.22 concerns extrabiblical traditions only, it will not be treated at this point. Instead, the present study will address itself to the writer and his source. For v.23, Ex 2:11a is called into service. The relationship between the two texts is as follows:

Acts 7:23	Ex 2:11
Ὡς δὲ ἐπληροῦτο αὐτῷ	Ἐγένετο δὲ ἐν ταῖς ἡμέραις
	ταῖς πολλαῖς ἐκείναις
τεσσερακονταέτης χρόνος,	μέγας γενόμενος Μωυσῆς
ἀνέβη ἐπὶ τὴν καρδίαν αὐτοῦ	ἐξῆλθεν
ἐπισκέψασθαι τοὺς ἀδελοὺς αὐτοῦ	πρὸς τοὺς ἀδελφοὺς αὐτοῦ
τοὺς υἱοὺς Ἰσραήλ.	τοὺς υἱοὺς Ισραηλ.

As was the case for the other verses of 7:17f., there is little doubt about the source of the concepts and the final phrase of the present verse. However, the two time formulae have nothing in common beyond introducing the subsequent episode in Moses' life, while the principal verbal structure, ἀναβαίνω . . . ἐπισκέψασθαι, appears to be his own. Furthermore, the change from ἐξέρχομαι πρός to ἐπισκέπτομαι + object is especially striking and will be vital to his purpose.

V.24. Once more the source for the final phrase of the verse is readily identified. However, the OT model has exerted influence beyond direct quotation.

Acts 7:24		Ex 2
	11b	κατανοήσας δὲ τὸν πόνον αὐτῶν
καὶ ἰδών		ὁρᾷ ἄνθρωπον Αἰγύπτιον
τινα ἀδικούμενον		τύπτοντά τινα Εβραῖον
		τῶν ἑαυτοῦ ἀδελφῶν τῶν υἱῶν Ισραηλ·
ἠμύνατο	12	περιβλεψάμενος δὲ ὧδε καὶ ὧδε
καὶ ἐποίησεν ἐκδίκησιν		οὐχ ὁρᾷ οὐδένα
τῷ καταπονουμένῳ		καὶ πατάξας τὸν Αἰγύπτιον
πατάξας τὸν Αἰγύπτιον.		ἔκρυψεν αὐτὸν ἐν τῇ ἄμμῳ.

The power of the source over the author of Acts can be seen in the following examples: ὁρᾷ ἄνθρωπον Αἰγύπτιον τύπτοντά τινα Εβραῖον upon ἰδών τινα ἀδικούμενον,[128] τὸν πόνον upon τῷ καταπονουμένῳ;[129] and τῷ ἀδικοῦντι of Ex 2:13 upon ἀδικούμενον

---

[128]The transformation from an active construction to a passive one is a common feature of the writer (e.g., see vv.13, 26, 29, etc.).

[129]Καταπονέω, which is rare both in the LXX (only 2 and 3 Mc) and in the NT (Acts 7:24 and 2 P 2:7), can best be explained in relation to Ex 2:11 especially since the author so often

and ἐκδίκησιν (see also ἀδικεῖτε of v.26 and ἀδικῶν of v.27). From this it is clear that the writer returns to a more consistent use of his OT model, as he did earlier in the speech. As is true of the other verses of this section of his text, though, the structure and inspiration are his own.

After the nonbiblical, obviously redactional assertion of v.25, he resumes the story of Moses at the point where he momentarily abandoned his source. Once more the relationship between the two texts is evident, although not very close structurally.

Acts 7:26	Ex 2:13
	ἐξελθὼν δὲ
<u>τῇ</u> τε ἐπιούσῃ <u>ἡμέρᾳ</u>	<u>τῇ ἡμέρᾳ</u> τῇ δευτέρᾳ
<u>ὤφθε</u> αὐτοῖς μαχομένοις,	<u>ὁρᾷ</u> δύο ἄνδρας Εβραίους
καὶ συνήλλασσεν αὐτοὺς	διαπληκτιζομένους
εἰς εἰρήνην	
εἰπών·	καὶ λέγει τῷ <u>ἀδικο</u>ῦντι
ἄνδρες, ἀδελφοί ἐστε·	
ἱνατί <u>ἀδικε</u>ῖτε ἀλλήλους;	Διὰ τί σὺ τύπτεις τὸν πλησίον;

The change of τῇ ἡμέρᾳ τῇ δευτέρᾳ to τῇ τε ἐπιούσῃ ἡμέρᾳ is to be understood in light of the use of ἔπειμι, which appears only in Acts. In every case (7:26; 16:11; 20:15; 21:18; 23:11) it means "on the next day," while only in the first instance is the term ἡμέρα employed. In other words, the OT text suggests a favorite expression to the author[130] and further influences

---

adds or drops prepositional prefixes while using his source. The term is not a very common one in any period of Greek literature. However, there appears to have been an increase in its use in late Greek generally (see Liddell-Scott-Jones, <u>Lexicon</u>, s.v. "καταπονέω"); in some of the late books of the LXX, in the NT, in Codes Bezae (καταπονέω for διαπονέω of Acts 4:2), and in the papyri (Moulton-Milligan, <u>Vocabulary</u>, s.v. "καταπονέω," give three examples, two of which are passive participles). Also, it must be noted that the noun καταπονήσις appears in Symmachus' translation of Ex 3:7 [Frederick Field, <u>Origenis hexaplorum quae supersunt; sive veterum interpretum graecorum in totum vetus testamentum fragmente</u>, 2 vols. (Oxford: Clarendon Press, 1875), 1:85], a verse quoted in Acts 7:34.

[130]It should be pointed out, however, that ביום השני of the MT is rendered by ܠܝܘܡܐ ܐܚܪܢܐ in Syriac (identical form in Acts 7:26). While it is possible that the Greek version used by the author of Acts had a similar reading, the evidence is

him to the extent that he retains ἡμέρα. Again there occurs a transfer from the active construction of the LXX (ὁρᾷ) to a passive structure (ὤφθη),[131] as well as from a particular, to a more generalized description of an episode.[132] Since the structure owes more to redaction than to the influence of the OT, its analysis will be made later.

There are two further elements to be discussed which have a bearing upon the relationship between the LXX and Acts 7:26. The first concerns the use in Acts of μαχομένοις in place of διαπληκτιζομένους. For a number of reasons I am led to the conclusion that the OT model itself employed μαχομένοις. In effect, the term in question represents the Hebrew נצה, which is regularly translated in the LXX by μάχομαι[133] not διαπληκτίζομαι, a <u>hapax legomenon</u>.[134] Also it can hardly be coincidental that both in Aquila and Symmachus the נצים of Ex 2:13 should be rendered by διαμαχομένους.[135] In light of these, the evidence from the Syriac takes on new importance, namely, that both Ex 2:13 and Acts 7:26, in speaking of the fighting men, should employ the same term, ܢܨܐ.

The second element to be considered here is the influence of Gn 13:8, along with Ex 2:13, upon Acts 7:26.[136]

---

too slight for such a conclusion. Furthermore, the writer's liking for the phrase τῇ ἐπιούσῃ suggests a redactional solution.

[131]<u>Supra</u>, n. 128.

[132]Similar phenomena occur regularly in the speech: vv.5 (twice), 6, 9-10, 11, etc.

[133]Of the five occurrences of נצה in the niphal (only the reflexive construction concerns us here), four are rendered by μάχομαι (Ex 21:22; Lv 24:10; Dt 25:11; 2 S 14:6) and only one, Ex 2:13, by διαπληκτίζομαι. Also, the noun מצה is translated by μάχη: Is 58:4; Pr 17:19.

[134]Other facts should be pointed out in this regard. While διαπληκτίζομαι is employed once in the LXX, the root never appears. Furthermore, the term which the author of Acts allegedly avoided is rather rare and its usage a late phenomenon in the history of the language. Apart from the example given from Ex 2:13 other instances date from the time of Plutarch and later (see Liddell-Scott-Jones, <u>Lexicon</u>, s.v. "διαπληκτίζομαι."

[135]Field, <u>Hexapla</u>, 1:82 (already pointed out by Wilcox, <u>Semitisms</u>, pp. 42-43).

[136]Eberhard Nestle, <u>ExpT</u> 23 (1911-12): 528, in a short note pointed out this relation a long time ago.

εἶπεν δὲ Αβραμ τῷ Λωτ
Μὴ ἔστω μάχη ἀνὰ μέσον ἐμοῦ ...
ὅτι ἄνθρωποι ἀδελφοὶ ἡμεῖς ἐσμέν.

What may appear as an unusual statement in the Stephen speech would seem less so in light of the above, both from the point of view of style and idea. The transformation of ἄνθρωπος to ἀνήρ is to be seen as owing to the author's stylistic tendencies,[137] while the meaning of the texts is approximately the same, that is, there should be no strife among brothers. Of course this last statement is barely implied in Ex 2:13 and was inserted within the story of Moses by the redactor.

Vv.27-28. For the first time within this part of the speech, except perhaps for v.18, the author draws substantially upon his source. However, even in this instance the OT model furnishes only a secondary element. The quotation demonstrates one of the writer's key ideas, expressed verbally by ἀπώσατο (see also v.39).

	Acts 7		Ex 2
27	ὁ δὲ ἀδικῶν τὸν πλησίον ἀπώσατο αὐτὸν	13b	καὶ λέγει τῷ ἀδικοῦντι Διὰ τί σὺ τύπτεις τὸν πλησίον;
	εἰπών· τίς σε κατέστησεν ἄρχοντα	14	ὁ δὲ εἶπεν Τίς σε κατέστησεν ἄρχοντα
	καὶ δικαστὴν ἐφ' ἡμῶν;		καὶ δικαστὴν ἐφ' ἡμῶν;
28	μὴ ἀνελεῖν με σὺ θέλεις ὃν τρόπον ἀνεῖλες ἐχθὲς τὸν Αἰγύπτιον;		μὴ ἀνελεῖν με σὺ θέλεις, ὃν τρόπον ἀνεῖλες ἐχθὲς τὸν Αἰγύπτιον;

The first part of v.27 illustrates once more the author's sometime minute stylistic borrowing from the LXX. The OT speech formula, ὁ δὲ εἶπεν, is modified sufficiently to be incorporated within the new composition and still serve its original function, i.e., prefacing direct speech. The remainder of vv.

137The expression ἄνδρες ἀδελφοί is employed no less than fourteen times in Acts, and only there in the NT. Also the double use of the expression in the speech (7:2 and 26) seems intentional. Furthermore, the author either eliminates ἄνθρωπος or utilizes ἀνήρ in its place on several occasions; see the discussion of this point on pp. 117(7:40 = Ex 32:1), 130 (7:45-46 in relation to Ps 89:21, compare n. 244), and finally 272 (Acts 6:3 and the author's use of Gn 41:33).

27-28 needs no comment at this point since it is a faithful quotation of the LXX.

V.29. The author of Acts omits Ex 2:14b and 15a, thereby modifying the motivation of what follows. Instead, he returns to his source where he borrows a few items from v.15b.

Acts 7:29	Ex 2:15b
ἔφυγεν δὲ Μωϋσῆς	ἀνεχώρησεν δὲ Μωυσῆς
ἐν τῷ λόγῳ τούτῳ,	ἀπὸ προσώπου Φαραω
καὶ ἐγένετο πάροικος ἐν γῇ Μαδιάμ,	καὶ ᾤκησεν ἐν γῇ Μαδιαμ.
οὗ ἐγέννησεν υἱοὺς δύο.	

Closer examination indicates that the structure of the verse is also taken from the model. Three elements (not underlined), though differing philologically from the LXX text, are nevertheless situated within the original pattern. The final clause, though, is an addition based on Ex 2:22 and 18:3f. The modification of ᾤκησεν to ἐγένετο πάροικος is readily understood in the light of the author's purpose (see in particular the introduction of the πάροικος theme in Acts 7:6 where Gn 15:13 and Ex 2:22 are conflated). In effect, καὶ ἐγένετο πάροικος ἐν γῇ Μαδιάμ becomes a parallel to and a fulfillment of the prophecy of 7:6: ἔσται τὸ σπέρμα αὐτοῦ πάροικον ἐν γῇ ἀλλυτρίᾳ.[138] Furthermore, according to the writer's logic, not only does Moses--the σπέρμα of Abraham--but also his two children, become sojourners in the foreign land.[139]

The addition of ἐν τῷ λόγῳ τούτῳ is related to the τὸ ῥῆμα τοῦτο (employed both in Ex 2:14b and 15a) of the LXX text. However, the editing on the part of the NT author has necessitated further changes. In the OT text Moses leaves Egypt because the affair (ῥῆμα) is known to the Pharaoh. Owing to the omission of Ex 2:14b-15a, the motivation for Moses' departure is now related to the double question (7:27-28) of the Hebrew worker. The change from ῥῆμα to λόγος ensues.

---

[138]Instead of the simple root οἰκέω the author utilizes a paraphrastic construction with the compound term πάροικος.

[139]It will be noted that both Gn 15:13 (Acts 7:6) and Ex 2:15b (7:29) undergo the influence of Ex 2:22: καὶ ἐπωνόμασεν Μωυσῆς τὸ ὄνομα αὐτοῦ Γηρσαμ λέγων ὅτι πάροικος εἰμι ἐν γῇ ἀλλοτρίᾳ. While employing Ex 2:22 in composing Acts 7:29, the writer is led to a supplementary text, Ex 18:3f., where another

Finally, the relationship between ἔφυγεν and ἀνεχώρησεν must be considered. In the first place, nothing within the Stephen story seems to motivate such a change.[140] Secondly, the term used in Acts renders more faithfully the Hebrew original, ויברח משה מפני פרעה, than does the LXX, which has weakened the text from "flee" to "depart."[141] An examination of the LXX data reveals, at best, that the translators were very inconsistent in their translation of ברח and in their use of φεύγω and ἀναχωρέω, both of which, in the Pentateuch, stand for ברח.[142] For these reasons, and based on the available evidence, I conclude that the Greek text used by the author of Acts probably employed φεύγω, and that the writer is following his model. This solution is further supported by the use of ܥܪܩ in the Syriac Old and New Testaments.[143]

3) <u>Vv.30-34</u>

With v.29 the writer has terminated an important part of the life of Moses and has set the stage for the central episode of the speech: the theophany and mission. For this section of his narrative he makes abundant use of Ex 3, leaving aside however most anecdotal detail of the source. After a time formula, the author in v.30 directs his attention to the key elements of the story.

---

son is mentioned.

[140]Both verbs occur twice in Acts, φεύγω once in the Stephen story. Neither term would appear to be favored over the other, so that the willful substitution of one for the other remains unexplained, at least based on the evidence we possess.

[141]The targums follow the MT (<u>Onkelos</u>, <u>Pseudo-Jonathan</u>, <u>Neofiti 1</u>). This is also true for the Samaritan Pentateuch, Hebrew, and Aramaic texts.

[142]In the Pentateuch ברח is translated once as ἀναχωρέω (Ex 2:15), twice as φεύγω (Ex 14:5 and Nb 24:11), but more commonly by ἀποδιδράσκω, while in other books φεύγω is by far the most common, ἀναχωρέω being employed only twice for ברח. Note, however, that the translator(s) of a single book is not fully consistent: Jer 4:29 (ἀναχωρέω) and 26:21 (φεύγω).

[143]The interchange in manuscripts between the two Greek terms should be mentioned in passing: Jdg 4:17 (A: ἀνεχώρησεν; B: ἔφυγεν) and Jn 6:15 (most manuscripts: ἀνεχώρησεν; א* lat sy^{c}: φεύγει).

Acts 7:30	Ex 3
καὶ πληρωθέντων ἐτῶν τεσσεράκοντα	1 καὶ ἤγαγεν τὰ πρόβατα
	ὑπὸ τὴν ἔρημον καὶ ἦλθεν εἰς τὸ ὄρος Χωρηβ.
ὤφθη αὐτῷ	2 ὤφθη δὲ αὐτῷ
ἐν τῇ ἐρήμῳ τοῦ ὄρους Σινὰ	
ἄγγελος	ἄγγελος κυρίου
ἐν φλογὶ πυρὸς βάτου.[144]	ἐν φλογὶ πυρὸς ἐκ τοῦ βάτου.

At a glance one can see that he has borrowed the structural elements furnished by the OT text, and has merely supplemented this by adding a prepositional phrase, in which he utilizes the details given in the preceding verse of his model. The expression, ἐν τῇ ἐρήμῳ τοῦ ὄρους Σινά, is never found in the LXX and appears only in the present verse in the NT. This particular construction, then, is probably due to the author. The substitution of Σινά for Χωρηβ, since it is supported by no known textual evidence, must also be considered a modification by the writer and an intentional one, if one takes v.38 into consideration.[145] I accept, with Aland,[146] the omission of κυρίου (which seems to be deliberate and intimately related to the structure of this section), and the reading ἐν φλογὶ πυρός rather than ἐν πυρὶ φλογός. But see below (pp. 150-52) for further discussion of textual problems.

144The divergence between the text and its source: the genitive for ἐκ τοῦ. . . is probably due to the writer's style (see v.35, ἐν τῇ βάτῳ) rather than other causes since the LXX and other versions represent more faithfully the MT מתוך. Note the same phenomenon in v.33 quoting Ex 3:5.

145By insisting upon intentional modification, I mean simply that the author must have known that the sacred mountain was often referred to as Horeb but following later tradition adopts the name Sinai, as does Josephus, Ant. 11.264-65: χρόνῳ δ' ὕστερον νέμων ἐπὶ τὸ Σιναῖον καλούμενον ὄρος ἄγει τὰ ποίμνια· τοῦτο δ' ἐστὶν ὑψηλότατον τῶν ταύτῃ ὀρῶν. The targums in their midrashic additions to the biblical text usually use Sinai, see Pseudo-Jonathan, Dt 1:1, even if the appellation Horeb will be retained in close proximity (Dt 1:2). Furthermore, the name Sinai is by far the more common in the OT in Jewish tradition, and the only one used in the NT; see Eduard Lohse, "Σινᾶ," in TDNT, 7:282-86.

146NT Graece, p. 317. See also Aland et al., Gk NT, p. 442; and Merk, NT, p. 417.

V.31. Even if it is sufficiently clear that for this text the source being used is Ex 3:2b-4, the relationship of the verse to the OT model is still problematic.

Acts 7:31		Ex 3
ὁ δὲ Μωϋσῆς ἰδὼν	2b	καὶ ὁρᾷ ὅτι ὁ βάτος καίεται πυρί,
		ὁ δὲ βάτος οὐ κατεκαίετο.
ἐθαύμαζεν τὸ ὅραμα·	3	εἶπεν δὲ Μωυσῆς
προσερχομένου δὲ αὐτοῦ		Παρελθὼν ὄψομαι τὸ ὅραμα τὸ μέγα τοῦτο,
κατανοῆσαι		τί ὅτι οὐ κατακαίεται ὁ βάτος.
	4	ὡς δὲ εἶδεν κύριος
		ὅτι προσάγει ἰδεῖν,
ἐγένετο φωνὴ κυρίου·		ἐκάλεσεν αὐτὸν κύριος ἐκ τοῦ βάτου
		λέγων Μωυσῆ, Μωυσῆ.
		ὁ δὲ εἶπεν Τί ἐστιν;

The texts bear no resemblance structurally to one another; instead the author seems to have gone out of his way to summarize and totally reformulate the same ideas. Such radical transformations, especially of terminology, are unusual for this writer, as noted throughout the study. For this reason careful analysis is required on two counts: the possible influence of the OT on the vocabulary being used, and structural and stylistic elements as they reveal the purpose of the passage. The first will be considered immediately, while the second will be seen below.

The author is interested in summarizing the very repetitious OT account, as the phrase ἰδὼν ἐθαύμαζεν τὸ ὅραμα indicates. The first and third terms are borrowed from the source, while the second derives from the writer's personal vocabulary,[147] and describes a reaction which is only implied in the model. The analysis of the remainder of the verse, however, is more troublesome. Προσερχομένου . . . κατανοῆσαι is practically identical in meaning to both παρελθὼν ὄψομαι of v.3 and

[147] θαυμάζω which is a common word in the NT, occurs five times in Acts. The strikingly similar passage of Dn 8:27 (Theod.), καὶ ἐθαύμαζον τὴν ὅρασιν, should be noted in this

προσάγει ἰδεῖν of v.4, and could very well be the equivalent of either. Nevertheless, it is one of these LXX terms which is at the basis of προσέρχομαι of Acts. This conclusion follows since the Greek version has modified the sense of the Hebrew from "turn aside"[148] (סור in both verses) to "draw near." While this may explain the semantic relationship between the texts, it still does not account for the change imposed upon the source. In view of the author's translation techniques (the root ἔρχομαι is preserved), of his stylistic tendencies (frequent transformation of prepositional prefixes), and of the semantic evolution of παρέρχομαι (it no longer means "to go near" in the NT[149]), the relationship between the LXX text and v.31 is greatly clarified. I conclude that the author is quoting the Greek OT, but that he modifies its archaic terminology (παρέρχομαι > προσέρχομαι).[150] Κατανοῆσαι will be discussed below since it recurs in v.32 of the Stephen speech.

Finally, the background of the expression ἐγένετο φωνὴ κυρίου, unique in the NT, requires considerable attention as regards its relation to the OT and the author's style. No doubt the use of φωνή for the divinity is in accordance with OT, late Jewish, and even pagan Greek practice.[151] But, neither its appearance in this particular context nor its form is accounted for. Since the writer is obviously editing Ex 3:3-4, it would seem logical to seek some clarification in relation to

---

regard.

[148]The Syriac and other Aramaic versions follow the MT.

[149]Arndt-Gingrich, <u>Lexicon</u>, s.v. "παρέρχομαι."

[150]The change was no doubt facilitated by the special meaning which this verb exhibits: "approach the divinity for worship" in Heb 4:16; 7:25; etc. See Moulton-Milligan, <u>Vocabulary</u>, s.v. "παρέρχομαι": "The semi-technical use of this verb of the approach of the worshipper to God is frequent in the LXX, and is found <u>septies</u> in Heb, twice (10.1, 22) without an obj.; cf. P. Giss <u>I.20.24</u> (beg. ii/A.D.) . . . of worship to be performed at a private shrine of the Dioscuri. See also Dio Cassius lvi.9 τοῖς θεοῖς προσερχώμεθα."

[151]Arndt-Gingrich, <u>Lexicon</u>, s.v. "φωνή." See especially the article of Otto Betz, "φωνή," in <u>TDNT</u> 9:278-309, where the literary/theological practice of referring to the divinity as φωνή is amply documented for the Greek world, the OT, Palestinian, rabbinic, and Hellenistic Judaism, and the NT.

that text, ἐκάλεσεν αὐτὸν κύριος ἐκ τοῦ βάτου λέγων.[152] The transformation would then be seen in the light of contemporary idiom,[153] as well as due to LXX influence, particularly Gn 15: 4: καὶ εὐθὺς φωνὴ κυρίου ἐγένετο πρὸς αὐτὸν λέγων.[154]

Vv.32-33. After the introductory formula discussed above, the writer returns once again to more direct use of his source for the two following verses:

Acts 7	Ex 3
31 ἐγένετο φωνὴ κυρίου·	5 καὶ εἶπεν Μὴ ἐγγίσῃς ὧδε·
32 ἐγὼ ὁ θεὸς τῶν πατέρων σου,	λῦσαι τὸ ὑπόδημα ἐκ τῶν ποδῶν σου·
ὁ θεὸς Ἀβραὰμ καὶ Ἰσαὰκ καὶ Ἰσκώβ.	ὁ γὰρ τόπος, ἐν ᾧ σὺ ἕστηκας γῆ ἁγία ἐστίν.
ἔντρομος δὲ γενόμενος Μωϋσῆς	6 καὶ εἶπεν αὐτῷ
οὐκ ἐτόλμα κατανοῆσαι.	Ἐγώ εἰμι ὁ θεὸς τοῦ πατρός σου,

---

[152]It might be tempting to appeal to the targums for evidence, particularly the frequent rendering of the divine name as ממרא דייי (Neofiti 1, e.g., Ex 3:4 and often Onkelos, e.g., Gn 3:8; Pseudo-Jonathan, e.g., Gn 3:8, 10). However, their late date warrants caution. See n. 151 above as well as the discussion of the targums at the end of the present chapter.

[153]Whether or not we refer to the late Jewish traditions concerning the Bath qol (Strack and Billerbeck, Kommentar, vol. 1: Das Evangelium nach Matthaus erläutert aus Talmud und Midrash, pp. 125-32) in explaining such texts as Mk 1:11, φωνὴ ἐγένετο ἐκ τῶν οὐρανῶν or 9:7, ἐγένετο φωνὴ ἐκ τῆς νεφέλης (and parallels), they are nevertheless indicative of contemporary literary as well as theological idiom throughout NT literature. Reference might also be made to the author's own construction in Acts 10:13, ἐγένετο φωνὴ πρὸς αὐτόν. Finally, I would also point out that only in Acts, in the NT, is either φωνὴ κυρίου (7:31) or θεοῦ φωνή (12:22) found.

[154]It will be remembered that Gn 15:2 is used in Acts 7:5 and Gn 15:13-14 extensively quoted in Acts 7:6-7. Thus, the text referred to above would have been familiar to the writer. However, further observations are in order. The LXX text referred to above, Gn 15:4, stands for the following Hebrew clause: והנה דבר־יהוה אליו לאמר. An almost identical text appears in Gn 15:1: . . . היה דבר־יהוה but is translated as follows in the LXX: ἐγενέθη ῥῆμα κυρίου. In like manner, similar texts (e.g., 2 S 7:4; 1 K 6:11; 1 Ch 17:3; etc.) are variously translated but generally follow the Hebrew word order, γίνομαι + φωνή (λόγος, ῥῆμα) + κυρίου, precisely that of Acts 7:31.

33 εἶπεν δὲ αὐτῷ ὁ κύριος·	θεὸς Αβρααμ καὶ θεὸς Ισαακ καὶ θεὸς Ισκωβ.
λῦσον τὸ ὑπόδημα τῶν ποδῶν σου·	ἀπέστρεψεν δὲ Μωυσῆς τὸ πρόσωπον αὐτοῦ·
ὁ γὰρ τόπος ἐφ' ᾧ ἕστηκας γῆ ἁγία ἐστίν.	εὐλαβεῖτο γὰρ κατεμβλέψαι ἐνώπιον τοῦ θεοῦ.
	7 εἶπεν δὲ κύριος πρὸς Μωυσῆν...

The most obvious modification is the order in which the author quotes Ex 3:5 and 6, but since the reasons for such a change concern structure and purpose primarily, this will be discussed later. V.32 draws directly from Ex 3:6, the only text which could provide it with the four parts (and order) of its overall structure:

a ἐγώ

b ὁ θεὸς τῶν πατέρων σου

c ὁ θεὸς Αβραὰμ καὶ 'Ισαὰκ καὶ 'Ισκώβ

d remainder of verse.

The differences between Acts and Exodus are both interesting and difficult to resolve because of three problem areas: NT textual considerations, the character of the LXX version employed, and the degree of the author's originality. The analysis of this text is rendered even more difficult since all three areas mentioned are further complicated by the nature of the evidence available: the occurrence within the NT, within Acts itself, and the OT of a number of similar texts. Such a situation obviously enhances the likelihood of conflation and assimilation. With this circumstance in mind, it is necessary to consider each part of v.32 separately.

In part a we note the strange omission of εἰμί[155] from the LXX text. This could be explained as a minor case of editing by the author; the evidence, however, indicates otherwise. By the elimination of εἰμί, Acts 7:32 is in fact closer to the MT and, an even more serious consideration, the independent quotation in Mk 12:26 of the same reading[156] leads to the conclusion

---

[155]See Jacquier, Actes, p. 221: "Εἰμί, Septante, Ex. iii, 6, est omis comme dans le texte hébreu. Cette omission est rare en grec à la 1re personne." See also Blass and Debrunner, Gk Grammar, p. 71: "Εἰμί, ἐσμέν, and εἶ are not often omitted, and when they are, the personal pronoun is usually present."

[156]The Markan text is a direct quotation of Ex. 3:6, al-

that some form of the LXX, without εἰμί, was utilized for these two NT quotations.

The next section of v.32, ὁ θεὸς τῶν πατέρων σου, is in clear contrast both to the LXX, τοῦ πατρός σου, and the MT, אביך. Appeal could be made, as Wilcox in fact does,[157] to the Samaritan authorities (Pentateuch: Hebrew text אבתיך and targum אבהתך) to support an original reading in the plural (Acts 3:13 is also offered here as evidence, but see below). The data from Acts 7:32 and the Samaritan texts could be explained in terms of conflation, since both betray harmonizing tendencies[158] and would have used any of the following passages: Ex 3:13, 15, 16 or 4:5 in conjunction with Ex 3:6. To this argument one should add that the phrase, ὁ θεὸς τῶν πατέρων, appears no less than four times in Acts,[159] while the expression "our/your fathers" is clearly a favorite theme of the author, not only in the Stephen speech but throughout the work. Thus, one could conclude that the writer is quoting Ex 3:6, but that he has imposed a slight modification, at least grammatically, upon his source. Nonetheless, appeal should be made once more to textual evidence. Paul Kahle a long time ago called attention to this data,[160] which can be summed up as follows: in support of the plural reading we have Acts 7:32 and a solid OT textual tradition: the Samaritan texts, LXX manuscripts k and m, the Bohairic and Ethiopic (codex C) traditions, as well as

---

though the phrase, θεὸς τοῦ πατρός σου, is omitted. It should be noted that the addition by the Matthean version (22:32; Lk 20:37 employs an indirect statement) of εἰμί further supports the conclusion stated above.

[157] Semitisms, pp. 29-30.

[158] The tendency within Acts 7:2-53 to repeatedly combine OT texts has often been noted in this study. In regard to "the harmonizing, expansionist nature of the Samaritan text," Patrick W. Skehan notes, after giving several examples: ". . . the words used to fill out a particular passage are those of the Bible itself," "Texts and Versions," in The Jerome Biblical Commentary, eds. Raymond E. Brown, Joseph A. Fitzmyer, and Roland E. Murphy, 2 vols. (Englewood Cliffs, New Jersey: Prentice-Hall, 1968), 2:566 and 564 respectively.

[159] 3:13; 5:30; 7:32; and 22:14.

[160] The Cairo Geniza, Schweich Lectures (London: Oxford University Press, 1947), pp. 144-45.

[161] Brooke and McLean, Old Testament, 1:161.

confirmation from Eusebius, Cyprian, and Justin Martry.[161] It is safe to conclude, therefore, that the author of Acts was relying upon a Palestinian textual tradition of his time.[162]

Part *c* of v.32 presents problems of a different nature. Since the phrase referred to appears several times in the OT source and in the NT corpus--two of which occur in Acts--an ideal situation for harmonization eventuated. After having surveyed the available data, it seems possible to arrive only at a tentative solution. This owes to the interrelation of the problems involved and to the increase in uncertainty as one attempts to work back step by step through the difficulties. There are 1) the textual problems regarding the actual NT readings (especially for Acts 3:13 and 7:32), 2) the relation of such a conjectural reading to the LXX text (whether a quotation of Ex 3:6 or a text conflated by the author), and 3) the nature of the LXX model itself (particularly the modification of Ex 3:16 to conform to 3:6 and 4:5). Only after having resolved these difficulties will it be possible to examine the redactional process.

Textual criticism in dealing with the present situation is proffered some difficult choices. The phrase, "the God of Abraham . . . ," occurs five times in the NT, but in what appears to be two different traditions: the synoptic gospels (Mk 12:26 and parallels) and Acts. The former is stable and reflects accurately the LXX readings. The latter, however, presents major problems. The manuscript data are as follows:

ὁ θεός preceding 'Ισαάκ and 'Ιακώβ:

Acts 3:13 P^{74} ℌ A D *pc* lat Ir^{lat}

Acts 7:32 𝔎 E 33 *pm* and D gig vg[163]

without θεός (Aland and Merk readings)[164]

Acts 3:13 B 𝔎 E *pl* gig h sy

Acts 7:32 P^{74} ℌ *al*

While commentators and editors often opt for the reading without ὁ θεός both for Acts 3:13 and 7:32, we must note the lack

---

[162]Now see Richard, "Acts 7: An Investigation of the Samaritan Evidence," p. 199-202.

[163]D adds anarthrous θεός (gig and vg: deus) in accordance with Ex 3:6.

[164]*NT Graece*, pp. 305 and 317-18 and *NT*, pp. 402 and 418.

of logic involved. If one follows what is generally admitted to be the more important manuscripts (P^{74} and 𝔐), then one would have to opt for different readings for the two passages indicated above,[165] with ὁ θεός for Acts 3:13 and without ὁ θεός for 7:32. For the first text it could be argued that the addition of ὁ θεός was done under the influence either of the consistent LXX tradition or of the synoptic gospels or both; however, the nature of the text would seem to argue for an original ὁ θεός before each proper name.[166] Acts 3:13 does not constitute a quotation from a specific verse or verses of Exodus, but rather the justaposition of two well-known biblical phrases often found in Ex 3 and 4.[167] For Acts 7:32 one could argue for an original ὁ θεός--admittedly on weaker manuscript evidence--on the assumption that the author is faithfully quoting from Ex 3:6. However, the omission of ὁ θεός would seem to resolve more difficulties (textually), and to be consistent with the tendencies ascribed throughout this study to the writer of the Stephen speech (method of quoting OT and purpose). The more important manuscripts are to be followed[168] and the minor readings (of both Acts 3:13 and 7:32) explained as being due to harmonization. The reading without ὁ θεός is then understood in terms of the conflation of Ex 2:6 and 16 (arguing for a LXX reading in conformity with the MT text of Ex 2:16,

---

[165]The only major manuscript which would seem to demand the choice of one and the rejection of the other reading is in this case Vaticanus. It would be possible to conclude that the B scribe is consistent in omitting ὁ θεός in both texts.

[166]Aland et al., Gk NT, p. 426, choose this reading, but enclose ὁ θεός in brackets. See Metzger, Commentary, p. 310, for a statement of the committee's deliberations.

[167]It is especially the order of the components (ὁ θεὸς τῶν πατέρων ἡμῶν, a favorite phrase of his, following upon ὁ θεὸς 'Αβραάμ) and the absence of ἐγώ [εἰμι] which indicate that the author is not quoting Ex 3:6 as he does in Acts 7:32. However, see "Acts 7: An Investigation of the Samaritan Evidence," p. 201.

[168]Position also of Aland et al., Gk NT, p. 442. Metzger, Commentary, p. 349, expresses this opinion in the following way: "A majority of the Committee judged that the combination of P^{74} ℵ A B C Ψ 81 614 $syr^{p,h}$ cop^{sa} was superior to the several witnesses which attest the other readings."

i.e., omitting אלהי prior to Isaac and Jacob).[169] This solution is further supported by an appeal to the influence of Ex 2:24, καὶ ἐμνήσθη ὁ θεὸς τῆς διαθήκης αὐτοῦ τῆς πρὸς Αβρααμ καὶ Ισαακ καὶ Ιακωβ (see Acts 7:8 and 17). And, finally, it will be argued below that the omission of ὁ θεός fits well into the author's thematic schema.

The remainder of v.32 (part d) presents still further problems. Its relationship to Ex 3:6 is unmistakable in idea. However, the terminology and structure require careful analysis. For convenience the problems are assembled into two areas: 1) the relation between ἔντρομος . . . γενόμενος / οὐκ ἐτόλμα and ἀπέστρεψεν . . . τὸ πρόσωπον αὐτοῦ / εὐλαβεῖτο and 2) that between κατανοῆσαι and κατεμβλέψαι.

The LXX text, ἀπέστρεψεν . . . τὸ πρόσωπον αὐτοῦ, renders the MT פניו . . . ויסתר, and is apparently a mistranslation. Our author does not seem to have drawn from this expression. Instead, the following LXX verb, εὐλαβέομαι (MT ירא), appears to be related, at least in idea, to both expressions used in Acts: ἔντρομος . . . γενόμενος and οὐκ ἐτόλμα. The term εὐλαβέομαι is frequent in the LXX and rare in the NT[170] while ἔντρομος and τολμάω are not often used in the Greek OT but frequently, at least the latter, in the NT.[171] In view of these facts, one can conclude that the modifications probably owe to the work of the author, who employed contemporary idiom rather than adhere too closely to the archaic terminology of this passage of his source.[172]

---

[169]Only the LXX among the versions does not follow the MT. Furthermore, the conflation of Ex 3:6 and 16 would apply also to the plural construction: "your father" of part b discussed earlier.

[170]This term, which occurs only once in the NT (Heb 11:7), translates in the LXX a variety of Hebrew verbs.

[171]Τολμάω occurs only in Esther and Job in the OT and often throughout NT literature. Regarding ἔντρομος, Bruce states: "The adj. is post-classical; it is found in LXX, Plutarch, and the Palatine Anthology," Acts, p. 170; and I might add not very often in the LXX.

[172]This is particularly true of the construction ἔντρομος . . . γενόμενος. The term ἔντρομος occurs no more than five times in the LXX, but twice (Ps 17:7 and 76:18) it takes the form of this particular construction. Similarly, of the three occurrences of the adjective in the NT, the two passages in Acts (7:32 and 16:29) also adopt this structure. Finally, it

The relation of κατανοῆσαι to κατεμβλέψαι may at first appear to be no more than the substitution by the author of Acts of a common NT term--one well known to him (4 occurrences in Acts)--for a <u>hapax legomenon</u> in the LXX. This would be reinforced by the use of the same verb in the previous verse of the speech. The verb κατεμβλέπω is used only once in the LXX, Ex 3:6, where it renders the Hebrew term נבט. The latter, however, in at least eight cases is translated in the Greek OT by κατανοέω.[173] In all probability, the LXX used by the author of Acts furnished him with the term κατανοέω.[174]

V.33. Because vv.5 and 6 of Ex 2 are inverted, it is clear that the first line of v.7, following immediately upon the text just discussed, served the author in introducing the next element of direct speech.

The speech formula of 7:33, εἶπεν δὲ αὐτῷ ὁ κύριος, while having some features in common with its source, Ex 3:7a, εἶπεν δὲ κύριος πρὸς Μωυσῆν, nevertheless reveals the author's independence in composing his own formulae.[175] The second part of v. 33 is a literal quotation; but three differences between the texts in question must be noted: λῦσαι > λῦσον, ἐκ τῶν > genitive construction, and ἐν ᾧ > ἐφ' ᾧ. Recently Wilcox has proposed that the ἐφ' ᾧ of Acts might be explained via Aquila (ἐπ' αὐτοῦ for Hebrew עלו), as being akin to ". . . a Greek version

---

might be added that the LXX adjective τρόμος twice represents the Hebrew term מורא (Gn 9:2 and Dt 11:25), a construct of the verb ירא, the term here being considered. Even though the author's tendency to augment or reduce verbal expressions is well documented, the evidence is too slight to postulate a LXX version utilizing an original τρόμος for ירא.

[173]Of about 23 occurrences of κατανοέω in the LXX, 9 represent ראה, 8 נבט and 6 a variety of verbs. It will be noted in all fairness that נבט is often translated by ἐμβλέπω (see for example Is 5:12, κατανοέω = ראה and ἐμβλέπω = נבט) or a compound of that root (Gn 19:17 and 26). At the same time Ex 3:3 or 4 (both rendered by ὁράω) quoted in 7:31 does represent ראה in both cases, a term often also translated in the LXX by κατανοέω. This last suggestion I reject since the five occurrences of ראה in Ex 3:2-4 would probably all have been rendered by the translators by some form of ὁράω.

[174]The LXX reading καταβλέψαι for κατεμβλέψαι by "b c f h q u a_2 Cyr-ed$\frac{2}{3}$-cod$\frac{1}{3}$ Thd" should be noted; see Brooke and McLean, <u>Old Testament</u>, I:161. Furthermore, the author will have encountered the verb κατανοέω in Ex 2:11^b (see Acts 7:24).

[175]See the treatment of speech formulae in chapter three.

other than the LXX, which has here preserved the form of the Hebrew more literally than our LXX," or possibly as related directly to the Hebrew text.[176] As attractive as such a solution might be, the analysis of the author's quoting techniques has furnished, I believe, the necessary clue to a better explanation. It has often been noted that the writer is easily led by an idea or a particular passage to a similar or complementary concept or text elsewhere in the sacred text. Thus a comparison between the following quotations is in order.

Acts 7:33	λῦσον τὸ ὑπόδημα τῶν ποδῶν σου·
	ὁ γὰρ τόπος ἐφ᾽ ᾧ ἕστηκας γῆ ἁγία ἐστίν.
Ex 3:5	λῦσαι τὸ ὑπόδημα ἐκ τῶν ποδῶν σου·
	ὁ γὰρ τόπος, ἐν ᾧ σὺ ἕστηκας, γῆ ἁγία ἐστίν.
Jos 5:15	Λῦσαι τὸ ὑπόδημα ἐκ τῶν ποδῶν σου·
	ὁ γὰρ τόπος, ἐφ᾽ ᾧ σὺ ἕστηκας, ἅγιός ἐστιν.

From the above texts it is logical to conclude that the ἐφ᾽ ᾧ of Jos 5:15 has brought about the grammatical modification of the original source.

The second change, from ἐκ τῶν to a genitive construction, should be seen as a stylistic tendency of the author.[177] The transformation of λῦσαι to λῦσον, i.e., from the middle to the active voice could probably be explained in relation to the saying of Jesus (note Acts 13:25 where the logion occurs), but there is ample textual evidence to conclude that the author of Acts was simply quoting a LXX text of his day.[178]

V.34. Again we are dealing with an extended quotation. While the author has greatly reduced the original, he has borrowed the entire structure from his source. The relation between the texts is as follows:

---

[176] Semitisms, p. 42.

[177] See vv. 30 and 35 of the speech. Confer also n. 144 above.

[178] For the reading λῦσον at Ex 3:5 we have: "b h m q u w y Acts Eus-codd$\frac{1}{3}$ Cyr-ed$\frac{1}{8}$-cod$\frac{1}{8}$" and at Jos 5:15: "A Δ_8 e h j m q y $d_2\frac{1}{2}$ Eus-codd$\frac{1}{3}$ Thdt," Brooke and McLean, Old Testament, 1:161 and 690. One could also refer to the LXX manuscript Alexandrinus which reads λῦσον for λῦσαι in Jos 5:15 and eliminates συ in its version of Ex 3:5. I am led to suspect these changes as later modifications based upon the NT passage. See p. 154 below.

Acts 7:34		Ex 3
ἰδὼν εἶδον τὴν κάκωσιν τοῦ λαοῦ μου	7	Ἰδὼν εἶδον τὴν κάκωσιν τοῦ λαοῦ μου
τοῦ ἐν Αἰγύπτῳ, καὶ τοῦ στεναγμοῦ αὐτῶν		τοῦ ἐν Αἰγύπτῳ καὶ τῆς κραυγῆς αὐτῶν
ἤκουσα,		ἀκήκοα ἀπὸ τῶν ἐργοδιωκτῶν· οἶδα γὰρ τὴν ὀδύνην αὐτῶν·
καὶ κατέβην ἐξελέσθαι αὐτούς·	8	καὶ κατέβην ἐξελέσθαι αὐτοὺς ἐκ χειρὸς Αἰγυπτίων καὶ ἐξαγαγεῖν αὐτοὺς ἐκ τῆς γῆς ἐκείνης καὶ εἰσαγαγεῖν αὐτούς ...
	9	καὶ νῦν ἰδοὺ κραυγὴ τῶν υἱῶν Ισραηλ ἥκει πρός με, κἀγὼ ἑώρακα τὸν θλιμμόν, ὃν οἱ Αἰγύπτιοι θλίβουσιν αὐτούς.
καὶ νῦν δεῦρο ἀποστείλω σε εἰς Αἴγυπτον.	10	καὶ νῦν δεῦρο ἀποστείλω σε πρὸς Φαραω βασιλέα Αἰγύπτου, καὶ ἐξάξεις τὸν λαόν μου τοὺς υἱοὺς Ισραηλ ἐκ γῆς Αἰγύπτου.

In terms of dependence upon the LXX, there are only two minor alterations which call for immediate attention. The first is the conflation of a phrase from Ex 2:24[179] with Ex 3:7.

Ex 3:7	καὶ τῆς κραυγῆς αὐτῶν ἀκήκοα ἀπό ...
Ex 2:24	καὶ εἰσήκουσεν ὁ θεὸς τὸν στεναγμὸν αὐτῶν, καί ...
Acts 7:34	καὶ τοῦ στεναγμοῦ αὐτῶν[180] ἤκουσα καί ...

---

[179]See also Ex 6:5, καὶ ἐγὼ εἰσήκουσα τὸν στεναγμὸν τῶν υἱῶν Ισραηλ. It is equally possible that the author is utilizing this particular text. However, it seems more likely that the use of Ex 2:24 in composing 7:34 has brought to mind the very similar text of Ex 6:5, whose context, particularly v.6, is employed in formulating 7:35, see below.

[180]Contrary to Nestle and Aland, NT Graece, p. 318, it is preferable to follow the major and large majority of manuscripts in reading αὐτῶν rather than αὐτοῦ. Metzger, Commen-

This is an excellent example to illustrate the extent to which the LXX exerts its influence upon the author. While he rejects the above phrase from Ex 3:7 in favor of 2:24, he still retains the genitive with the verb ἀκουω, and the word order of the first text. However, from the new text he borrows the form of the verb[181] and the term στεναγμός.[182]

The second point concerns the addition of εἰς Αἴγυπτον. The occurrence of "Egypt" at the beginning and the end of v.34 (the same is true of Shechem in 7:16) and the use of the same as both introduction (v.17) and conclusion (v.34) to the Egyptian sojourn, are clearly structural features. The architectural aspects of the discourse will be discussed in the next chapter; presently, however, it should be noted that the building blocks are from the OT model, but the construction is solely that of the author.

b. Vv.17-34: Quoting Process

The story of Moses occupies a central place in the speech. This is clearly indicated by the amount of space and attention given his birth and rearing, his visit to his brethren, and his meeting with God. These themes are intimately related to the sojourn in Egypt, which serves as the background and framework

---

tary, p. 349, in defense of Aland et al., Gk NT, p. 442 [also the reading of Merk, NT, p. 419], states: "Since the singular number αὐτοῦ (B D 321 1838 syr^{p}) is the more correct form grammatically (it refers to τοῦ λαοῦ), it is probable that αὐτῶν (P^{74} ℵ A C E H P nearly all minuscules and versions) is the original reading which was altered by punctilious scribes."

[181]The author's attitude toward compound verbs has often been discussed, see vv.12, 24, 29, 31, etc. At the same time the influence of Jer 4:31, ὅτι φωνὴν ὡς ὠδινούσης ἤκουσα, τοῦ στεναγμοῦ σου . . . , should not be discounted.

[182]Because of the above research I opt for conflation and restructuring of the text by the author rather than some other possible influence of the LXX upon him because of two negative conclusions. First of all the Hebrew term צעקה translated as κραυγή is never rendered in the LXX by the term employed in Acts: στεναγμός. Secondly the combination of κάκωσις--στεναγμός never appears in the Greek OT. Furthermore, I might point out in favor of the utilization of Ex 2:24 at this point that Ex 2 has been amply employed from 7:20f., that Ex 2:22 has already been cited at 7:6 and made use of in 7:29, that Ex 2:24 has probably been of service in formulating 7:32c, and finally that Ex 2:23, μετὰ δὲ τὰς ἡμέρας τὰς πολλὰς ἐκείνας is related to the time formula of Acts 7:30.

within which the author has depicted the role of Moses. As mentioned earlier, the entire episode begins with the birth of Moses ἐν Αἰγύπτῳ and ends with his mission εἰς Αἴγυπτον.

In earlier parts of this study, while discussing the quoting process, it was necessary to examine carefully the procedure by which the author selected his OT quotations. This was especially important since the choice of passages ranged over a considerable portion of the book of Genesis. In this particular case, the situation is entirely different. As indicated above, the entire section, vv.17-34, consists of the editing of the first three chapters of Exodus. It is evident that in composing 7:17-19, 20-29, and 30-34, the writer used Ex 1:7-22, 2:2-15, and 3:1-8 respectively. The actual source of the quotations then is less problematic. It is the editing process which will require special attention later.

Still, a few general comments concerning quoting techniques and the relation of vv.17-34 to the OT model need to be made. At the end of his account of the patriarchal story, the writer had followed his source to the end of Genesis and had even borrowed elements from Ex 1:5-6 to compose vv.14 and 15 of the speech. At this very point he picks up his source once more in formulating the prelude to the life and mission of Moses. The first two verses of this section borrow both their content and their structure from the model. From v.19 onward the author modifies his source in a more radical way, choosing words, phrases, and ideas but providing an entirely new framework. The OT text now plays a more subordinate role, as the author's purpose requires greater control of the narrative elements. The text of Exodus provides key terms, biblical coloring, and tone as well as historical content; structural and thematic factors, however, increase in importance.

The quoting techniques in this part of the speech are basically the same as those encountered earlier. The author follows his source rather consistently, choosing key elements to incorporate into his own composition. He is faithful often in the most minute details, but, as seen previously, modifies his source rather readily for stylistic, structural or thematic reasons. On some occasions he conflates OT passages; in other instances he borrows the idea and retains no more than a word or phrase. At the same time there are several extended quotations within this part of the speech. It is particularly with vv. 30-34, the description of the theophany and mission, that he returns to more systematic use of his source.

The role played by the OT text will be examined in greater detail both in the following chapter from a structural and stylistic point of view, and in the last chapter, in relation to the author's purpose and method of composition. At this point, it suffices to point out that the first three chapters of Exodus and the events they record are crucial to an understanding of the speech. Since these episodes of the history of Israel occupy so sizable a portion of the discourse, their analysis reveals major concerns of the author, while the choices and omissions of elements from the OT model give further indications of his purpose.

3. Thematic Section: 7:35-50

V. 35 marks the beginning of a new concern on the author's part. In place of the careful rewriting of sacred history, where his main interest seemed the retelling of Jewish history, one now finds a more polemical and thematic expose centered first upon Moses (35-41), then upon God and his people (42-50). With the change in perspective there corresponds a distinctive approach to the OT text. The choice factor and the structure of the section become more central to this study. The main concern now is to examine the use the author makes of his OT model.

a. Vv. 35-41: Moses and the Fathers

1) Vv.35-41: Textual Relation to OT

Just as vv.32-33 mark a climax in the composition of the speech, so vv.35f. indicate through their style, structure, and posture vis-à-vis the OT text, a new direction and goal. The biblical text continues to furnish the writer with valuable data for his work, but its function acquires an increasingly demonstrative, illustrative, and polemic character.

V.35. The structure of this verse, the repeated use of οὗτος throughout this section, and the relation of v.35 to the preceding division of the speech will be examined later. It is clear though that they explain in great part the nature of the OT quotations found in vv.35-41. By means of a reiterative technique (this Moses, that one, the one who . . .), the author both concentrates on particular details through repetition and selection and summarizes the historical and thematic elements of the biblical account which he considers important.

Both OT citations found in v.35 are, in effect, taken from earlier passages of the speech, and ultimately from the LXX. The first one,

Acts 7:35 . . . ὃν ἠρνήσαντο εἰπόντες·
τίς σε κατέστησεν ἄρχοντα καὶ
δικαστήν;

7:27 . . . ἀπώσατο αὐτὸν εἰπών·
τίς σε κατέστησεν ἄρχοντα καὶ
δικαστὴν ἐφ' ἡμῶν;

Ex 2:14 ὁ δὲ εἶπεν
Τίς σε κατεστησεν ἄρχοντα καὶ
δικαστὴν ἐφ' ἡμῶν;

reveals two important features, both of which are of a stylistic nature and elucidate the author's purpose. By means of such repetition either of a term, phrase or theme, the writer draws particular attention to the components central to his views. Secondly, the singular/plural contrast (εἰπόντες/εἰπών - εἶπεν) is clearly intentional and provides valuable assistance in analysis of the writer's message.

The second quotation is likewise borrowed from an earlier passage of the speech.

Acts 7:35 σὺν χειρὶ ἀγγέλου
τοῦ ὀφθέντος αὐτῷ ἐν τῇ βάτῳ

7:30 ὤφθη αὐτῷ ... ἄγγελος ἐν φλογὶ πυρὸς βάτου

Ex 3:2 ὤφθη δὲ αὐτῷ ἄγγελος κυρίου ἐν φλογὶ πυρὸς
ἐκ τοῦ βάτου.

While the modifications imposed owe to structural considerations, one in particular indicates further influence by the OT text: ἐν τῇ βάτῳ from ἐν φλογὶ πυρὸς ἐκ τοῦ βάτου.[183]

---

[183]Under the heading of metaplasm, Blass and Debrunner, Gk Grammar, p. 28, discuss the gender fluctuation of βάτος and λιμός. A careful examination of the NT evidence reveals the following data. Each term occurs twice in Acts. Both are clearly feminine: βάτος in 7:35 and λιμός in 11:28. Further, on two occasions, the terms are indistinguishable as to gender. It is reasonable to conclude that the terms consistently are of the feminine gender for the author of Acts. The situation for

Lastly, the relation of τοῦτον ὁ θεὸς καὶ ἄρχοντα καὶ λυτρωτὴν ἀπέσταλκεν to the biblical text merits some attention at this point. Ἄρχοντα is repeated from the previous clause, itself a quotation. Ἀπέσταλκεν, as well as the general idea, is borrowed from v.34, also a biblical citation. The appearance of λυτρωτήν in this particular context will require careful consideration later in this study (infra, pp. 334-37). Nevertheless, it is necessary to note at this point the influence of Ex 6:6, καὶ λυτρώσομαι ὑμᾶς ἐν βραχίονι ὑψηλῷ καὶ κρίσει μεγάλῃ.[184] Just as God is the one who acts in the OT text, so the author is careful to note: God . . . sent him both as leader and deliverer σὺν χειρὶ ἀγγέλου. In a similar way in v.25, where he has also inserted the concept of salvation/redemption, he also insists: ὁ θεὸς διὰ χειρὸς αὐτοῦ δίδωσιν σωτηρίαν αὐτοῖς.

V.36. The author continues to dwell upon Moses, connecting his statements by the repeated use of οὗτος. For the content of these statements he continues to draw upon his OT source. There are several problems to be considered in relation to this verse:

a οὗτος ἐξήγαγεν αὐτοὺς
b ποιήσας τέρατα καὶ σημεῖα
c ἐν γῇ Αἰγύπτῳ
d καὶ ἐν ἐρυθρᾷ θαλάσσῃ
e καὶ ἐν τῇ ἐρήμῳ
f ἔτη τεσσεράκοντα.

The first part presents a concept which would have been familiar to the author since it is found both in Ex 3:8 and 10, which texts he used in composing 7:34. Furthermore, the same idea is found in Ex 3:11 and 12 and again in Ex 6:6; 7:26, 27; 7:4, 5. It is probable that he has drawn his text from Ex 3:

---

the third gospel is slightly different. On the one hand approximately the same situation occurs in regard to βάτος since in Lk 20:37 it is clearly feminine, while in 6:44 it is indistinguishable. However, in regard to λιμός one has the following data: masculine 4:25, feminine 15:14 and indistinguishable 15:17 and 21:11. So we conclude that the term metaplasm should be applied strictly only to the gospel of Luke (in regard to λιμός).

[184]It will be noted that Ex 6:5 has probably been called into service, or at least called to mind while composing 7:34,

10, καὶ ἐξάξεις τὸν λαόν μου τοὺς υἱοὺς Ισραηλ, since of the texts mentioned above, only Ex 3:10, 11, 12 speak of Moses as agent, and since the author would have picked up his source at the very point where he had ended his quoting activity for 7:34, i.e., Ex 3:10b.[185] Several texts, because of their similarity, have led the author to different passages within his source. The texts mentioned above, where ἐξάγω is employed, help in understanding both the quoting process (discussed below) and the source of the quotation (see also the ἐξάγω of v. 40 = Ex 32:1/23).

Through the intermediary of ἐξάγω--used of the Exodus event--the author is led to Ex 6:26:

> οὗτος Ααρων καὶ Μωυσῆς, οἷς εἶπεν αὐτοῖς ὁ θεὸς ἐξαγαγεῖν τοὺς υἱοὺς Ισραηλ ἐκ γῆς Αἰγύπτου σὺν δυνάμει αὐτῶν· 27 οὗτοί εἰσιν οἱ διαλεγόμενοι πρὸς Φαραω βασιλέα Αἰγύπτου καὶ ἐξήγαγον τοὺς υἱοὺς Ισραηλ ἐξ Αἰγύπτου· αὐτὸς Ααρων καὶ Μωυσῆς.

It is there I believe that he found a stylistic feature, the resumptive οὗτος...οἷς...οὗτοί εἰσι οἱ...αὐτός..., which appealed to him, and he combined this with his more usual construction, τοῦτον...ὃν...τοῦτον... of 7:35 (see pp. 192-96 below for stylistic and structural considerations).

In discussing v.36b-f, commentators usually refer to Ex 7:3, καὶ πληθυνῶ τὰ σημεῖά μου καὶ τὰ τέρατα ἐν γῇ Αἰγύπτῳ, and Nb 14:33, οἱ δὲ υἱοὶ ὑμῶν ἔσονται νεμόμενοι ἐν τῇ ἐρήμῳ τεσσαράκοντα ἔτη. They often conclude their analysis by referring to the strikingly similar passage of <u>Assump</u>. <u>Mos</u>. 3.11, "moyses . . . qui multa passus est in Aegypto et in mari rubro et in heremo annix xl."[186] However, the problems are not so readily dismissed. The use of ποιέω, the word order τέρατα καὶ σημεῖα, and the agency of Moses are left unexplained.

The use of the verb ποιέω in the present context could be

---

see n. 179 above.

[185] It is possible that Ex 3:11 or 12 could have been used since they are structurally similar and in such proximity. It will be remembered that part of Ex 3:12 was employed in 7:7.

[186] <u>Beginnings</u>, 4:77-78, followed by Bruce, <u>Acts</u>, p. 171; Wilson, "Theologian and Historian," pp. 180-81; <u>Bihler</u>, <u>Stephanusgeschichte</u>, pp. 56-57; Haenchen, <u>Acts</u>, p. 283; Conzelmann, <u>Apostelgeschichte</u>, p. 54.

explained in relation to the Johannine expression ποιέω σημεῖα[187] (found once in Acts 8:6); but for several reasons, it seems best to see here the author's own stylistic preferences in regard to σημεῖον and σημεῖον/τέρας, including word order,[188] the influence of the OT source upon this text, and the intended parallelism of Acts 6:8 and 7:36. At this point only the second element concerns us. It seems clear that Ex 7:3 has suggested the basic elements of the quotation, but since similar concepts and expressions were found elsewhere, particularly employing ποιέω, the author would have been susceptible to conflating passages and nuances of thought.

In this regard it is especially the book of Deuteronomy,[189] with its characteristic phraseology and theology, which attracts him. The combination σημεῖον and τέρας occurs ten times, five of these with ποιέω,[190] and generally with God as agent. Attention will be given later to the influence which these passages (Dt 4; 7; and 11) along with Dt 1:1f. and 18:15f. have exerted upon Acts 7:35-41. At present the two following texts call for immediate consideration. Dt 13:1-2 warns against following a potential false prophet, one who advocates false gods, indeed even one who performs (δίδωμι) signs and wonders. In words reminiscent of this passage, the author will return to the theme of prophecy in Acts 7:37 (see below). However, it is the concept of a human agent, no doubt encountered in Ex 11:9-10, where Moses and Aaron are said to perform signs

---

187The construction is found fourteen times in the fourth gospel, always with Jesus as agent (except 10:41: Ἰωάννης μὲν σημεῖον ἐποίησεν οὐδέν) and four times in Revelation, all in apocalyptic contexts. In the one occurrence in Acts it is said of Philip.

188A survey of all Deuteronomic passages listed in n. 190 below reveals no LXX data for the word order of Acts 7:36b (see Brooke and McLean, Old Testament, loc. cit.).

189Jer 39:21f. presents an interesting textual parallel to Acts 7:36, but it is the preponderant influence of Deuteronomy, not without close ties to Jeremiah [see Henri S. Cazelles, "Jérémie et Deutéronome," RSR 39 (1951):5-36], which is the more compelling.

190Dt 4:34; 6:22; 7:19; 11:3; 13:1, 2; 26:8; 28:46; 29:3; and 34:11 (the underlined passages employ ποιέω).

and wonders,[191] which interests us here. This is further illuminated by a second passage, all the more important since it forms the conclusion of the Torah: Dt 34:10

καὶ οὐκ ἀνέστη ἔτι προφήτης ἐν Ισραηλ ὡς Μωυσῆς,
ὃν ἔγνω κύριος αὐτὸν πρόσωπον κατὰ πρόσωπον, 11
ἐν πᾶσι τοῖς σημείοις καὶ τέρασιν, ὃν ἀπέστειλεν
αὐτὸν κύριος ποιῆσαι αὐτὰ ἐν γῇ Αἰγύπτῳ Φαραω καὶ
τοῖς θεράπουσιν αὐτοῦ καὶ πάσῃ τῇ γῇ αὐτοῦ, 12
τὰ θαυμάσια τὰ μεγάλα καὶ τὴν χεῖρα τὴν κραταιάν,
ἃ ἐποίησεν Μωυσῆς ἔναντι παντὸς Ισραηλ.

Again we are confronted with the theme of Moses the prophet as well as wonder worker, but one sent by God (see Acts 7:34-35).[192] It is clear, therefore, that Ex 7:3 has provided the basic source and structure of the text, but owing to the influence of Dt 34:11, ποιέω replaces πληθύνω, and Moses is given a more active role.

The remaining part of v.36 (c, d, e, and f), consisting of four distinct elements, three local (each introduced by ἐν) and one temporal expression, is insufficiently explained by referring to Ex 7:3 and Nb 14:33,[193] since the expression ἐν ἐρυθρᾷ θαλάσσῃ is nowhere mentioned. Again it appears that the author has had recourse to a familiar technique, that of conflating texts. The concepts expressed in the first part of the verse lead him to a similar, but fuller statement of events:

---

[191] Πληθύνων πληθύνω μου τὰ σημεῖα καὶ τὰ τέρατα ἐν γῇ Αἰγύπτῳ. 10 Μωυσῆς δὲ καὶ Ααρων ἐποίησαν πάντα τὰ σημεῖα καὶ τὰ τέρατα ταῦτα ἐν γῇ Αἰγύπτῳ. The similarity of this text to the original source of the quotation is obvious, thereby facilitating the conflation of the two.

[192] In light of the author's quoting techniques--the complementary use of a second text to add nuances of meaning--the objections of Haenchen [*Acts*, p. 283: "According to Exod. 7.3 it was God himself who promised to perform 'many wonders and signs [*sic*!] in the land of Egypt'"] and Conzelmann [*Apostelgeschichte*, p. 54: "Das Motiv erwächst aus Ex 7.3 (wo Gott der Täter ist)"] are rendered less cogent, since the change is one of choice between two biblical concepts of Moses rather than the introduction of one alien to scripture.

[193] The similarity to *Assump*. *Mos*. will be discussed below, p. 148.

Dt 11:3 . . . τὰ σημεῖα αὐτοῦ καὶ τὰ τέρατα αὐτοῦ,
ὅσα ἐποίησεν ἐν μέσῳ Αἰγύπτου
4 . . . ὡς ἐπέκλυσεν τὸ ὕδωρ τῆς θαλάσσης τῆς
ἐρυθρᾶς
5 . . . καὶ ὅσα ἐποίησεν ὑμῖν ἐν τῇ ἐρήμῳ ....

This passage suggests itself for several reasons. All the elements used are readily found there (the time formula no doubt was a standard phrase, especially in relation to ἐν τῇ ἐρήμῳ, see Nb 14:33, Am 5:25 = Acts 7:42).[194] Furthermore, the sequel, particularly Dt 11:8-9, shares several concepts with the speech: entrance into and inheritance of the land, and promise to the fathers to give the land to them and their seed after them. However, a very important reason in terms of the quoting process is that the author probably already utilized Dt 10:22 in composing 7:14 (see p. 72 above).

In this regard reference should also be made to the possible influence of Dt. 1:1f. where such phrases are found, ἐν τῇ ἐρήμῳ; πλησίον τῆς ἐρυθρᾶς θαλάσσης [the form adopted by the author]; and ἐν τῷ τεσσαρακοστῷ ἔτει, which would correspond to Acts 7:35. Dt 1:8 bears great resemblance to Acts 7:5, 17, and 32. In v.3 one finds a key to the beginning of Acts 7:37, see below. And finally, it should be mentioned, in passing, that the targum Pseudo-Jonathan,[195] in its midrashic additions to Dt 1:1, bears striking resemblances to the present text (for further treatment of this subject confer p. 149 below).

V.37. By means of a construction encountered in Ex 6:26-27 (see p. 105 above), the writer introduces both vv. 37 and 38, οὗτός ἐστιν ὁ. . . . Starting from Dt 1:3, ἐλάλησεν Μωυσῆς πρὸς πάντας υἱοὺς Ισραηλ, he is probably led to compose his own speech formula, ὁ εἴπας τοῖς υἱοῖς 'Ισραήλ. This conclusion is further indicated by the usual freedom he exhibits in composing such formulae, and in the fact that "sons of Israel" appears here for the second and last time in the entire speech. The construction, then, is clearly redactional and this particular

---

[194]Reference should be made to Dt 29:4; Neh 9:21; Am 2:10, and also to related passages such as Dt 2:7; Ez 29:12-13, and perhaps to Jos 5:5 (see 7:33 above where the influence of Jos 5:15 upon that verse is discussed).

[195]Ginsburger, Pseudo-Jonathan, p. 300.

appellation of the Hebrews intentional. In relation to this I am led to consider Dt 1:3 as the ultimate source of the text.

The remaining part of v.37 is an extended quotation of Dt 18:15. Owing to differences in word order between the two, the influence of 18:18 should probably be considered at this point. The textual relationship, then, would be as follows:

Dt 18:15 προφήτην ἐκ τῶν ἀδελφῶν σου ὡς ἐμὲ ἀναστήσει
σοι κύριος ὁ θεός σου, αὐτοῦ ἀκούσεσθε

18 προφήτην ἀναστήσω αὐτοῖς ἐκ τῶν ἀδελφῶν αὐτῶν
ὥσπερ σε...

Acts 7:37 προφήτην ὑμῖν ἀναστήσει ὁ θεὸς ἐκ τῶν ἀδελφῶν
ὑμῶν ὡς ἐμέ.

Moreover, the appearance of the same text in Acts 3:22 is not without interest for the discussion, but see below. A comparison of the texts given above demonstrates clearly enough that the LXX translation of v.15 is being quoted, but it seems equally indicated that v.18 has provided the word order. The modification of κύριος ὁ θεός to ὁ θεός is explained by the author's preference for the latter (vv.2, 3, 6, 7, 9c, 17, etc.). The change from the singular (σου. . .σοι) of Dt 18:15 to the plural (ὑμῖν. . .ὑμῶν) is satisfactorily explained in relation to Dt 18:18 (αὐτοῖς. . .αὐτῶν), but textual data require comment and a degree of caution. While the MT, LXX, and most versions, including the Peshitta, read the second person singular (אלהיך ... לך ... מקרבך מאחיך ...) for Dt 18:15, the targum Pseudo-Jonathan presents the entire verse in the second person plural, נבייא מביניכון מן אחיכון דדמי לי ברוח קודשא יקים לכון ה׳ אלהכון. . . .[196] Vööbus, in a recent study, has presented additional evidence for such a Textgestalt from Syriac, Arabic, and Armenian manuscripts.[197] From this evidence it

---

[196]Ibid., p. 332. It should be pointed out that in the previous verse the targum calls the prophet, נביא תריציא, a phrase which, I believe, sheds light on the understanding of 7:52: περὶ τῆς ἐλεύσεως τοῦ δικαίου; but see chapter four.

[197]Peschitta und Targumim des Pentateuchs, neues Licht zur Frage des Herkunft des Peschitta aus dem altpalästinischen Targum, Handschriftstudien, Papers of the Estonian Theological Society in Exile, no. 9 (Stockholm: ETSE, 1958), pp. 28 and 32. Note that Brooke and McLean, Old Testament, 1:613, list the following: "u y 𝔄-codd Eus$\frac{1}{3}$ Cyr-cod$\frac{1}{8}$" as evidence for the reading ἐκ τῶν ἀδελφῶν ὑμῶν.

seems logical to accept a late textual tradition, perhaps even contemporary to Acts, which contained such readings.

The quotation of Dt 18:15f. in Acts 3:22-23 furnishes corroborating data in understanding the author's quoting process.

Acts 3:22 Μωϋσῆς μὲν εἶπεν ὅτι προφήτην ὑμῖν ἀναστήσει κύριος ὁ θεὸς ἡμῶν[198] ἐκ τῶν ἀδελφῶν ὑμῶν ὡς ἐμέ· αὐτοῦ ἀκούσεσθε κατὰ πάντα ὅσα ἂν λαλήσῃ πρὸς ὑμᾶς.

23 ἔσται δὲ πᾶσα ψυχὴ ἥτις ἐὰν μὴ ἀκούσῃ τοῦ προφήτου ἐκείνου ἐξολεθρευθήσεται ἐκ τοῦ λαοῦ.

The word order is identical to that found in 7:37 and so would also indicate the influence of Dt 18:18, while the plural pronouns, ὑμῖν . . . ἡμῶν[199] . . . ὑμῶν, would tend to support a textual solution as reflected in the targum Pseudo-Jonathan and a variety of manuscripts. The speech formula, apparently a creation of the writer, indicates his preference for the verb λέγω rather than λαλέω. The remainder of Acts 3:22 and 23 betrays the type of editorial work encountered in the earlier part of the speech: a mosaic-like use of Dt 18:14-22 (see 7:19) and the conflation of biblical texts, Dt 18:15f. with Lv 23:29 (see especially 7:34).

V.38. It is particularly difficult to assess the rela-

---

[198]I choose to read ἡμῶν along with ℵ* C 𝔎 E pm (and the corroboration of A D al Ir[lat]: ὑμῶν--clearly a scribal correction of an original ἡμῶν) rather than omit the possessive pronouns as do the manuscripts: B h p (the reading of Nestle and Aland, NT Graece, p. 305). Against the last option, Metzger, Commentary, p. 315, states: "The quotation is from Dt 18:15f. (where the Septaugint reads ὁ θεός σου) and Lv 23.29. It appears that the Alexandrian text, with its usual tendency toward parsimoniousness, has eliminated the pronoun after θεός." Metzger continues (in support of the committee's choice of ὑμῶν, see Aland et al., Gk NT, p. 427): "In view of the interchange of ἡμῶν and ὑμῶν through itacism it is difficult to decide between the two chief readings; a majority of the Committee, however, judged that external evidence seems to support ὑμῶν." I believe, nevertheless, that internal and external evidence weighs in favor of ἡμῶν (see also Merk, NT, p. 403). For further textual considerations see below pp. 150-52.

[199]The change from "you" to "our" would not seem to be objectionable to the author of Acts, see especially 7:51-53. For the discussion of an alleged Samaritan solution to Acts 7:37, see Richard, "Acts 7: An Investigation of the Samaritan Evidence," pp. 202-6.

tionship between this verse and the OT narrative, owing to the degree of redactional activity by the writer. The structural and stylistic aspects of the study are primary and will be treated later. Nevertheless, the role of the LXX text is not neglibible. Acts 7:38 reads as follows:

a οὗτός ἐστιν ὁ γενόμενος
b ἐν τῇ ἐκκλησίᾳ
c ἐν τῇ ἐρήμῳ
d μετὰ τοῦ ἀγγέλου τοῦ λαλοῦντος αὐτῷ ἐν τῷ ὄρει Σινὰ
e καὶ τῶν πατέρων ἡμῶν
f ὃς ἐδέξατο λόγια ζῶντα δοῦναι ὑμῖν.[200]

Part _a_ seems patterned upon Ex 6:27, οὗτοί εἰσιν οἱ διαλεγόμενοι (see v.37 above), while the awkwardly attached relative clause of part _f_ recalls 7:20 and 44-45. Beyond this, however, v.38 presents problems. Since it serves as a historical summary in a similar way and as a parallel to v.36, one can expect the components to have been drawn from a number of OT passages.

Owing to more general considerations, discussed in relation to v.39 below, I am led to consider Dt 18:15-21 as the principal source for this text. Following upon the quotation

---

200The manuscript evidence for this particular reading renders a final solution difficult. In A C 𝔄 D _pm_ we read ἡμῖν and in P^{74} B ℵ _al_ p Ir we find ὑμῖν. Jacquier, _Actes_, p. 224 notes the problem but fails to reach a final decision. Bihler, _Stephanusgeschichte_, p. 67, opts for ὑμῖν primarily because, in his opinion, the author is borrowing from Dt 9:10 and there encounters that precise reading. Ropes, _Beginnings_, 3:69, states: "ημιν A C 81 D Antiochian seems preferable to υμιν B ℵ minn perp Iren. The variation being probably due to accident, the intrinisc evidence of fitness to the context (cf. οι πατερες ημων) is to be accepted." This last opinion is hardly acceptable since ὑμῖν is quite admissible intrinsically (for a contrary opinion see Metzger, _Commentary_, pp. 350-51) since the speaker addresses the audience several times: 7:2, 4, 38, 51f. In each case the second person plural is in close proximity to first person plural elements. The author is not reluctant to mix such constructions, no more than is his OT source (_infra_, p. 113). Internal evidence fully supports ὑμῖν. But more importantly, such a solution follows the major manuscripts (also the position of Nestle and Aland, _NT Graece_, p. 318 and Merk, _NT_, p. 419). Finally, it should be pointed out that the unanimous Coptic tradition (Sahidic, Bohairic, and G67) in supporting ὑμῖν is significant since it renders less compelling the witness of D or of the non-Western manuscripts.

of Dt 18:15, 18 for v.37, the author draws from v.16 of his model, ἐν Χωρηβ τῇ ἡμέρᾳ τῆς ἐκκλησίας to compose his text. The mention of the mountain, already transformed from Horeb to Sinai in 7:30, readily leads him to the concepts of "desert," "angel," and the theophany of Sinai, while that of ἐκκλησία, found only in Deuteronomy within the Torah, no doubt brought to mind the giving of the Law. Each of these statements requires further comment.

That the reference to the sacred mountain of revelation, see vv.30, 33, and 35, should conjure up related concepts is hardly surprising since these themes are so important to the author's purpose. The role of the angel(s), related to late Jewish and Christian preoccupations with angelology,[201] is a prominent factor throughout the Stephen material: 6:15, 7:30, 35, 38, 53. The particular nuance (μετὰ τοῦ ἀγγέλου) of v.38 is probably related to that of Exodus (23:20f.; 32:34; 33:2),[202] where an angel is sent/goes before the face of Moses. The author of the speech seems to accept the fully intermediary role of the angel and even to render Moses subordinate to him.[203] His presence then within the community during the desert sojourn is taken literally.[204]

The quoting process for v.38d is very similar to that of

---

[201]See the excellent study of Joseph P. Schultz, "Angelic Opposition to the Ascension of Moses and the Revelation of the Law," _JQR_ 61 (1970-71): 282-307, but more particularly pp. 282-87, where the author examines a large variety of literature dealing with ". . . the presence of angels at the revelation of the Law on Mount Sinai . . ." (282); the targums _Onkelos_ and _Pseudo-Jonathan_, the LXX, the _Book of Jubilees_, Philo, Josephus, the _Biblical Antiquities of Philo_, the Samaritan Memar Marqah and early Talmudic, Midrashic, and NT literature. See also James D. Purvis, "The Fourth Gospel and the Samaritans," _NT_ 17 (1975): 176.

[202]Ex 32:1/23 is extensively quoted in 7:40, and Ex 33:1f. has some bearing upon several passages of the remaining part of the speech.

[203]See 7:35 and probably 7:44. The primacy of the angel is not without OT background; note Ex 23:20f., especially 23: πορεύσεται γὰρ ὁ ἄγγελός μου ἡγούμενός σου καὶ εἰσάξει σε.

[204]I agree with Haenchen, _Acts_, p. 283: "As in Acts 9.19 and 20.18, γίγνομαι μετά means 'to be together with'." I would also agree with his dissent from the views of the editors of _Beginnings_, 4:78 (μετά + double genitive renders Hebrew: בין . . . ובין) and of Schmiedel (ἐν τῇ ἐκκλησίᾳ goes before τῶν πατέρων).

7:35, where twice the author quotes earlier sections of his own text, but more particularly the second, which also involves the angel:

Acts 7:38 μετὰ τοῦ ἀγγέλου
τοῦ λαλοῦντος αὐτῷ ἐν τῷ ὄρει Σινά
30 ὤφθη αὐτῷ ἐν τῇ ἐρήμῳ τοῦ ὄρους Σινὰ ἄγγελος
Ex 3:1-2 . . .ὑπὸ τὴν ἔρημον ... εἰς τὸ ὄρος Χωρηβ.
ὤφθη δὲ αὐτῷ ἄγγελος κυρίου.

The same stylistic link is utilized here as in v.35, namely, an appositional phrase consisting of a participle and selected elements from Acts 7:30. The influence, however, of Ex 31:18 is to be noted, λαλῶν αὐτῷ ἐν τῷ ὄρει τῷ Σινα (see 7:40 below where the author quotes extensively from the following verse of the OT text).

The relation between ἐκκλησία and the giving of the Law referred to above is to be seen within the context of the quoting process. The word here utilized for "community" is fully within LXX usage, and is due to Deuteronomic influence upon the writer. From τῇ ἡμέρᾳ τῆς ἐκκλησίας of Dt 18:16 he is led to 31:30 καὶ ἐλάλησεν Μωυσῆς εἰς τὰ ὦτα πάσης ἐκκλησίας Ισραηλ τὰ ῥήματα τῆς ᾠδῆς ταύτης ... and the final addresses of Moses to the people before his death.[205] There he encountered the very striking passages:

Dt 32:46 . . . ἐντελεῖσθε τοῖς υἱοῖς ὑμῶν φυλάσσειν
καὶ ποιεῖν πάντας <u>τοὺς λόγους τοῦ νόμου τούτου</u>·
47 ὅτι οὐχὶ λόγος κενὸς οὗτος ὑμῖν, <u>ὅτι αὕτη ἡ ζωὴ ὑμῶν</u> ...
Dt 33:2 κύριος ἐκ Σινα ἥκει ...
ἐκ δεξιῶν αὐτοῦ ἄγγελοι μετ' αὐτοῦ
3 καὶ <u>ἐδέξατο</u> ἀπὸ τῶν <u>λόγων</u> αὐτοῦ
4 νόμον, ὃν <u>ἐνετείλατο ἡμῖν Μωυσῆς</u>,
κληρονομίαν συναγωγαῖς Ιακωβ.
5 και ἔσται ἐν τῷ ἠγαπημένῳ ἄρχων
συναχθέντων ἀρχόντων λαῶν
ἅμα φυλαῖς Ισραηλ.

Once again the writer has chosen a variety of terms and concepts from his source(s) and has composed his own narrative.

---

[205]See also Bruce, <u>Acts</u>, p. 172 and Haenchen, <u>Acts</u>, p. 283.

The process is familiar: the form of the verb comes directly from the LXX text, λόγοι suggests λόγια (see 7:12, σῖτος σιτία--confer n. 96), and the concept of "giving" is readily taken from ἐντέλλω. The use of ὑμῶν in Dt 32:47 and of ἡμῖν in 33:4 should be noted in regard to the textual problem of Acts 7:38, but see the discussion below at 7:51, also supra n. 200).

Two concluding remarks need to be made here. The first concerns the appearance of angels in Dt 33:2 in relation to the giving of the Law. This point will not be lost on the writer who will return to it in the final verse of the speech, ἐλάβετε τὸν νόμον εἰς διαταγὰς ἀγγέλων (7:53).

The second concerns the relation mentioned earlier between "assembly" and the giving of the Law. The same process occurs in the targum Pseudo-Jonathan, Dt 18:16, ביומא דאתכנשו שבטיא למקבלא אורייתא. The appearance there of שבטיא shows that, like Acts 7:38, the influence of Dt 33:4-5 easily led either to midrashic interpretation or to the conflation of texts and concepts.[206]

V.39. The author then describes the reaction of the Hebrews to Moses in forceful terms:

> ᾧ οὐκ ἠθέλησαν ὑπήκοοι γενέσθαι οἱ πατέρες ἡμῶν,
> ἀλλὰ ἀπώσαντο
> καὶ ἐστράφησαν ἐν ταῖς καρδίαις αὐτῶν εἰς Αἴγυπτον.

Earlier scholars[207] have often sought to explain this verse in relation to Ezekiel. Jacquier's treatment represents the most serious attempt to do this:

> V 39) Cf. Nombr. XIV,4. Ce passage reproduit les idées et même les paroles d'Ezéchiel: c'est donc par lui qu'il faut l'expliquer: Sur οὐκ ἠθέλησαν ὑπήκοοι γενέσθαι, cf. Ez. XX.8; οὐκ ἠθέλησαν εἰσακοῦσαί μοι; sur ἀπώσαντο, cf. Ez. XX, 13, 24; τὰ δικαιώματά μου ἀπώσαντο; sur ἐστράφησαν ἐν ταῖς καρδίαις αὐτῶν εἰς Αἴγυπτον,

---

[206]See below for a more detailed treatment of the targums.

[207]Authors such as Weiss, Wendt (the former according to Beginnings, 4:78; the latter according to Haenchen, Acts, p. 283), Preuschen, Apostelgeschichte, p. 42, the editors of Beginnings (though hesitatingly), 4:78, but recently also Wilson "Theologian and Historian," p. 182 and Conzelmann, Apostelgeschichte, p. 55.

cf. Ez. XX, 7, 8.[208]

Linguistically the first parallel is striking, especially in light of the author's freedom in treating compound verbs (ὑπακούω/εἰσακούω). The other relations, however, are not very convincing. This theory has not won considerable support in recent years,[209] since the textual relationship is tenuous at best, and especially since the contexts are so different. Furthermore, the quoting process seems to indicate another solution.

It was noted in the analysis of 7:37 above that the author, while quoting Dt 18:15, has ended his quotation before the words αὐτοῦ ἀκούσεσθε, but in Acts 3:22 has proceeded to borrow the entire text. In the present case he has simply returned to his source after having inserted a number of historical facts (v.38). The process involved here is characteristic of him. The command to "listen to him" (ἀκούω) has prompted a contrary response in the form of a conclusion: "they did not wish to be subject to him" (ὑπακούω)[210] (see also the analysis of 7:5). The stylistic features of this text are clearly those of the author. The paraphrastic construction of γίνομαι with a participle is common within the speech (13, 29, 32, 39) and in Acts generally (9:42; 10:4, 10; 12:23; 16:27, 29; 19:17, etc.). The verb θέλω must be seen in light of its double use within the speech: 28 (=Ex 2:14) and 39.[211] This is even more persuasive since ἀπωθέω also appears only twice in the discourse: 27 and 39.

---

[208]Actes, p. 224.

[209]That scholars such as Foakes-Jackson, Acts, p. 63 (1931); Bruce, Acts, p. 172 (1953) and Bihler, Stephanusgeschichte, pp. 67-68 (1963) should refer only to Nb 14:2-3 and avoid any mention of Ezekiel is significant. Moreover, Haenchen, Acts, p. 283 (1965) explicitely rejects such a solution, however, without presenting an alternate explanation: "According to Wendt (146) this verse is based on Ezek.20. Ἀπώσαντο certainly occurs there in verses 13, 16 and 24 (with reference to God's commandments), but ἐστράφησαν εἰς Αἴγυπτον reflects Num. 14.3 . . ."

[210]Note the use of this verb in Acts 6:7.

[211]The influence of a LXX expression such as Ez 20:8 ἠθέλησαν εἰσακοῦσαί μοι upon the author's formulation of this verse need not be discounted. However, the conclusion above concerns the quoting process.

In regard to the last verb, there is no known source. Although ἀπωθέω occurs in Ezekiel, there is no thematic or structural reason to posit a relationship with Acts 7:39.[212] Further, the appearance of this term in Am 5:21 in close proximity to a quoted passage (5:25-27 = Acts 7:42-43) might call for special attention. However, it is the context once more which leads me to reject this. Instead, it appears that the concept as well as the term is due to the author's redaction (7:27 is a parallel to the present text; see also 13:46)[213] and will be examined later.

For the final part of v.39 the author once more finds a clue in the ensuing text of Dt 18. But since the influence of this source is much more pervasive, it is necessary to dwell for an instant upon the quoting process. From Dt 18:9 he learns that God will take vengeance (ἐγὼ ἐκδικήσω ἐξ αὐτοῦ--see Acts 7:24) upon the man who will not listen (μὴ ἀκούσῃ). In response to this he composes 7:42. In Dt 18:20 he reads that the prophet who impiously speaks in God's name a word (λαλέω. . .ῥῆμα--see 6:11 and 13) not commanded by him or in the name of other gods (θεῶν ἑτέρων--see 7:40) will die. And finally Dt 18:21, ἐὰν δὲ εἴπης ἐν τῇ καρδίᾳ σου, prompts him to modify the well-known biblical account of the people's attitude in the desert (Nb 14:3, ἀποστραφῆναι εἰς Αἴγυπτον) by an expression which recalls his own construction of 7:23.[214] Once again his attitude toward his source in regard to compound verbs is clear.

---

[212]After having quoted extensively from Ez 20, Lake and Cadbury, Beginnings, 4:78, conclude: "Apparently there are no nearer analogies in the LXX."

[213]The term is rare in the NT (six occurrences, three of which appear in Acts). In this connection it is strange, to say the least, to read Karl L. Schmidt's statement, "ἀπωθέω," in TDNT 1:448: "The only passage of significance for biblical theology is R. 11:1, 2: μὴ ἀπώσατο ὁ θεὸς τὸν λαὸν αὐτοῦ."

[214]The expression does not, contrary to Haenchen's opinion, Acts, p. 283, "spiritualize" the people's return to Egypt. Instead it represents, in relation to θέλω, a stylistic trait of the author. By this word combination (see also 7:23 and 28 where the same phenomenon occurs) the author lays particular stress on the intention and willfulness of the act considered.

V.40. This verse consists of an extended quotation of the classic formulation of Israel's idolatry:

Acts 7:40	Ex 32:1 (v.23 identical)
εἰπόντες τῷ 'Ααρών·	... ἐπὶ Ααρων καὶ λέγουσιν αὐτῷ
ποίησον ἡμῖν θεοὺς	'Ανάστηθι καὶ ποίησον ἡμῖν θεούς,
οἳ προπορεύσονται ἡμῶν·	οἳ προπορεύσονται ἡμῶν·
ὁ γὰρ Μωϋσῆς οὗτος,	ὁ γὰρ Μωυσῆς οὗτος ὁ ἄνθρωπος,
ὃς ἐξήγαγεν ἡμᾶς ἐκ γῆς Αἰγύπτου,	ὃς ἐξήγαγεν ἡμᾶς ἐξ Αἰγύπτου,
οὐκ οἴδαμεν τί ἐγένετο αὐτῷ.	οὐκ οἴδαμεν, τί γέγονεν αὐτῷ.

The speech formula once again is his own creation. At the same time the combination of ideas (the turning to Egypt and making of gods) is also his own and furnishes added clues in understanding his point of view.

The differences between the texts are minimal and easily accounted for in view of tendencies already noted. "Ανθρωπος has been replaced twice by ἀνήρ (supra, p. 85 and n. 137), so its elimination here is not surprising (see the two strategic occurrences of the former in the Stephen material, 6:13 and 7:56). The addition of γῆς could be explained as the inadvertent substitution of one common LXX expression for another or as due to the influence of the reading of Alexandrinus (both for Ex 32:1 and 23). I propose here an original LXX reading more in conformity with the MT (מארץ מצרים), the versions, and textual evidence.[215] Finally, for the modification of γέγονεν to ἐγένετο, despite the assimilation to the LXX by 𝔐 D pm, reference should be made to the author's frequent use of this form, no less than six times within the Stephen material.

V.41. The writer continues to draw from his source elements for this passage:

a καὶ ἐμοσχοποίησαν ἐν ταῖς ἡμέραις ἐκείναις

b καὶ ἀνήγαγον θυσίαν τῷ εἰδώλῳ,

c καὶ εὐφραίνοντο ἐν τοῖς ἔργοις τῶν χειρῶν αὐτῶν.

---

[215]For Ex 32:1 we have: "A b f i q u w 𝔅 𝔈 𝔖 𝔏^{z} Acta Cyr" and for 32:32: "A e g j q s(txt) u v z(txt) 𝔅 𝔈 𝔖 𝔏^{wz} ," Brooke and McLean, Old Testament, 1:265 and 266 respectively. Furthermore, the phrase "land of Egypt" is relatively rare in the NT, Acts 7:40 (=Ex 32:1?); 13:17 (=an OT formula?); Heb 8:9 (=Jer 31:32) and Jd 5, so that its occurrence here strongly

The technique of drawing various ideas or texts from the OT and reformulating them into a series of independent clauses connected by καί has been noted before: 7:8, 9-10, 13, 15-16. The writer draws the elements for the first part of the verse from Ex 32, where he encounters the combination ποιέω μόσχον four times: vv.4, 8, 20, 35. It is generally the first, καὶ ἐποίησεν αὐτὰ μόσχον χωνευτόν, which attracts the attention of commentators. Vv.8 and 20, in attributing this action to the people, also seem to have some bearing upon this text,[216] although the author's use of contrasting singular/plural constructions is not to be overlooked in this context.[217] It is possible that Ex 32:35, καὶ ἐπάταξεν κύριος τὸν λαὸν περὶ τῆς ποιήσεως τοῦ μόσχου, οὗ ἐποίησεν Ααρων, has exerted some influence upon the author's formulation of 7:41a, but the opinion of Lake and Cadbury probably remains the best:

> The Greek ἐμοσχοποίησεν appears to be found only here and in later writers commenting on Amos v. 25, but the recurrence of μοσχοποιία [sic] in Justin's Dialogue with Trypho (xix.5, lxxiii.6, cii. 6, cxxxii.1), which is not directly dependent on Acts, indicates that it was not merely the creation of the author of Acts.[218]

The time formula is also due to the author's activity.

The following part of v.41 seems clearly to be related to Ex 32:6, ἀνεβίβασεν ὁλοκαυτώματα καὶ προσήνεγκεν θυσίαν σωτηρίου, by reason of context and textual dependence. Still the modification of προσφέρω to ἀνάγω requires critical attention. In the first place the latter is rarely employed in a sacrificial sense: Herodotus 2:48, 60, etc.; 1 K 3:15; OGIS 764.47 (127 B.C.); and Acts 7:41.[219] Furthermore, the Hebrew

---

suggests a source.

[216]Jacquier, Actes, p. 225, oddly enough states: "Etienne attribue à tout le peuple la fabrication du veau d'or, bien qu'elle soit l'oeuvre d'Aaron, Ex. xxxii.3; le peuple y avait participé quisqu'il l'avait demandée." Note also the statements of Haenchen, Acts, p. 283 and Conzelmann, Apostelgeschichte, p. 55.

[217]The contrast between the actions of one Hebrew 7:24-28 and those of the Hebrews is clearly intentional.

[218]Beginnings, 4:78-79.

[219]See Liddell-Scott-Jones, Lexicon, s.v. "ἀνάγω"; Preuschen (and later commentators), Apostelgeschichte, p. 43; Moulton-Milligan, Vocabulary, s.v. "ἀνάγω" (for OGIS 764.47).

underlying ἀνάγω of 1 K 3:15 is ויעל, which verb is translated by ἀνεβίβασεν in the text under consideration (Ex 32:6).[220] Since the Hebrew expression literally corresponds to the Greek term, ἀνάγω, it is possible to postulate the following as the LXX reading used by the author of Acts: ἀνήγαγον/-εν ὁλοκαυτώματα καὶ προσήνεγκαν/-εν θυσίαν σωτηρίου. The writer would then have chosen the necessary elements to form his text, a process facilitated no doubt by the possible, though rare, sacrificial meaning of ἀνάγω. I hesitate to choose between an original singular or plural subject. The standard LXX diverges from the MT in this regard. Since one characteristic of the Greek version used by the author of Acts is often a more faithful rendering of the Hebrew, one could insist on a plural subject. Knowing, however, the writer's redactional intent (the Hebrews contrasted to the Israelite of vv.24-28), I am not willing to disregard the possibility of an intentional change.

The reference to the idol in v.41b does not relate to the OT source. One can still easily understand how the very subject of Acts 7:40-41 would call to mind the sacred prohibition either of Ex 20:4 or Dt 5:8: οὐ ποιήσεις σεαυτῷ εἴδωλον.

The last part of v.41 is related in idea to Ex 32:6 (the continuation of the verse quoted above), καὶ ἐκάθισεν ὁ λαὸς φαγεῖν καὶ πιεῖν καὶ ἀνέστησαν παίζειν. The writer goes far beyond his source in commenting upon the people's reaction. This text is clearly related to a major theme of this part of the speech, vv.40-50, namely, the concept of "making" or of "handmade things."

2) Vv.35-41: Quoting Process

Contrary to the procedure followed earlier, it has been necessary in examining the textual relation of vv.35-41 to the OT model, to anticipate on numerous occasions factors that concern more properly the quoting process and even structural and stylistic elements. This was demanded by the nature of the text. For that reason the treatment will be brief, since a few general considerations will now suffice to provide an overall

---

[220]Note that Aquila and Symmachus transform this LXX reading to ἀνήνεγκαν and Theodotion to ἤνεγκαν. This has also been pointed out by Wilcox, Semitisms, p. 43.

view of the author's methodology.

In view of the following chart, several areas require particular attention. In the first instance it will be noted that the writer pursues the narrative sequence of his source. In other words, in spite of the polemical and thematic nature of vv.35f., he none the less returns to his OT model at the exact place where he had abandoned it. V.35 reiterates the concept of mission (see v.34 = Ex 3:10), while v.36 draws more extensively from the early chapters of Exodus (generously supplemented with quotations from Deuteronomy). After a thematic excurses, vv.37-39 (a midrashic treatment of Dt 18:15-21), the author returns to the narrative sequence of his source in vv.40-41. This is, in fact, consistent with what has been observed throughout the speech, namely, that the writer wishes to present a valid account of the biblical story and, to that effect, is faithful to the narrative sequence of the OT account.

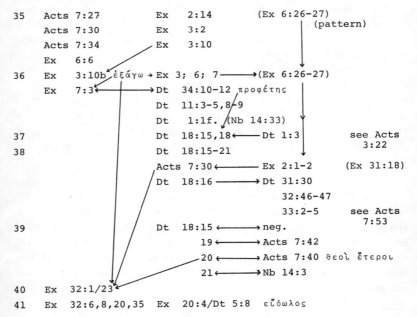

35	Acts 7:27	Ex 2:14	(Ex 6:26-27) (pattern)	
	Acts 7:30	Ex 3:2		
	Acts 7:34	Ex 3:10		
	Ex 6:6			
36	Ex 3:10b ἐξάγω →	Ex 3; 6; 7 →	(Ex 6:26-27)	
	Ex 7:3 ↔	Dt 34:10-12 προφέτης		
		Dt 11:3-5,8-9		
		Dt 1:1f. (Nb 14:33)		
37		Dt 18:15,18 ←	Dt 1:3	see Acts 3:22
38		Dt 18:15-21		
		Acts 7:30 ←	Ex 2:1-2	(Ex 31:18)
		Dt 18:16 →	Dt 31:30	
			32:46-47	
			33:2-5	see Acts 7:53
39		Dt 18:15 ↔	neg.	
		19 ↔	Acts 7:42	
		20 ↔	Acts 7:40 θεοὶ ἕτεροι	
		21 ↔	Nb 14:3	
40	Ex 32:1/23			
41	Ex 32:6,8,20,35	Ex 20:4/Dt 5:8	εἴδωλος	

A second element noted in passing only, since it is primarily stylistic in nature, is the author's use of the OT through the intermediary of his own text. On four separate occasions he quotes his own composition, texts which are ultimately derived from the biblical narrative.

Thirdly, the influence of the book of Deuteronomy should be examined briefly. The role played by this work may seem preponderant, even though scholars have seldom noted more than the citation of Dt 18:15 in Acts 7:37. The chart given above places its influence within its proper perspective: first in vv.36 and 41 as a second source used by the author to supplement his narrative (i.e., conflation of texts), and second in vv.37-39 as an excursus on Moses the prophet in the midst of the fathers, based upon Dt 18:15-21.

Finally, reference should be made to several quoting peculiarities already encountered in the earlier parts of the speech, such as conflation of texts, stream-of-consciousness technique, positive/negative contrast, stylistic imitation (note the pattern borrowed from Ex 6:26-27). These tend to confirm the writer's constancy of composition as well as purpose.

b. Vv.42-50: God and the Fathers

1) Vv.42-50: Textual Relation to OT

This section of the speech is clearly delineated structurally (ὁ θεός of v.42 and the divine names of vv.48 and 49 form an evident inclusio), and marks a new attitude toward the OT. More than anywhere else in the speech, the author seems the slave of an idea. The concepts expressed, the texts quoted, the unity of the passage--all seem governed by what he considers the successive stages of Israel's rebellion against God.

V.42. After having described in detail the ultimate point of Israel's unfaithfulness (v.40), and having insisted upon the intentional and perverse character of this episode (v.41), the writer finally notes the rupture of the relationship between God and his people (v.42):

ἔστρεψεν δὲ ὁ θεὸς
καὶ παρέδωκεν αὐτοὺς λατρεύειν τῇ στρατίᾳ τοῦ οὐρανοῦ.

The first clause once caused considerable debate: was the construction transitive or intransitive?[221] More recently commen-

---

[221]Jacquier, Actes, p. 226, gives the opinions of earlier scholars and, relying primarily upon the work of Loisy, presents his reasons for choosing the second option. In concluding his commentary he makes the two following pertinent re-

tators simply affirm its intransitive nature.[222] I agree with this tendency and propose further that the OT background for this text is the expression ἀποστρέψω τὸ πρόσωπόν μου ἀπ' αὐτῶν of Dt 31:18 and 32:19.[223] From the threatening statements of Ex 32:10f.--God's response to the making of the calf--the author is led to the concluding chapters of Deuteronomy, where he borrows a more appropriate term to describe God's reaction to his people's infidelity. The modification of ἀποστρέφω to στρέφω is understandable in light of the author's usual redactional tendencies. It is further explained in terms of the antithesis between v.39, the fathers who turn to Egypt in their hearts and 42, God who, as the result of their faithlessness, turns away. Not only did Ex 32:10f. suggest other biblical statements of God's anger with his people, but v.15 even provided the necessary term, ἀποστρέφω.[224]

The second part of v.42 introduces the audience of the speech to the consequences of the ultimate rupture in the relationship between God and Israel. The context of this particular clause however is problematic. On the one hand, the best analogue to παραδίδωμι is surely Rm 1:24, 26, 28, where the concept is also expressed "that God punishes sinners by handing them over to worse sins."[225] On the other hand, "the

---

marks: "Mais dans la Bible les dérivés seuls de ἔστρεψεν: ἀναστρέφειν, ἐπιστρέφειν, ἀποστρέφειν ont ce sens. Remarquons cependant qu'il y a une sorte d'antithèse entre ἔστρεψεν et ἐστράφησαν, v.39: Dieu s'est détourné des Israélites comme ceux-ci s'étaient détournés dans leur coeurs." Both observations, I believe, receive ample clarification throughout this study. On the opinions of earlier scholars, note also *Beginnings*, 4:79.

222 Bruce, *Acts*, p. 173; Haenchen, *Acts*, p. 283; and Conzelmann, *Apostelgeschichte*, p. 55.

223 Both texts deal with God's response to the apostasy of Israel.

224 The context is very different, but it has often been noted that the author is most susceptible to the least influence of his source, borrowing minute details of grammar, vocabulary or ideas.

225 *Beginnings*, 4:79. Haenchen's (*Acts*, p. 284) insistence that Paul refers to "punishment" and Acts to "consequence" in relating God's action goes counter to the meaning of Acts 7:42, which in no uncertain terms insists upon God's active role. See Arndt-Gingrich, *Lexicon*, s.v. "παραδίδωμι," who insist that the verb speaks "of God who punishes evil-doers."

worship of the host of heaven" as an example of idol worship, though not a very common concept, is still found in several books of the OT. But the situation is rendered more complex by the nature of the LXX version. Acts 7:42 speaks of λατρεύειν τῇ στρατιᾷ τοῦ οὐρανοῦ, an expression which, as Haenchen has pointed out,[226] is not found in the Greek version.

A closer examination of the OT passages which refer to "the host of heaven" reveals some interesting facts. The Hebrew phrase צבא השמים is rendered in a variety of ways by the LXX translators: a) as στρατιὰ τοῦ οὐρανοῦ (2 Chr 33:3, 5; Jer 8:2; 19:13;[227] Zeph 1:5); b) by δύναμις τοὺ οὐρανοῦ (2 K 23:5); and finally c) by κόσμος τοῦ οὐρανοῦ Dt 4:19 and 17:3). In the last instance, Aquila renders both texts by στρατιὰ τοῦ οὐρανοῦ.[228] Furthermore, the combination of Hebrew verbs, עבד and שחה, also demands attention. The latter is invariably translated by προσκυνέω, while the former is represented both by δουλεύω (2 Chr 33:3 and Jer 8:2) and λατρεύω (Dt 4:19 and 17:3).

As a result of these observations, I conclude that the author of Acts employs Dt 17:3, καὶ ἐλθόντες λατρεύσωσιν θεοῖς ἑτέροις καὶ προσκυνήσωσιν αὐτοῖς, τῷ ἡλίῳ ἢ τῇ σελήνῃ ἢ παντὶ τῶν ἐκ [τῆς στρατιᾶς] τοῦ οὐρανοῦ, ἃ οὐ προσέταξεν, to formulate his accusation against the Hebrews. Furthermore, under the influence of a very similar passage from Dt 4:19, καὶ μὴ ἀναβλέψας εἰς τὸν οὐρανὸν καὶ ἰδὼν τὸν ἥλιον καὶ τὴν σελήνην καὶ τοὺς ἀστέρας καὶ πάντα [τὴν στρατίαν] τοῦ οὐρανοῦ πλανηθεὶς προσκυνήσῃς αὐτοῖς καὶ λατρεύσῃς αὐτοῖς, he is led to the one text in the OT where a false god and a star are associated--Am 5:26. The use of λατρεύω in 7:42 in relation to "the host of heaven," the addition within the text of Am 5:26 (note Acts 7:43) of the verb προσκυνέω, the tendency of the writer to

---

226 Acts, p. 284: "Such service of the stars is held against Israel in Deut. 4.19 and other places, though apart from the λατρεύειν to be found there the wording is not reminiscent of the present verse. On the other hand, Jer. 7.18 and 19.13 LXX mention the 'host of heaven', which in LXX is never named in conjunction with λατρεύω." Other scholars apparently have not noted the difficulties involved.

227 The difficult passage of Jer 7:18, למלכת השמים, is also rendered by στρατιὰ τοῦ οὐρανοῦ.

228 See Field, Hexapla, 1:279 and 297.

conflate texts and ideas as well as his "stream-of-conscious" quoting technique, lead me to propose the above as the most plausible analysis of the passage under consideration. To further underscore this conclusion, it should be noted that "the host of heaven" and "the star of god Raiphan" form a doublet as do λατρεύω and προσκυνέω. Lastly, the ultimate source of the idea of "star worship" is probably Ex 32:13, where Moses is promised a posterity, ὡσεὶ τὰ ἄστρα τοῦ οὐρανοῦ τῷ πλήθει. From this clue the author is led to further passages in Deuteronomy and Amos dealing with worship of the heavenly bodies (infra, p. 136).

The second part of v.42 consists of an introductory formula and the intitial portion of the quotation from Amos. The former, καθὼς γέγραπται ἐν βίβλῳ τῶν προφητῶν, owes to the author and will be examined later, while the latter requires immediate attention. The relation between the prophetic text and the NT passage is clearly shown in the juxtaposition of the two texts from Acts and Amos.

a	42	μὴ σφάγια	25	μὴ σφάγια
b		καὶ θυσίας προσηνέγκατέ μοι		καὶ θυσίας προσηνέγκατέ μοι
c		ἔτη τεσσεράκοντα ἐν τῇ ἐρήμῳ,		ἐν τῇ ἐρήμῳ τεσσαράκοντα ἔτη,
d		οἶκος 'Ισραήλ,		οἶκος Ισραηλ;
e	43	καὶ ἀνελάβετε τὴν σκηνὴν τοῦ Μόλοχ	26	καὶ ἀνελάβετε τὴν σκηνὴν τοῦ Μολοχ
f		καὶ τὸ ἄστρον τοῦ θεοῦ ὑμῶν Ραιφάν[229]		καὶ τὸ ἄστρον τοῦ θεοῦ ὑμῶν Ραιφαν,

---

[229] I choose to read ὑμῶν along with P^{74} ℌ 𝔄 E pl h vg sy^h (also the reading of Aland et al., Gk NT, p. 443--in brackets) against B D pc gig sy^p Ir Or (choice of Nestle and Aland NT Graece, p. 319 and Merk, NT, p. 419) in omitting the possessive pronoun. The Aland reading (NT Graece, p. 319) Ρομφα, supported only by B is also rejected in favor of the LXX text, Ραιφαν (choice of Aland et al., Gk NT, p. 443), along with P^{74} A pc (also Aland et al., Gk NT, p. 443) and the corroborating witness of C E al sy, Ρεφαν (reading of Merk, NT, p. 419). See the statement of Ropes, Beginnings, 3:70 and Haenchen, Acts, p. 284, n. 1.

g	τοὺς τύπους οὓς ἐποιήσατε		τοὺς τύπους [αὐτῶν],[230] οὓς ἐποιήσατε
h	<u>προσκυνεῖν αὐτοῖς</u>;		<u>ἑαυτοῖς</u>.
i	καὶ μετοικιῶ ὑμᾶς	27	καὶ μετοικιῶ ὑμᾶς
j	ἐπέκεινα <u>Βαβυλῶνος</u>.		ἐπέκεινα <u>Δαμασκοῦ</u>, λέγει κύριος, ὁ θεὸς ὁ παντοκράτωρ ὄνομα αὐτῷ.

The extended quotation presents few serious problems. The differences between Acts and the LXX text of Amos are readily understood in light of textual evidence or the author's theological concerns. The contrast between the two Greek texts in part <u>c</u> is notable only because the LXX column is taken from Rahlfs' edition. While there is great variety in the LXX manuscript tradition in regard to parts <u>c</u> and <u>d</u>, the text type represented by Acts 7:42 (τεσσαράκοντα ἔτη ἐν τῇ ἐρήμῳ) is well attested among the witnesses.[231] Furthermore, even though the author is consistent throughout the book of Acts in placing before the ordinal both the term for day and year, we should probably also attribute the order: ἔτη τεσσαράκοντα to the manuscript tradition, since this stylistic feature is well attested in the LXX witnesses.[232]

The addition in part <u>h</u> of προσκυνεῖν, and the consequent modification of ἑαυτοῖς to αὐτοῖς, owes no doubt to the author's desire, on the one hand, to stress his accusation against Israel for having disobeyed the condemnation of idol

---

[230]Αὐτῶν is omitted by the following: "A-Q^{txt} <u>L</u>$^{''}$-36 <u>C</u>-68 Bo Iust. Th. Tht. I 205;" see Joseph Ziegler, ed., <u>Duodecim prophetae</u>, vol. 13 of <u>Septuaginta Vetus Testamentum Graecum Auctoritate Societatis Litterarum Gottingensis</u> (Göttingen: Vandenhoeck & Ruprecht, 1943), p. 195. For the Bohairic text of Am 5:26, see William Grossouw, <u>The Coptic Versions of the Minor Prophets: A Contribution to the Study of the Septuagint</u>, Monumenta biblica et ecclesiastica, no. 3 (Rome: Pontifical Biblical Institute, 1938), p. 37.

[231]"L$'$-763-613 Aeth^{p} Th," (Ziegler, <u>Duodecim prophetae</u>, p. 195).

[232]Ziegler, <u>ibid</u>., does not give variants for this particular feature in relation to Amos 5:25; however, see n. 45 above for manuscript evidence for Gn 15:13 (= Acts 7:6). Also confer both Brooke and McLean, <u>Old Testament</u> and Wevers, <u>Genesis</u>, for variants in relation to Gn 11:10-32.

"worship" (Ex 20:4 and Dt 5:8, see Acts 7:41) and, on the other, to reflect more faithfully the fact that the Hebrews both "served" (v.42) and "worshipped" (v.43) the host of heaven. The change seems his own since no other text imposes such a modification upon the text of Amos.

Finally, the substitution of Babylon for Damascus seems--and most commentators agree--best explained as a post-exilic correction.[233] The modification appears logical in such a context and is understandable in light of the author's repeated tendency to conflate texts, episodes, and themes.

V.44. This particular verse has received considerable attention by commentators, although these considerations have been primarily of a structural nature. Many have wanted to see v.44 as the beginning of a new theme[234] or section[235] of the speech, while others have attempted to relate this verse to what they considered the neutral history of 7:2-34.[236] It is also my contention that the structural considerations are primary in analyzing the entire section of the speech, vv.42-50.

---

[233]The influence of Is 52:4, "Thus says the Lord: my people went down to Egypt first to sojourn there and were carried away by force to the Assyrians [εἰς Ἀσσυρίους]," upon the Amos quotation should not be discounted, especially since Is 52-53 has played such an important role in the composition of the Stephen story (<u>infra</u>, p. 351) and Acts 3:13. Note also the reference in the targum <u>Jerushalmi</u> (Ex 34:10) to "captivity along the river of Babel" (reference given by Strack and Billerbeck, <u>Kommentar</u>, 2:683). It is obvious that similar processes have left their mark upon Acts 7:43 and the targum.

[234]Bihler, <u>Stephanusgeschichte</u>, p. 71: "Mit v.44 beginnt ein neues Thema." See also Jacquier, <u>Actes</u>, p. 229 (although he does point out the connections between vv.43 and 44).

[235]Renié, <u>Actes</u>, p. 120; Richard J. Dillon and Joseph A. Fitzmyer, "Acts of the Apostles" in <u>JBC</u> 2:183-84; Javier Colmenero Atienza," Hechos 7,17-43 y las corrientes cristológicas dentro de la primitiva comunidad cristiana," <u>EstBib</u> 33 (1974): 42-43.

[236]Haenchen, <u>Acts</u>, p. 284. Conzelmann, <u>Apostelgeschichte</u>, p. 55 expresses a very similar point of view: "V.44 and 42 gehen nicht zusammen. Es entsteht die Seltsamkeit, dass zwei Zelte mitgeführt werden. Offenbar kehrt der Verfasser hier nach einem Einschub zur Vorlage zurück (Stilwechsel!); der Anschluss an v 38 (oder 34?) wäre glatt; die formale Verknüpfung wird durch das Stichwort σκηνή gewonnen, wodurch eben die merkwürdige und vom Verfasser kaum beachtete Verdoppelung entsteht."

Presently it should be noted that v.44 is intimately related to the preceding verses of the discourse and is indeed a midrashic expansion of the quotation of Amos. At the same time, it serves as an intentional contrast between the negative (idolatry) and positive (fidelity) aspects of Hebrew history.[237] The persistent influence of Ex 32-33 indicates a similar conclusion.

The relation of v.44,

a 'Η σκηνὴ τοῦ μαρτυρίου ἦν τοῖς πατράσιν ἡμῶν ἐν τῇ ἐρήμῳ,

b καθὼς διετάξατο ὁ λαλῶν τῷ Μωϋσῇ

c ποιῆσαι αὐτὴν κατὰ τὸν τύπον ὃν ἑωράκει

to the OT requires special attention. The phrase ἡ σκηνὴ τοῦ μαρτυρίου, used in contrast to the ἡ σκηνὴ τοῦ Μόλοχ of v.43, is borrowed from Ex 33:7, while ἐν τῇ ἐρήμῳ which doubtless could be related to a number of OT texts, is more properly viewed as a quotation from his own text, vv.42, 38, 36, 30, but particularly the first.

Part b of this verse is more properly understood in terms of stylistic considerations and has no immediate relation to the OT source. Section c of v.44, however, is a quotation drawn from Ex 25:40, ὅρα ποιήσεις κατὰ τὸν τύπον τὸν δεδειγμένον σοι ἐν τῷ ὄρει. The exact relation between the text of Acts and its source is rendered more complex by the very nature of the data. The author adds αὐτήν, obviously referring to the tabernacle, while the LXX does not have a direct object. It is clear from the context that the source is referring not to the tabernacle but to its implements (true also of the Hebrew text). Other texts, however, do speak of making the tabernacle or sanctuary (ἁγίασμα) according to the pattern shown to Moses. The terms for pattern, however, are παράδειγμα (Ex 25:9) or

---

[237]Earlier scholars have not been unaware of such contrasts. Bruce, Acts, p. 174 states: "By contrast with 'the tabernacle of Moloch' (ver. 43)" and p. 175 "This τύπος may be contrasted with the idolatrous τύποι of ver. 43." Much earlier Preuschen, Apostelgeschichte, p. 43, had made similar observations. Furthermore, Haenchen's comment regarding v. 44 (Acts, p. 284: "It is astonishing that the fathers nevertheless, during their time in the wilderness, possessed the σκηνὴ τοῦ μαρτυρίου, made in conformity with the ordinance of God"), is very much to the point, but unfortunately he does not develop the idea. This I believe is precisely the intended meaning of the writer, see pp. 324-30.

εἶδον (26:30) or the circumlocution, κατὰ τὸ παραδειχθέν σοι (27:8). Again it seems that we should see here a tendency, pointed out several times already, of the author to conflate texts taken from his source. He is interested in the passage from his model which utilizes the term τύπος even if he is obliged to modify this text.[238]

I opt for a modification by the author rather than seek a possible solution in relation to the nature of the LXX Vorlage for several reasons, one of which involves the conclusion of section c, ὃν ἑωράκει. This clause should be seen not as a quotation of Ex 25:40 (τὸν δεδειγμένον σοι ἐν τῷ ὄρει), but as a reformulation by the author of the idea found in his source. In effect, he has remodeled this part of v.44 upon his own text:[239]

v.43 τοὺς τύπους οὓς ἐποιήσατε
44 κατὰ τὸν τύπον ὃν ἑωράκει.

While it might have been possible to seek in the LXX rendering of וראה ועשה בתבניתם אשר־אתה מראה בהר some justification of the use in Acts of ὁράω rather than δείκνυμι, i.e., some LXX textual tradition in support of such a reading, the evidence seems to indicate otherwise. The texts of Exodus, which speak of Moses being shown some "pattern" by God, invariably employ the latter (25:9, 40; 26:30) or a compound, παραδείκνυμι (27:8). Note that the quotation of Ex 25:40 in Heb 8:5, ὅρα γάρ φησιν, ποιήσεις πάντα κατὰ τὸν τύπον τὸν δειχθέντα σοι ἐν τῷ ὄρει, supports such a conclusion.

V.45. The relationship between the various elements of this verse and the OT narrative should be considered secondary, since a number of ideas and terms employed could ultimately be ascribed to an OT source:

---

[238]The expression τύπος is very rare in the LXX, appearing only twice: Am 5:26 and Ex 25:40 (both of which are used by the author!). The first involves problems of LXX translation while the second translates the Hebrew term תבנית, the same word found in Ex 25:9, but rendered as παραδείγμα.

[239]The procedure is related to the midrashic technique so much in evidence here. The doublets, the plural/singular contrast, the overall relation between vv.42-43 and 44 constitutes important structural elements of the text.

ἣν καὶ εἰσήγαγον	Jos 3:14
διαδεξάμενοι οἱ πατέρες ἡμῶν	Jos 18:1
μετὰ 'Ιησοῦ	Dt 34:9
ἐν τῇ κατασχέσει τῶν ἐθνῶν	Gn 17:8; 48:4; Jos 1:1f.
ὧν ἐξῶσεν ὁ θεὸς ἀπὸ προσώπου τῶν πατέρων ἡμῶν,	Dt 7:1, 22
ἕως τῶν ἡμερῶν Δαυίδ.	

In reality the author's own text is the primary source for several of these. His tendency to use doublets to express contrast, promise-fulfillment, parallelism, etc., suggests the following:

εἰσάγω	ἐξάγω	vv.36, 40
διαδέχομαι	δέχομαι	v.38
κατάσχεσις	κατάσχεσις	v.5
ἐξωθέω	ἀπωθέομαι	vv.27, 39

All the correspondences indicated above, except the last one, involve OT quotations.

In any event, three passages call for further commentary in view of their OT background, all of which involve the persistent influence of Ex 33 in the process of composition. The first, found in v.11 of his source, is the reference to Joshua, who appears only in this text and in Heb 4:8 in the NT.[240] The second concerns the "driving out of the nations by God." Ex 33:2 provided him with the following text: καὶ ἐκβαλεῖ τὸν Αμορραῖον καί. . . . Since this passage refers to an angel as the one who will drive out the peoples, it is logical to assume that the writer would have had recourse to several other passages which express the same concept but present God as the agent: Ex 34:11 or Dt 7:1. However, the relationship between ἐξωθέω of Acts and ἐκβάλλω (Ex 33:2 and 34:11 both = גרש) or ἐξαίρω (Dt 7:1 = נשל) of the alleged sources is clearly problematic. The difficulty is compounded by several factors. The verb ἐξωθέω occurs only twice in the NT, both in Acts (7:45 and 27:39). However, the latter is a technical, nautical term: "to beach or run a ship ashore." At the same time, the author often uses the same verbs, but with different prefixes, e.g., ἐξωθέω and ἀπωθέω. In the present case his source would have

---

[240]On the role of Joshua, see chapter four.

provided the prefix. Furthermore, neither Hebrew verb, גרש or נשל,[241] is ever rendered in the LXX by ἐξωθέω or a related form.[242]

The third passage concerns the introduction at this point of David into the narrative. The passages of Ex 33:12-17, which speak of Moses "finding favor," have brought to mind the one par excellence who found favor with God--King David.[243]

V.46. The writer directs his attention to the figure of David and, in contrast to him, to that of his son Solomon--both of whom played a role in relation to "the place" mentioned in the accusations (6:13-14), as well as in the evolution of the relationship between God and his people. His attitude toward David is fully consistent with the view he will express in Acts 13:22, where he will insist upon God's approval of David in terms quite similar to v.46. Acts 13:22 reads as follows: ᾧ καὶ εἶπεν μαρτυρήσας· εὗρον Δαυὶδ τὸν τοῦ Ἰεσσαί, ἄνδρα κατὰ τὴν καρδίαν μου, ὃς ποιήσει πάντα τὰ θελήματα μου. A similar process has occurred in the formulation of Acts 7:46 and 13:22. In both cases the basic source is I S 13:14, καὶ ζητήσει κύριος ἑαυτῷ ἄνθρωπον κατὰ τὴν καρδίαν αὐτοῦ, καὶ ἐντελεῖται κύριος αὐτῷ εἰς ἄρχοντα ἐπὶ τὸν λαὸν αὐτοῦ. In both texts the author has been led to reformulate and supplement the original idea by means of other biblical texts referring to David's good fortune. In the case of Acts 13:22 he borrows from Ps 89:21 the expression εὗρον Δαυίδ, retains ἄνθρωπον (> ἄνδρα)[244] κατὰ τὴν καρδίαν αὐτοῦ from I S 13:14, and further supplements his text

---

241 This term according to Francis Brown, Samuel R. Driver and Charles A. Briggs, A Hebrew and English Lexicon of the Old Testament (Oxford: Clarendon Press, 1968), s.v. "נשל," is employed three times in the bible with the meaning "clear away nations": Dt 7:1, 22 and 2 K 16:6. These are translated in the LXX by ἐξαίρω, καταναλίσκω, and ἐκβάλλω respectively.

242 Note that Acts 13:19, a text consisting of a conflation of OT quotations, presents different problems. In this case ἔθνη ἑπτά indicates Dt 7:1, while the verb καθελών is easily explained in relation to ἐξάρῃ, in terms both of the writer's quoting techniques and the occurrence of the verb καθαίρω in Dt 7:5.

243 See the discussion in chapter four of the role of David.

244 The transformation of ἄνθρωπος to ἀνήρ has been pointed out before; see n. 137 above.

by adopting a phrase from Is 44:28.

As regards 7:46, εὗρεν χάριν ἐνώπιον τοῦ θεοῦ, he has reformulated God's approval of David (note the contrast/response in relation to ζητήσει of I S 13:14) in terms reminiscent of LXX usage,[245] and at the same time as an intended parallel to 7:10, καὶ ἔδωκεν αὐτῷ χάριν καὶ σοφίαν ἐναντίον Φαραώ. . . . In a way similar to that described for Acts 13:22, the writer also uses a psalm to supplement his source and to illustrate his theme.[246] The textual relationship between the two texts is as follows:

Acts 7:46	Ps 131:5
καὶ ᾐτήσατο εὑρεῖν	ἕως οὗ εὕρω τόπον τῷ κυρίῳ,
σκήνωμα τῷ θεῷ 'Ιακώβ.	σκήνωμα τῷ θεῷ Ιακωβ.

Apart from structural considerations there is one major problem to be discussed, a textual one. I have opted for the reading τῷ θεῷ (A C 𝔎 E *pl* lat sy) rather than τῷ οἴκῳ (P^{74} B ℵ* D H).[247] The manuscript evidence is admittedly complex and inconclusive at best.[248] Therefore, other aspects of the problem must be given due consideration. On the one hand, I agree with more recent scholarship that the context, especially vv.47f.

---

[245]Εὑρίσκω (also δίδωμι) χάριν is a common expression in the OT and is usually followed by the preposition ἐναντίον (throughout Genesis and Exodus). 'Ενώπιον, though less frequent, is also employed (Ex 33:17; 34:9, once in Numbers, 1 Esdras, Tobit, and twice in Esther). The author's choice of the latter owes to his preference (also that of all NT writers) for this preposition (ἐναντίον occurs twice in Acts, both in OT quotations) and to the influence of Ex 33:17 (see the numerous references to Ex 31-33 in the commentary of Acts 7:38-48).

[246]No doubt he is led to this new text through the use of the verb εὑρίσκω. A similar process occurs in 7:5 and the result is structurally comparable:

οὐκ ἔδωκεν . . .	εὗρεν . . .
καὶ ἐπηγγείλατο δοῦναι . . .	καὶ ᾐτήσατο εὑρεῖν . . . .

See also the discussion of 7:46b.

[247]The first reading is followed by Merk, *NT*, p. 420; the second, by Nestle and Aland, *NT Graece*, p. 319 and Aland et al., *Gk NT*, p. 443.

[248]See the lengthy discussion of Metzger, *Commentary*, pp. 351-53, who in evaluating the pertinent evidence, presents both external and internal factors in defense of the reading τῷ οἴκῳ.

seems to require τῷ θεῷ,[249] in particular the αὐτῷ of v.47.[250] On the other hand, for structural reasons--an intended parallel between v.46a and b (on the pattern of 7.5a and b)[251]--the LXX reading, I believe, is the original one.

V.47. The precise source of this verse is a matter for debate, leading scholars to propose several passages from 1 K 5:1f.; 6:2; 8:20). In effect 1 K 6:2 furnishes most data required (καὶ ὁ οἶκος ὃν ᾠκοδόμησεν ὁ βασιλεὺς Σαλωμων τῷ κυρίῳ), while 6:14 (not found in manuscripts B L† nor represented in the MT), καὶ ᾠκοδόμησεν Σαλωμων τὸν οἶκον, comes closest to the form represented by our text, Σολομὼν δὲ οἰκοδόμησεν αὐτῷ οἶκον. Assuming that the author has employed the first text, or even a combination of several passages, two characteristics of v.47 attract our attention. By the omission of the article the writer lifts the line of argument to a philosophical level (a habitation or house) as opposed to a historical one (the house, this place of 6:13-14). This line of thought he has already encountered in the text quoted from Ps 131:5, εὕρω. . . σκήνωμα. It is true that Solomon says in 1 K 5:17 (note an almost identical text in v.19): ὅτι οὐκ ἐδύνατο οἰκοδομῆσαι οἶκον τῷ ὀνόματι κυρίου θεοῦ μου, and that our author could very well have borrowed from this source. Regardless, it is the writer's mode of expression which matters most.

In the second place the word order is significant, namely, . . . αὐτῷ οἶκον. From 1 K 5:3, 5 or even 6:2 we would expect the opposite. However, by placing οἶκος in final position the author draws particular attention upon the term and further stresses the contrast between v.46b and 47, between σκήνωμα and οἶκος, between David and Solomon.[252]

V.48. The first part of this verse, ἀλλ' οὐχ ὁ ὕψιστος ἐν χειροποιήτοις κατοικεῖ, could conceivably be explained in rela-

---

[249]Bruce, Acts, p. 175; Wilson, "Theologian and Historian," p. 185; Bihler, Stephanusgeschichte, p. 74; Conzelmann, Apostelgeschichte, p. 56; Colmenero Atienza, "Hechos 7," p. 42, n. 43.

[250]See Haenchen, Acts, p. 285; "Verse 47: αὐτῷ--i.e., θεῷ."

[251]See the study of parallelism in the following chapter.

[252]Techniques to achieve contrast will be studied in the following chapter.

tion to Isaiah. In effect, vv.49-50 consist of an extended quotation of Is 66:1-2, while the terms ὕψιστος and χειροποίητος are also perceived in Isaian terms. Of ten OT occurrences the latter appears eight times in Isaiah, generally of idols but once (16:12) of pagan sanctuaries (translating the MT, מקדשו). The former is clearly less frequent in Isaiah (three occurrences). However, in this work the background for Acts 7:48 is to be sought. Indeed Is 57:15,

> Τάδε λέγει κύριος ὁ ὕψιστος
> ὁ ἐν ὑψηλοῖς κατοικῶν τον αἰῶνα,
> ἅγιος ἐν ἁγίοις ὄνομα αὐτῷ,
> κύριος ὕψιστος ἐν ἁγίοις ἀναπαυόμενος,

furnishes in positive terms what the author of the speech expresses in a very negative way.

It is my contention that the text quoted above has exerted its influence upon v.48, but that the text of Mk 14:58 is even more fundamental to the writer's purpose. The Markan version of the trial of Jesus is extensively used in formulating Acts 6:8-15. The accusation brought against Jesus, Mk 14:58, ὅτι ἡμεῖς ἠκούσαμεν αὐτοῦ λέγοντος ὅτι ἐγὼ καταλύσω τὸν ναὸν τοῦτον τὸν χειροποίητον καὶ διὰ τριῶν ἡμερῶν ἄλλον ἀχειροποίητον οἰκοδομήσω, is intimately related to that leveled against Stephen (6:14). The author employs the second part of the saying to counter the accusation leveled against Stephen (speaking against the holy place) and to underscore his argument: God does not dwell in human habitations.[253] The latter had been made sufficiently clear by Isaiah. In fact, the author of Acts makes a similar point in 17:24, where the influence of Isaiah is very obvious:

Acts 17:24	Is 42:5
ὁ θεὸς	κύριος ὁ θεὸς
ὁ ποιήσας τὸν κόσμον	ὁ ποιήσας τὸν οὐρανὸν
καὶ πάντα τὰ ἐν αὐτῷ,	καὶ πήξας αὐτόν,
οὗτος οὐρανοῦ καὶ γῆς ὑπάρχων κύριος	ὁ στερεώσας τὴν γῆν καὶ τὰ ἐν αὐτῇ
οὐκ ἐν χειροποιήτοις ναοῖς κατοικεῖ.	καὶ διδοὺς πνοὴν τῷ λαῷ τῷ ἐπ' αὐτῆς.

---

[253]This point is further developed in chapter four.

Apart from the interesting stylistic parallels with the Stephen speech (choice of ὁ θεός, ὁ ποιήσας . . . οὗτος, see 7:35f.), this text illustrates a point made above that the thought of Isaiah, while contributing to the author's point of view, is utilized as a commentary upon Jesus' statement. Acts 7:48a emphatically states this thesis in response to the accusation brought both against Stephen and Jesus (use of Mk 14:58), while 48b introduces a corroborating text from the prophet. It should also be pointed out that the omission in Acts 7:48 of the noun ναός is significant in light of the author's purpose.[254] Finally, the introductory formula of v.48b, as is usual throughout the speech, is due principally to the redactive process.

Vv.49-50. The next two verses constitute an extended OT quotation:

Acts 7	Is 66
	1 Οὕτως λέγει κύριος
49 ὁ οὐρανός μοι θρόνος,	Ὁ οὐρανός μοι θρόνος,
ἡ δὲ γῆ ὑποπόδιον τῶν	ἡ δὲ γῆ ὑποπόδιον τῶν
ποδῶν μου·	ποδῶν μου·
ποῖον οἶκον οἰκοδομήσετέ	ποῖον οἶκον οἰκοδομήσετέ
μοι,	μοι;
λέγει κύριος,	
ἢ τίς τόπος τῆς	ἢ ποῖος τόπος τῆς
καταπαύσεώς μου;	καταπαύσεώς μου;
50 οὐχὶ ἡ χείρ μου ἐποίησεν	2 Πάντα γὰρ ταῦτα ἐποίησεν ἡ
ταῦτα πάντα;	χείρ μου,
	καὶ ἔστιν ἐμὰ πάντα ταῦτα,
	λέγει κύριος.

In grammatical terms the modifications are relatively minor, τίς replaces ποῖος (this also occurs in Barn 16:2),[255] and a

---

[254]The absence of ναός could be explained as the result of homoioteleuton on the part of an early scribe; however, the omission seems to form part of the author's overall purpose.

[255]Two observations are in order. On the one hand, since the relatively rare expression of the MT, אי זה, is regularly rendered by ποῖος and never τίς as is here the case, the change does not seem to be due to the LXX Vorlage. On the other hand, the occurrence, in Barn 16:2 of the same form in an apparently independent quotation of Is 66:1, points to a more complex textual situation than our present evidence allows us to resolve.

declarative statement is transformed into a question.

Finally, the modification of word order should be noted:

Acts 7:50 οὐχὶ ἡ χείρ μου ἐποίησεν ταῦτα πάντα;

Is 66:2 πάντα γὰρ ταῦτα ἐποίησεν ἡ χείρ μου.

This can be explained in terms of a tendency often noted throughout the speech, that of conflating texts. The passage in question is Is 41:20, ὅτι χεὶρ κυρίου ἐποίησεν ταῦτα πάντα. The word order, then, of this text is imposed upon the original quotation. The textual difficulties regarding ταῦτα πάντα of Is 41:20 require attention. Rahlfs follows the reading of A C, but notes the different order of Q S^{c} and the omission of πάντα (following the MT) by B S* L.[256] This textual problem has no direct bearing upon the present analysis, since it is the transformation of Is 66:2 which concerns us (41:20 has furnished the word order only) and also since the author of Acts is following contemporary idiom in writing ταῦτα πάντα--the usual order of the gospels, especially Matthew--and a well attested LXX manuscript tradition for Is 66:2.[257]

2) Vv.42-50: Quoting Process

The second thematic section of the speech presents clear structural lines, even in its approach to the OT model. On the following page is a schema which, I believe, does justice to the quoting process which occurred during the composition of vv.42-50.

This chart makes clear that the writer persists in following the narrative sequence of his OT source. After having drawn from Ex 32:1 the account of Israel's horrendous betrayal of God (v.40), he follows the clues offered by its ensuing verses, supplementing constantly as he is wont to do. Thus, in

---

On this last point see Lake and Cadbury, Beginnings, 4:81-82 as well as Haenchen, Acts, p. 285, n. 4, who expresses reservations regarding to the conclusions drawn from this evidence. Confer also Joseph Ziegler, Isaias, vol. 14 of Septauginta Vetus Testamentum Graecum Auctoritate Societatis Litterarum Gottingensis (Göttingen: Vandenhoeck & Ruprecht, 1939), p. 364, who gives the following witnesses for the reading found in Acts 7:49: "28-86^{txt} 534 Barn. Cypr."

[256]Rahlfs, Septauginta, 2:622; see also Ziegler, Isaias, p. 275.

[257]Ziegler, Isaias, p. 364.

Ex 31:18		Acts 7:38		
Ex 32:1/23		Acts 7:40		
Ex 32:6,8		Acts 7:41 ←	Ex 32:35	
Ex 32:10f.	God's response	Acts 7:42 ←	Dt 31:17-18; 32:19	
Ex 32:13f.	τὸ ἄστρα τοῦ οὐρανοῦ	Acts 7:42 →	Dt 17:3 λατρεύω & προσκυνέω	
			Dt 4:19 ἀστήρ	
		Acts 7:42-43 =	Am 5:25-27 σκηνή	
			τύπος	
Ex 32:15	ἀποστρέφω	Acts 7:42		
Ex 32:20,35	calf making	Acts 7:41		
Ex 33:2	angel before your face →		Acts 7:38,53	
	casting out nations	Acts 7:45		
Ex 33:3,5	stiff-necked →		Acts 7:51	
Ex 33:7	σκηνὴ τοῦ μαρτυρίου	Acts 7:44 ←	Ex 25:40	
Ex 33:7	Joshua	Acts 7:45 ↔	Dt 34:9	see Acts 6:6-7
Ex 33:12-17	find favor	Acts 7:45-46 (David) ↔	(1 S 13:14) ←	Ps 131:5
		Acts 7:47 ↕ Neg.	(Solomon) ← 1 K 6:2f.	οἰκοδομέω οἶκον
	Acts 6:14 ↔	Acts 7:48	Is 57:10 ↔ Mk 14:58	see Acts 17:24
		Acts 7:49-50	Is 66:1-2 ← Is 41:20	↔ Is 42:5

this part of the speech, even though the thematic elements predominate, they are none the less situated within their narrative sequence: the years in the desert, the time of Joshua, David, and Solomon.

The quoting techniques are similar to the ones encountered in earlier parts of the discourse. At the same time, the author's dependence upon his OT model continues to be important in his method of composition. However, as structural and thematic elements increase in frequency, it is clear that the quoting process, since it depends greatly upon these, must await further analysis later in this study.

4. Invective Against Audience 7:51-51: Relation to OT

The final verses of the speech have always claimed considerable attention from scholars. This has been particularly true for two reasons: 1) the unique Christological reference of the discourse occurs in v.52, περὶ τῆς ἐλεύσεως τοῦ δικαίου[258] and 2) the obvious severity of the ending and the apparent disjunction between Acts 7:2-50 and 51-53 have often been noted. Both aspects will be dealt with; but, presently, the role played by the OT narrative--beyond a simple listing of possible sources--demands immediate attention.

Vv.51-53 mark a new and final section of the speech. Its attitude toward the audience, its goal, and use of sources is markedly different from what precedes. The author now causes Stephen to address himself directly to his audience. At the same time, the choice of biblical materials becomes more selective and fragmentary, making use of terms and ideas rather than of any particular OT passage.

V.51. It is the first verse of this section,

a Σκληροτράχηλοι
b καὶ ἀπερίτμητοι καρδίαις καὶ τοῖς ὠσίν,
c ὑμεῖς ἀεὶ τῷ πνεύματι τῷ ἁγίῳ ἀντιπίπτετε,
d ὡς οἱ πατέρες ὑμῶν καὶ ὑμεῖς.

which merits most consideration in relation to its background.

---

[258]With this text scholars generally associate Acts 7:37. See Martin Rese, Alttestamentliche Motive in des Christologie des Lukas, Studien zum Neuen Testament, no. 1 ([Gütersloh]: Gütersloher Verlagshaus G. Mohn, [1969]), pp. 78-80 and 132.

> The language of the invective is thoroughly OT; for σκληροτράχηλοι cf. Ex. xxxiii.5; for ἀπερίτμητοι καρδίαις cf. Lev. xxvi.41; Dt x.16; Jer. iv.4; ix.26; Ezek. xliv.7; for ἀπερίτμητοι . . . τοῖς ὠσίν cf. Jer. vi.10.[259]

In addition, reference is generally made to Nb 27:14 and Is 63:10 to explain v.51c. The very nature of the passage being discussed requires such an explanation, no doubt, since the author appears to have as his goal to list as many accusations as possible against the Judaism of NT times.

To this should be added a few comments about the writer's method of procedure. In the discussion of 7:40, 44-6, the important role played by Ex 32-33 in the composition of the speech was especially stressed. At Ex 33:2 and 5 God Himself accuses the Hebrews of being "a stiff-necked people." This passage leads him to the text crucial to the composition of v. 51, namely, Dt 10:16, καὶ περιτεμεῖσθε τὴν σκληροκαρδίαν ὑμῖν καὶ τὸν τράχηλον ὑμῶν οὐ σκληρυνεῖτε ἔτι,[260] and in turn to the stark image of Jer 6:10, ἰδοὺ ἀπερίτμητα τὰ ὦτα αὐτῶν, καὶ οὐ δύνανται ἀκούειν. At this point we lose trace of the author's sources. V.51c, although it utilizes the rare verb ἀντιπίπτω (found in Nb 27:14) and refers to "the Holy Spirit" (Is 63:10: "they disobeyed and provoked his holy spirit"), is not adequately explained in relation to OT sources. Instead, the allusion to the Spirit here should be understood in light of the role played by the Holy Sprit throughout the Stephen material: 6:3, 5, 10; 7:51, 55. The intended contrast is clear: Stephen and the other appointees are full of the Spirit, but the early Hebrews and the present generation of Jews are not and indeed "resist" Him.

V.52. The writer pursues his goal by listing further accusations against his audience. This particular passage,

a τίνα τῶν προφητῶν οὐκ ἐδίωξαν οἱ πατέρας ὑμῶν;

b καὶ ἀπέκτειναν τοὺς προκαταγγείλαντας περὶ τῆς ἐλεύσεως τοῦ δικαίου,

---

[259] Bruce, <u>Acts</u>, p. 177.

[260] <u>Beginnings</u>, 4:82: "For 'uncircumcised in ear' cf. Jer. vi.10. But the combination in Acts resembles most nearly Deut. x.16." See also Conzelmann, <u>Apostelgeschichte</u>, p. 56.

c οὗ νῦν ὑμεῖς προδόται
καὶ φονεῖς ἐγένεσθε,

has been discussed in relation to NT, late Jewish, and early Christian background, with particular emphasis on Jewish sources.[261] These studies have been concerned with the martyrdom of the prophets and the suggestion in v.52 that all or most of God's envoys were killed. For this reason, it has been customary to investigate various OT passages and early rabbinic commentaries of these for evidence of the martyrdom of prophets.[262]

While such studies are valuable as background for the existence of such notions during NT times, the more immediate sources are to be sought in passages from Matthew and Luke. Further, the formulation of the verse owes primarily to the activity of the writer. The persecution (διώκω, Mt 5:12; 23:34; Lk 11:49) and killing of the prophets (ἀποκτείνω, Mt 23:34, 37, Lk 11:47, 48, 49; 13:34) is clearly an accusation attributed to Jesus in Matthew and Luke. Furthermore, the expression of Mt 23:35, ὅπως ἔλθῃ ἐφ' ὑμᾶς πᾶν αἷμα δίκαιον . . . ἀπὸ τοῦ αἵματος Ἄβελ τοῦ δικαίου, is not without interest for several passages within the speech, 7:11 (ἔρχομαι ἐπί followed by the accusative); 52a (implying "all the prophets," which expression Lk 11:50 renders even more explicit--ἐκζητηθῇ τὸ αἷμα πάντων τῶν προφητῶν); and 52b ("the Just One"). Προδόται. . . ἐγένεσθε probably recalls Lk 6:16 (Ἰούδαν . . . ὃς ἐγένετο προδότης). Finally, twice in relation to the prophets, Matthew (23:31, 35) speaks of "murder" (φονεύω). He is also the only evangelist to use the term φονεύς, which passage is obviously related to the present text--Mt 22:7 ὁ δὲ βασιλεὺς ὠργίσθη, καὶ πέμψας τὰ στρατεύματα αὐτοῦ ἀπώλεσεν τοὺς φονεῖς ἐκείνους.

The style and formulation of 7:52, however, owe to the

---

[261]See Beginnings, 4:82, for a discussion of early Christian writings which deal with the martyrdom of the prophets. See also Haenchen, Acts, p. 286, n. 1, for references particularly to Strack and Billerbeck and H. J. Schoeps and also Conzelmann, Apostelgeschichte, p. 57, for additional information.

[262]As an example of this particular interest, see Haenchen, Acts, p. 286, n. 1: "Jer. 2.30 may well have appeared to represent being murdered as the normal lot of a prophet."

author. It can hardly be coincidental that most of the terms of the verse are also employed in an earlier speech of Acts, ἀποκτείνω (Acts 3:15); προκαταγγέλλω (3:18); δίκαιος (3:14); and φονεύς (3:14). The structure is also his own.

V.53. The final verse of the lengthy speech has also claimed its share of attention. This owes particularly to the intermediary role assigned to angels in the giving of the Law. Scholars have rightly pointed to similar concepts in the NT (Gal 3:19 and Heb 2:2) and in contemporary Jewish documents. In the words of Bruce:

> This angelic mediation of the Law does not appear in OT, but is mentioned in Jos. Ant. xx.5.3 (ἡμῶν δὲ τὰ κάλλιστα τῶν δογμάτων καὶ τὰ ὁσιώτατα τῶν ἐν τοῖς νόμοις δι' ἀγγέλων παρὰ τοῦ θεοῦ μαθόντων); Philo (De somniis i.141ff.), the 'Testaments of the Twelve Patriarchs' (Test. Dan vi.2), and Jubilees i.29.[263]

Such considerations, however, address themselves to one aspect only of the verse, in reality a secondary one.

To bring his accusations to a fitting conclusion, the author uses carefully chosen expressions to serve as connecting links to earlier parts of his text. The first part of v.53, ἐλάβετε τὸν νόμον, recalls v.38, ἐδέξατο λόγια ζῶντα δοῦναι ὑμῖν; and one of its OT sources, Dt 32:46, ἐντελεῖσθε τοῖς υἱοῖς ὑμῶν φυλάσσειν καὶ ποιεῖν πάντας τοὺς λόγους τοῦ νόμου τούτου. The last-mentioned text suggests to the author the ultimate accusation, καὶ οὐκ ἐφυλάξατε. Νόμος harks back to the accusation of Acts 6:13 (the term appears twice in the Stephen material), while οὐ φυλάσσω, addressed to the accusers, constitutes a sharp counter-accusation to charges brought against Stephen (6:11, 13-14).

C. The Speech, the OT, and Related Problems

It is my intention here to investigate two principal areas relating to the author's use of the OT in composing the speech. Both of these are secondary when compared to the primary role played by the LXX text itself (this was the goal of the chapter

---

[263] Acts, p. 178. See also further references in relation to Acts 7:38 in Beginnings, 4:78; Bruce, Acts, p. 172; Haenchen, Acts, p. 283, n. 2; Conzelmann, Apostelgeschichte, pp. 54-55. Lastly see the article of Schultz, "Angelic Opposition," especially pp. 282-95 (work cited in n. 201 above).

up to this point). However, a number of problems have presented themselves, whose analysis has been postponed until now. These involve "other sources" utilized by the writer and "textual considerations" encountered in the study.

1. Other Sources

Obviously the Stephen speech is fundamentally a synopsis of Israel's history. While it is possible to find in the Torah and other biblical books the data required in composing such a historical summary, the OT itself contains numerous "histories" of Israel. These, of course, can also be found in Jewish works of the intertestamental period, whether canonical, sectarian or apocryphal in nature. On the one hand, it is necessary to investigate whether the author of Acts might have employed such a summary of Hebrew history or have been influenced by such a tradition. On the other hand, the question of supplementary sources must be taken seriously, since there are obvious additions to the biblical story and aberrant traditions found in the Stephen speech.

a. Histories of Israel

Few scholars have failed to note the similarity between Acts 7:2-53 and the many recapitulations of Hebrew history, whether in the OT or in late Jewish works. Recently, in a section of his monograph entitled "Versuch einer Ortsbestimmung der in der Rede verarbeiteten Tradition," Holtz has given the following, convenient list of such histories:

- credal summaries: Dt 6:20-24; 26:5-9; Jos 24:2-13
- texts presenting the stages of salvation: Ps 78; 105; 106; 135; 136
- historical synopses: Neh 9:6-31 (note: Ez 20:5-29)
- histories from late Jewish writings: Jdt 5:6-18; 1 Mc 2:52-60; 3 Mc 2:2-20; Josephus, Ant. 3.86f. (5.3); 4.43-45 (3.2); JW 5.379-419 (9.4); and Heb 11 (note 4 Esdras 3:4-36; 14:29-31; and from Qumran CD 2.14-6.11).[264]

In view of the historical summaries just presented, it is imperative to examine the views of modern scholars on the relationship these have to the Stephen speech. In his monograph on Stephen, the speech, and the Hellenists, Simon scrutinizes a variety of OT and Pseudepigraphic histories, ". . . texts which

---

264 Untersuchungen, pp. 100-1.

may have formally influenced its [Acts 7:2-53] composition . . ." and concludes ". . . that Stephen's speech, while reproducing the same pattern when it sketches the main stages of Israelite history, has a very different emphasis."[265] The Jewish texts, according to him, exhibit the mercy of God and thereby present an optimistic view of history, while that of Stephen is diametrically opposed. Acts 7:2-53, then, has little in common with these histories in orientation. Simon does not examine any possible relation in terms of form or style.

Following upon Dibelius' theory that the author of Acts has edited an old historical document and inserted this into the martyrdom of Stephen, a number of recent scholars have further pursued this line of investigation. The neutral document hypothesis will be discussed later. I shall treat presently the opinions of Holtz, since he lends special attention to the sources of the Stephen speech in terms of "histories" of Israel.

Traugott Holtz ia interested primarily in finding the "Ortsbestimmung" of the discourse and, to that end, examines a considerable variety of biblical and apocryphal literature. He concludes

> . . . dass sowohl der Form wie der Theologie nach das in Frage stehende Stück seinen Platz im Judentum der beiden Jahrhunderte um Chr. sehr wohl gehabt haben kann. . . . dass es tatsächlich aus dem Judentum dieser Zeit stammt.[266]

Like Simon, he is more interested in themes and theology than in stylistic and structural considerations, thus neglecting to investigate the real relationship of Acts 7, either to synopses of Hebrew history or the OT text directly.

In studying the Stephen speech and its OT background, it was necessary to investigate repeatedly its possible relationship to a large variety of historical summaries. That Acts 7:2-53 should find its inspiration in, or be influenced by, various elements of this literary tradition could not <u>a priori</u> be

---

265<u>Stephen</u>, p. 41. Simon refers particularly to Ps 104:12-43; 105:6-42; Jos 24:2-13; Neh 9:7-31; and Jdt 5:6-18.

266<u>Untersuchungen</u>, p. 109.

excluded, since "dahinter steht eine lange Tradition"[267] of this genre. To investigate such a possibility it seemed necessary to consider the question in a structural, thematic/lexical, and stylistic manner, since the most cursory analysis indicated that historical surveys were not of a single structural type. Indeed, they varied according to purpose, function, audience, literary genre, etc.

Structurally, histories seem of two very different classes: one based upon the sequence of the biblical narrative, and the other centered upon a succession of OT personalities. The latter is the domain of sapiential and didactic literature, while the former admits a greater variety of functions. The Stephen speech could conceivably be seen as a history of successive personalities: Abraham, Joseph, Moses, David-Solomon. However, it is clearly not as didactic as 1 Mc 2:52-60 or Heb 11, or as poetic as Sir 44. Instead, like the majority of such historical synopses, it is modeled upon the well-known sequence of the biblical narrative, and like these proves to be quite selective in its choice of episodes.

From a structural point of view the Stephen speech is independent of presently known historical summaries. In light of this, it should be noted that alleged similarities between Acts 7 and Ps 104 are no more striking than contacts with other histories, e.g., Neh 9:6-31 or Jdt 5:6-18. A close examination indicates that, by virtue of subject matter and common source (the Pentateuchal narrative), a number of parallels do exist, but that these are not of a structural nature.

The relation of Acts 7 to historical summaries has also been investigated from thematic/lexical and stylistic points of view, the results of which study indicate that the author of the discourse borrows directly from the LXX text of the bible. A comparison between the Stephen speech and its closest historical analogue, in my opinion, Jdt 5:16-18, only underscores the independence of the writer in his selection of quotations and episodes, editing process, and method of composition. Both texts have as their goal the oratorical formulation of Israel's history; both borrow freely from the OT narrative; and both

---

[267]Conzelmann, Apostelgeschichte, p. 57.

follow the sequence of the biblical narrative. Beyond this, the two histories of Israel have little in common.

The present discussion will be concluded by giving examples from four well-known histories of Israel to illustrate the above conclusions. The first example, drawn from Jos 24, is as follows:

> 4 . . . καὶ Ιακωβ καὶ οἱ υἱοι αὐτοῦ κατέβησαν εἰς Αἴγυπτον καὶ ἐγένοντο ἐκεῖ εἰς ἔθνος μέγα καὶ πολὺ καὶ κραταίον. 5 καὶ ἐκάκωσαν αὐτοὺς οἱ Αἰγύπτιοι, καὶ ἐπάταξεν κύριος τὴν Αἴγυπτον ἐν οἷς ἐποίησεν αὐτοῖς.

The events here described are also found in Acts 7:15, 17, 19, and 36. There is, however, little or no relation between these texts beyond dependence upon a common biblical tradition.

The second example is taken from Ps 104:

> 16 καὶ ἐκάλεσεν λιμὸν ἐπὶ τὴν γῆν,
> πᾶν στήριγμα ἄρτου συνέτριψεν·
> 17 ἀπέστειλεν ἔμπροσθεν αὐτῶν ἄνθρωπον,
> εἰς δοῦλον ἐπράθη Ιωσηφ.

The Stephen speech also retells the Joseph episode (vv.9f.), but the two histories have little in common philologically. Furthermore, each utilizes the vocabulary proper to its genre, either poetry or historical prose.

From Neh 9 (2 Esd 19), we note the following excerpt from the speech of Esdras to the assembled community:

> 9 καὶ εἶδες τὴν ταπείνωσιν τῶν πατέρων ἡμῶν ἐν Αἰγύπτῳ καὶ τὴν κραυγὴν αὐτῶν ἤκουσας ἐπὶ θάλασσαν ἐρυθράν. 10 καὶ ἔδωκας σημεῖα ἐν Αἰγύπτῳ ἐν Φαραω καὶ ἐν πᾶσιν τοῖς παισὶν αὐτοῦ καὶ ἐν παντὶ τῷ λαῷ τῆς γῆς αὐτοῦ, ὅτι ἔγνως ὅτι ὑπερηφάνησαν ἐπ' αὐτούς.

The terminology of this text is closer to that of the Stephen speech than that of the earlier examples noted. The increased degree of similarity is due primarily to a greater use of the OT narrative. The difference lies in the quoting process, the style, and goal of the respective writers. Finally, it is clear that the speech of Stephen could never have been written on the basis of such a narrative, and that only the OT text could have furnished the author the necessary data.

The fourth and final example is drawn from the late work, Jdt 5:

7 καὶ παρῴκησαν τὸ πρότερον ἐν τῇ Μεσοποταμίᾳ,
ὅτι οὐκ ἐβουλήθησαν ἀκολουθῆσαι τοῖς θεοῖς τῶν
πατέρων αὐτῶν, οἱ ἐγένοντο ἐν γῇ Χαλδαίων...
10 καὶ κατέβησαν εἰς Αἴγυπτον, ἐκάλυψεν γὰρ τὸ
πρόσωπον τῆς γῆς Χανααν λιμός, καὶ παρῴκησαν
ἐκεῖ μέχρις οὗ διετράφησαν· καὶ ἐγένοντο ἐκεῖ
εἰς πλῆθος πολύ, καὶ οὐκ ἦν ἀριθμὸς τοῦ γένους
αὐτῶν. 11 καὶ ἐπανέστη αὐτοῖς ὁ βασιλεὺς
Αἰγύπτου καὶ κατεσοφίσατο αὐτοὺς ἐν πόνῳ καὶ
πλίνθῳ, ἐταπείνωσαν αὐτοὺς καὶ ἔθεντο αὐτοὺς
εἰς δούλους.

On the one hand, this speech manifests a considerable degree of similarity in vocabulary and phraseology with Acts 7; on the other hand, it reveals as distinct an approach to OT history as one would expect from a totally different author. The two writers draw directly from the biblical narrative, but, owing to the great variety of choice within that source and owing also to the originality of each, the resultant compositions are considerably different and independent.

b. <u>Supplementary Sources</u>

The analysis of this entire chapter has demonstrated clearly enough, I believe, that the author of Acts has utilized the biblical text directly in composing this unique history of Israel. It is the OT narrative which has furnished him with the events, their sequence, the terminology, and, to a great extent, the themes exposed throughout the speech. An objective of this study has been to examine the writer's sources and the quoting process which occurred in the course of composition. While it has been possible to establish direct use of the LXX version of the OT narrative, the recurrence of a series of anomalies, i.e., traditions which do not correspond to the standard biblical story, has often been noted.

The aberrant traditions of the Stephen speech are well known and are alluded to in most commentaries. For the present study I will draw extensively from Cadbury's excellent list.

a) "In the Old Testament God appeared to Abraham at Haran and told him to migrate. In Acts he appeared to Abraham before his earlier migration from Ur of the Chaldees to Haran. [vv.2-3]

b) "In the Old Testament the account of Abraham's leaving Haran is told after his father's death, and so Acts definitely dates his departure. But the chronology of Genesis if examined dates it before his father's death. [v.4]

c) "In the Old Testament Jacob's family is reckoned as seventy persons, in Acts as seventy-five. [v.14]

d) "In the Old Testament Abraham buys a burial place from Ephron at Machpelah and Jacob buys a piece of ground near Shechem from the sons of Hamor, while in Acts Abraham buys a tomb at Shechem from the sons of Emmor (Hamor) or buys a tomb from Shechem the father of Hamor. [v.16]

e) "In the Old Testament Jacob is buried at Hebron, Joseph at Shechem. In Acts both they and all the patriarchs are buried at the same place, namely Shechem." [v.16]

The following, according to Cadbury, "are not in the Old Testament at all." (The next items constitute a continuous sentence in Cadbury's text.)

f) "As an infant he was beautiful before God; [v.20]

g) "he was educated in the wisdom of the Egyptians; [v.22]

h) "he was forty years old when he fled to Midian and it was forty years later when he returned; [vv.23, 30]

i) "the sea in which Pharaoh was overthrown was the Red Sea; [v.36]

j) "and the law as delivered to Moses by an angel."[268] [v.53]

This list could be considerably lengthened, e.g., the circumcision of Isaac's immediate descendants (v.8), the selling of Joseph by the brothers (v.9), the exposing of the children (v. 19), Moses being mighty in words (v.22), etc.

The source(s) of these traditions is, admittedly, a subject of debate. Some differences are only apparent, since a closer examination of the variety within the OT narrative will often reveal the required data. Three such examples will suffice: 1) The selling of Joseph is said to be attributed to the Midianites in Gn 37; however, later in Gn (45:4) this action is assigned to the brothers; 2) The chronology regarding Thera's death (b) is related to problems with the OT tradition itself.

---

[268]<u>Book of Acts</u>, pp. 102-3.

Later tradition (Acts, the Samaritan texts,[269] and Philo[270]) witnesses to this "aberrant" reading of Genesis;[271] and 3) The migration in two stages from Ur to Haran to Canaan is the standard view of the biblical account. Nevertheless, Gn 15:7, as well as Neh 9:7, states that God led Abraham from Ur to Canaan, with no mention of Haran. This is apparently the view adopted in Acts since the appearance to Abraham occurs in Ur. Similar traditions are found in Philo and Josephus.[272]

A considerable number of variations between the OT and Acts 7, particularly in matters of vocabulary and exactness of quotations, is related to textual problems. However, others (c and i above, for example) are explained in relation to the LXX Vorlage (supra, commentary on vv.14 and 36). Several of the variants mentioned above find parallels in Philo, Josephus, the Assumption of Moses, the Testaments of the Twelve Patriarchs, the Book of Jubilees,[273] the Damascus Document,[274] a variety of Qumran scrolls (1QapGn, 4QFlor, 4QPsJos, and 4Q-Test),[275] and the targum Pseudo-Jonathan.

---

[269]Both Hebrew and Aramaic Pentateuch note (Gn 11:32) that Thera died at the age of 145, instead of 205, thereby correcting the inconsistencies of the biblical tradition; already noted in Beginnings, 4:98.

[270]Migr. Abr., 177.

[271]See Paul Kahle, Cairo Geniza, pp. 143-44. Now see Richard, "Acts 7: An Investigation of the Samaritan Evidence," pp. 196-97.

[272]For the former see Abr. 62f. (contrast Migr. Abr., 176) and for the latter confer Ant., 1.154.

[273]See Cadbury, Book of Acts, pp. 103f., for further references to these works and also Strack and Billerbeck, Kommentar, 2:666-84.

[274]See particularly the work of Jan de Waard, A Comparative Study of the Old Testament Text in the Dead Sea Scrolls and in the New Testament, Studies on the Texts of the Desert of Judah, no. 4 (Leiden: Brill, 1965 and Grand Rapids, Mich.: Eerdmans, 1966), pp. 41-47, where the quotation of Am 5:26-27 in CD 7.14-15 and Acts 7:43 is examined in detail; confer also the author's more general conclusions regarding Acts 7 and 15 on pp. 78-81. I would also note the article of A. F. J. Klijn, even though I do not share his conclusions, "Stephen's Speech," pp. 25-31, which examines at length the relationship between Acts 7 and the Damascus Document.

[275]See Joseph A. Fitzmyer, The Genesis Apocryphon of Qumran Cave 1: A Commentary, Biblica et Orientalia, no. 18A, 2d rev. ed. (Rome: Biblical Institute Press, 1971) and idem,

The author of Acts was a writer of his time conversant with the literature of the NT period. That he was influenced by this theological tradition seems obvious. Further, that he should have borrowed from contemporary idiom has been systematically illustrated, particularly through references to the papyri and other NT writings. To conclude this part of the study, I would like to examine briefly, by way of example, three "contemporary" compositions to further clarify the statement that the author of Acts was fully a writer of his time.

The first work to be considered is the Assumption of Moses. Aside from the central role of Moses in both works (as mediator in Assump. Mos. 1.14) and the importance of Joshua ("a man approved of the Lord") in regard to the tabernacle of the testimony and the entrance into the land, there are numerous themes and verbal parallels which speak of contemporaneity. Note the following: the convenant, oath spoken by the Lord, the visitation by which the Lord will visit his people, promise to the fathers (a common appellation for the Hebrews), setting up of idols in the sanctuary to worship them, calling upon the 'God of Abraham, God of Isaac, and God of Jacob,' and, finally, the striking parallel to Acts 7:36 (supra, pp. 105-07 and n. 193).[276] It is hardly surprising that the Stephen speech should make generous use of the theological and historical idiom of its day.

In a similar way, the Book of Jubilees yields considerable data for an understanding of the phraseology and thematic concerns of the author of Acts. The giving of the Law takes place on Mount Sinai (prologue; 1.2), where the voice of God speaks to Moses. The following terms and expressions are prominent: the glory of the Lord; the covenant; oath to the fathers, to

---

"'4Q Testimonia' and the New Testament," TS 18 (1957): 513-37 [also in Essays on the Semitic Background of the New Testament (London: Geoffrey Chapman, 1971)]. Confer also Fitzmyer's convenient guide to the vast bibliography on the scrolls: The Dead Sea Scrolls: Major Publications and Tools for Study, Sources for Biblical Study, no. 8 ([Missoula, Montana]: Society of Biblical Literature and Scholars Press, 1975).

[276]Robert H. Charles, The Apocrypha and Pseudepigrapha of the Old Testament, 2 vols. (Oxford: Clarendon Press, 1913), 2:414-24.

Abraham, Isaac and to Jacob; the inheritance; Ur of the Chaldees; etc. All the quotations of Acts 7:2-8 are cited in full in this work (12:22f.; 14:13f.). The role of the "angel of the presence" deserves note (1:27f.) in relation to Acts 7:36 and 53, while the story of the sojourn in Egypt and that of Moses (chapters 46-48) furnish numerous parallels to Acts 7:17f. Finally, the Book of Jubilees (1.22-23) presents a stark parallel to Acts 7:51f.:

> I know their contrariness and their thoughts and their stiffneckedness. . . . And after this they will turn to Me in all uprightness and with all (their) heart and with all (their) soul, and I will circumcise the foreskin of their heart and the foreskin of the heart of their seed, and I will create in them a holy spirit, and I will cleanse them so that they shall not turn away from Me from that day unto eternity.[277]

The third and final text to be examined is the targum Pseudo-Jonathan, to which numerous references have been made throughout the chapter. In approaching this brief survey, it is not my intention to discourse on the dating of the targum or on problems relating to the "Palestinian Targum."[278] The targum is very unreliable (though not absolutely) for textual problems, owing to its penchant for literary embellishment and thematic expansion. Nevertheless, many of its midrashic amplifications are of considerable interest to the reader of the Stephen story, not as a source for the author of Acts, but as an example of early interpretation, conflation of particular themes and texts, and midrashic idiom. See the references made above to this targum in studying vv.36 (Dt 1:1f.), 37 (Dt 18:14), and 38 (Dt 18:16 and 33:4-5).

In discussing "other sources" for the Stephen speech, an attempt was made to examine a large variety of histories and Jewish literature available to the author, or at least texts that reflected the idiom and concerns of NT times. From this survey, the conclusion emerges even more clearly that the writer made direct use of the Greek version of Hebrew history, and further, that he enjoyed a respectable acquaintance with con-

---

[277]Ibid., pp. 1-82. The quotation is taken from p. 12.

[278]See Rober Le Déaut, "The Current State of Targumic Studies," BTB 4 (1974): 3-32.

temporary theological thought.

2. Textual Considerations

It is the conclusion of this study that the LXX is the major source of Acts 7:2-53. This point has been made consistently throughout the present chapter. In this regard there has emerged from the study a number of textual problems related to the LXX which were dealt with as they arose. It is deemed necessary to assemble this data and to formulate the results of the present research.

a. Textual Criticism and LXX Quotations

A recurring problem encountered in this study has been the role which the LXX should play in evaluating OT quotations. On the one hand, there exists a precept of textual criticism stating that conformity to OT readings is most likely the product of scribal activity and that departure from the LXX should be viewed as original. Assimilation to the Greek OT is always a possibility. On the other hand, fidelity to the OT source is very likely when dealing with explicit citations. The Stephen speech is a case in point. The author is very conscientious and very exact in the use of his model. It, therefore, seems reasonable to be more discerning in the use of the precept mentioned above when discussing Acts 7.

The concept "conformity to the LXX" is itself a matter of discussion in light of recent proto-LXX study. For that reason both assimilation to and quotation of the LXX are to be determined on an individual basis upon the available evidence. In this context the evaluation of manuscripts and their reliability is important.

In light of these considerations I have been led to examine the list of variants which occur in the Stephen speech within direct quotations. [Note: the Aland readings (Nestle and Aland, NT Graece) are listed first for each verse; the choices made during the present study are indicated by an asterisk; Acts 3:22 (no. 12) is not included in the statistical observations.]

The following statistics (see chart on next page) are pertinent to the present study. Aland rejects LXX readings in 11

	vv.	Readings	Witnesses	LXX
(1)	v.3	omit 2nd ἐκ	B D sa	
		*read 2nd ἐκ	rell	X
(2)	v.7	read δουλεύσουσιν	P^{74} A C D pc sa	
		*read δουλεύσωσιν	B א 𝔎 E pl	X
(3)	v.10	omit ἐφ'	B 𝔎 D al	
		*read ἐφ'	P^{74} 𝔥 E pm	X
(4)	v.13	read ἐγνωρίσθη	B A p t vg	
		*read ἀνεγνωρίσθη	rell	X
(5)	v.18	*read ἐπ' Αἴγυπτον	rell	X
		omit ἐπ' Αἴγυπτον	P^{45vid} 𝔎 D E pm gig	
(6)	v.18	*read ᾔδει τόν	rell	X
		read ἐμνήσθη τοῦ	D E gig p	
(7)	v.30	*omit κυρίου	rell	
		read κυρίου	𝔎 D pl e p w sy	X
(8)	v.30	*read φλογὶ πυρός	rell	X
		read πυρὶ φλογός	P^{74} A C E pc t vg sy^p	
(9)	v.32	*omit ὁ θεός twice	P^{74} 𝔥 al	
		read θεός twice	D gig vg	X
		read ὁ θεός twice	𝔎 E 33 pm	
(10)	v.34	read αὐτοῦ	B D sy^p	
		*read αὐτῶν	P^{74} 𝔥 𝔎 E pl	X
(11)	v.36	*read ἐν γῇ Αἰγύπτῳ	א A 𝔎 E al	X
		read ἐν τῇ Αἰγύπτῳ	B C al	
		read ἐν γῇ Αἰγύπτου	P^{74} D al lat sy	
(12)	v.37→3:22	omit pronoun	B h p	
		*read ἡμῶν	א* C 𝔎 E pm	(Dt 18.16?)
		read ὑμῶν	A D al Ir^{lat}	(σου)
(13)	v.40	*read ἐγένετο	rell	
		read γέγονεν	𝔎 D pm	X
(14)	v.43	omit ὑμῶν	B D pc gig sy^p Ir Or	
		*read ὑμῶν	P^{74} 𝔥 𝔎 E pl h vg sy^h	X
(15)	v.43	read Ῥομφά	B	
		*read Ῥαιφάν	P^{74} A pc	X
		read Ῥεφάν	C E al sy	
		read Ῥομφάν	א*	
		read Ῥεμφάμ	D lat Ir^{lat}	
		read Ῥεμφάν	1 429 pm Or	
		read Ῥεμφά	81 Ir^{arm}	
(16)	v.46	read τῷ οἴκῳ Ἰακώβ	P^{74} B א* D H	
		*read τῷ θεῷ Ἰακώβ	A C 𝔎 E pl lat sy	X
(17)	v.49	*read μοι	rell	X
		read μου	P^{74} D	
(18)	v.49	*read ἡ δέ	rell	X
		read καὶ ἡ	B h sy^p	

cases out of 17 noted above.[279] In all of these, except nos. 2 and 11, B is a supporting witness against the OT greek text. Further, the editor agrees with the LXX against Vaticanus in only two cases, nos. 11 and 18.

Codex B departs from the OT text in 12 out of 17 instances; Bezae 11; A 6; P^{74} and א 5 each. From these facts I conclude that Vaticanus and D are especially tendentious in that regard. If the evidence is as convincing as it seems to be, then the weight of B as a textual witness is considerably lessened and, in fact, this particular manuscript may even be less than trustworthy in relation to OT quotations.

Finally, it should be noted that Vaticanus is the major witness in practically all the passages underlined in the above list. In four cases it is joined by Bezae. In each case, except no. 16 (contrast the commentary of 7:46 supra),[280] the manuscript evidence is not convincing and, I believe, in light of this study, the underlined readings are rendered even less probable.

b. LXX Used by the Author of the Stephen Speech

The study of the Stephen speech has led me on many occasions to dwell briefly upon the nature of the OT text used by the author of Acts. This preoccupation with the character of the Greek OT owes to the present interest and considerable advances in LXX studies.[281] Because of the discoveries of Qumran and their bearing upon Samaritan, LXX, and Proto-LXX research,[282] study of OT quotations has become increasingly more

---

[279]The committee in charge of making textual decisions (in Aland et al., Gk NT) reject LXX readings in five cases: 2, 7, 9, 13, and 16, while Merk, NT, disagrees in six instances: 2, 3, 7, 9, 13, and 15. In the present study I have disregarded LXX readings in three cases: 7, 9, and 13.

[280]I have stated my conclusions concerning B and D and note that while א is not a negligible witness in regard to quotations, the early correction of the reading is significant. The manuscript evidence then is not very compelling (note that H is a Koine text).

[281]S. P. Brock, C. T. Fritsch, and Sidney Jellicoe, A Classified Bibliography of the Septaugint (Leiden: Brill, 1973).

[282]See among others: Frank M. Cross, "A New Qumran Biblical Fragment Related to the Original Hebrew Underlying the Septaugint," BASOR 132 (1953): 15-26; William F. Albright, "New Light on Early Recensions of the Hebrew Bible," BASOR 140

complex. This is clearly related to the nature of the data. Indeed, the analysis of pre-Masoretic manuscripts has demonstrated the great variety of OT textual tradition. The existence of a Palestinian text type has not only been proved, but provided with numerous fragments and sources. The LXX is recognized as belonging to this particular tradition and has received extraordinary corroboration from Qumran finds.

Furthermore, the Greek translation of the OT has undergone a variety of successive revisions, so that the text utilized by the author of Acts is not always the one provided by the present manuscripts. This particular fact places the Stephen speech in an enviable position, since, along with other representatives of the Palestinian textual tradition underlying the LXX, it becomes an important source of proto-LXX evidence.

Analysis of the quotations of the discourse has demonstrated the author's fidelity in utilizing his sources. Because of this, it has often seemed reasonable to seek textual evidence for variants rather than to assign these to "loose" quoting methods, citations "from memory" or other such factors. In most instances disagreement of the LXX with the MT and versions has confirmed my suspicion. On other occasions, I have relied upon the consistency, or lack thereof, of the LXX translators in rendering the underlying Hebrew text. This is, admittedly, a tenuous area of research, but proper methodology and reevaluation of the data is indeed possible and desirable.[283] I have proposed textual evidence for the following

---

(1955): 27-33; Patrick W. Skehan, "Exodus in the Samaritan Recension from Qumran," JBL 74 (1955): 182-87; Frank M. Cross, Library, (1958); idem, "The History of the Biblical Text in the Light of Discoveries in the Judaean Desert," HTR 57 (1964): 281-99; Peter Katz, "Septaugint Studies in the Mid-century: Their Links with the Past and Their Present Tendencies," in New Testament and Its Eschatology, pp. 176-208; John W. Wevers, "Proto-Septaugint Studies," in The Seed of Wisdom: Essays in Honour of T. J. Meek, ed. W. S. McCullough (Toronto: University of Toronto Press, 1964), pp. 58-77; Dominique Barthélemy, "Pourquoi la Torah a-t-elle été traduite en grec?" in On Language, Culture, and Religion: In Honor of Eugene A. Nida, ed. Matthew Black and W. A. Smalley (The Hague/Paris: Mouton, 1974), pp. 23-41.

[283]Contra Wilson, "Theologian and Historian" p. 297, n.11: "One is not in a position either to prove or to disprove the theory that when Luke does vary from the Septaugint according to the extant manuscripts he may be following a lost reading."

verses of the speech: 5, 6, 8, 10, 19, 26, 29, 32, 32, 34, 37, 40, 41, 42, and 44. The present study of this phenomenon is preliminary in nature and is not central to the overall goal of the dissertation; therefore, observations have been intentionally limited to general statements.

The OT Greek text employed within the speech is clearly that of the LXX. Further, the particular LXX Vorlage used tends, in some cases, to be closer to the MT. However, in some instances where independent evidence has been available, it has been possible to discover in the discourse what is ostensibly proto-LXX data (i.e., of a Palestinian type).

Finally, it is necessary to treat of another problem related to the LXX used in the speech: the relation of the Alexandrian text to the quotations of Acts 7. It has often been maintained that A was the LXX manuscript most in agreement with NT quotations. It has also been recognized that this particular witness was the most susceptible to Christian editing. In the words of Filson: "One odd illustration of such influence may exist in Ps. 14, where LXX manuscripts inserted after v.3 the chain of Old Testament passages which in Rom. 3:13-18 follows the quotation of Ps. 14:1-3."[284] Another obvious example of this tendency is the addition in the OT manuscripts S* A C (Is 40:14) of a phrase from Rm 11:35[285] and the use of this text type in Palestinian Syriac.[286] In several passages (v.14: addition of πέντε to Dt 10:22; v.13: addition of Ιωσηφ to Gn 45:1; v.15: Ιακωβ made to follow verb in Gn 46:6; and v.33: omission of σου in Ex 3:5 and the modification of λῦσαι to λῦσον in Jos 5:15), the tendency of this codex to agree with the NT text was noted. I am therefore led to the conclusion that the conformity between these is due to Chrisitan editing of A rather than dependence of the NT writer upon codex Alexandrinus. This codex, therefore, must be considered in relation to the entire LXX manuscript tradition.

---

[284]Floyd V. Filson, "The Septaugint and the New Testament," BA 9 (1946): 40.

[285]Rahlfs, Septuaginta, 2:620.

[286]Matthew Black, ed. "Palestinian Syriac," in An Aramaic Handbook, Porta Linguarum Orientalium, ed. Franz Rosenthal, 2 vols. (Wiesbaden: Harrassowitz, 1967), 2/1:12.

With this task accomplished, attention will now be directed to a stylistic and structural analysis of the discourse. The role played by the OT text, as well as the modifications imposed upon that source, has indicated several areas for further research. This will be the goal of chapter three.

CHAPTER III

Functional Character of Stylistic Data

From the previous chapter, it has become increasingly clear that stylistic considerations play a major role in the composition of the speech. The author has used the OT from beginning to end of his discourse. However, throughout this process he has imposed a variety of modifications upon his source and has indulged his stylistic preferences in varying degrees. At the same time, he has pursued his goal of structuring his historical survey to suit his purpose. At every step he has left traces of his redactional activity. My intention at this point is to examine more systematically the variety of techniques, tendencies, and patterns employed in the speech and, by extension, throughout the narratives of the Stephen material.[1]

A. Presentation of Stylistic Data: The Corpus

From chance observation of the repeated use of various verbs and nouns within the speech, I was led to make a systematic survey of this phenomenon. It became evident that this tendency was a characteristic feature of the speech and of the narrative.[2] I now wish to present the data in a strictly de-

---

[1] I have made repeated use of the work of Henry J. Cadbury, who has been over the years the scholar most concerned with literary and stylistic factors in studying the author of Acts. See the bibliographical references above, p. 8, nn. 29 and 31. For this chapter, I am especially indebted to his article "Four Features of Lucan Style," in _Studies_, eds Keck and Martyn, pp. 87-102.

[2] F. Neirynck's series of articles, "Mark in Greek" and "Duality in Mark," _ETL_ 47 (1971): 144-98 and 394-463 respectively and "Duplicate Expressions in the Gospel of Mark," _ETL_ 48 (1972): 150-209, have been most helpful in establishing some of the categories adopted in this study. Also of assistance in this task was Morgenthaler, _Geschichtsschreibung_, 1:16-91, who lists and analyzes a large variety of stylistic patterns and features of Luke and Acts (approximately the same material referred to above, i.e., chapters one and two, was published in a short work, _Das Zweiheitsgesetz im Lukanischen Werke: Eine_

scriptive way, avoiding functional and structural tendencies at this point. To that end, the three following general headings will be used: 1) categories of a grammatical nature, 2) those of a lexical nature, and 3) those relating to a variety of patterns.

1. Grammatical Categories

a. Verb Followed by Cognate Substantive

6:11 λαλοῦντος ῥήματα βλάσφημα
6:13 λαλῶν ῥήματα
7:17 ἐπαγγελίας ἧς ὡμολόγησεν
7:47 οἰκοδόμησεν αὐτῷ οἶκον
7:49 οἶκον οἰκοδομήσετέ μοι
7:57 κράξαντες δὲ φωνῇ μεγάλῃ
7:60 ἔκραξεν φωνῇ μεγάλῃ

Less Obvious Cases:

6:2 διακονεῖν τραπέζαις
6:6 ἐπέθηκαν αὐτοῖς τὰς χεῖρας
6:8 ἐποίει τέρατα καὶ σημεῖα μεγάλα
7:10 ἔδωκεν αὐτῷ χάριν καὶ σοφίαν
7:10 κατέστησεν αὐτὸν ἡγούμενον
7:22 ἐπαιδεύθη Μωϋσῆς πάσῃ σοφίᾳ
7:27 κατέστησεν ἄρχοντα καὶ δικαστήν
7:35 κατέστησεν ἄρχοντα καὶ δικαστήν
7:36 ποιήσας τέρατα καὶ σημεῖα
7:46 εὗρεν χάριν
7:54 διεπρίοντο ταῖς καρδίαις αὐτῶν
7:54 ἔβρυχον τοὺς ὀδόντας
7:60 θεὶς δὲ τὰ γόνατα
8:2 ἐποίησαν κοπετὸν μέγαν
8:4 εὐαγγελιζόμενοι τὸν λόγον

b. Compound Verb Followed by the Same Preposition

7:3 ἔξελθε ἐκ
7:4 ἐξελθὼν ἐκ
7:10 ἐξείλατο ... ἐκ
7:40 ἐξήγαγεν ... ἐκ
7:58 ἐκβαλόντες ἔξω

---

stilkritische Untersuchung (Zurich: Zwingli-Verlag, 1949).

c. Singular/Plural

6:1 πληθυνόντων τῶν μαθητῶν
6:2 προσκαλεσάμενοι ... τὸ πλῆθος τῶν μαθητῶν

6:1 πληθυνόντων τῶν μαθητῶν
6:7 ἐπληθύνετο ὁ ἀριθμὸς τῶν μαθητῶν

6:1 ἐν τῇ διακονίᾳ τῇ καθημερινῇ
6:2 διακονεῖν τραπέζαις
6:3 ἐπὶ τῆς χρείας ταύτης

6:2 οἱ δώδεκα
6:2 τὸ πλῆθος τῶν μαθητῶν

6:2 τὸν λόγον τοῦ θεοῦ
6:2 διακονεῖν τραπέζαις

6:2 οὐκ ἀρεστόν ἐστιν ἡμᾶς
6:5 ἤρεσεν ὁ λόγος ἐνώπιον παντὸς τοῦ πλήθους

6:3 ἄνδρας ... πλήρεις
6:5 ἄνδρα πλήρη

6:5 ἐνώπιον παντὸς τοῦ πλήθους
6:5 ἐξελέξαντο

6:12 εἰς τὸ συνέδριον
6:15 πάντες οἱ καθεζόμενοι ἐν τῷ συνεδρίῳ

6:14 τὸν τόπον τοῦτον
6:14 τὰ ἔθη

6:15 ἀτενίσαντες ... εἶδον
7:55 ἀτενίσας ... εἶδεν

6:15 πρόσωπον ἀγγέλου
7:53 εἰς διαταγὰς ἀγγέλων

7:4 μετῴκισεν αὐτόν
7:43 μετοικιῶ ὑμᾶς

7:6 ἔσται τὸ σπέρμα αὐτοῦ ... δουλώσουσιν αὐτό
7:7 τὸ ἔθνος ᾧ ἐὰν δουλεύσωσιν

7:6 κακώσουσιν
7:19 οὗτος ... ἐκάκωσεν τοὺς πατέρας

7:7 τὸ ἔθνος ... κρινῶ ἐγώ
7:45 ἐν τῇ κατασχέσει τῶν ἐθνῶν

7:10 ἐξείλατο αὐτόν
7:34 κατέβην ἐξελέσθαι αὐτούς

7:10 ἐκ πασῶν τῶν θλίψεων αὐτοῦ
7:11 θλῖψις μεγάλη

7:11 οὐχ ηὕρισκον χορτάσματα οἱ πατέρες ἡμῶν
7:46 ᾐτήσατο εὑρεῖν σκήνωμα

7:13 ἀνεγνωρίσθη Ἰωσὴφ τοῖς ἀδελφοῖς αὐτοῦ
7:13 φανερὸν ἐγένετο τῷ Φαραὼ τὸ γένος Ἰωσήφ

7:18 βασιλεὺς ἕτερος ... ὃς οὐκ ᾔδει τὸν Ἰωσήφ
7:40 οὐκ οἴδαμεν τί ἐγένετο αὐτῷ

7:19 κατασοφισάμενος τὸ γένος ἡμῶν
7:19 ἐκάκωσεν τοὺς πατέρας

7:19 τοῦ ποιεῖν τὰ βρέφη ἔκθετα αὐτῶν
7:21 ἐκτεθέντος δὲ αὐτοῦ

7:22 πάσῃ σοφίᾳ Αἰγυπτίων
7:22 ἐν λόγοις καὶ ἔργοις αὐτοῦ

7:23 ὡς δὲ ἐπληροῦτο αὐτῷ τεσσερακονταέτης χρόνος
7:30 πληρωθέντων ἐτῶν τεσσεράκοντα

7:24 τινα ἀδικούμενον
7:26 ἱνατί ἀδικεῖτε
7:27 ὁ δὲ ἀδικῶν τὸν πλησίον

7:27 ὁ δὲ ἀδικῶν τὸν πλησίον ἀπώσατο αὐτόν
7:39 οἱ πατέρες ἡμῶν ἀλλὰ ἀπώσαντο

7:27 εἰπών· τίς σε κατέστησεν ἄρχοντα καὶ δικαστὴν ἐφ' ἡμῶν
7:35 εἰπόντες· τίς δε κατέστησεν ἄρχοντα καὶ δικαστήν

7:28 μὴ ἀνελεῖν με σὺ θέλεις
7:39 ᾧ οὐκ ἠθέλησαν ὑπήκοοι γενέσθαι οἱ πατέρες ἡμῶν

7:34 ἰδὼν εἶδον τὴν κάκωσιν τοῦ λαοῦ μου τοῦ ἐν Αἰγύπτῳ
7:34 τοῦ στεναγμοῦ αὐτῶν
7:34 κατέβην ἐξελέσθαι αὐτούς

7:37 προφήτην ὑμῖν ἀναστήσει ὁ θεός
7:42 καθὼς γέγραπται ἐν βίβλῳ τῶν προφητῶν
7:48 καθὼς ὁ προφήτης λέγει
7:52 τίνα τῶν προφητῶν οὐκ ἐδίωξαν οἱ πατέρες ὑμῶν

7:39 ἐστράφησαν ἐν ταῖς καρδίαις αὐτῶν
7:42 ἔστρεψεν δὲ ὁ θεός

7:40 ποίησον ἡμῖν θεοὺς οἳ προπορεύσονται ἡμῶν
7:42 ἔστρεψεν δὲ ὁ θεός

7:41 ἐμοσχοποίησαν
7:41 θυσίαν τῷ εἰδώλῳ
7:41 ἐν τοῖς ἔργοις τῶν χειρῶν αὐτῶν

7:41 ἀνήγαγον θυσίαν
7:42 μὴ σφάγια καὶ θυσίας προσηνέγκατέ μοι

7:41 εὐφραίνοντο ἐν τοῖς ἔργοις τῶν χειρῶν αὐτῶν
7:50 οὐχὶ ἡ χείρ μου ἐποίησεν ταῦτα πάντα

7:42 λατρεύειν τῇ στρατιᾷ τοῦ οὐρανοῦ
7:43 προσκυνεῖν αὐτοῖς

7:42 τῇ στρατιᾷ τοῦ οὐρανοῦ
7:43 τὸ ἄστρον τοῦ θεοῦ ὑμῶν 'Ραιφάν

7:43 τὴν σκηνὴν τοῦ Μόλοχ
7:43 καὶ τὸ ἄστρον τοῦ θεοῦ ὑμῶν 'Ραιφάν
7:43 τοὺς τύπους οὓς ἐποιήσατε

7:47 Σολομὼν δὲ οἰκοδόμησεν αὐτῷ οἶκον
7:49 ποῖον οἶκον οἰκοδομήσετέ μοι

7:47 Σολομὼν δὲ οἰκοδόμησεν αὐτῷ οἶκον
7:48 ἀλλ' οὐχ ὁ ὕψιστος ἐν χειροποιήτοις κατοικεῖ

7:48 οὐχ ὁ ὕψιστος ἐν χειροποιήτοις κατοικεῖ
7:49 ὁ οὐρανός μοι θρόνος
7:49 ἡ δὲ γῆ ὑποπόδιον τῶν ποδῶν μου
7:49 ποῖον οἶκον οἰκοδομήσετέ μοι
7:49 ἢ τίς τόπος τῆς καταπαύσεώς μου
7:50 οὐχὶ ἡ χείρ μου ἐποίησεν ταῦτα πάντα

7:55 ἀτενίσας εἰς τὸν οὐρανόν
7:56 θεωρῶ τοὺς οὐρανοὺς διηνοιγμένους

7:57 κράξαντες δὲ φωνῇ μεγάλῃ
7:60 ἔκραξεν φωνῇ μεγάλῃ

8:1 διωγμὸς μέγας ἐπὶ τὴν ἐκκλησίαν τὴν ἐν 'Ιεροσολύμοις
8:1 πάντες δὲ διεσπάρησαν

d. Redundancy

6:13,14	οὗτος ... τούτου ... αὐτοῦ ... τοῦτον
6:14	Ἰησοῦς ὁ Ναζωραῖος οὗτος
6:15	εἰς αὐτόν ... τὸ πρόσωπον αὐτοῦ
6:15	τὸ πρόσωπον αὐτοῦ ὡσεὶ πρόσωπον ἀγγέλου
7:2,3, 4,5	ἐν τῇ Μεσοποταμίᾳ ... ἐν Χαρράν ... ἐκ τῆς γῆς σου ... εἰς τὴν γῆν ἥν ... ἐκ γῆς Χαλδαίων ... ἐν Χαρράν ... κἀκαῖθεν ... εἰς τὴν γῆν ταύτην εἰς ἥν ... ἐν αὐτῇ ... αὐτήν
7:3	σου ... σου ... σοι
7:4,5	αὐτοῦ ... αὐτόν ... αὐτῷ ... αὐτῷ ... τῷ σπέρματι αὐτοῦ μετ' αὐτόν ... αὐτῷ
7:9,10	μετ' αὐτοῦ ... αὐτόν ... αὐτοῦ ... αὐτῷ ... αὐτόν
7:9,10, 11,12	εἰς Αἴγυπτον ... Αἰγύπτου ... ἐπ' Αἴγυπτον ... ἐφ' ὅλην τὴν Αἴγυπτον ... εἰς Αἴγυπτον
7:15	Ἰακώβ ... αὐτός
7:17,18	ἐν Αἰγύπτῳ ... ἐπ' Αἴγυπτον
7:19	τὸ γένος ἡμῶν ... τοὺς πατέρας ... αὐτῶν
7:21	αὐτοῦ ... αὐτόν ... αὐτόν ... εἰς υἱόν
7:21	ἡ θυγάτηρ Φαραὼ καὶ ἀνεθρέψατο ... ἑαυτῇ
7:22	Μωϋσῆς ... αὐτοῦ
7:23	αὐτῷ ... αὐτοῦ ... αὐτοῦ
7:25	τοὺς ἀδελφούς ... αὐτοῖς ... οἱ
7:26	αὐτοῖς μαχομένοις ... αὐτούς
7:31	ὁ δὲ Μωϋσῆς ... αὐτοῦ
7:32,33	Μωϋσῆς ... αὐτῷ
7:34	τοῦ λαοῦ μου ... αὐτῶν ... αὐτούς
7:34	ἐν Αἰγύπτῳ ... εἰς Αἴγυπτον
7:35-40	τοῦτον τὸν Μωϋσῆν ὅν ... σε ... τοῦτον ... οὗτος ... οὗτός ἐστιν ὁ Μωϋσῆς ὁ ... ἐμέ ... οὗτός ἐστιν ὁ ... ὅς ... ᾧ ... ὁ γὰρ Μωϋσῆς οὗτος, ὅς ... αὐτῷ
7:38	ἐν τῇ ἐκκλησίᾳ ... καὶ τῶν πατέρων ἡμῶν
7:39	οἱ πατέρες ἡμῶν ... αὐτῶν
7:39-40	εἰς Αἴγυπτον ... ἐκ γῆς Αἰγύπτου
7:40	ἡμῖν ... ἡμῶν ... ἡμᾶς
7:45	οἱ πατέρες ἡμῶν ... τῶν πατέρων ἡμῶν
7:45,46, 47,48	ὁ θεός ... ἐνώπιον τοῦ θεοῦ ... τῷ θεῷ Ἰακώβ ... αὐτῷ ... ὁ ὕψιστος
7:49,50	μοι ... μου ... μοι ... μου ... μου

7:51 ὑμεῖς ... ὑμῶν ... ὑμεῖς ... ὑμῶν ... ὑμεῖς ... οἵτινες
7:51,52 οἱ πατέρες ὑμῶν ... οἱ πατέρες ὑμῶν
7:58 οἱ μάρτυρες ... αὐτῶν
8:2 τὸν Στέφανον ... ἐπ' αὐτῷ

e. Negative/Positive

6:2 οὐκ ἀρεστόν ἐστιν ἡμᾶς
6:5 ἤρεσεν ὁ λόγος ἐνώπιον παντὸς τοῦ πλήθους

6:2 οὐκ ἀρεστόν ἐστιν ἡμᾶς
6:4 ἡμεῖς δὲ τῇ προσευχῇ

6:9 συζητοῦντες τῷ Στεφάνῳ
6:10 οὐκ ἴσχυον ἀντιστῆναι

6:13 ὁ ἄνθρωπος οὗτος οὐ παύεται λαλῶν
6:14 ἀκηκόαμεν γὰρ αὐτοῦ λέγοντος

7:4 εἰς τὴν γῆν ταύτην εἰς ἣν ὑμεῖς νῦν κατοικεῖτε
7:5 καὶ οὐκ ἔδωκεν αὐτῷ κληρονομίαν ἐν αὐτῇ

7:5 οὐκ ἔδωκεν αὐτῷ
7:5 ἐπηγγείλατο δοῦναι αὐτῷ

7:5 δοῦναι ... τῷ σπέρματι αὐτοῦ μετ' αὐτόν
7:5 οὐκ ὄντος αὐτῷ τέκνου

7:11 οὐχ ηὕρισκον χορτάσματα οἱ πατέρες ἡμῶν
7:12 ἀκούσας δὲ 'Ιακὼβ ὄντα σιτία εἰς Αἴγυπτον

7:19 τοῦ ποιεῖν τὰ βρέφη ἔκθετα αὐτῶν
7:19 εἰς τὸ μὴ ζῳογονεῖσθαι

7:25 ἐνόμιζεν δὲ συνιέναι τοὺς ἀδελφούς
7:25 οἱ δὲ οὐ συνῆκαν

7:31 προσερχομένου δὲ αὐτοῦ κατανοῆσαι
7:32 ἔντρομος δὲ γενόμενος Μωϋσῆς οὐκ ἐτόλμα κατανοῆσαι

7:39 ᾧ οὐκ ἠθέλησαν ὑπήκοοι γενέσθαι οἱ πατέρες ἡμῶν
7:39 ἀλλὰ ἀπώσαντο

7:46 καὶ ᾐτήσατο εὑρεῖν σκήνωμα
7:47 Σολομὼν δὲ οἰκοδόμησεν αὐτῷ οἶκον
7:48 ἀλλ' οὐχ ὁ ὕψιστος ἐν χειροποιήτοις κατοικεῖ

7:49 ποῖον οἶκον οἰκοδομήσετέ μοι
7:49 ἢ τίς τόπος τῆς καταπαύσεώς μου
7:50 οὐχὶ ἡ χείρ μου ἐποίησεν ταῦτα πάντα

7:52 τίνα τῶν προφητῶν οὐκ ἐδίωξαν οἱ πατέρες ὑμῶν
7:52 ἀπέκτειναν τοὺς προκαταγγείλαντας

7:53 οἵτινες ἐλάβετε τὸν νόμον
7:53 οὐκ ἐφυλάξατε

7:59 κύριε Ἰησοῦ, δέξαι τὸ πνεῦμά μου
7:60 κύριε, μὴ στήσῃς αὐτοῖς ταύτην τὴν ἁμαρτίαν

8:1 πάντες δὲ διεσπάρησαν
8:1 πλὴν τῶν ἀποστόλων

The data of this first division, as seen by the degree of frequency, vary from one category to another. Even the most cursory perusal of the corpus indicates that categories a and b play a relatively minor role in comparison to the others.

Stylistically, a and b are negligible in terms of redaction. Analysis has shown that they are either of a mechanical nature or represent ready-made phrases borrowed from the LXX.

Owing to their frequency and varied functions, singular/plural contrasts (c), as used by the author, rarely seem mechanical. In most cases, some structural or functional purpose reveals itself. Presently, it suffices to note the writer's inclination to employ this particular stylistic feature.

The frequency of category d, redundancy, points to a second characteristic of the author's style. This type of repetitiveness occurs only in certain sections of the story and in relation either to OT episodes or particular themes. In other words, the use of redundancy, or what may be considered as undue repetition of pronouns, antecedents or even ideas, appears as a conscious imitation of OT sources in some cases, and in others as a method to enhance a given theme or a person's role.

A third feature of importance in terms of occurrence is that of negative/positive combinations (e). Its significance is further enhanced by its frequent association with categories 2 (lexical) and 3 (patterns). To be fully understood, this group must be seen in relation to other techniques of contrast used by the author.

This first division, therefore, plays a considerable role in the author's method of composition. An examination of its function will appear later in the chapter.

2. Lexical Categories[3]

a. Cognate Expressions: Verbal, Substantive, and Adjectival

Within Consecutive Blocks of Material:

6:1,2,5,7	πληθυνόντων; τὸ πλῆθος; τοῦ πλήθους; ἐπληθύνετο
6:1,7	πληθυνόντων; ἐπληθύνετο
6:1,2, 7	τῶν μαθητῶν; τὸ πλῆθος τῶν μαθητῶν; ὁ ἀριθμὸς τῶν μαθητῶν
6:1,2,4	ἐν τῇ διακονίᾳ τῇ καθημερινῇ; διακονεῖν; τῇ διακονίᾳ
6:2,5	το πλῆθος τῶν μαθητῶν; ἐνώπιον παντὸς τοῦ πλήθους
6:2,5	ἀρεστόν ἐστιν; ἤρεσεν ὁ λόγος
6:2,4, 7	τὸν λόγον τοῦ θεοῦ; τῇ διακονίᾳ τοῦ λόγου; ὁ λόγος τοῦ θεοῦ; 8:4 τὸν λόγον
7:3,5	ἄνδρας; ἄνδρα
6:3,5,8	πλήρεις; πλήρη; πλήρης
6:3,5,10	πνεύματος; πνεύματος ἁγίου; τῷ πνεύματι
6:3,6	καταστήσομεν; ἔστησαν
6:4,6	τῇ προσευχῇ; προσευξάμενοι
6:5,6	ἐνώπιον; ἐνώπιον
6:5,7	πίστεως; τῇ πίστει
6:6,9,10, 12,13	ἔστησαν; ἀνέστησαν; ἀντιστῆναι; ἐπιστάντες; ἔστησαν
6:8,12	ἐν τῷ λαῷ; τὸν λαόν
6:10,11,13	ἐλάλει; αὐτοῦ λαλοῦντος; λαλῶν
6:11,13,14	λέγοντας; λέγοντας; λέγοντος
6:11,14	ἀκηκόαμεν; ἀκηκόαμεν
6:11,13	ῥήματα; ῥήματα
6:12,15	εἰς τὸ συνέδριον; ἐν τῷ συνεδρίῳ
6:13,14	κατὰ τοῦ τόπου τοῦ ἁγίου τούτου; τὸν τόπον τοῦτον
6:15	τὸ πρόσωπον αὐτοῦ ὡσεὶ πρόσωπον ἀγγελου

---

[3]Cadbury ("Four Features," pp. 88 and 97) has treated some of these phenomena under the headings: "repetition and variation" and "distribution and concentration." It is interesting to note that most of his data are lexical in nature. See also Morgenthaler, Geschichtsschreibung, 1:16-47, on lexical categories.

7:2,4 κατοικῆσαι; κατῴκησεν: κατοικεῖτε
7:3,4, ἐκ τῆς γῆς σου; εἰς τὴν γῆν; ἐκ γῆς Χαλδαίων; εἰς τὴν
6 γῆν ταύτην; ἐν γῇ ἀλλοτρίᾳ
7:5,8,10 ἔδωκεν; δοῦναι; ἔδωκεν; ἔδωκεν
7:5,6 τῷ σπέρματι αὐτοῦ; τὸ σπέρμα αὐτοῦ
7:6,7 δουλώσουσιν; δουλεύσουσιν
7:8 περιτομῆς; περιέτεμεν
7:8,9 τοὺς δώδεκα πατριάρχας; οἱ πατριάρχαι
7:9,10 ἀπέδοντο; ἔδωκεν
7:10,11 πασῶν τῶν θλίψεων αὐτοῦ; θλῖψις μεγάλη
7:10,11 ὅλον τὸν οἶκον αὐτοῦ; ἐφ' ὅλην τὴν Αἴγυπτον
7:11,12, οἱ πατέρες ἡμῶν; τοὺς πατέρας ἡμῶν; οἱ πατέρες
15 ἡμῶν
7:12,14 ἐξαπέστειλεν; ἀποστείλας
7:16 μετετέθησαν; ἐτέθησαν
7:17,23 ὁ χρόνος; χρόνος
7:19,22 κατασοφισάμενος; πάσῃ σοφίᾳ; also 7:10
7:19,21 τὰ βρέφη ἔκθετα αὐτῶν; ἐκτεθέντος δὲ αὐτοῦ
7:20,21 ἀνετράφη; ἀνεθρέψατο
7:23,30 ἐπληροῦτο; πληρωθέντων
7:23,30 τεσσερακονταέτης χρόνος; ἐτῶν τεσσεράκοντα
7:23,25, τοὺς ἀδελφοὺς αὐτοῦ; τοὺς ἀδελφοὺς αὐτοῦ; ἄνδρες,
26 ἀδελφοί ἐστε
7:24,26, τινα ἀδικούμενον; ἐποίησεν ἐκδίκησιν; ἀδικεῖτε;
27 ὁ ... ἀδικῶν
7:25 συνιέναι; συνῆκαν
7:28 ἀνελεῖν; ἀνεῖλες
7:31,32 κατανοῆσαι; κατανοῆσαι
7:34,35 ἀποστείλω; ἀπέσταλκεν
7:35,38 σὺν χειρὶ ἀγγέλου; μετὰ τοῦ ἀγγέλου; also 7:30
7:35 ἄρχοντα; ἄρχοντα
7:36,40 οὗτος ἐξήγαγεν; ὃς ἐξήγαγεν
7:36,38 ἐν τῇ ἐρήμῳ; ἐν τῇ ἐρήμῳ
7:38,39 τῶν πατέρων ἡμῶν; οἱ πατέρες ἡμῶν
7:41,42 θυσίαν; θυσίας
7:42,49 τῇ στρατιᾷ τοῦ οὐρανοῦ; ὁ οὐρανός μοι θρόνος
7:42,48,52 τῶν προφητῶν; ὁ προφήτης; τῶν προφητῶν
7:42,44 ἐν τῇ ἐρήμῳ; ἐν τῇ ἐρήμῳ
7:43,44,46 τὴν σκηνὴν τοῦ Μόλοχ; ἡ σκηνὴ τοῦ μαρτυρίου; σκήνωμα

7:43,44 τοὺς τύπους; κατὰ τὸν τύπον
7:43,44,50 ἐποιήσατε; ποιῆσαι; ἐποίησεν
7:44,45 τοῖς πατράσιν ἡμῶν; οἱ πατέρες ἡμῶν; τῶν πατέρων ἡμῶν
7:46 εὗρεν; εὑρεῖν
7:47,48,49 οἰκοδόμησεν ... οἶκον; κατοικεῖ; οἶκον οἰκοδομήσετε
7:47,49 οἰκοδόμησεν; οἰκοδομήσετε
7:48,50 ἐν χειροποιήτοις; ἡ χείρ μου ἐποίησεν
7:48,49 λέγει; λέγει
7:51,54 καρδίαις; ταῖς καρδίαις αὐτῶν
7:51,57 τοῖς ὠσίν; τὰ ὦτα αὐτῶν
7:51,55 τῷ πνεύματι τῷ ἁγίῳ; πνεύματος ἁγίου
7:51,52 οἱ πατέρες ὑμῶν; οἱ πατέρες ὑμῶν
7:51,52 ὑμεῖς; καὶ ὑμεῖς; ὑμεῖς
7:55,56 εἰς τὸν οὐρανόν; τοὺς οὐρανοὺς διηνοιγμένους; also 7:42,49
7:55,56 Ἰησοῦν ἑστῶτα ἐκ δεξιῶν τοῦ θεοῦ; τὸν υἱὸν τοῦ ἀνθρώπου ἐκ δεξιῶν ἑστῶτα τοῦ θεοῦ
7:57,60 κράξαντες δὲ φωνῇ μεγάλῃ; ἔκραξεν φωνῇ μεγάλῃ
7:58,59 ἐλιθοβόλουν; ἐλιθοβόλουν
7:58,60 ἀπέθεντο; θείς
7:59,60 κύριε; κύριε
8:1,2 διωγμὸς μέγας ἐπί; κοπετὸν μέγαν ἐπ' ...
8:1,3 ἐπὶ τὴν ἐκκλησίαν; τὴν ἐκκλησίαν; also 7:38
8:1,4 πάντες δὲ διεσπάρησαν; οἱ μὲν οὖν διασπαρέντες

Throughout the Stephen Material:

6:1;7:56 παρεθεωροῦντο; θεωρῶ
6:2;7:8 οἱ δώδεκα; τοὺς δώδεκα πατριάρχας
6:3;7:23 ἐπισκέψασθε; ἐπισκέψασθαι
6:3;7:2,13, 23,25,26,37 ἀδελφοί; ἄνδρες ἀδελφοί, τοῖς ἀδελφοῖς αὐτοῦ, τοὺς ἀδελφοὺς αὐτοῦ; τοὺς ἀδελφούς; ἄνδρες, ἀδελφοί ἐστε; ἐκ τῶν ἀδελφῶν ὑμῶν
6:3,5,11; 7:2,26;8:2,3 ἄνδρας; ἄνδρα; ἄνδρας; ἄνδρες ἀδελφοί; ἄνδρες, ἀδελφοί ἐστε; ἄνδρες εὐλαβεῖς; ἄνδρας
6:3,13; 7:44,58 μαρτυρουμένους ἑπτά; μάρτυρας ψευδεῖς; ἡ σκηνὴ τοῦ μαρτυρίου; οἱ μάρτυρες
6:3,10 σοφίας; τῇ σοφίᾳ; also 7:19,22
6:3;7:10,27,35 καταστήσομεν; κατέστησεν; κατέστησεν; κατέστησεν
6:6;8:1 ἐνώπιον τῶν ἀποστόλων; πλὴν τῶν ἀποστόλων

6:7;7:17 ηὔξανεν; ηὔξησεν

6:8;7:10,46 χάριτος; χάριν; χάριν

6:8;7:22 δυνάμεως; δυνατός

6:8;7:36 ἐποίει τέρατα καὶ σημεῖα μεγάλα; ποιήσας τέρατα καὶ σημεῖα

6:9;7:18,37 ἀνέστησαν; ἀνέστη; ἀναστήσει

6:13;7:56 ὁ ἄνθρωπος οὗτος; τὸν υἱὸν τοῦ ἀνθρώπου

6:13;7:33 κατὰ τοῦ τόπου τοῦ ἁγίου τούτου; γῆ ἁγία ἐστίν; also 6:5;7:51,55

6:13;7:53 τοῦ νόμου; τὸν νόμον

6:14;7:42,8:3 παρέδωκεν, παρέδωκεν; παρεδίδου

6:15;7:55 ἀτενίσαντες εἰς αὐτόν; ἀτενίσας εἰς τὸν οὐρανόν

6:15;7:53 ὡσεὶ πρόσωπον ἀγγέλου; εἰς διαταγὰς ἀγγέλων; also 7:30,35,38

7:1,7,50,54 εἰ ταῦτα οὕτως ἔχει; μετὰ ταῦτα; ταῦτα πάντα; ἀκούοντες δὲ ταῦτα

7:2,12,34,54 ἀκούσατε; ἀκούσας; ἤκουσα; ἀκούοντες

7:2,55 ὁ θεὸς τῆς δόξης; δόξαν θεοῦ

7:3,14 τῆς συγγενείας σου; πᾶσαν τὴν συγγένειαν

7:3,34 καὶ δεῦρο; καὶ νῦν δεῦρο

7:4,43 μετῴκισεν; μετοικιῶ

7:5,17 ἐπηγγείλατο; ὁ χρόνος τῆς ἐπαγγελίας

7:5,45 εἰς κατάσχεσιν; ἐν τῇ κατασχέσει τῶν ἐθνῶν

7:6,29 πάροικον ἐν γῇ ἀλλοτρίᾳ; πάροικος ἐν γῇ Μαδιάμ

7:6,19,34 κακώσουσιν; ἐκάκωσεν; τὴν κάκωσιν τοῦ λαοῦ

7:7,45 τὸ ἔθνος; ἐν τῇ κατασχέσει τῶν ἐθνῶν

7:7,42 λατρεύσουσιν; λατρεύειν

7:7,33,49 ἐν τῷ τόπῳ τούτῳ; ὁ ... τόπος; τόπος τῆς καταπαύσεώς μου, also 6:13,14

7:10,34 ἐξείλατο; ἐξελέσθαι

7:10,18 ἐναντίον Φαραὼ βασιλέως Αἰγύπτου; βασιλεὺς ἕτερος ἐπ' Αἴγυπτον

7:13,19 τὸ γένος 'Ιωσήφ; τὸ γένος ἡμῶν

7:15,34 κατέβη 'Ιακώβ; κατέβην

7:17,34 ὁ λαός; τὴν κάκωσιν τοῦ λαοῦ μου; also 6:8,12

7:18,40 οὐκ ᾔδει; οὐκ οἴδαμεν

7:22,41 ἔργοις αὐτοῦ; ἐν τοῖς ἔργοις τῶν χειρῶν αὐτῶν

7:23,39 ἐπὶ τὴν καρδίαν αὐτοῦ; ἐν ταῖς καρδίαις αὐτῶν; also 7:51,54

7:23,37 τοὺς ἀδελφοὺς αὐτοῦ τοὺς υἱοὺς 'Ισραήλ; τοῖς υἱοῖς 'Ισραήλ ... ἐκ τῶν ἀδελφῶν ὑμῶν

7:25,35 διὰ χειρὸς αὐτοῦ; σὺν χειρὶ ἀγγέλου

7:25,38 δίδωσιν; δοῦναι; also 7:5,8,10

7:27,39 ἀπώσατο; ἀπώσαντο

7:28,39 θέλεις; οὐκ ἠθέλησαν

7:30,35 ὤφθη αὐτῷ ... ἄγγελος ἐν φλογὶ πυρὸς βάτου; σὺν χειρὶ ἀγγέλου τοῦ ὀφθέντος αὐτῷ ἐν τῇ βάτῳ

7:30,38 ὤφθη αὐτῷ ἐν τῇ ἐρήμῳ τοῦ ὄρους Σινὰ ἄγγελος; μετὰ τοῦ ἀγγέλου τοῦ λαλοῦντος αὐτῷ ἐν τῷ ὄρει Σινά

7:36,42 ἔτη τεσσεράκοντα; ἔτη τεσσεράκοντα; also 7:23,30

7:38,59 ἐδέξατο; δέξαι

7:39,42 ἐστράφησαν; ἔστρεψεν

7:44,53 διετάξατο; εἰς διαταγὰς ἀγγέλων

7:52;8:1 οὐκ ἐδίωξαν; διωγμὸς μέγας

b. Proper Names and Titles

θεός 6:2,7,11; 7:2,6,7,9,17,20,25,32,32,35,37,(40),42,(43), 45,46,46,55,55,56

Στέφανος 6:5,8,9; 7:59; 8:2

ἐν 'Ιερουσαλήμ 6:7; ἐν 'Ιεροσολύμοις 8:1

Μωϋσῆς 6:11,14; 7:20,22,29,31,32,35,37,40,44

'Ιησοῦς 6:14; 7:55,59

'Αβραάμ 7:2,16,17,32

Χαρράν 7:2,4

'Ισαάκ 7:8,8,32

'Ιακώβ 7:8,8,12,14,15,32,46

'Ιωσήφ 7:9,13,13,14,18

Αἴγυπτος 7:9,10,10,11,12,15,17,18,34,34,36,39,40

Φαραώ 7:10,13,21

Συχέμ 7:16,16

Αἰγύπτιος 7:22,24,28

υἱοὶ 'Ισραήλ 7:23,37; οἶκος 'Ισραήλ 7:42

ὄρος Σινά 7:30,38

κύριος 7:31,33,49,59,60

Σαῦλος 7:58; 8:1,3

c. Synonymous Terms, Phrases, and Proper Names[4]

6:1	γογγυσμός; παρεθεωροῦντο
6:1,2,3	ἐν τῇ διακονίᾳ τῇ καθημερινῇ; διακονεῖν τραπέζαις; ἐπὶ τῆς χρείας ταύτης
6:2,6	οἱ δώδεκα; ἐνώπιον τῶν ἀποστόλων
6:2,5,7	τὸ πλῆθος; παντὸς τοῦ πλήθους; ὁ ἀριθμός; πολύς ... ὄχλος
6:2,4,6	τὸν λόγον τοῦ θεοῦ; τῇ προσευχῇ καὶ τῇ διακονίᾳ τοῦ λόγου; προσευξάμενοι
6:3,5-6	ἐπισκέψασθε; ἐξελέξαντο ... οὓς ἔστησαν ἐνώπιον
6:3,5	ἑπτά; [7 proper names]
6:3,5,8	πλήρεις πνεύματος καὶ σοφίας; πλήρη πίστεως καὶ πνεύματος ἁγίου; πλήρης χάριτος καὶ δυνάμεως
6:3,6	οὓς καταστήσομεν; ἐπέθηκαν αὐτοῖς τὰς χεῖρας
6:7	ηὔξανεν; ἐπληθύνετο
6:8	τέρατα; σημεῖα μεγάλα
6:11,13	ὑπέβαλον ἄνδρας λέγοντας; ἔστησάν τε μάρτυρας ψευδεῖς λέγοντας
6:11,13	λαγοῦντος ῥήματα βλάσφημα εἰς; λαλῶν ῥήματα κατά
6:11,13,14	εἰς Μωϋσῆν καὶ τὸν θεόν; κατὰ τοῦ τόπου τοῦ ἁγίου τούτου καὶ τοῦ νόμου; τὸν τόπον τοῦτον ... τὰ ἔθη ἃ παρέδωκεν ... Μωϋσῆς
7:2,3,4	ἐν τῇ Μεσοποταμίᾳ; ἐκ τῆς γῆς σου; ἐκ γῆς Χαλδαίων
7:5	ἔδωκεν αὐτῷ κληρονομίαν ἐν αὐτῇ; δοῦναι αὐτῷ εἰς κατάσχεσιν αὐτήν
7:5	τῷ σπέρματι αὐτοῦ; αὐτῷ τέκνου
7:6	δουλώσουσιν; κακώσουσιν
7:11	λιμὸς ἐφ' ὅλην; θλῖψις μεγάλη
7:11,12	χορτάσματα; σιτία
7:13	ἀνεγωρίσθη; φανερὸν ἐγένετο
7:13	τοῖς ἀδελφοῖς αὐτοῦ; τὸ γένος 'Ιωσήφ
7:17	ηὔξησεν ὁ λαός; ἐπληθύνθη
7:19	τὸ γένος ἡμῶν; τοὺς πατέρας
7:21	ἀνείλατο; ἀνεθρέψατα ... ἑαυτῇ
7:24	ἠμύνατο; ἐποίησεν ἐκδίκησιν

---

[4]This category is described by Cadbury ("Four Features," p. 92) as "the habit of combining synonyms in pairs" and is further characterized by him as being a feature of Greek style.

7:25,35	σωτηρίαν; λυτρωτήν
7:31,32	ἐθαύμαζεν; ἔντρομος δὲ γενόμενος
7:34	τὴν κάκωσιν τοῦ λαοῦ; τοῦ στεναγμοῦ αὐτοῦ
7:36	τέρατα; σημεῖα
7:39	οὐκ ἠθέλησαν ὑπήκοοι γενέσθαι; ἀπώσαντο
7:41	ἐμοσχοποίησαν; τῷ εἰδώλῳ; ἐν τοῖς ἔργοις τῶν χειρῶν αὐτῶν
7:42,43	λατρεύειν; προσκυνεῖν
7:42,43	τῇ στρατιᾷ τοῦ οὐρανοῦ; τὸ ἄστρον τοῦ θεοῦ ὑμῶν Ῥαιφάν
7:42	σφάγια; θυσίας
7:48,49	ὁ ὕψιστος; κύριος
7:51	σκληροτράχηλοι; ἀπερίτμητοι καρδίαις καὶ τοῖς ὠσίν
7:52	τῶν προφητῶν; τοὺς προκαταγγείλαντας
7:52	ἐδίωξαν; ἀπέκτειναν
7:52	προδόται; φονεῖς
7:54	διεπρίοντο ταῖς καρδίαις αὐτῶν; ἔβρυχον τοὺς ὀδόντας ἐπ' αὐτόν
7:57,60	κράξαντες δὲ φωνῇ μεγάλῃ; συνέσχον τὰ ὦτα αὐτῶν
7:59	ἐπικαλούμενον; λέγοντα
7:59,60	κύριε Ἰησοῦ; κύριε

d. <u>Substantive Followed by Apposition</u>

6:3	ἄνδρας ἐξ ὑμῶν - μαρτυρουμένους ἑπτά
6:5	Στέφανον - ἄνδρα πλήρη
6:5	Νικόλαον - προσήλυτον Ἀντιοχέα
6:9	ἐκ τῆς συναγωγῆς - τῆς λεγομένης Λιβερτίνων
6:14	Ἰησοῦς - ὁ Ναζωραῖος οὗτος
7:2	τῷ πατρὶ ἡμῶν - Ἀβραάμ
7:5	κληρονομίαν ἐν αὐτῇ - οὐδὲ βῆμα ποδός
7:14	Ἰακὼβ - τὸν πατέρα αὐτοῦ
7:23	τοὺς ἀδελφοὺς αὐτοῦ - τοὺς υἱοὺς Ἰσραήλ
7:32	ὁ θεὸς τῶν πατέρων σου - ὁ θεὸς Ἀβραὰμ καὶ Ἰσαὰκ καὶ Ἰακώβ
7:34	τοῦ λαοῦ μου - τοῦ ἐν Αἰγύπτῳ
7:35	σὺν χειρὶ ἀγγέλου - τοῦ ὀφθέντος αὐτῷ ἐν τῇ βάτῳ
7:38	μετὰ τοῦ ἀγγέλου - τοῦ λαλοῦντος αὐτῷ ἐν τῷ ὄρει Σινά
7:43	τὴν σκηνὴν ... καὶ τὸ ἄστρον... - τοὺς τύπους ...
7:58	παρὰ τοὺς πόδας νεανίου - καλουμένου Σαύλου
8:1	ἐπὶ τὴν ἐκκλησίαν - τὴν ἐν Ἱεροσολύμοις

Also to be Added here is the Appositional Adjective: πλήρης

6:3 ἄνδρας ἐξ ὑμῶν ... - πλήρεις πνεύματος καὶ σοφίας

6:5 ἄνδρα - πλήρη πίστεως καὶ πνεύματος ἁγίου

6:8 Στέφανος δὲ - πλήρης χάριτος καὶ δυνάμεως

Lexical repetition--by far the most discernible of the categories--plays a major role in the author's method of composition. From the above lists, it is clear that we are dealing with more than the chance repetition of a few words and roots. Indeed, the use of cognate terms or synonymous expressions in close succession is characteristic of the entire Stephen story. This is obviously a preferred technique of the writer. A number of general observations are called for at this point.

The large number of doublets (words, terms, roots) occurring in the Stephen material is truly unusual. Of added significance, though, is the fact that many occur only once in the immediate context of the Stephen speech, the book of Acts itself, or even in the entire NT. This phenomenon seems to indicate the importance of particular expressions in relation to given themes and episodes. More fundamentally, such stylistic features demonstrate the writer's inclination to employ double expressions: repetition of the same word, same or similar idea, contrasting concepts. Far from being an occasional feature of composition, repetitiveness in the form of doublets and more complex structures constitutes a major stylistic characteristic of the author.

In light of the author's preference for doublets, the occurrence throughout the Stephen material of various cognates, expressions, and names--not very convincing in themselves--take on added importance. Further analysis will make clear that the majority of these reiterated elements bear a significant relation to the central themes of the story.

The frequency and variety of lexical repetition, then, apart from their functional and structural purpose, clearly demonstrate a characteristic feature of the author. His need to imitate, to contrast, and to clarify is related to his stylistic tendencies and preferences, among others, his constant repetition of lexical elements throughout his text.

3. Categories Relating to a Variety of Patterns

a. Parallelismus Membrorum[5]

6:7 καὶ ἐπληθύνετο ὁ ἀριθμὸς τῶν μαθητῶν ἐν Ἰερουσαλὴμ
σφόδρα
πολύς τε ὄχλος τῶν ἱερέων ὑπήκουον τῇ πίστει

6:13 ἔστησάν τε μάρτυρας ψευδεῖς λέγοντας·
ὁ ἄνθρωπος οὗτος οὐ παύεται λαλῶν ῥήματα κατὰ τοῦ
τόπου τοῦ ἁγίου τούτου
καὶ τοῦ νόμου·

6:14 ἀκηκόαμεν γὰρ αὐτοῦ λέγοντος ὅτι
Ἰησοῦς ὁ Ναζωραῖος οὗτος καταλύσει τὸν τόπον
τοῦτον
καὶ ἀλλάξει τὰ ἔθη ἃ παρέδωκεν ἡμῖν Μωϋσῆς.

7:5 καὶ οὐκ ἔδωκεν αὐτῷ κληρονομίαν ἐν αὐτῇ
οὐδὲ βῆμα ποδός
καὶ ἐπηγγείλατο δοῦναι αὐτῷ εἰς κατάσχεσιν αὐτὴν καὶ
τῷ σπέρματι αὐτοῦ μετ' αὐτόν
οὐκ ὄντος αὐτῷ τέκνου

7:13 ἀνεγνωρίσθη Ἰωσὴφ τοῖς ἀδελφοῖς αὐτοῦ
καὶ φανερὸν ἐγένετο τῷ Φαραὼ τὸ γένος Ἰωσήφ

7:19 οὗτος κατασοφισάμενος τὸ γένος ἡμῶν
ἐκάκωσεν τοὺς πατέρας

7:21 ἀνείλατο αὐτὸν ἡ θυγάτηρ Φαραὼ
καὶ ἀνεθρέψατο αὐτὸν ἑαυτῇ εἰς υἱόν

7:24 καὶ ἰδών τινα ἀδικούμενον ἠμύνατο
καὶ ἐποίησεν ἐκδίκησεν τῷ καταπονουμένῳ

7:34 ἰδὼν εἶδον τὴν κάκωσιν τοῦ λαοῦ μου τοῦ ἐν Αἰγύπτῳ
καὶ τοῦ στεναγμοῦ αὐτοῦ ἤκουσα

---

[5]The article of Olof Linton, "Le _Parallelismus Membrorum_ dans le nouveau testament, simple remarques," in _Mélanges bibliques en hommage au R. P. Béda Rigaux_, eds. A. Descamps and A. de Halleux (Gembloux: Duculot, 1970), pp. 489-507, has been most helpful in the study of this stylistic phenomenon even though no reference is made to Acts or the occurrence there of parallelismus membrorum. See also Cadbury, "Four Features," pp. 92-93 and Morgenthaler, _Geschichtsschreibung_, 1:64-67. The latter's _Doppelsätze_ examples (pp. 48-80) provided considerable assistance in formulating the structural categories.

7:35 τίς σε κατέστησεν ἄρχοντα καὶ δικαστήν
τοῦτον ὁ θεὸς καὶ ἄρχοντα καὶ λυτρωτὴν ἀπέσταλκεν

7:49 ὁ οὐρανός μοι θρόνος
ἡ δὲ γῆ ὑποπόδιον τῶν ποδῶν μου

7:49 ποῖον οἶκον οἰκοδομήσετέ μοι, λέγει κύριος
ἢ τίς τόπος τῆς καταπαύσεως μου;

7:52 τίνα τῶν προφητῶν οὐκ ἐδίωξαν οἱ πατέρες ὑμῶν
καὶ ἀπέκτειναν τοὺς προκαταγγείλαντας περὶ τῆς
ἐλεύσεως τοῦ δικαίου

7:54 διεπρίοντο ταῖς καρδίαις αὐτῶν
καὶ ἔβρυχον τοὺς ὀδόντας ἐπ' αὐτόν

7:55 ἀτενίσας εἰς τὸν οὐρανόν
εἶδεν δόξαν θεοῦ
καὶ Ἰησοῦν ἑστῶτα ἐκ δεξιῶν τοῦ θεοῦ,
7:56 καὶ εἶπεν·
ἰδοὺ θεωρῶ τοὺς οὐρανοὺς διηνοιγμένους
καὶ υἱὸν τοῦ ἀνθρώπου ἐκ δεξιῶν ἑστῶτα τοῦ θεοῦ.

7:59 καὶ ἐλιθοβόλουν τὸν Στέφανον,
ἐπικαλούμενον καὶ λέγοντα·
κύριε Ἰησοῦ, δέξαι τὸ πνεῦμά μου.
7:60 θεὶς δὲ τὰ γόνατα
ἔκραξεν φωνῇ μεγάλῃ·
κύριε, μὴ στήσῃς αὐτοῖς ταύτην τὴν ἁμαρτίαν.

8:2 συνεκόμισαν δὲ τὸν Στέφανον ἄνδρες εὐλαβεῖς
καὶ ἐποίησαν κοπετὸν μέγαν ἐπ' αὐτῷ

b. Formulaic Repetition

Time Formulae

6:1 ἐν δὲ ταῖς ἡμέραις ταύταις
7:41 ἐν ταῖς ἡμέραις ἐκείναις
8:1 ἐν ἐκείνῃ τῇ ἡμέρᾳ

7:2 πρὶν ἢ κατοικῆσαι αὐτὸν ἐν Χαρράν
7:4 μετὰ τὸ ἀποθανεῖν τὸν πατέρα αὐτοῦ

7:8 τῇ ἡμέρᾳ τῇ ὀγδόῃ
7:26 τῇ τε ἐπιούσῃ ἡμέρᾳ

7:17	καθὼς δὲ ἤγγιζεν ὁ χρόνος τῆς ἐπαγγελίας	
7:23	ὡς δὲ ἐπληροῦτο αὐτῷ τεσσερακονταέτης χρόνος	
7:23	ὡς δὲ ἐπληροῦτο αὐτῷ τεσσερακονταέτης χρόνος	
7:30	καὶ πληρωθέντων ἐτῶν τεσσεράκοντα	
7:30	καὶ πληρωθέντων ἐτῶν τεσσεράκοντα	
7:36	ἔτη τεσσεράκοντα	
7:42	ἔτη τεσσεράκοντα	

Formulae Introducing Speech

6:11	ἄνδρας λέγοντας ὅτι	
6:13	μάρτυρας ψευδεῖς λέγοντας	
6:14	ἀκηκόαμεν γὰρ αὐτοῦ λέγοντος ὅτι	
7:1	εἶπεν δὲ ὁ ἀρχιερεύς	
7:2	ὁ δὲ ἔφη	
7:3	καὶ εἶπεν πρὸς αὐτόν	
7:6	ἐλάλησεν δὲ οὕτως ὁ θεός	
7:7	ὁ θεὸς εἶπεν	
7:26	συνήλλασσεν ... εἰπών	
7:27	ὁ δὲ ἀδικῶν ... ἀπώσατο αὐτὸν εἰπών	
7:35	ἠρνήσαντο εἰπόντες	
7:37	ὁ Μωϋσῆς ὁ εἴπας τοῖς υἱοῖς Ἰσραήλ	
7:39-40	ἐστράφησαν ... εἰπόντες τῷ Ἀαρών	
7:31	ἐγένετο φωνὴ κυρίου	
7:33	εἶπεν δὲ αὐτῷ ὁ κύριος	
7:49	λέγει κύριος	
7:42	καθὼς γέγραπται ἐν βίβλῳ τῶν προφητῶν	
7:48	καθὼς ὁ προφήτης λέγει	
7:49	λέγει κύριος	
7:56	καὶ εἶπεν	
7:59	ἐπικαλούμενον καὶ λέγοντα	
7:60	ἔκραξεν φωνῇ μεγάλῃ	

c. Local Expressions Introducing and Concluding Episodes

6:5	προσήλυτον Ἀντιοχέα	entire Stephen story
8:1	χώρας τῆς Ἰουδαίας καὶ Σαμαρείας	
6:7	ἐν Ἰερουσαλήμ	entire Stephen story
8:1	τὴν ἐν Ἱεροσολύμοις	

7:2	ἐν Χαρράν	God's command
7:4	ἐν Χαρράν	
7:9	εἰς Αἴγυπτον	Joseph story
7:15	εἰς Αἴγυπτον	
7:12	εἰς Αἴγυπτον	Jacob episode
7:15	εἰς Αἴγυπτον	
7:16	εἰς Συχέμ	burial episode
7:16	ἐν Συχέμ	
7:17	ἐν Αἰγύπτῳ	period of enslavement
7:34	εἰς Αἴγυπτον	
7:34	τοῦ ἐν Αἰγύπτῳ	vocation of Moses
7:34	εἰς Αἴγυπτον	
7:36	ἐν γῇ Αἰγύπτῳ	thematic excursus
7:39	εἰς Αἴγυπτον	
7:42	τῇ στρατιᾷ τοῦ οὐρανοῦ	thematic section
7:49	ὁ οὐρανός μοι θρόνος	

d. Lists

6:3 πνεύματος καὶ σοφίας
6:4 τῇ προσευχῇ καὶ τῇ διακονίᾳ
6:5 Στέφανον ... καὶ Φίλιππον καὶ Πρόχορον καὶ Νικάνορα καὶ Τίμωνα καὶ Πορμενᾶν καὶ Νικόλαον
6:5 πίστεως καὶ πνεύματος ἁγίου
6:8 χάριτος καὶ δυνάμεως
6:8 τέρατα καὶ σημεῖα μεγάλα
6:9 τινες τῶν ἐκ τῆς συναγωγῆς ... καὶ τῶν ἀπό ...
6:9 τῆς λεγομένης Λιβερτίνων καὶ Κυρηναίων καὶ Ἀλεξανδέων
6:9 τῶν ἀπὸ Κιλικίας καὶ Ἀσίας
6:10 τῇ σοφίᾳ καὶ τῷ πνεύματι
6:11 εἰς Μωϋσῆν καὶ τὸν θεόν
6:12 τὸν λαὸν καὶ τοὺς πρεσβυτέρους καὶ τοὺς γραμματεῖς
6:13 κατὰ τοῦ τόπου τοῦ ἁγίου τούτου καὶ τοῦ νόμου
7:3 ἐκ τῆς γῆς σου καὶ τῆς συγγενείας σου
7:5 αὐτῷ ... καὶ τῷ σπέρματι αὐτοῦ
7:10 χάριν καὶ σοφίαν
7:10 ἐπ' Αἴγυπτον καὶ ἐφ' ὅλον τὸν οἶκον αὐτοῦ
7:11 ἐφ' ὅλην τὴν Αἴγυπτον καὶ Χανάαν

7:14 Ἰακὼβ τὸν πατέρα αὐτοῦ καὶ πᾶσαν τὴν συγγένειαν
7:15 αὐτὸς καὶ οἱ πατέρες ἡμῶν
7:22 ἐν λόγοις καὶ ἔργοις αὐτοῦ
7:27 ἄρχοντα καὶ δικαστήν
7:32 ὁ θεὸς Ἀβραὰμ καὶ Ἰσαὰκ καὶ Ἰακώβ
7:35 ἄρχοντα καὶ δικαστήν
7:35 ἄρχοντα καὶ λυτρωτήν
7:36 τέρατα καὶ σημεῖα
7:36 ἐν γῇ Αἰγύπτῳ καὶ ἐν ἐρυθρᾷ θαλάσσῃ καὶ ἐν τῇ ἐρήμῳ
7:38 ἐν τῇ ἐκκλησίᾳ ἐν τῇ ἐρήμῳ
7:38 μετὰ τοῦ ἀγγέλου ... καὶ τῶν πατέρων ἡμῶν
7:42 σφάγια καὶ θυσίας
7:43 τὴν σκηνὴν τοῦ Μόλοχ καὶ τὸ ἄστρον τοῦ θεοῦ ὑμῶν Ῥαιφάν
7:51 Σκληροτράχηλοι καὶ ἀπερίτμητοι
7:51 καρδίαις καὶ τοῖς ὠσίν
7:51 ὡς οἱ πατέρες ὑμῶν καὶ ὑμεῖς
7:52 προδόται καὶ φονεῖς
7:55 δόξαν θεοῦ καὶ Ἰησοῦν ἑστῶτα
7:56 τοὺς οὐρανούς ... καὶ τὸν υἱὸν τοῦ ἀνθρώπου
7:59 ἐπικαλούμενον καὶ λέγοντα
8:1 τὰς χώρας τῆς Ἰουδαίας καὶ Σαμαρείας
8:3 ἄνδρας καὶ γυναῖκας

e. <u>Sequential Patterns</u>

6:1 πληθυνόντων
6:2 τὸ πλῆθος τῶν μαθητῶν
6:5 ἐνώπιον παντὸς τοῦ πλήθους
6:7 ἐπληθύνετο

6:1 τῶν μαθητῶν
6:2 τὸ πλῆθος τῶν μαθητῶν
6:5 παντὸς τοῦ πλήθους
6:7 ὁ ἀριθμὸς τῶν μαθητῶν

6:2 ἡμᾶς
6:3 ἐξ ὑμῶν
6:4 ἡμεῖς

6:3 πλήρεις πνεύματος καὶ σοφίας
6:5 πλήρη πίστεως καὶ πνεύματος ἁγίου
6:7 τῇ πίστει
6:10 τῇ σοφίᾳ καὶ τῷ πνεύματι

7:55 πλήρης πνεύματος ἁγίου

6:11 ῥήματα βλάσφημα εἰς Μωϋσῆν καὶ τὸν θεόν
6:13 ῥήματα κατὰ τοῦ τόπου τοῦ ἁγίου τούτου καὶ τοῦ νόμου
6:14 Ἰησοῦς ὁ Ναζωραῖος οὗτος καταλύσει τὸν τόπον τοῦτον
καὶ ἀλλάξει τὰ ἔθη ἃ παρέδωκεν ἡμῖν Μωϋσῆς

7:2 ἐν τῇ Μεσοποταμίᾳ ... κατοικῆσαι ... ἐν Χαρράν
7:4 ἐκ γῆς Χαλδαίων κατῴκησεν ἐν Χαρράν

7:8 ἐγέννησεν τὸν Ισαάκ
7:8 καὶ Ἰσαὰκ τὸν Ἰακώβ
7:8 καὶ Ἰακὼβ τοὺς δώδεκα πατριάρχας
7:9 καὶ οἱ πατριάρχαι

7:10 ἐναντίον Φαραὼ βασιλέως Αἰγύπτου
7:13 τῷ Φαραώ
7:18 βασιλεὺς ἕτερος ἐπ᾽ Αἴγυπτον
7:21 ἡ θυγάτηρ Φαραώ

7:12 πρῶτον
7:13 καὶ ἐν τῷ δευτέρῳ

7:27 ἀπώσατο αὐτόν
7:39 ἀπώσαντο καὶ ἐστράφησαν
7:42 ἔστρεψεν δὲ ὁ θεός

7:51 ὑμεῖς
7:51 οἱ πατέρες ὑμῶν
7:51 ὑμεῖς
7:52 οἱ πατέρες ὑμῶν
7:52 ὑμεῖς

7:57 ἐπ᾽ αὐτόν
7:58 νεανίου καλουμένου Σαύλου
7:59 τὸν Στέφανον
8:1 Σαῦλος
8:2 τὸν Στέφανον
8:3 Σαῦλος

f. Double Clusters

6:1 πληθυνόντων τῶν μαθητῶν
6:2-4 οἱ δώδεκα τὸ πλῆθος τῶν μαθητῶν
οὐκ ἀρεστόν ἐστιν ἡμᾶς
τὸν λόγον τοῦ θεοῦ

ἐπισκέψασθε ... ἄνδρας ἐξ ὑμῶν
μαρτυρουμένους ἑπτά
πλήρεις πνεύματος καὶ σοφίας
οὓς καταστήσομεν
τῇ προσευχῇ καὶ τῇ διακονίᾳ τοῦ λόγου

6:5-7a καὶ ἤρεσεν ὁ λόγος ἐνώπιον παντὸς τοῦ πλήθους
καὶ ἐξελέξαντο ... ἄνδρα πλήρη πίστεως καὶ πνεύματος ἁγίου
(names of 7 men elected)
προσήλυτον Ἀντιοχέα
οὓς ἔστησαν ἐνώπιον τῶν ἀποστόλων
καὶ προσευξάμενοι ἐπέθηκαν αὐτοῖς τὰς χεῖρας
καὶ ὁ λόγος τοῦ θεοῦ

6:7b ἐπληθύνετο ὁ ἀριθμὸς τῶν μαθητῶν

6:11
6:13 (accusations)

6:13,15 καὶ τοῦ νόμου ... ὡσεὶ πρόσωπον ἀγγέλου

6:15-7:2 καὶ ἀτενίσαντες εἰς ... εἶδον τὸ πρόσωπον
εἰ ταῦτα οὕτως ἔχει;
ἀκούσατε
ὁ θεὸς τῆς δόξης

7:53 τὸν νόμον εἰς διαταγὰς ἀγγέλων

7:54-5 ἀκούοντες δὲ ταῦτα
ἀτενίσας εἰς ... εἶδεν δόξαν θεοῦ καὶ Ἰησοῦν

7:2
7:4 see sequential patterns

7:5-6 καὶ ἐπηγγείλατο δοῦναι αὐτῷ ... καὶ τῷ σπέρματι αὐτοῦ
ἐλάλησεν δὲ οὕτως ὁ θεός
ὅτι ἔσται τὸ σπέρμα αὐτοῦ πάροικον ἐν γῇ ἀλλοτρίᾳ
καὶ κακώσουσιν

7:17,19 ὁ χρόνος τῆς ἐπαγγελίας ἧς ὡμολόγησεν ὁ θεὸς τῷ Ἀβραάμ
ηὔξησεν ὁ λαὸς καὶ ἐπληθύνθη ἐν Αἰγύπτῳ
ἐκάκωσεν τοὺς πατέρας

7:6 ἔσται τὸ σπέρμα αὐτοῦ πάροικον ἐν γῇ ἀλλοτρίᾳ

7:29 καὶ ἐγένετο πάροικος ἐν γῇ Μαδιάμ οὗ ἐγέννησεν υἱοὺς δύο

7:17-9 ηὔξησεν ὁ λαὸς καὶ ἐπληθύνθη ἐν Αἰγύπτῳ
ἀνέστη βασιλεὺς ἕτερος ἐπ' Αἴγυπτον
ἐκάκωσεν

7:34 εἶδον τὴν κάκωσιν τοῦ λαοῦ μου τοῦ ἐν Αἰγύπτῳ
ἀποστείλω σε εἰς Αἴγυπτον

7:25,27 ὁ θεὸς διὰ χειρὸς αὐτοῦ δίδωσιν σωτηρίαν αὐτοῖς
ἀπώσατο αὐτόν
εἰπών· τίς σε κατέστησεν ἄρχοντα καὶ δικαστὴν ἐφ' ἡμῶν;

7:35 ὃν ἠρνήσαντο
εἰπόντες· τίς σε κατέστησεν ἄρχοντα καὶ δικαστήν;
τοῦτον ὁ θεὸς καὶ ἄρχοντα καὶ λυτρωτὴν ἀπέσταλκεν
σὺν χειρὶ ἀγγέλου

7:31-32b Μωϋσῆς ... ἐθαύμαζεν ... κατανοῆσαι
ἐγένετο φωνὴ κυρίου
(quotation)

7:32c-33 ἔντρομος δὲ γενόμενος Μωϋσῆς ... κατονῆσαι
εἶπεν δὲ αὐτῷ ὁ κύριος
(quotation)

7:36 οὗτος ἐξήγαγεν αὐτούς

7:40 ὁ γὰρ Μωϋσῆς οὗτος, ὃς ἐξήγαγεν ἡμᾶς

The appellation "categories relating to a variety of patterns" admittedly encompasses disparate elements of duality and repetition; none the less the concept of pattern is appropriate. Although more difficult to demonstrate than earlier examples, these categories are extremely important since they tend less to support the work of accidental combination of elements than to illustrate the conscious activity and intention of the author. Since inherently these phenomena are functional and structural, the present observations of a more descriptive nature will be summary in form.

Each category listed above illustrates or further supports a number of conclusions. There is no doubt that the author favors formulaic expressions. These are rarely abused, though, each formula generally being employed twice. Such patterns of use as combinations of terms and sequential patterns illustrate both the writer's intentional attempt to achieve variety and his inclination to employ repetition. The occurrence of lists of synonymous expressions, particularly the technique of parallelismus membrorum and the existence of double clusters of repeated elements, further supports the earlier conclusion that duality is a major characteristic of the author's style. The dual use of local expressions to introduce and conclude episodes, while of great structural significance, requires the same judgment. The import of the category listed as "double clusters" suggests a vital area of study, namely, the relation of these elements to the themes of the Stephen story and, as a consequence, to the conclusions which can be drawn regarding the structure of the entire episode.

This ends the presentation of stylistic data which relate to duality. The observations and conclusions have been kept to a minimum since the immediate goal was presentation of a corpus of data to serve as basis for analysis throughout this chapter.

B. Stylistic Data Within the Speech

Analysis of the discourse has permitted me to observe a variety of stylistic and redactive tendencies which should be credited to the author of Acts. These features are particularly evident in the speech, so it is at this point that the investigation of their role and function within the composition will begin.

1. Distribution

Far from being a peculiarity of any specific section of the text, the characteristics referred to are persistently employed throughout the speech. The repetition of cognate expressions (category 2.a) is particularly striking in this regard, since this technique appears both within consecutive blocks of material and within different sections of the speech. In like manner stylistic features, formulae, lists, etc., are found throughout.

The distribution of these features merits particular attention. On the one hand a large number of the categories listed above pertain to dual or multiple elements which occur in close proximity. Indeed, for many of these, nearness constitutes an essential element: verb followed by cognate substantive, redundancy, substantive followed by apposition, parallelismus membrorum, lists, etc. For others it comprises an important factor in recognizing and especially in accepting constructions such as singular/plural, negative/positive contrasts, synonymous terms, and sequential patterns. Aside from the proximity required by the nature of the categories under discussion, it should be noted that the occurrence of dual or multiple elements within consecutive blocks of material and also the frequency of these patterns argue for structural and stylistic conclusions. Their distribution, then, is due to specific tendencies of the author's method of composition.

On the other hand one is impressed, as a result of systematic analysis, by another aspect of the distribution of these features, that is, their occurrence in different parts of the speech. Some terms, striking per se, are rendered doubly so by their twofold use within the speech (e.g., κατάσχεσις 5 and 45; πάροικος 6 and 29; ἐπαγγέλλω 5 and 17, etc.). Some occur in double clusters (category 3.f); some in apparently significant structural contexts (3.c local expressions introducing and concluding episodes); others in contrasting episodes (27 ἀπώσατο and 37 ἀπώσαντο).

In the following analysis, then, the stylistic data will be examined in relation to their distribution within the discourse. This factor will shed considerable light both upon the nature and the function of the various constructions being studied.

2. Nature and Function

Earlier in this chapter several lists of data were presented to serve as a basis for further study. My purpose, at this point, is to examine these to arrive at a better idea of the essential character or nature of the constructions employed by the author and, in light of this, to investigate their function within the discourse. Since the distribution of these throughout various parts of the speech has a direct bearing upon their basic make-up and role, I will proceed accordingly.

a. Within Consecutive Blocks of Material

1) Vv.2-8

The first section of the speech introduces one immediately to a host of stylistic features and patterns. Therefore, to begin this part of the study, attention should be drawn to the important data given above. The following categories should be noted:

1.b Compound verb followed by same preposition (7:3), (4)
1.c Singular/plural (6,7)
1.d Redundancy (2,3,4,5), (3), (4,5)
1.e Negative/positive (4,5), (5), (5)
2.a Cognate expressions (2,4), (3,4,4,6), (5), (5,6), (6,7), (8)
2.b Proper names (2,6,7), (2,4), (8), (8)
2.c Synonymous terms (2,3,4), (5), (5), (6)
2.d Substantive followed by apposition (2), (5)
3.a Parallelismus membrorum (5)
3.b Formulaic repetition: time (2,4); speech (3,6,7)
3.c Local expressions introducing and concluding episodes (2,4)
3.d Lists (3), (5)
3.e Sequential patterns (2,4), (8)
3.f Double clusters (2,4)

It is clear from this list that duality, repetition, and stylistic patterns play an important role in the author's method of composition. This is true from a strictly numerical point of view. The writer for many reasons uses the same, similar or parallel terms or structures, and does this consistently.

Attention should be drawn to four structural units within vv.2-8. 1) Vv.2-4 present a well-defined construction:

Appearance of God
    in Mesopotamia
    before dwelling in Harran
Quotation: command -- Go out . . .
[Response]
    move out of land of Chaldeans
    dwell in Harran.

This unit is particularly interesting--only here does Harran occur (twice) in the NT--since the pattern is one of inclusion framing the direct command from God, and since the main function of this structure seems to be directly related to the author's purpose here: the accomplishment of the divine imperative. 2) V.5 betrays a number of stylistic tendencies. The entire verse, "God did not give . . . ," is a polemical statement in direct response to the ending of v.4 (the land where the audience of the speech dwells).[6] Employing his καί-style

[6]This clearly invalidates the position of some modern commentators who insist that the first part of the speech, generally referring to 7:2-34, is nonpolemic or neutral. See Dibelius, "Speeches in Acts," p. 167: "It is not until 7.35 that we sense any polemic interest. From 2-34 the point of the speech is not obvious at all; we are simply given an account of the history of Israel. . . . This change from historical review to controversy becomes quite clear from 7.35 onwards . . ."

the author, making abundant use of the OT text, constructs a well-balanced parallelismus membrorum:

> καὶ οὐκ ἔδωκεν αὐτῷ κληρονομίαν ἐν αὐτῇ
> οὐδὲ βῆμα ποδός
> καὶ ἐπηγγείλατο δοῦναι αὐτῷ εἰς κατάσχεσιν αὐτὴν
> καὶ τῷ σπέρματι αὐτοῦ μετ' αὐτόν
> οὐκ ὄντος αὐτῷ τέκνου.

Such features of the verse as a negative statement followed by negative apposition, negative/positive contrast, double indirect object (the second of which is modified by a negative genitive absolute) are a clear indication of the writer's stylistic dexterity. The word order of the second member of the parallel has been modeled upon that of the first (see pp. 47-48). 3) The long quotation of vv.6-7 (Gn 15:13-14) is presented within the framework of a double speech formula: the first introduces the quotation, the second is inserted toward the end of the OT text. In effect, the structure is identical to that of 7:48-50, quoting Is 66:1-2:

6 ἐλάλησεν δὲ οὕτως ὁ θεός	48 καθὼς ὁ προφήτης λέγει
quotation	quotation
7 ὁ θεὸς εἶπεν	49 λέγει κύριος
end of quotation	end of quotation.[7]

4) Employing the καί-style once more, the writer introduces five brief clauses as a conclusion to the Abraham episode. Aside from the double reference to circumcision and the parallel clauses of birth and circumcision, the overall structure is that of genealogical texts. Furthermore, the structure does double duty since both birth and circumcision are implied in the final clauses.

From a stylistic point of view, the frequent occurrence of the same or similar terms in close succession can best be described as a *mot-agraffe* technique, a feature which is very common throughout the speech. Within vv.2-8 particular note should be taken of the double use of "seed" in vv.5 and 6 and the root for "circumcision" in 8. In the latter a functional element is equally evident, namely, that of covenant/command and fulfilment.

---

[7]See the study of these texts on pp. 49-54.

Finally, it is necessary to dwell upon a more general concern of this part of the speech, one which is stylistic and structural as well as thematic. The overriding notions of "land/place" and "posterity" have influenced every aspect of the Abraham story. The terminology of vv.2-8 is a veritable lexicon describing or qualifying the principal themes of the author. The OT passages are chosen with these in mind ("land, seed, possession") or modified ("a land not theirs" > "a foreign land," "on this mountain" > "in this place") for thematic reasons. These two primary concerns of the author have greatly contributed to the preponderant use of doublets; however, they have left clear structural traces. It is with the notion of "posterity" that the author crowns the Abraham episode and introduces the great descendants of the patriarch. The idea of "place or land" claims a central and strategic position within vv.2-8: ". . . into the land which I will show you" (v.4); ". . . into this land in which you now dwell" (v.4); ". . . and they will serve me in this place" (v.7).

2) <u>Vv.9-16</u>

The second section of the speech likewise makes generous use of repetitive elements. The following categories of the corpus are germane to the discussion:

- 1.a Verb followed by cognate substantive (7:10), (10)
- 1.b Compound verb followed by the same preposition (10)
- 1.c Singular/plural (10,11), (13)
- 1.d Redundancy (9,10), (9,10,10,11,12), (15)
- 1.e Negative/positive (11,12)
- 2.a Cognate expressions (9,10), (10,11), (10,11), (11,12 15), (12,14), (16)
- 2.b Proper names (9,13,13,14), (10,10,11,12,15), (10,13), (12,14,15), (16,16)
- 2.c Synonymous terms (11), (11,12), (13), (13)
- 2.d Substantive followed by apposition (14)
- 3.a Parallelismus membrorum (13)
- 3.c Local expressions introducing and concluding episodes (9,15), (12,15), (16,16)
- 3.d Lists (10), (10), (11), (14), (15)
- 3.e Sequential patterns (12,13)

The data are both numerous and constant, while the structural and functional considerations are even more impressive.

Owing to the author's greater freedom in the use of the OT--the result no doubt of a more polemical intent--we find clearer and more abundant structural and stylistic features. The frequent use of inclusio (3.c) is particularly noteworthy, while the fivefold reference to Egypt is both consistent with the writer's thematic concern and stylistic tendency. The latter is further underscored by the repeated reference, albeit in close succession, of the names of Jacob (vv.14-15) and Joseph (13-14). Other stylistic features are more meaningfully considered in their structural context.

The entire Joseph episode is situated within a very definable framework, that is, the stark contrast between v.9 (the Patriarchs sell Joseph into Egypt) and vv.14 (Joseph calls for his father and kindred) and 15 (Jacob goes down into Egypt). The first component introduces a very negative evaluation of "the fathers'" role in the history of Israel. This accusation is rendered even more polemical by the author's use of Gn 45:5 where the selling into Egypt is attributed directly to the brothers, in lieu of the standard and less negative version of Gn 37. This polemical thrust is highlighted even further. After the introductory statement of v.9, the writer takes great pains to contrast, rather to the disadvantage of the brothers, the status of Joseph with that of the other sons of Jacob. Vv. 9b-11 present a remarkable structural and thematic unit:

Positive aspect: Joseph
- God was with him
- he delivered him from all his tribulations (ϑλῖψις)
- he gave him favor and wisdom before Pharaoh King of Egypt
- he appointed him ruler over Egypt and his whole house

Negative aspect: the Patriarchs
- [God was not with them]
- but there came a famine upon all Egypt and Canaan
- [there came] great tribulation (ϑλῖψις)
- the fathers were unable to find sustenance.

The interpretation of this text will be seen later, but it should be pointed out that the same line of argument is found in Dt 31:17 and Ps 36:19. Presently, it is the structural and stylistic aspect of the text which demands attention. The double use of ϑλῖψις (with plural/singular contrast) is notable, while the totally positive or negative tone of the two sections is even more remarkable (note the positive/negative contrast, "he gave him . . ." and "they were unable to find . . ."). This point constitutes a serious objection to Dibelius' contention that the beginning of the speech is lacking in polemics.[8] God is with Joseph, but he is not with "the fathers."

Two final observations should be made regarding the composition of vv.9-11. The positive and negative portions of the text are not without structural links. The word order of v.9a and 11c is such that "the patriarchs" and "our fathers" form an inclusion, introducing and terminating the polemical unit. Furthermore, the writer joins the two portions of his text by the postpositive δέ and a remarkable stylistic parallel:

10 . . . ἡγούμενον ἐπ' Αἴγυπτον
καὶ ἐφ' ὅλον τὸν οἶκον αὐτοῦ
11 . . . λιμὸς ἐφ' ὅλην την Αἴγυπτον
καὶ Χανάαν.[9]

Following this structural unit, whose function is unmistakably polemical, the author returns more directly in v.12 to the historical sequence of the OT narrative. However, it is the final clause of v.11 which both leads him back to his OT model and furnishes him with some of the elements of v.12: "our fathers" and "sustenance" which, under the influence of Gn 42:2 (σίτος), becomes "food" (σιτία).

The sequential pattern πρῶτον καὶ ἐν τῷ δευτέρῳ of vv.12-13 betrays the author's tendency to employ doublets, as well as his desire to summarize elements of the story which he chooses not to overlook.[10] This technique allows him to draw particular attention to the important concept of v.13, for which he reserves his most striking parallelismus membrorum:

---

[8]See note 6 above.

[9]It will be noted that ὅλος is employed only in these two instances in the Stephen story.

[10]The editors of Beginnings, 4:73, have proposed that the first and second meetings of Joseph and his brothers be seen as announcing the two advents of Jesus. To support this interpretation they note that Moses is successful in his mission not the first time but only forty years later, after the Sinai event. It is preferable to see here no more than a stylistic device of the author in his effort to summarize the historical narrative. Such a technique is understandable in light of the data given in the corpus. I would note, nevertheless, that the appeal to the Moses event by the editors has not been without effect on this analysis. But the significance of the dual role of Moses should be seen in terms of the author's style and purpose, i.e., singular/plural contrasts.

ἀνεγνωρίσθη 'Ιωσὴφ τοῖς ἀδελοῖς αὐτοῦ
καὶ φανερὸν ἐγένετο τῷ Φαραὼ τὸ γένος 'Ιωσήφ.

In v.14 he states the second element of the contrast mentioned earlier (between vv.9 and 14-15). Here too he uses a mot-agraffe technique, i.e., the ἐξαποστέλλω of v.12 suggests the ἀποστέλλω of the present verse.

Finally, a few structural and functional observations must be made in regard to vv.15 and 16. The "into Egypt" of v.15 constitutes an inclusion both with v.9 for the entire Joseph episode and with v.12 for the role of Jacob within that incident. Vv.15b-16 serve as a fitting conclusion to this part of the history and constitute a faithful reflection of the concerns of Gn 50 (see also Ex 1:6), namely, the death and burial of the patriarchs. The double use of Shechem--only time mentioned in the NT--to form an inclusion can hardly be accidental, while the occurrence of μετατίθημι followed by τίθημι within v.16, is consistent with a stylistic tendency of the author[11] (see v.9 ἀποδίδωμι and v.10 δίδωμι, see also category 2.a).

3) Vv.17-34

From the corpus the following categories should be noted:

1.a Verb followed by cognate substantive (7:17), (22), (27)
1.c Singular/plural (19), (19,21), (22), (23,30), (24,26, 27), (34)
1.d Redundancy (17,18), (19), (21), (22), (23), (25), (26), (31), (32,33), (34), (34)
1.e Negative/positive (19), (25), (31,32)
2.a Cognate expressions (17,23), (17,34), (19,22), (19, 21), (20,21), (23,30), (23,30), (23,25,26), (24,26, 27), (25), (28), (31,32)
2.b Proper names (17,20,25,32,32), (17,32), (17,18,34, 34), (20,22,29,31,32), (22,24,28), (31,33)
2.c Synonymous terms (17), (19), (21), (24), (31,32), (34)
2.d Substantive followed by apposition (23), (32), (34)
3.a Parallelismus membrorum (19), (21), (24), (34)
3.b Formulaic repetition: time (17,23), (23,30); speech (31,33)
3.c Local expressions introducing and concluding episodes (17,34), (34)
3.d Lists (22), (27), (32)
3.f Double clusters (17-19,34), (31-32b,32c-33)

As in the first two sections of the speech, the categories

---

[11]See Morgenthaler, Geschichtsschreibung, 1:20.

listed above, as well as their generous distribution, testify to the importance of the data in the corpus. This part of the discourse is the longest by far. Because of the abundance of the data and the frequency of certain categories, the author's tendency to employ techniques of repetition and duality is particularly well demonstrated.

This segment of the speech consists of three subsections. In the previous chapter the following divisions were suggested: 17-19, 20-29, and 30-34, to facilitate the study of the author's use of his sources, i.e., the first three chapters of Exodus. For structural reasons, however, the section should be thus divided: 17-22, 23-29, and 30-34. This conclusion is particularly indicated by the time formulae introducing each part,

17 καθὼς δὲ ἤγγιζεν ὁ χρόνος τῆς ἐπαγγελίας

23 ὡς δὲ ἐπληροῦτο αὐτῷ τεσσερακονταέτης χρόνος

30 καὶ πληρωθέντων ἐτῶν τεσσεράκοντα,

and further confirmed by the inner structure of each division, each of which constitutes a fairly independent unit.

The first section, vv.17-22, offers a number of interesting features within an impressive structural and thematic construction. After the doubly formal introduction (ἐπαγγελία--ὁμολογέω) stating the difference between the period of growth and the new situation after Joseph's death (note the <u>mot-agraffe</u> technique, 17 ἐν Αἰγύπτῳ and 18 ἐπ' Αἴγυπτον), the writer indulges in his reformulation of the OT data, in a cleverly contrived, ironic contrast. V.19 states in very simple terms the intention of the Egyptian king: by exposing the children, he would exterminate the Hebrews. V.21 however dwells upon the irony of the outcome. The king's wishes are carried out, Moses is exposed (double use of ἐκτίθημι), but his own daughter saves the child. To add insult to injury she adopts him as her own son. The author revels further in his imagery and in v.22 responds to the Pharaoh's wise-dealing (v. 19 κατασοφισάμενος) by stating that the young Hebrew was instructed in all the wisdom (σοφία) of the Egyptians.[12]

---

[12]This contrast is even more noteworthy since v.22 in its entirety is an addition to the biblical story. The wisdom, eloquence, and prowess of Moses are amply attested in biblical

A final touch of irony might be seen in the comparison made in vv.20 and 21 between the rearing of Moses, first in his own Jewish milieu, and then in a foreign culture. The verb ἀνατρέφω is utilized in both verses, indicating the same goal. In fact, the author underscores the polemic possibilities of this event. After noting that Moses was brought up three months in his father's house, he describes his foreign upbringing not only by dwelling upon his Egyptian culture, but in v.23 states that this period lasted forty years.

Vv.23-29 recount an interesting episode in the life of Moses. The incident is drawn substantially from the OT source, but the author has restructured the entire passage. The threefold use of ἀδικέω is most instructive. The first and third occurrences draw a contrast between the "one being wronged" (v.24) and the "one causing the wrong" (v.27), while the second addresses them both (v.26 ἱνατί ἀδικεῖτε ἀλλήλους). Furthermore, each forms part of a structural unit. V.24 consists of a parallelismus membrorum where the negative element of the first member (ἀδικέω) is adroitly complemented by positive expression of the second (ποιέω ἐκδίκησιν):

. . . τινα ἀδικούμενον	ἠμύνατο
καὶ ἐποίησεν ἐκδίκησιν	τῷ καταπονουμένῳ . . .

The second occurrence of ἀδικέω is found within a statement/question construction: "Men, you are brothers, why then do you harm one another?" The final use of the term (v.27) once again introduces a contrast between the negative term ἀδικέω ("the evil-doer") and "the leader and judge" (δικαστῆς) of the quotation.

Structurally, the entire passage is very balanced:

v.23 Introduction to episode
  24 quarrelling among Hebrews
     Moses strikes the Egyptian
  25 he thought they would understand
       salvation from God
     but they did not understand
  26 quarrelling - urges peace
  27 rejection as leader and judge
  28 accused of killing Egyptian
  29 Conclusion.

(Sir 45:3) and extrabiblical literature (Philo, Moses 1.21; Josephus, Ant. 2.10; 3.13), so that one need not be surprised that the author should be acquainted with such traditions.

The occurrence of doublets is particularly impressive in this unit: ἀδικέω (mentioned earlier), συνίημι (25 twice), ἀναιρέω (23 twice), Αἰγύπτιος (24,28). The double use of συνίημι, by means of positive/negative juxtaposition, strikes a vehemently polemic note; that of ἀναιρέω demonstrates the author's penchant for such stylistic tendencies (he borrows this text from Ex 2:14); while that of Αἰγύπτιος manifests his rhetorical skill. The twofold use of the latter forms an inclusio. The first marks the intervention of Moses on behalf of his brothers; the second demonstrates not only the negative response and effect of this act, but also the positive rejection of salvation. In this regard, the doublet is clearly intended by the author to correspond to the positive/negative contrast of v.25.

Finally, the introduction and conclusion offer interesting contrasts. "Moses desiring to visit his brethren, the children of Israel" now becomes "Moses fleeing because of his brethren and becoming a sojourner in a foreign land."

The third and final section, vv.30-34, presents an even more striking thematic and structural framework:

	structural	thematic
30	- appearance	great theophany - an angel
31	reaction of Moses: wonderment	
	approaches - κατανοῆσαι	
	speech formula (Lord)	voice of the Lord
32	- quotation:	great revelation - "I am the God . . ."
	reaction of Moses: trembling	
	did not dare - κατανοῆσαι	
33	speech formula (Lord)	the Lord said
	- quotation:	place/holy ground (see vv.3,4, 5f.)
34		enslavement/salvation (see vv. 5,19,25)
		mission (see v.35).

The structural nature of the revelation theme is quite clear since the successive stages are carefully delineated: an angel, the voice of the Lord, and--after the revelation occurs (v.32)--the Lord himself. The other themes, since they involve interrelations between different parts of the speech, will be seen later in this chapter.

The doublets once more serve as stylistic and structural indicators of the nature of the text. The positive/negative use of κατανοέω (vv.31,32) forms an inclusio for the divine revelation, while the twofold occurrence of κύριος and the synonymous terms describing Moses' bewilderment betray the author's stylistic tendencies (the same is true of ὤφθη v.30 and τὸ ὅραμα v.31). Finally, it should be noted once more that "to Egypt" at the end of v.34 constitutes an inclusio both with "in Egypt" for the entire verse (see a similar structure involving Shechem in 7:16) and with "in Egypt" of v.17 for the complete Egyptian sojourn.

4) Vv.35-41

This new section of the speech introduces us to an increasingly thematic tendency on the part of the author. At the same time numerous stylistic features and patterns are encountered. Once again reference should be made to the following categories of the corpus:

1.a Verb followed by cognate substantive (7:35), (36)
1.b Compound verb followed by the same preposition (40)
1.c Singular/plural (41)
1.d Redundancy (35-40), (38), (39), (39), (40)
1.e Negative/positive (39)
2.a Cognate expressions (35,38), (35), (36,40), (36,38), (38,39)
2.b Proper names (35,37,40), (35,37,40), (36,39,40)
2.c Synonymous terms (36), (39), (41)
2.d Substantive followed by apposition (35), (38)
3.a Parallelismus membrorum (35)
3.c Local expressions introducing and concluding episodes (36,39)
3.d Lists (35), (35), (36), (38), (38)
3.f Double Clusters (36,40)

In this part of the speech, as in others, there is approximately the same distribution of categories. Cognate expressions (2.a) and proper names (2.b) predominate, while redundancy (1.d) and lists (3.d) also appear frequently. These categories, however, apart from their frequency and regular distribution, are more significant from structural, stylistic, and thematic points of view. The repeated use of οὗτος has not escaped the attention of scholars who have seen this phenomenon as an indication of an abrupt change of style[13] or as a techni-

---

[13]Haenchen, Acts, p. 283. He explains in n. 3: "A sign of this is the heavily stressed, repeated τοῦτον, taken up again in verses 36-8 by the threefold οὗτος. Cf. Norden, Agnostos Theos, 164f. and 222ff. Luke employs the style of the encomium, originally devised for the praise of a god, for the eulogy

que employed by the author to underscore a typological relation between Moses and Joseph[14] or Moses and Jesus.[15] Commentators have often referred to the work of Norden to support their conclusion that Acts 7:35f. is an encomium delivered in honor of Moses.[16] Indeed, the following example from the papyri is most striking:

οὗτός ἐστιν ὁ κύριος τῆς οἰκουμένης
οὗτός ἐστιν ὃν οἱ ἄνεμοι φοβοῦνται
οὗτός ἐστιν ὁ ποιήσας φωνὴν προσ-
τάγματι ἑαυτοῦ παντακύριε βασιλεῦ.[17]

Norden classifies this particular stylistic composition as "der 'er'Stil des Prädikation" and gives numerous Hellenistic and Jewish examples of it.[18] I believe that Acts 7:35f. forms part of this same literary tradition. The relation of this text to Ex 6:26-27 has already been noted (supra, pp. 104-5), but it should be pointed out that the former passage has not received the attention it deserves.

To understand the text better, it is necessary to examine its role within the overall structure of this part of the speech.

v.35 τοῦτον τὸν Μωϋσῆν
  ὃν ἠρνήσαντο
    εἰπόντες + quotation
  τοῦτον . . .
36 οὗτος . . . ποιήσας

---

of Moses, the man of God, as did Philo for the emperor (Leg. ad Gaium, C.-W. VI, 145ff.)." See the similar statements of Conzelmann, Apostelgeschichte, p. 54; Wilson, "Theologian and Historian," p.180; and Bihler, Stephanusgeschichte, pp. 57-58.

14 Beginnings, 4:77: "The point is that, just as in the case of Joseph, God chose him whom the Israelites rejected, and it is emphasized by the six-fold repetition of οὗτος in vss. 36, 37, 38 and 40."

15 Bruce, Acts, p. 171: "Note the emphatic use of οὗτος (as in ii.23, etc.) five times in vv. 35-38. Both Moses and Jesus, though rejected by their brethren, were chosen by God to deliver them." He insists upon this conclusion by pointing out the parallel between 7:35 (Moses) and 5:31 (Jesus).

16 See n. 13 above.

17 Agnostos Theos, p. 188.

18 Ibid., pp. 163-66; 177-201.

37 οὗτός ἐστιν ὁ Μωϋσῆς
ὁ εἴπας . . . + quotation
38 οὗτός ἐστιν ὁ γενόμενος
ὃς ἐδέξατο
39 ᾧ οὐκ ἠθέλησαν
ἀλλὰ ἀπώσαντο
καὶ ἐστράφησαν
40 εἰπόντες + quotation [ὁ γὰρ Μωϋσῆς
οὗτος ὅς . . .]
41 καὶ ἐμοσχοποίησαν
καὶ ἀνήγαγον
καὶ εὐφραίνοντο.

The entire unit seems to consist of three stylistic entities which the author has combined: 35, 36-39a, 39b-41. They will be examined in reverse order, starting with the one which presents the least difficulty.

After having treated the accomplishments of Moses, consequent upon his mission, the author directs his polemic against the fathers, ἀλλὰ ἀπώσαντο. This important accusation (foreshadowed in v.27) he illustrates by four successive statements introduced by καί. The first relates Israel's great sin. The author further emphasizes the gravity of this act by a quotation followed by three restatements of the people's apostasy. This stylistic unit, then, is devoted entirely to a negative theme.

The second unit consists of an encomium-like structure extolling Moses. Each of three statements, introduced by οὗτος, allows the author to present added information concerning him. This structure, suggested to him by his OT source, is hardly new to him since analogous stylistic constructions are also found in Acts 4:9-11; 9:20-22; and 18:24-26. The primary feature of all four passages, including 7:36-39a, is the repeated use of οὗτος to introduce successive but interrelated components. In the present context it should be noted that the first and third sections (vv.36 and 38), in a manner similar to Acts 7:2 and 4, form an interesting parallel in their list-like accumulation of elements.

The first part, v.35, presents perhaps the most striking features of all. The structure of the verse, τοῦτον τὸν

Μωϋσῆν, ὃν . . . τοῦτον . . ., is clearly one which the author favors since similar constructions occur in Acts 2:22-24, (Ἰησοῦν τὸν Ναζωραῖον . . . τοῦτον . . . ὃν . . .); 3:13-14 (Ἰησοῦν ὃν . . . ὑμεῖς δὲ τὸν ἅγιον καὶ δίκαιον . . . τὸν δὲ ἀρχηγόν . . . ὃν . . .); 4:10 (Ἰησοῦ Χριστοῦ τοῦ Ναζωραίου ὃν . . . ὃν . . .); 5:30-31 (Ἰησοῦν ὃν . . . τοῦτον . . .); 10: 38-40 (Ἰησοῦν τὸν ἀπὸ Ναζαρέθ . . . ὃν . . . τοῦτον . . .); and, finally, 16:1-3 (. . . μαθητής . . . Τιμόθεος . . . ὅς . . . τοῦτον . . .). All of these parallels would merit further attention in relation to various aspects of the author's style; but only the most striking example will be further analyzed:

7:35	5:30-31
see 7:32	ὁ θεὸς τῶν πατέρων ἡμῶν ἤγειρεν
τοῦτον τὸν Μωϋσῆν	Ἰησοῦν
ὃν ἠρνήσαντο	ὃν ὑμεῖς διεχειρίσασθε
εἰπόντες· τίς σε	κρεμάσοντες ἐπὶ ξύλου·
κατέστησεν	
ἄρχοντα καὶ δικαστήν,	
τοῦτον ὁ θεὸς καὶ ἄρχοντα καὶ	τοῦτον ὁ θεὸς ἀρχηγὸν καὶ
λυτρωτὴν ἀπέσταλκεν	σωτῆρα ὕψωσεν
σὺν χειρὶ ἀγγέλου ...	τῇ δεξιᾷ αὐτοῦ ...

The similarity of ideas, especially within the second clause, would be evident even to a casual observer; it is the stylistic affinity, however, which is most impressive.

The writer, then, has brought together three stylistic units to present his binary, but antithetic theme: Moses the envoy of God--rejection and apostasy. He has taken pains, furthermore, to interrelate these units. To this effect note the threefold occurrence of the name of Moses (35, 37, 40), as well as the three quotations involving a plural/singular/plural pattern (v.35 εἰπόντες, 37 ὁ εἴπας, 40 εἰπόντες), and the two-fold references to the angel (35, 38) and to Egypt (36, 39). Similarly, the effective parallel between vv.

36 οὗτος ἐξήγαγεν αὐτούς . . . ἐν γῇ Αἰγύπτῳ

40 . . . ὁ γὰρ Μωϋσῆς οὗτος, ὃς ἐξήγαγεν ἡμᾶς ἐκ γῆς Αἰγύπτου.

should be pointed out. The relationship between the role of Moses and the people's infidelity, i.e., the second and third parts of the passage being studied, is well orchestrated. The author terminates the passage on Moses and his mission with a double relative construction, ὅς . . . ᾧ . . ., but does this on a negative note, ᾧ οὐκ ἠθέλησαν ὑπήκοοι γενέσθαι οἱ πατέρες ἡμῶν, thereby introducing and slightly anticipating the second part of his theme. A further link between the stylistic units of this section is brought about by the writer's technique of contrast. In v.35, to underscore Moses' role as the envoy of God, he already interjects the people's negative reaction to him, ὃν ἠρνήσαντο.

Finally, a few stylistic features of vv.35-41 should be pointed out to illustrate further the author's redactional tendencies. The double reference in this section to the angel is all the more striking owing to the likeness of construction:

v.35 σὺν χειρὶ ἀγγέλου τοῦ ὀφθέντος αὐτῷ ἐν τῇ βάτῳ
38 μετὰ τοῦ ἀγγέλου τοῦ λαλοῦντος αὐτῷ ἐν τῷ ὄρει Σινά.

The lists of vv.36 and 38 are consistent with the writer's style, while the parallelismus membrorum of v.35,

τίς σε κατέστησεν ἄρχοντα καὶ δικαστήν;
τοῦτον ὁ θεὸς καὶ ἄρχοντα καὶ λυτρωτὴν ἀπέσταλκεν,

with its a b/c d - b a/d c structure, illustrates once more his tendency both to utilize doublets and to imitate his own style in successive passages (see v.5 in particular).

5) Vv.42-50

This part of the speech, in spite of its special features (e.g., two extensive OT quotations), nevertheless presents repetitive techniques similar to the ones already encountered. The following categories are germane to the present discussion:

1.a Verb followed by cognate substantive (7:46), (47), (49)
1.c Singular/plural (42,43), (42,43), (43), (47,49), (48, 49,50)
1.d Redundancy (45), (45,46,47,48), (49,50)
1.e Negative/positive (46,47,48), (49,50)
2.a Cognate expressions (42,49), (42,48), (42,44), (43, 44,46), (43,44), (43,44,50), (44,45), (46), (47,48, 49), (47,49), (48,50), (48,49)
2.b Proper names (42,43,45,46)
2.c Synonymous terms (42,43), (42,43), (42), (48,49)
2.d Substantive followed by apposition (43)
3.a Parallelismus membrorum (49), (49)
3.b Formulae: speech (42,48)
3.c Local expressions introducing and concluding episodes (42,49)
3.d Lists (42), (43).

Once more the distribution of categories is approximately what has been noted for other sections of the speech. These stylistic features must be seen in their structural context. Note that the exceptionally large number of cognate expressions will be given particular attention later.

The key to defining the framework of vv.42-50 is the threefold use of καθώς in vv.42, 44, and 48, each term responding to the statement immediately preceding it.[19] The following outline is therefore proposed:

v.42 statement introduced by δέ
καθώς + quotation (τῶν προφητῶν)
v.44 statement/midrash upon σκηνή of v.43
καθώς + "quotation": divine command.
v.48 statement (neg) introduced by ἀλλά
καθώς + quotation (ὁ προφήτης).

Each section presents significant interrelationships, an added indication of the author's consistent use of doublets. Within vv.42-43 it is clear that he wishes to draw a parallel between "serving the host of heaven" (v.42) and the gods Moloch and Raiphan (v.43). This is further indicated by the addition to the OT quotation of the following phrase: προσκυνεῖν αὐτοῖς. The double occurrence of εὑρίσκω (v.46 mot-agraffe technique), the contrast between father and son (David and Solomon), and the threefold reference to "our fathers" indicates the writer's heavy style, an occasional consequence of his constant use of repetitive elements throughout the speech. The final section contributes more stylistic features: the double speech formula of vv. 48 and 49 (already discussed supra, p. 184) and the parallel between ἐν χειροποιήτοις of v.48 and οὐχὶ ἡ χείρ μου ἐποίησεν ταῦτα πάντα (see v.50). The latter constitutes a very effective inclusio, which is rendered more dramatic as a twofold negative statement.

As noted before, the author takes great pains to interrelate the various sections of his narrative. The threefold occurrence of ποιέω (vv.42, 44, 50) betrays his thematic preoccupation in relation to the making of the calf, while the

---

19Morgenthaler, Geschichtsschreibung, 1:70, has noted the first and third elements of this structure.

double reference to the prophets, as well as prophetic quotations (vv.42 and 48) and the parallel phrases, ἡ στρατιὰ τοῦ οὐρανοῦ (v.42) and ὁ οὐρανός μοι θρόνος (v.49), indicate both structural and thematic solicitude. The overall effect is greater unity within vv.42-50. Furthermore, sections two and three present added links which contribute on the one hand to the author's purpose, v.47 "Solomon built him a house" (note the rejoinder of v.48) and v.49 "what house will you build me?" On the other hand, they illustrate his stylistic dexterity, namely, the progressively adversive nature of vv.46 (καί), 47 (δέ), and 48 (ἀλλά).

Finally, the relationship between vv.42-43 (quotation of Am 5:25-27) and 44-47 deserves special attention. In the structural outline above this relation was qualified as a midrash. In effect, the double use of τύπος (along with ποιέω, vv.43, 44) and ἔρημος (42, 44), as well as the twofold reference to σκηνή (43, 44 see also σκήνωμα v.46),[20] lend support to such an affirmation. In addition, the manifest midrashic character of the LXX text of Amos in relation to the Hebrew text, and the equally midrashic use made of this text in the <u>Damascus Document</u>, justify the above statement.[21] However, the author is more interested in the contrasts which this material presents than in finding allegorical meanings for the various elements of the quotation. He draws particular attention, by means of this technique, to the paradoxical reality of Jewish

---

[20]Cadbury, "Four Features," p. 95, notes the use of these three terms; however, his designation of these as "3 passages from LXX" is both incorrect and misleading. The first case, v.43, is part of a quotation from Am 5:26. The second, v.44, is unrelated to the OT text, even though it is a midrashic comment upon the first term and is undoubtedly influenced by LXX idiom (<u>supra</u>, pp. 127f.). The third example, v.46, is a quotation of Ps 131:5. The combination of the passages as well as the use of the cognate terms in successive verses is clearly the work of the author.

[21]The textual relationship between Acts 7:43 and Am 5:26-27 (MT, LXX, later Greek versions, and CD) is studied at length by de Waard, <u>OT Text</u>, pp. 41-47. No contact with Qumran or the <u>Damascus Document</u> is proposed here (also de Waard, p. 44). Instead, one should see this particular use of Amos as an example of both Greek and Hebrew exegesis. This is further enhanced by the added reference in CD 7.16 (also 4QFlor 1.12) and Acts 15:16 of Am 9:11 concerning the tabernacle of David.

history, namely, the contemporaneity of their idolatry and infidelity (bearing the tabernacle and star of handmade gods) and God's presence in their midst (bearing the tabernacle of testimony made according to the heavenly model). This purpose explains the thematic development of vv.45-50.

6) Vv.51-53

The following categories from the corpus should be noted as a preliminary to the discussion of the invective:

1.d Redundancy (7:51), (51,52)
1.e Negative/positive (52), (53)
2.a Cognate expressions (51,52), (51,52)
2.c Synonymous terms (51), (52), (52), (52)
3.a Parallelismus membrorum (52)
3.d Lists (51), (51), (51), (52)

The paucity of categories and the seemingly few examples of these are explained by the brevity and the nature of the passage in question.

A structural analysis of vv.51-53 will reveal interesting and generally unnoticed features. These will be more readily understood in light of what appears to be its structure:

Address/accusation

σκληροτράχηλοι v.51
καὶ ἀπερίτμηλοι καρδίαις
καὶ τοῖς ὠσίν
ὑμεῖς ἀεὶ τῷ πνεύματι τῷ ἁγίῳ ἀντιπίπτετε

Lesson of history: 1) ὡς οἱ πατέρες ὑμῶν 2) καὶ ὑμεῖς

1) τίνα τῶν προφητῶν οὐκ ἐδίωξαν οἱ πατέρες ὑμῶν v.52
καὶ ἀπέκτειναν τοὺς προκαταγγείλαντας
περὶ τῆς ἐλεύσεως τοῦ δικαίου
2) οὗ νῦν ὑμεῖς προδόται
καὶ φονεῖς ἐγένεσθε
οἵτινες ἐλάβετε τὸν νόμον εἰς διαταγὰς ἀγγέλων v.53
καὶ οὐκ ἐφυλάξατε.

In the invective, as in earlier parts of the discourse, the affinity of the author for doublets is evident. In the present case, these consist of lists, synonymous terms, and negative/positive contrasts. The striking parallelismus membrorum (abc/ba) of v.52 takes on added importance in such a short and allegedly different text. It has been usual to see the concluding verses as presenting an abrupt change from the rest of the speech.[22] On the basis of this observation, earlier scholarship has attempted to find a solution to this anomaly in a precise historical situation,[23] while more recent commentators have explained this in terms of other passages from Acts.[24]

The present study of the invective demands that considerations of overall structure (the relation of the conclusion to the entire discourse) be anticipated.[25] The author addresses his audience directly, not for the first time however (see vv. 2, 4, and 38). After having accused his hearers in very strident terms of being obstinate and recalcitrant in their rebellion, he then states in one short phrase (ὡς οἱ πατέρες ὑμῶν καὶ ὑμεῖς) a methodological principle which confers actuality to the entire historical survey of the speech. In effect, the discourse is a history of the fathers beginning with "our father Abraham" (v.2). Following his general conclusion, he illustrates concretely both aspects of the principle: the role of the Fathers and that of the present generation (vv.52-53). Stylistically he renders very clearly the historical relation between the two: the precursors of the Just One were killed by the Fathers, while the Just One Himself was murdered by the audience.[26] The structure of the invective, then, presents a fitting conclusion to Stephen's long history of Israel's dealings with God, while its style is consistent with that of earlier parts of the discourse.

---

[22]See Foakes Jackson, Acts, p. 65; Haenchen, Acts, p. 286.

[23]Renié, Actes, p. 122 presents the position of earlier scholars: "Plus d'un exégète a supposé que les dernières paroles de l'orateur ayant provoqué les murmures de son auditoire, il aurait brusqué sa conclusion." In more recent years, Bruce, Acts, pp. 176-77, holds a very similar view (1953).

[24]See Bihler, Stephanusgeschichte, p. 81; Wilson, Gentiles, p. 135.

[25]Note the interesting structural observation of R.P.C. Hanson, "Studies in Texts," pp. 144-45; "Verses 51 and 53 make the whole meaning of Stephen's speech clear. The speech does not break off abruptly, as so many critics assume; the verses are a summary of the foregoing verses, drawing the moral."

[26]Renié, Actes, states this in very clear terms: "Passant à l'offensive, il invective ceux qui l'écoutent: la génération présente a vraiment mis le comble à l'iniquité des ancêtres; ceux-ci avaient égorgé les prophètes par qui était annoncée la venue du Messie, eux, ils ont crucifié le Messie lui-même!"

From a structural point of view, the invective is masterfully conceived. The author begins with an address consisting of a series of denunciations couched in LXX terms. These accusations are presented in a succession of doublets. V.51 ends with the climactic phrase "as your fathers also you." The writer returns to the charge by further illustrating this dual historical judgment. First he speaks of the fathers' role (v. 52) in the form of a parallelismus membrorum and then of the audience's part in this history (v.53), once again utilizing a series of doublets. Structurally, therefore, the invective is by the same hand as the rest of the discourse.

b. Throughout the Speech

After having isolated structural and stylistic features relating to the smaller units of the speech, attention must now be directed to the entire discourse. We are confronted with very similar tendencies, namely, the occurrence of many of the same categories. To begin the discussion reference should be made to the corpus, in particular to the following categories: 1.c Singular/plural; 2.a Cognate expressions (throughout the Stephen material); 3.b Formulaic repetition (both time and speech); 3.e Sequential patterns; 3.f Double clusters. Each of the above contributes to an overall impression that the writer wishes to interrelate various parts of his text, that he is interested in certain techniques of contrast, and that he seeks to emphasize and reiterate certain themes and concepts. But it is necessary to investigate this conclusion in greater detail.

These various elements, as they occur throughout the speech, are best viewed under three headings: structural, stylistic, and thematic. In the first case, it is important to observe how the writer has carefully inserted connecting links between the various parts of the speech. In three instances a mot-agraffe technique is imployed to insure the continuity of the narrative. The double use of πατριάρχαι in vv.8 and 9 unites the Abraham (vv.2-8) and Joseph episodes (vv.9-16); of 'Αβρααμ in vv.16 and 17 the Joseph and Moses story (vv.17f.); and of ἀποστέλλω in vv.34 and 35 the first (vv.17-34) and second parts (vv.35-41) of the Moses episode. The two important thematic sections, vv.35-41 and 42-50, are brought together in a very effective way by the use of the adversative conjunction δέ and contrasting plural/singular constructions involving the verb στρέφω. Two other connecting links, however, require more detailed examination.

First, it is clear that the author subscribes to a 120 year span for the life of Moses,[27] but more important is the structural use of the data. After introducing the Egyptian setting of the story (vv.17-19) and the birth and rearing of Moses (vv.20-22), the writer inserts within the biblical narrative a first forty-year formula to introduce Moses' initial encounter with his people (vv.23-29), a second one to preface the encounter with God at Sinai (vv.30-34), and a third (v.36),[28] whose function is less structural than thematic.

Secondly, the invective, vv.51-53, due to the nature of its structure and function, bears a different relation to other parts of the speech. The author jars his audience by providing no transitional element. However, the ending verses are carefully linked to the entire discourse. The following interconnections should be noted in this regard: "circumcision" vv.8 and 51; "the fathers" throughout and v.51; "the prophets" vv. 42, 48, and 52; "the angels" vv.30, 35, 38, and 53; "living words/the Law" vv.38 and 53. Furthermore, the ὡς οἱ πατέρες ὑμῶν of v.51 implies that the entire speech has been presented as introduction and proof of the accusations of vv.51-53.

Finally, the speech formulae must be considered at some length because of their structural nature and significance. In recent years, OT quotations in the NT have received considerable attention, and along with these methods of citing and interpreting the scriptures have also been examined. It has become increasingly clear that NT writers generally utilize formulae introducing speech similar to those found at Qumran[29]

---

[27]See Strack and Billerbeck, Kommentar, 2:679-80 and the major commentaries, most of which refer to the work just mentioned.

[28]An additional reference to the forty-year sojourn in the desert v.42 (quotation of Am 5:25), does not form part of the 120-year span of Moses' life, but rather constitutes a further parallel between the two thematic sections: 35-41 and 42-50.

[29]JOseph A. Fitzmyer, "The Use of Explicit Old Testament Quotations in Qumran Literature and in the New Testament," NTS

and in early rabbinic literature, particularly the Mishnah.[30] It should be stated further that the formulae occurring in the speech, especially vv.3, 6, 7 and 42, 48, 49, find numerous parallels in various books of the NT. However, a broader perspective is necessary since the writer of the discourse employs additional formulae to introduce direct speech. The list below presents all the data. An examination of these shows that

1	v.3	καὶ εἶπεν πρὸς αὐτόν
	6	ἐλάλησεν δὲ οὕτως ὁ θεός, ὅτι
	7	ὁ θεὸς εἶπεν
2	26	... εἰς εἰρήνην εἰπών
	27	... ἀπώσατο αὐτὸν εἰπών
3	31	ἐγένετο φωνὴ κυρίου
	33	εἶπεν δὲ αὐτῷ ὁ κύριος
4	35	ὃν ἠρνήσαντο εἰπόντες
	37	... ὁ Μωϋσῆς ὁ εἴπας τοῖς υἱοῖς Ἰσραήλ
	39-40	... εἰς Αἴγυπτον, εἰπόντες τῷ Ἀαρών
5	42	καθὼς γέγραπται ἐν βίβλῳ τῶν προφητῶν
	48	καθὼς ὁ προφήτης λέγει
	49	λέγει κύριος

their primary function is structural since each type is limited to a single part of the speech. Furthermore each of the five categories reveals additional stylistic or thematic features. The stylistic similarities between the first and fifth group have already been pointed out.[31] The second category underscores the difference between Moses who advocates peace, and the Hebrew who rejects both peace and its advocate, while the

---

7 (1960-61): 297-333; idem, "Jewish Christianity in Acts in Light of the Qumran Scrolls," in Studies, eds. Keck and Martyn, pp. 251-57. See also de Waard, OT Text, pp. 78-84.

[30]Bruce M. Metzger, "The Formulas Introducing Quotations of Scripture in the NT and the Mishnah," JBL 70 (1951): 297-307.

[31]See p. 184 where the structural similarities of vv.6-7 and 48-49 were contrasted. The more complete formulaic framework of vv.3-7 (εἶπεν . . . ὁ θεός . . . ὁ θεὸς εἶπεν) and 42-49 (τῶν προφητῶν . . . ὁ προφήτης λέγει . . . λέγει) should be noted. Furthermore, the occurrence of οὕτως in v.6 must be related to its threefold use in the Stephen material (7:1, 6, and 8) and that of καθώς in vv.42 and 48, likewise to its threefold occurrence in the entire Stephen material (vv.42, 44, and 48).

fourth group uses a plural/singular/plural technique to contrast the role of Moses and that of the fathers. Finally, the speech formulae of vv.31 and 33 form part of the author's concept of gradual revelation: the angel v.30, the voice v.31, and the Lord v.33.

The second area for consideration is the stylistic nature of the data as they occur throughout the speech. Under this heading are to be included: doublets, patterns, and contrasts which indicate the author's various stylistic tendencies. While a large number of the singular/plural contrasts (1.c of the corpus) betrays some structural or thematic function, many of them do not. Owing to their number and distribution, it is safe to conclude that they represent a peculiarity of the writer. The same explanation applies to a large number of cognate expressions (2.a) which occur only twice in the speech, terms whose function is not otherwise indicated.

To the above should be added a category whose stylistic nature is more obvious, namely, sequential patterns (3.e), particularly the alternating structure of the following: 1) Pharaoh, king of Egypt (v.10); Pharaoh (v.13); king over Egypt (v.18); and daughter of Pharaoh (v.21); and 2) ἀπώσατο (v.27); ἀπώσαντο καὶ ἐστράφησαν (v.39); ἔστρεψεν (v.42 including a singular/plural/singular contrast). The first and last reference to Egypt, vv.9 and 40, although both betraying a negative situation of the Hebrews, seem to indicate a stylistic bias of the author. Similarly the double use of δεῦρω in vv.3 and 34 should be pointed out, as well as the analogous expressions of vv.23, ἀνέβη ἐπὶ τὴν καρδίαν αὐτοῦ ἐπισκέψασθαι, and 39, ἐστράφησαν ἐν ταῖς καρδίαις αὐτῶν εἰς Αἴγυπτον.

Finally, it should be stated that most categories by the very fact that they appear throughout the speech indicate definite stylistic tendencies on the part of the author.

The third and final area to be considered, the thematic function, is also the most important. However, since a detailed analysis of this aspect of the speech would demand that considerable attention be given to interpretation, the present investigation will be limited to elements of duality and repetitiveness, as they relate to the author's thematic concerns.

By means of cognate expressions the writer draws parallels, contrasts or a variety of relationships between persons, episodes, and themes. Between the period of Abraham and other parts of the speech, a number of such relationships exist. First of all, reference should be made to the corpus, 3.f double clusters, for connections between vv.5-6 and 17, 19 (note also the use of κάκωσις in v.34) and between vv.6 and 29. I would note the double use of μετοικίζω (4 and 43 with singular/plural as well as positive/negative contrast), of κατάσχεσις (5 and 45), of λατρεύω (7 and 42 also presenting a positive/negative contrast), and, finally, of περιτομή (also περιτέμνω) and ἀπερίτμητοι (8 and 51). The function of these parallels is clearly thematic, whether promise/fulfilment or positive/negative contrasts between Abraham and his descendants.

The author draws further links between the Joseph episode, vv.9-16, and later periods. In particular one should note the following parallels: ἐξαιρέω (10 and 34), δίδωμι χάριν and εὑρίσκω χάριν (10 and 46), σοφία (10 and 22), and καθίστημι (10, 27, and 35). Once again the thematic nature of the doublets is clear. The author wishes to interrelate Hebrew history by drawing comparisons between its principal personalities. Joseph and David are presented as Jews who had God's favor. However, the major parallels which the author draws are between Joseph and Moses (three of the four doublets given above). In light of this a further comparison between the two should be pointed out. V.9 states that the patriarchs, through envy, sold Joseph into Egypt. V.39 presents a clear parallel when it states that the fathers would not be subject to Moses, but instead pushed him away and returned in their hearts to Egypt. The Abraham and Joseph episodes are further interconnected by the twofold occurrence of the name of Abraham (2 and 16) and συγγένεια (3 and 14), the latter involving a rather paradoxical theme.

There is no doubt that Moses occupies a central position in the Stephen speech both in a strategic and a proportional sense. It is equally clear that two important sections of the discourse have been devoted to him, vv.17-34 and 35-41, the second of which is considerably more thematic. Careful analysis of the doublets and repetitive elements provided by these sections indicates well-orchestrated interrelations between the two. First, reference must be made to the corpus (3.f double clusters) for the parallel between vv.25, 27, and 35 (note also the singular/plural contrasts). To these should be added the following: "words and works" (v.22) and "wonders and signs . . . living words" (vv.36 and 38); "works" (22 and 41); "sons of Israel" (23 and 37); "give" salvation/words (25 and 38); ἀπωθέω (27 and 39 with a singular/plural contrast). In several cases the doublets consist of parallels whose function is that of underscoring an important concept. In most, however, the constant use of singular/plural constructions suggests that the author places great value on these episodes and their thematic significance.

The interconnections between vv.42-50 and the preceding sections of the speech are numerous. Many of these have already been pointed out particularly in relation to the Abraham story and earlier in the chapter in speaking of the structural unity between the various parts of the discourse. Finally, the invective (vv.51-53) has already been dealt with earlier in the chapter (see pp. 199-201).

3. Relation to OT Model

Throughout the present chapter it has become increasingly clear that the stylistic data abound in every part of the speech. At the same time, the analysis in the previous chapter has also indicated how greatly the author relied upon his OT source. At this point then it is necessary to correlate the data from the two parts of this study (chapters two and three) to determine as precisely as possible the degree to which either the writer or the OT model is to be credited with the doublets, repetitive elements, and patterns of the corpus.

a. Grammatical Categories

1) Category 1.a Verb followed by cognate substantive

Observations:

a) Of 10 examples 2 (7:17 and 22) are unrelated to the OT

b) Acts 7:10--based on a hypothetical LXX model: κατέστησεν αὐτὸν [ἡγούμενος]; see pp. 63-64

2) Category 1.b Compound verb followed by the same preposition

Observations:

a) Of 4 examples 2 (7:3 and 40) are OT quotations

b) Acts 7:4: ἐξελθὼν ἐκ, a parallel based upon 7:3

c) Acts 7:10: ἐξείλατο . . . ἐκ, probably based upon an OT model; see p. 62

3) Category 1.c Singular/plural

Observations:

a) Of 30 examples 6 are related to the OT

b) 3 are found within an extended quotation (7:6-7,34,43)

c) In 3 cases (7 and 45, 18 and 40, 47 and 49) both elements are taken from the OT, but the combination, i.e., the singular/plural contrast, is due to the author

4) Category 1.d Redundancy

Observations:

a) Of 28 examples 6 (7:3,15,34,39-40,40,49-50) are taken from the OT

b) In 12 examples 1 or several elements are from the OT source: (2,3,4,5), (4,5), (9,10), (17,18), (21), (21), (23), (31), (32,33), (34), (35-40), (45,46,47,48)

c) On 1 occasion (9,10,11,12) all elements are from the OT but the combination is due to the author

d) 7 examples (19,22,25,26,38,39,45) represent minor cases of redundancy (i.e., 2 elements)

5) Category 1.3 Negative/positive

Observations:

a) Of 12 examples 2 (7:5 and 5) are from the OT (both positive/negative elements), but since these are from diverse passages of the source, the combination is due to the author of Acts; see p. 46

b) In 3 cases 1 element is drawn from the model 4-5 (neg.), 11-12 (pos.), 46-47 and 48 (pos.)

c) On 1 occasion (49,49,50) all three statements are borrowed from Isaiah, but the author has inserted the negative particle, οὐχί.

GENERAL CONCLUSIONS REGARDING CATEGORY 1

1. Categories a and b are generally related to the OT and, due to their small number, indicate a relatively minor

influence of biblical Greek style.

2. Examples of redundancy, i.e., category d, generally appear in texts where the author borrows generously from his source, and are due or related to OT passages.

3. Categories c and e demonstrate clearly the writer's penchant for techniques of contrast. And more important still, from the above data it is clear that these owe not to the model being used but to the author's redaction.

b. Lexical Categories

1) Category 2.a Cognate expressions (within consecutive blocks of material)

Observations:

a) Of 45 examples 2 (7:6-7 and 28) occur within an extended quotation

b) In 9 cases the cognate expressions are drawn from the OT but from different passages (5,6), (8), (9,10), (36,40), (42, 49), (43,44), (43,44,50), (46), (47,49). The combination then is the work of the writer.

c) For the remaining examples, 19 show a partial relation to the OT model (usually 1 term is from the OT) and 15 do not

(throughout the speech)

Observations:

d) Of 34 examples 12 are borrowed from the OT, i.e., each component is taken from the biblical source (7:2,12,35), (3,14), (6,19,34), (7,45), (7,50), (7,42), (10, 34), (10,46), (10,18), (10,27,35), (18, 37), (18,40), (36,42). It must be noted, however, that the choice factor plays a major role: the author has utilized 2 or more passages from his model, among the many examples available, and has inserted these within the structure of his text.

e) Of the remaining examples, 15 are partly related to the OT (at least 1 is supplied by the writer) and 7 are totally independent of it. In both cases the role of the author is especially evident.

2) Category 2.b Proper names

Observations:

a) The following are the proper names and titles employed more than once in the speech: God, Abraham, Harran, Isaac, Jacob, Egypt, Pharaoh, Shechem, Moses,

Egyptian, Israel, Mount Sinai, Lord

b) Very few, "Shechem" (v.16 twice) and "Mount Sinai" (vv.30 and 38), in at least some of their occurrences, bear no direct relation to the OT text.

c) All of the proper names and titles listed above involve important structural or stylistic considerations. The names, God, Egypt, and Moses, for example, are generally present or implied in the OT model. However, the use made of these within the discourse is due to the work of the author: inclusio, various techniques of contrast, parallelismus membrorum, etc. Particular attention has been given to the examples of this category throughout chapters two and three, and further consideration will be given to them in chapter four since they play a significant role in the interpretation of the entire Stephen story

3) <u>Category 2.c</u> Synonymous terms

Observations:

a) Of 26 examples 4 (7:6,17,36,42) occur within extended quotations, while a fifth (34) involves a conflation of 2 biblical texts. The last example is due to OT influence; see pp. 99-100

b) In 6 examples all the synonymous terms are derived from the biblical source (5, 5,41,42-43,42-43,51), but since these involve different quotations, the particular combination within the speech is due to the author. The first and fourth cases will be examined at greater length below.

c) On 9 occasions at least 1 of the elements is unrelated to the OT source (2,3,4), (11), (11,12), (13), (13), (19), (21), (25,35), (48-49), while in the 6 remaining cases none of the synonymous terms is taken from the model

4) <u>Category 2.d</u> Substantive followed by apposition

Observations:

a) Of 9 examples 5 (7:5,23,32,34,43) occur within OT quotations

b) The remaining 4 cases are good illustrations of the author's use of biblical Greek (2,14,35, and 38)

GENERAL CONCLUSIONS REGARDING CATEGORY 2

1. Category <u>d</u> (along with categories 1.a, b, and d) il-

lustrates a relatively minor but real influence of LXX style upon the writer, and exemplifies to a lesser extent his imitation of biblical Greek idiom.

2. The examination of cognate (a) and synonymous (c) terms indicates that these are most often due to the author's redactional activity. Only in rare instances are they entirely borrowed from the OT. Furthermore, even when the writer quotes from his model, at least one element of the doublet or repetitive construction is his own creation.

3. Category b, along with a and c, underscores the prominent role which the structural and stylistic data should play in the interpretation of the speech, since they repeatedly draw attention to the personalities, episodes, and themes germane to the author's purpose.

c. Categories Relating to a Variety of Patterns

1) Category 3.a Parallelismus membrorum

Observations:

a) Of 10 examples 3 (7:34,49,49) are borrowed directly from the OT text. The first involves a conflation of two biblical passages, although the structure is still that of the original quotation; see pp. 99-100. The second 2 pairs are drawn from an extended quotation of Isaiah and will be discussed below

b) 1 text (5) consists of 3 separate OT passages; 5 others (13,19,21,24,35) employ some elements from the biblical source, and a final example (52) bears no direct relation to the LXX. In these instances it is clear that the actual formulation of the structure classified as parallelismus membrorum is the work of the author. Whether he borrows all the elements or just a few, the combination is his own.

2) Category 3.b Formulaic repetition (time formulae)

Observations:

a) Of 5 groups of formulae only 1 (7:8 and 26) relates entirely to the OT, although the second construction has been slightly modified; see p. 83

b) Another group corresponds to OT passages, but only in part since the first example is introduced by the author into the biblical narrative

c) The remaining groups of time formulae (2, 4), (17,23), (23,30) are unrelated to the LXX

(formulae introducing speech)

Observations:

d) None of the 4 formulae groups is taken directly from the OT model (7:3,6,7), (26, 27,35,37,39-40), (31,33,49), (42,48)

e) 1 formula offers a partial relation with the biblical source in the first (3) and third (33) groups, and 2 in the second (27,35), while only the third series has borrowed a complete speech formula from the LXX (49 λέγει κύριος -- note that for structural reasons the author has displaced the expression from its original context; see p. 133)

f) Other formulae have no relation to the OT text

3) <u>Category 3.c</u> Local expressions introducing and concluding episodes

Observations:

a) Of 8 examples 6 have borrowed both elements from the OT source (7:2,4), (9,15), (12,15), (34), (36,39), (42,49). However, the local expressions are taken from different biblical passages. Only v.34 relates to a single OT quotation, but the writer has transformed an original ἀποστείλω σε πρὸς Φαραὼ βασιλέα Αἰγύπτου to ἀποστείλω σε εἰς Αἴγυπτον. From this the conclusion follows that the resulting structure in all 6 cases (inclusio) is due to the author

b) The 2 remaining examples show even greater freedom on the part of the writer. The double occurrence of Shechem (v.16) is clearly of the same pattern as 34 discussed above, and is fully his work since he has added the entire episode to the biblical narrative. The final example (17,34) has resulted from an insertion of the first local element within the text of Exodus quoted in v.17

4) <u>Category 3.d</u> Lists

Observations:

a) Of 22 lists, i.e., double or triple elements 8 (7:3,5,27,32,35,36,42,43) are taken fully from the OT, 2 of which involve the same passage (27 and 35)

b) In 5 cases (10,11,36,51,51) all the elements originate in the OT, but from different passages

c) In 5 cases the author has borrowed only 1 element from his source (10,14,15,35,38)

d) Finally, 4 examples are unrelated to the biblical narrative (22,38,51,52)

5) Category 3.e Sequential patterns

Observations:

a) All 5 patterns are the work of the author since none bears relation structurally to the OT text

b) In most instances 1 or more elements are borrowed from the OT narrative (7:2,4), (8,9), (10,13,18,21), (12,13--only the concept), (27,39,42)

6) Category 3.f Double clusters

Observations:

a) Of 7 examples of double clusters, 2 consist entirely of OT quotations (7:6 and 29) and (17-19 and 34). The modifications imposed upon the first, and the structural use made of the second, underscore the author's stylistic tendencies as they relate to his purpose

b) The remaining examples (2,4), 5,6, and 17, 19), (25,26, and 35), (31-32b and 32c-33), and (36 and 40) relate to the biblical model in varying degrees: the first and last rely heavily upon the LXX; the second and third are due as much to the author as to the source; the fourth relates minimally to the OT text

GENERAL CONCLUSIONS REGARDING CATEGORY 3

1. Time and speech formulae (b) rarely bear any relation to the OT model. They are clearly the work of the author both structurally and functionally.

2. For category c (local expressions) the writer relies greatly upon his model for the elements used. However, the functional nature of these expressions, i.e., inclusio, is due entirely to his redaction.

3. The study of sequential patterns (e), double clusters (f), and lists (d) indicates the important role played by the source in furnishing the writer with a large variety of redactive elements. The structures are almost always the result of the author's composition. For the last-mentioned category it is important to note that he both borrows lists from his source and, more significant, expands his model by adding elements to construct lists.

4. The distribution of category a (parallelismus membrorum) throughout the speech clearly indicates that this is a favorite stylistic construction of the writer. Furthermore, the very nature of this structure makes its frequent use all the more significant.

Although it would be interesting to consider each example from the above data, a detailed examination at this point is impossible owing to the space required. However, study of this phenomenon is not complete since in chapter two this matter was analyzed from a perspective which did not include stylistic and structural features. A few examples of the data just discussed will be examined to determine more precisely their structural relation to the OT text.

Category 3.d (lists) provides short and very illuminating examples. Observe the following relationship:

Acts 7:10b καὶ ἔδωκεν αὐτῷ χάριν καὶ σοφίαν ἐναντίον ...
Gn 39:21 καὶ ἔδωκεν αὐτῷ χάριν ἐναντίον ...

One element of the list is from the LXX text, but the second is added to the quotation by the author. 7:10 and 11 provide two lists. All four elements employed in constructing these lists are drawn from different OT passages (Gn 41:40, 43, 54; 42:5). Thus the building blocks all originate in the LXX, but the resulting structures owe to the author of Acts.

Even in the extended quotations of the speech, the writer adjusts the OT model by omitting from, adding to or restructuring the original. In v.3 (quoting Gn 12:1) he eliminates a phrase and adds δεῦρο.[32] Later in citing Ex 23:1 (v.40) he omits ἄνθρωπος, but places the phrase ὁ γὰρ Μωυσῆς οὗτος ὅς... within the long encomium-like structure of vv.35-41.[33] Still later, v.43, he adds προσκυνεῖν to the text of Am 5:26 to construct a parallel with λατρεύω of 7:42.

Finally, the modifications imposed upon Is 66:1-2 in 7:49-50 should be referred to. Various aspects of these transformations have already been pointed out (*supra*, pp. 134-35, 197, and 207), so the following observations will be brief. The

---

[32]See pp. 41-42.

[33]See the discussion of this text, pp. 102f. and 193f.

text of Isaiah, both Greek and Hebrew, is composed of six lines cast into three parallelismi membrorum and two speech formulae. The author retains two of the parallel pairs, but transforms the second one into a double question. Of the third pair from the source he retains one member which he also casts into an interrogative form. The effect is most striking: two declarative statements, two rhetorical questions, and a final indictment also in the form of a question. The last mentioned is further transformed by the addition of οὐχί, which underscores, by means of a negative particle, the affirmative response expected. Lastly, the insertion of λέγει κύριος--in reality borrowed from the source--within the quotation, finds an excellent parallel in 7:6-7 (already noted <u>supra</u>, p. 184), where another OT quotation is interrupted by a speech formula. In fact, the similarity is even greater when one observes the double formulae in both cases: one introducing the citation and one toward the end emphasizing the divine origin of the text.

From the above analysis, it has become increasingly clear that the stylistic data listed in the corpus owe in large measure to the activity of the author. In spite of considerable and often minute borrowing from the OT, he has imposed his peculiar style upon the material. Duality, repetition, contrast, etc., are rarely a result of the quoting process, instead it is my conclusion, that they constitute structural, stylistic or thematic tendencies of the author.

C. <u>Nature and Function of the Stylistic Data within the Narrative</u>

Up to this point the study has dealt solely with the speech. This was done first by an analysis of the quotations to distinguish as precisely as possible what was simply taken from the OT model and what owed to the author's creativity both as original composition and as editing of his source. In light of this, a number of structural and stylistic data began to emerge.

Presently it is possible to investigate the narratives of the Stephen story from the same point of view. The same categories, as well as method, will be utilized to that end. Since stylistic, thematic, and structural tendencies similar to those encountered in the lengthy discourse have emerged from the analysis of the narrative, this part of the study is a corroboration of the conclusions stated above.

1. Acts 6.1-7

The initial section of the Stephen story introduces the reader fully into a community quarrel. The apparent abruptness of the narrative has caused considerable comment among scholars, since the previous chapters of Acts consistently stressed the harmonious relations between the early Christians. While it is not my purpose to dwell upon the many facets of this particular problem, it is my belief that the following analysis will provide new data for understanding both the composition and purpose of the passage under consideration.

The first part of the narrative makes generous use of doublets and repetitive elements. The data provided by the corpus are as follows:

1.a Verb followed by cognate substantive (6:2), (6)
1.c Singular/plural (1,2), (1,7), (1,2,3), (2), (2,5), (2), (3,5), (5)
1.e Negative/positive (2,5), (2,4)
2.a Cognate expressions (1,2,5,7), (1,7), (1,2,7), (1,2,4), (2,5), (2,5), (2,4,7), (3,5), (3,5), (3,6), (4,6), (5,6), (5,7)
2.b Proper names (2,7)
2.c Synonymous terms (1), (1,2,3), (2,6), (2,5,7), (2,4,6), (3,5), (3,5), (3,5), (3,6), (7)
2.d Substantive followed by apposition (3), (3), (5), (5), (5)
3.a Parallelismus membrorum (7)
3.d Lists (3), (4), (5), (5)
3.e Sequential patterns (1,2,5,7), (1,2,5,7), (2,3,4)
3.f Double clusters (1,2-4 and 5-7a, 7b)

From a strictly numerical point of view, it is clear that the stylistic data presented above play a prominent role within the text being examined. The distribution is consistent with that observed for the various parts of the speech, that is, cognate expressions, synonymous terms, singular/plural contrasts, and lists generally predominate. Other categories such as negative/positive contrasts, verb followed by cognate substantive, parallelismus membrorum, sequential patterns, and double clusters proffer approximately the same frequency. Finally, the absence of redundancy and the rarity of proper names are understood in relation to the nature of the text. The former has generally been associated with close dependence upon the OT, while the latter has been central to the author's method throughout the speech.

Of far greater significance is the occurrence of the data within their structural context. The large number of elements interconnecting the two sections of this passage (vv.1-4 and 5-7) is truly striking. Due to the complexity of the overall framework, it seems best to examine the passage in the following fourfold division: 1) vv.1 and 7; 2) vv.2 and 5a; 3) vv.3 and 5b-6a; and 4) vv.4 and 6b.

The introductory and concluding verses of this part of the Stephen story form an evident structural and thematic inclusio. V.1 πληθυνόντων τῶν μαθητῶν and v.7 ἐπληθύνετο ὁ ἀριθμὸς τῶν μαθητῶν are obvious parallels. 'Εν δὲ ταῖς ἡμέραις ταύταις, introducing the first phrase and ἐν 'Ιερουσαλήμ, following directly upon the second, reinforce the conclusion that vv.1 and 7 constitute an inclusio. In effect, "the days" (v.1) refers to the time of the Jerusalem community (Acts 1-5). The author, in his concern to portray the pristine character of the early Church, begins and ends a troublesome episode by affirming the growth, thereby implying the unity of that institution. After a brief statement concerning the increase of members, he introduces a problem which the Church had to encounter. By the use of a time formula followed by a genitive absolute, he seems to suggest a temporal rather than a causal relationship between the growth in numbers and the internal problems. Modern scholars are probably not wrong in discerning clues of more serious questions within this construction.[34] However, of greater concern here is the writer's goal. He presents a problem (v.1), proposes a solution (vv.2-4) and its adoption (vv.5-6), and, finally, dwells upon the successful resolution of the grievance (v.7). In fact, the final verse by its threefold repetition of the theme of growth, allows the author to reiterate several concepts germane to his purpose: "word of God," "The multiplication of disciples," adherence to "the faith." At the same time, v.7 clearly displays some of the writer's stylistic tendencies: the use of the biblical doublet "increase and multiply" in v.7a and b (see the discussion of 7:17), and of a parallelismus membrorum in v.7b and c. V.7, then, by its

---

[34]See Haenchen, Acts, pp. 264-69; Schmithals, Paul and James, pp. 16-37; Trocmé, Livre des Actes, pp. 188-91.

repetitive character successfully terminates, at least in the mind of the author, a relatively independent episode of the Church's early history.

Before proceeding to a discussion of the remaining sections of 6:1-7, the following synopsis is necessary:

2	προσκαλεσάμενοι δὲ οἱ δώδεκα	5	
	τὸ πλῆθος τῶν μαθητῶν εἶπαν		καὶ ἤρεσεν ὁ λόγος
	οὐκ ἀρεστόν ἐστιν ἡμᾶς		ἐνώπιον παντὸς τοῦ πλήθους,
	καταλείψαντος τὸν λόγον τοῦ θεοῦ		
	διακονεῖν τραπέζαις		
3	ἐπισκέψασθε δέ, ἀδελφοί,		καὶ ἐξελέξαντο
	ἄνδρας ἐξ ὑμῶν		Στέφανον, ἄνδρα
	μαρτυρουμένους		πλήρη πίστεως καὶ πνεύματος ἁγίου,
	ἑπτὰ		καὶ Φίγιππον καὶ Πρόχορον καὶ Νικάνορα καὶ Τίμωνα καὶ Παρμενᾶν
	πλήρεις πνεύματος καὶ σοφίας,		καὶ Νικόλαον προσήλυτον Ἀντιοχέα,
	οὓς καταστήσομεν ἐπὶ τῆς χρείας ταύτης·	6	οὓς ἔστησαν ἐνώπιον τῶν ἀποστόλων,
4	ἡμεῖς δὲ τῇ προσευχῇ		καὶ προσευξάμενοι ἐπέθηκαν αὐτοῖς τὰς χεῖρας.
	καὶ τῇ διακονίᾳ τοῦ λόγου προσκαρτερήσομεν.		

The relationship between vv.2 and 5 is particularly underscored by the negative/positive contrast as well as cognate doublet: οὐκ ἀρεστόν ἐστιν and καὶ ἤρεσεν ὁ λόγος and the repetition of πλῆθος.

The third structural component, vv.3 and 5b-6a, reveals a more complex but also more striking parallelism. The expressions, "select" and "they chose," function as command/fulfilment and introduce the elements prescribed and those executed. The relationship between the two passages, however, is more elaborate still. The plural terms, ἄνδρας, μαρτυρουμένους, and πλήρεις correspond to singular statements, Στέφανον ἄνδρα, πλήρη, and Νικόλαον προσήλυτον. The first two parallels are obvious, but the last needs comment. The combination μαρτυρέω - πλήρης with its complementary statement in v.5 must be understood in light of the author's stylistic tendencies. The description of Cornelius, Acts 10:22, is particularly instructive in this regard:

Κορνήλιος ἑκατοντάρχης, ἀνὴρ δίκαιος καὶ φοβούμενος τὸν θεόν, μαρτυρούμενός τε ὑπὸ ὅλου τοῦ ἔθνους τῶν Ἰουδαίων ...

The participle of μαρτυρέω functions in both texts as a term qualifying the person in question: in Acts 10:22 along with "just and God-fearing," and in 6:3 with "full of Spirit and wisdom." The use of μαρτυρέω in both passages is strikingly similar: "believers" are presented with the best Jewish recommendation possible.[35] In light of these considerations, the structural similarities between vv.3 and 5 are greatly enhanced,

v.3 ἄνδρας ... μαρτυρουμένους + ἑπτά + πλήρεις ...
v.5 Στέφανον ἄνδρα + πλήρη ... + [list] + Νικόλαον προτήλυτον,

and further underscored by the final clause of each text, οὓς καταστήσομεν (v.3) and οὓς ἔστησαν ἐνώπιον τῶν ἀποστόλων (6a). Of particular interest is the double use of ἵστημι (once with a prepositional prefix) and the twofold reference to the apostles--as subject in v.3 and as object in v.6.

The relationship between vv.4 and 6b is structurally and stylistically significant. Apart from the cognate doublet, τῇ προσευχῇ and προσευξάμενοι, which serves to emphasize the principal role of the Twelve, the author draws special attention to another function of the apostles. In v.3 he states that they are the ones who will appoint the Seven. This command, the writer tells us, is fulfilled in two successive steps: 1) the presentation before the apostles, and 2) the laying of hands (a phrase borrowed from the LXX, Dt 34:9).

The overall unity of 6:1-7 requires more extensive analysis. The inclusio-like nature of vv.1 and 7 has already been noted. The completeness and relative independence of the epi-

---

[35]Acts 22:12, Ἁνανίας δέ τις, ἀνὴρ εὐλαβὴς κατὰ τὸν νόμον, μαρτυρούμενος ὑπὸ πάντων τῶν κατοικούντων Ἰουδαίων, ἐλθὼν ..., presents an identical stylistic parallel. See also

sode have also been pointed out. Furthermore, in v.4 (τῇ διακονίᾳ τοῦ λόγου προσκαρτερήσομεν), the author adroitly relates the theme of the "word of God" (λόγος τοῦ θεοῦ vv.2 and 7) with that of "table service" (vv.1, 2, 3--the first and second of which use διακονία and διακονέω respectively). The motif of "word-service" forms an inclusio, introducing and concluding the speech of the Twelve. Finally, the twofold reference to the leaders of the community, v.2 (οἱ δώδεκα) and v.6 (τῶν ἀποστόλων) functions as an inclusio for the passage dealing with the solution of the controversy (vv.2-6); but also serves to emphasize that the initiative and central role within the assembly rests with those same leaders.

2. Acts 6:8-7:2a

A new section of the narrative begins at v.8 and introduces the reader to a new episode in the history of the Jerusalem community. Once again it is not my intention to review the host of problems which have claimed the attention of generations of scholars, but instead to examine the data provided by the corpus to seek new insights in the author's purpose and method of composition.

The pertinent categories are as follows:

1.a Verb followed by cognate substantive (6:8), (11), (13)
1.c Singular/plural (12,15), (14)
1.d Redundancy (13,14), (14), (15), (15)
1.e Negative/positive (9,10), (13,14)
2.a Cognate expressions (8,12), (9,10,12,13), (10,11,13), (11,13,14), (11,14), (11,13), (12,15), (13,14), (15)
2.b Proper names (8,9), (11,14)
2.c Synonymous terms (8), (11,13), (11,13), (11,13,14)
2.d Substantive followed by apposition (8), (9), (14)
3.a Parallelismus membrorum (13,14)
3.b Formulaic repetition: speech (11,13,14), (7:1,2)
3.d Lists (8), (8), (9), (9), (9), (10), (11), (12), (13)
3.e Sequential pattern (11,13,14)
3.f Double cluster (11 and 13)

The distribution and frequency of the stylistic data are consistent with other parts of the narrative, as well as different sections of the discourse. The increase in category 3.d (lists) is particularly noteworthy since no other part of the Stephen material, with the possible exception of the invective, vv.51-53, exhibits such a high ratio.

16:1-2.

Of far greater significance, however, in the analysis of this text, is the distribution of the stylistic data within the structure of the passage. To achieve this objective the narrative will be examined according to its threefold division: 1) 6:8-12a, the pretrial confrontation of Stephen with his opponents; 2) 12b-15, the accusation before the Sanhedrin; and 3) 7:1-2a, the interrogation by the high priest.

The first part deals with Stephen's work among the people and, in fact, is delineated by the double use of λαός in vv.8 and 12a. The entire section betrays the author's characteristic modes of composition.[36] Vv.8 and 9 present the protagonists: Stephen and his opponents in dispute with him. The author begins his text by his accustomed use of doublets. Stephen is represented as having "grace and power" and achieving "wonders and great signs." His antagonists are introduced in a twofold group, one of three: Libertines, Cyrenians, and Alexandrians, and one of two: Cilician and Asians. Furthermore, the first and last element of the text is the name of Stephen, the only occurrences of the name in 6:8-7:2a. The writer, by a positive/negative technique (v.10), then proceeds to the central concern of his narrative, the accusations brought against Stephen. The opponents take the initiative because they are overpowered by the "wisdom and Spirit by which he spoke." By means of a mot-agraffe (λαλέω), the author presents the first accusation (against Moses and God, v.11) and concludes his text by stating the successful outcome of the episode: "they stirred up the people, the elders and the scribes." (12a)

The second part of the narrative (vv.12-15) presents a second stage in the charges brought against Stephen since he is led before the Sanhedrin, which section is delineated by the expressions, εἰς τὸ συνέδριον (v.12b) and ἐν τῷ συνεδρίῳ (v. 15). The initiative is now taken by a larger and more official group that accuses Stephen before the court. Witnesses are brought forth and there follow double sets of indictments, both

---

[36]Reference should be made to the parallel with the Philip story, 8:5-8, where "Samaria" forms a doublet with "that city," in effect delineating the first part of the episode. See a further discussion of this parallel in chapter four.

consisting of doublets: v.13 against the holy place and the Law, and v.14 regarding "the place" and the customs of Moses. The writer then terminates this part of his narrative by introducing the first of two statements (v.15) concerning Stephen's transfiguration (see 7:55-56).

The third part (7:1-2a) presents in abbreviated form an interrogation of the accused. By this means the writer is able to introduce the long discourse which follows.[37]

The various segments of the narrative under consideration are carefully orchestrated by the writer. He employs a variety of stylistic features to interrelate the themes and episodes of his text. Characteristic of his redactive tendencies is the double use in the first and second parts of his narrative of the following cognates: ἀνέστησαν (9), ἀντιστῆναι (10), ἐπιστάντες (12b), and ἔστησαν (13). Equally important stylistically is the threefold use of λαλέω; however, its structural function is probably more striking. V.10 dwells upon Stephen's eloquence (use of λαλέω) and the opponents' inability to gainsay his arguments. The author then employs the same term in obvious contrast, i.e., in a negative sense, to formulate both accusations (vv.11 and 13).

The charges require considerable attention. They constitute the central focus of the introductory narrative, both within the informal forum of the crowd scene (vv.8-12a), and within the trial before the Sanhedrin (12b-15). However the second accusation is in reality a doublet, since vv.13 and 14 constitute a parallelismus membrorum. In light of this, it is possible to speak of a threefold indictment whose introductory formulae are strikingly similar:

11 τότε ὑπέβαλον ἄνδρας λέγοντας ὅτι ...

13 ἔστησάν τε μάρτυρας ψευδεῖς λέγοντας ...

14 ἀκηκόαμεν γὰρ αὐτοῦ λέγοντος ὅτι ...

Apart from the three occurrences of the participle of λέγω, the following doublets should also be pointed out: ἀκούω (vv.11 and 14), λαλέω ῥήματα (11 and 13), Moses (11 and 14), and "this

---

[37]The same interrogation process occurs in Acts 5:27-28 (by the high priest) and is followed by a response in the form of a speech. See the analysis of the post-speech structure of the Stephen episode below, pp. 225-27.

place" (vv.13 and 14). It is obvious, then, that these charges are stylistically related and betray clear traces of the author's redactive tendencies.

In this regard, a final point should be made concerning the structural disposition of the accusations. Not only are there three denunciation statements, but there are three sets of accusers: the speakers of v.11, the false witnesses of v. 13, and Stephen himself in v.14. Indeed, the third accusation is given in the form of testimony "we have heard him saying. . . ." The author cleverly makes Stephen himself a witness and, therefore, an accuser. In spite of the threefold character of these indictments, 1) against Moses and God v.11; 2) against the holy place and the Law v.13; and 3) regarding the holy place and the customs from Moses v.14, there are only two charges made against Stephen: one concerning Moses and the Law, and the other concerning God and the temple.[38] The author states these accusations in three different passages whose structure presents a pattern often seen throughout the Stephen material. A survey of practically all the parallelismi membrorum noted in the corpus will reveal a similar situation, namely, an intentional link between one part of the parallel structure, usually the first, and an earlier element of the text.[39] One example suffices to illustrate this stylistic feature:

7:13 καὶ φανερὸν ἐγένετο τῷ Φαραὼ τὸ γένος Ἰωσήφ
19 οὗτος κατασοφισάμενος τὸ γένος ἡμῶν
ἐκάκωσεν τοὺς πατέρας ...

It is noteworthy that γένος occurs only twice in the entire Stephen story. The accusations, then, reveal a similar structure:

---

[38]See Haenchen, Acts, p. 271, who refers approvingly to Loisy in this regard.

[39]Similar constructions occur throughout the Stephen story: 6:1 and 7: "multiplication of disciples"; 6:3 and 6: καταστήσομεν - ἔστησαν; 7:19 and 34: "ill-treatment"; 7:20 and 21: ἀνατρέφω; 7:27 and 35: OT quotation; 7:42 and 49: "building a house"; 7:51 and 54: "hearts"; 7:51 and 52: "your fathers." In the case of 7:24 and 26 the parallelismus membrorum precedes the use of ἀδικέω in v.26.

v.11 ἀκηκόαμεν αὐτοῦ λαλοῦντος ῥήματα βλάσφημα εἰς Μωϋσῆν
καὶ τὸν θεόν

v.13 ὁ ἄνθρωπος οὗτος οὐ παύεται λαλῶν ῥήματα κατὰ τοῦ
τόπου τοῦ ἁγίου τούτου
καὶ τοῦ νόμου

v.14 Ἰησοῦς ὁ Ναζωραῖος οὗτος καταλύσει τὸν τόπον τοῦτον
καὶ ἀλλάξει τὰ ἔθη ἃ παρέδωκεν ἡμῖν Μωϋσῆς.

Vv.13 and 14 represent a restatement by the author in the form of a parallelismus membrorum of the indictment brought against Stephen before the Sanhedrin (note the links between the two statements: double accusations, οὗτος, "this place," Law-Moses). None the less, the similarity is even greater between the charges made in vv.11 and 13, so much so that I am led to the conclusion that the latter has been modeled upon the former (this will be treated further in the next chapter).

In concluding the discussion of Acts 6:8-7:2a, it is necessary to point out the large number of stylistic features which the text has in common with Acts 3:1f. and 5:17f. The first passage, after an introductory verse, reads καί τις ἀνήρ . . . (see also 4:36-5:1) in a manner similar to 6:9. In 3:4 and 12 note the double use of ἀτενίζω (see 6:15 and 7:55). The speech of 3:12f. bears numerous contacts with the Stephen speech.[40] Finally, the opponents of the apostles in 4:1 and 5 (groups of three) are very similar to those of Stephen, 6:12. Acts 5:17f. likewise reveals great continuity of style with the passage under question. The use of ἀνίστημι in 5:17 is identical to that of 6:9; while λαλέω . . . πάντα τὰ ῥήματα of 5:20 is to be related to 6:11 and 13: ἀγαγόντες δὲ αὐτοὺς ἔστησαν ἐν τῷ συνεδρίῳ of 5:27 to 6:12; the interrogation by the high priest of 5:27 to 7:1; and the subsequent speech, particularly v.30 to 7:32 and 35. To anticipate a bit, the reaction to Peter's words, οἱ δὲ ἀκούσαντες διεπρίοντο καὶ ἐβούλοντο ἀνελεῖν αὐτούς (v.33), is very similar to that provoked by Stephen's words in 7:54, ἀκούοντες δὲ ταῦτα διεπρίοντο ταῖς καρδίαις αὐτῶν, followed by the death scene. Finally, the beginning phrase of 5:34, ἀναστὰς δέ τις ἐν τῷ συνεδρίῳ Φαρισαῖος

---

[40]Note in particular 3:13 and 7:32; 3:13-15 and 7:35 (see 3:20-21 also); 3:22 and 7:37.

ὀνόματι Γαμαλιήλ, bears a close resemblance to 6:9.[41]

3. Acts 7:54-8:4

The final narrative serves both as a conclusion to the speech and to the Stephen story: the termination of the trial and the ensuing death scene. At the same time, the author has introduced a totally new element within the history of the Jerusalem community, namely, the early activities of Saul. The following elements of the stylistic corpus should be noted:

1.a Verb followed by cognate substantive (7:54), (54), (57), (60), (60), (8:2), (4)
1.b Compound verb followed by same preposition (58)
1.c Singular/plural (55,56), (57,60), (8:1)
1.d Redundancy (58), (8:2)
1.e Negative/positive (59,60), (8:1)
2.a Cognate expressions (55,56), (55,56), (57,60), (58, 59), (58,60), (59,60), (8:1,2), (1,3), (1,4)
2.b Proper names (55,59), (55,55,56), (58; 8:1,3), (59, 60)
2.c Synonymous terms (54), (59)
2.d Substantive followed by apposition (58), (8:1)
3.a Parallelismus membrorum (54), (55,56), (59,60), (8:2)
3.b Formulaic repetition: speech (56,59,60)
3.d Lists (55), (56), (59), (8:1), (3)
3.e Sequential pattern (57,58,59; 8:1,2,3)

The distribution of the categories is consistent with the other sections of the Stephen story. Once again the functional nature of the data requires careful attention, and it will be necessary to examine these in their structural context.

This part of the narrative has been particularly troublesome to commentators since it raises a host of historical and theological problems. While it is not possible to review these even briefly, it is nevertheless plausible that a new perspective could shed some light on the author's purpose and method of composition. To begin this discussion reference should be made to one particular problem raised recently by scholars.

> Despite the views attributed to Stephen in his speech, it does not appear that even those were sufficient to ensure his condemnation and death. The climax is reached in 7:56, when he claims to see the Son of Man, so that like his Master before him he provides the final provocation which leads to his death. In the end it is not

---

[41]One should note the obvious positive/negative contrast which the author makes within the Gamaliel episode between the Pharisee who is τίμιος (v.34) and the apostles who finally become worthy to be dishonored (ἀτιμασθῆναι), v.41.

> his attitude to the Law and the Temple, but his confession of Christ which, in Luke's view, is the final cause of his death.[42]

Such observations may at first glance seem quite convincing. In effect, the non-Christian character of the long discourse[43] is compensated for by insisting upon the centrality of the Christological verses (55-56) of the narrative. The only justification for such a conclusion is precisely the failure of the Jews to react appropriately, following the bitter invective of vv.51-53. However, such an approach is far from satisfactory, since this conclusion relegates the Stephen speech to a relatively minor role. This is particularly bothersome in view of the length of the discourse, which one would have to conclude is irrelevant or unsuited to its present context.[44]

An analysis of the overall structure of the narrative, and with this an examination of the stylistic data presented in the corpus, reveals generally unnoticed features of the author's method of composition. Since 7:54-8:4 follows immediately upon a speech and in fact constitutes the audience's response, it has seemed logical to survey the book of Acts from that point of view. In at least five instances (2:37f., 5:33f., 7:54f., 11:18f., and 13:48f.) after a speech the writer resumes his text with a participial form of the verb ἀκούω followed by a finite verb expressing the hearers' reaction. While each of these passages could assist one in understanding the sequel to the Stephen speech--it is the second (5:33f.) which will retain prolonged attention.

After Peter's brief speech (5:29-32), which has important

---

[42]Wilson, <u>Gentiles</u>, p. 136. See a similar statement by Haenchen, <u>Acts</u>, p. 295. David M. Hay, <u>Glory at the Right Hand: Psalm 110 in Early Christianity</u>, Society of Biblical Literature, Monograph Series, no. 18 (Nashville: Published for the Society of Biblical Literature by Abingdon Press, [1973]), p. 74 and n. 97, draws analogous conclusions.

[43]O'Neill, <u>Theology</u>, dwells at length upon this aspect not only of the speech but also of the entire Stephen story; see p. 25, n. 89 above for a discussion of his views.

[44]The length of the discourse and its apparent inappropriateness within the Stephen story have been repeatedly pointed out by scholars, who have usually had recourse, in solving the problem, to the less-than-perfect editing of an old document or source by the author of Acts; see the discussion of this point in chapter four.

links with 7:35 (see the discussion above), the author expresses the hearers' response as follows: v.33 οἱ δὲ ἀκούσαντες διεπρίοντο καὶ ἐβούλοντο ἀνελεῖν αὐτούς. Instead of an immediate statement of the punishment meted out to the apostles, the writer presents a sequel, vv.34f. (involving narrative v.34 and discourse vv.35-39), and a second reaction by the audience v. 40. It is only at this point that the episode is resolved, δείραντες παρήγγειλαν μὴ λαλεῖν ἐπὶ τῷ ὀνόματι τοῦ Ἰησοῦ καὶ ἀπέλυσαν. The author then terminates the entire section, prior to the Stephen story, with the two following verses:

41 οἱ μὲν οὖν ἐπορεύοντο χαίροντες ἀπὸ προσώπου τοῦ συνεδρίου, ὅτι κατηξιώθησαν ὑπὲρ τοῦ ὀνόματος ἀτιμασθῆναι·

42 πᾶσάν τε ἡμέραν ἐν τῷ ἱερῷ καὶ κατ' οἶκον οὐκ ἐπαύοντο διδάσκοντες καὶ εὐαγγελιζόμενοι τὸν χριστον Ἰησοῦν.

A comparison then of chapters 5:29-42 and 7:2-8:4 reveals the following framework:

Speech	7:2-53	5:29-32
1st reaction	54	33
sequel: narrative	55	34
discourse	56	35-39
2nd reaction & resolution	57-8:3	40
conclusion	8:4	41-42

Furthermore, the various parts of the structure bear remarkable similarities. The relationship between the speeches has already been noted. 5:33, διεπρίοντο recalls 7:54, διεπρίοντο ταῖς καρδίαις αὐτῶν, while the remainder of v.33, ἐβούλοντο ἀνελεῖν αὐτούς, relates not to the first sequel of the Stephen story, but to the resolution (see the use of ἀναίρεσις in 8:1). The difference clearly owes to the demands of the context: in chapter five Gamaliel dissuades the audience from carrying the death penalty, while in chapter seven the death scene plays a prominent role. The sequel in both cases consists of narrative followed by discourse, which discourse provokes a second reaction on the part of the hearers. Once again the difference between the two texts, particularly as regards the nature of the reaction, is due to the needs of the narrative. In 5:40 the response is one of moderation as indicated by the resolution, while in 7:57 it is violent, and indeed serves as an appropriate prologue to the death of Stephen. The sequel in the first case is brief and without repercussions; however, in the second it involves Stephen's execution and its consequences both in terms of persecution and dispersion. Finally the conclusion of each passage begins with the expression, οἱ μὲν οὖν . . . , followed in 5:41 by a finite verb and participle, and in 8:4 by a participle and finite verb. It terminates with similar expressions 5:42 εὐαγγελιζόμενοι τὸν χριστὸν Ἰησοῦν and 8:4 εὐαγγελιζόμενοι τὸν λόγον.

Further confirmation of the stylistic patterns indicated above is forthcoming from 2:37f. and 11:18f. In the first instance, the reaction of the audience is expressed in terms reminiscent of 7:54, ἀκούσαντες δὲ κατενύγησαν τὴν καρδίαν. The sequel is considerably different from the pattern described above. However, in 2:41 the author introduces his conclusion as follows: οἱ μὲν οὖν ἀποδεξάμενοι. . . . In the second passage the response of the hearers is positive (ἡσύχασαν καὶ ἐδόξασαν τὸν θεόν 11:18; see also 13:48) and brief (expressed in direct discourse). The conclusion[45] which follows immediately is practically identical with that of the Stephen story:

8:4	11:19
οἱ μὲν οὖν διασπαρέντες	οἱ μὲν οὖν διασπαρέντες
	ἀπὸ τῆς θλίψεως
	τῆς γενομένης ἐπὶ Στεφάνῳ
διῆλθον	διῆλθον
	ἕως Φοινίκης καὶ Κύπρου καὶ Ἀντιοχείας,
εὐαγγελιζόμενοι τὸν λόγον.	μηδενὶ λαλοῦντες τὸν λόγον
	εἰ μὴ μόνον Ἰουδαίοις.

The reference to Stephen in this context is most significant.

In light of the preceding analysis, therefore, one can only conclude that the double reaction of the audience, once following the speech and again after the twofold statement of

[45]It is possible to speak either of conclusion or introduction in relation to οἱ μὲν οὖν, "a favourite formula of Acts in opening a new story which is nevertheless connected with what goes before" *Beginnings*, 4:7 (see Haenchen, *Acts*, p. 143, n.6, for a complete list of the occurrence of this phrase in Acts.)

the heavenly vision, is intimately related to the author's method of composition, rather than owing to a poor combination of sources. He has followed a pattern similar to that found in chapter five.

Within this structure numerous doublets occur which require comment. The two reactions of the audience end with the expression, ἐπ' αὐτόν (vv.54 and 47). The twofold statement of the vision, vv.55-56, apart from being a narrative/discourse pattern corresponding to Acts 5:34 and 35-39, constitutes a parallelismus membrorum-like construction:

ὑπάρχων δὲ πλήρης πνεύματος ἁγίου
ἀτενίσας εἰς τὸν οὐρανὸν
εἶδεν δόξαν θεοῦ
καὶ 'Ιησοῦν ἑστῶτα ἐκ δεξιῶν τοῦ θεοῦ,
καὶ εἶπεν·
ἰδοὺ θεωρῶ τοὺς οὐρανοὺς διηνοιγμένους
καὶ τὸν υἱὸν τοῦ ἀνθρώπου ἐκ δεξιῶν ἑστῶτα τοῦ θεοῦ.

The various links between the two passages, cognate as well as structural doublets should be noted. The above construction in turn bears a relationship with 6:15. Like the accusations, the vision/transfiguration of Stephen receives a threefold assertion.

7:57-8:3, the section called "2nd reaction and resolution" above, requires special attention because of its length and peculiar character. While the threefold insertion of elements from the Saul tradition (58b; 8:1, and 3) has considerably lengthened the post-speech narrative, it has left intact the continuity of the death scene. However, it should be noted that these additions are not extraneous elements, nor are they to be considered as later interpolations, since each seems to have been intentionally situated within its present context. The stoning of Stephen, v.58a, allows the writer to insist upon the judicial nature of the execution (a second reference to the witnesses, see 6:13) and upon Saul's role in this affair (see Acts 22:19-20). By means of a resumptive technique the author repeats ἐλιθοβόλουν and pursues his goal. Furthermore, the death of Stephen (7:60 ἐκοιμήθη) calls to mind that Saul consented to his killing (8:1 Σαῦλος δὲ ἦν συνευδοκῶν τῇ ἀναιρέσει αὐτοῦ; see Acts 22:20 once more). After dwelling upon the consequences of this turn of events for the Jerusalem community, he returns once again to the Stephen story, only to pursue once more in 8:3 the fate of the assembly (ἐκκλησία, 8:1 and 3). The passages drawn from the Saul tradition then are linked to the death scene by the author, using his usual stylistic techniques. The threefold reference to Saul further supports this conclusion. 8:1 and 3, both introduced by Σαῦλος δέ, constitute a doublet whose relation to 7:58b is evident. Also it should be pointed out that the entire passage presents a salient alternating pattern, 7:57 "him," 58b "Saul," 59 "Stephen," 8:1 "Saul," 2 "Stephen," and 3 "Saul."

The overall structure of Acts 7:54-8:4, then owes to the author's method of composition, as evidenced in other parts of Acts. The unity of the passage is further enhanced by cognate (7:57 κράξαντες δὲ φωνῇ μεγάλῃ and 60 ἔκραξεν φωνῇ μεγάλῃ; 8:1 and 3, ἐκκλησία; 8:1 and 4 διασπείρω) and structural doublets (lists and constructions such as the twofold reaction of the audience, and statement of the vision, the threefold reference to Saul, and the two sayings of Stephen as he dies:

59 κύριε Ἰησοῦ, δέξαι τὰ πνεῦμά μου

60 κύριε, μὴ στήσῃς αὐτοῖς ταύτην τὴν ἁμαρτίαν[46]).

D. Relation between the Narratives and the Speech

From the above analysis it has become increasingly clear that the various parts of the Stephen story bear numerous stylistic, structural, and thematic tendencies and peculiarities in common. Through the examination of the corpus and the functional role of the data, it was possible to deduce important considerations for a study of the author's method of composition. However, one aspect of the research has been delayed until now, namely, interconnections between the discourse of Stephen and the rest of the story. To conclude this study it is necessary therefore to examine the relationship between the narratives and the speech from a stylistic point of view.

1. The Stephen Speech and Its Immediate Narrative Context

The long historical discourse of Acts 7 and its position

---

[46]See Morganthaler, Geschichtsschreibung, 1:48-49. The structural analysis of 7:55-56 will be seen later (pp. 293-98), since questions of source and redaction must first be discussed.

within the Stephen story requires further clarification. Careful scrutiny of the data does not reveal that it has been carelessly inserted into its present position. Instead there is much evidence to the contrary.

While it would be possible to cite a number of cognate doublets which link the speech to its immediate context, it is preferable to present this data as constituting a double cluster (see category 3.f). In effect the pertinent data are as follows:

6:13,15	καὶ τοῦ νόμου ... ὡσεὶ πρόσωπον ἀγγέλου
6:15;7:2	καὶ ἀτενίσαντες εἰς ... εἶδον τὸ πρόσωπον ...
	εἰ ταῦτα οὕτως ἔχει;
	... ἀκούσατε
	ὁ θεὸς τῆς δόξης ...
7:53	... τὸν νόμον εἰς διαταγὰς ἀγγέλων
7:54-5	ἀκούοντες δὲ ταῦτα
	ἀτενίσας εἰς ... εἶδεν δόξαν θεοῦ καὶ Ἰησοῦν ...

The speech, then, in its present condition is not an isolated text. In 7:1 the author places the following question in the mouth of the high priest, εἰ ταῦτα οὕτως ἔχει, and then resumes immediately after the discourse, ἀκούοντες δὲ ταῦτα . . . (7:54). Furthermore, to the introductory statement of the discourse, ἄνδρες ἀδελφοὶ καὶ πατέρες ἀκούσατε (7:2), corresponds the ἀκούοντες δὲ ταῦτα (7:54) of the audience's reaction. The important phrase, ἀτενίσαντες εἰς . . . εἶδον (6:15), is taken up once again after the speech, in a plural/singular contrast, to introduce the vision of Stephen, ἀτενίσας εἰς . . . εἶδεν. Finally, at the very beginning of the discourse (7:2), the writer presents a startling expression borrowed from Ps 28:3, ὁ θεὸς τῆς δόξης. It should be noted that he returns to this theme in 7:55, where he presents Stephen in the following manner, εἶδεν δόξαν θεοῦ.

Further considerations should be noted in this regard. The author's tendency to further expand the range of the parallelismus membrorum by positing an added link to another part of his composition has already been pointed out (see pp. 222-23). Presently it should be noted that 7:54, διεπρίοντο ταῖς καρδίαις αὐτῶν, is related to 7:51, ἀπερίτμητοι καρδίαις, and that 7:55-6, the double statement of Stephen's vision (note ἀτενίζω), refers back to 6:15, the reference to Stephen's transfigured face (note once more the use of ἀτενίζω). Further illustrations of the relation between the discourse and its introductory, as well as concluding, narrative are forthcoming. The author has cannily commented upon the invective of 7:51, ἀπερίτμητοι . . . τοῖς ὠσίν, by stating of the enraged crowd, συνέσχον τὰ ὦτα αὐτῶν (7:57). During the trial scene Stephen has been accused of speaking κατὰ τοῦ τόπου τοῦ ἁγίου τούτου (6:13), and Jesus of threatening to destroy τὸν τόπον τοῦτον. The author unites this theme to the beginning of Stephen's discourse by stating in 7:7, λατρεύσουσίν μοι ἐν τῷ τόπῳ τούτῳ, in effect modifying the text of Ex 3:12 to accomplish this (see p. 51).

Finally, the sequel to the Stephen speech, particularly the reaction of the audience, is consistent with the writer's method of composition as demonstrated earlier. This further emphasizes the conclusion that the historical discourse of Acts 7 forms an integral part of the entire Stephen episode.

2. The Interrelations Between the Various Parts of the Stephen Story

In a more general way it is possible to examine Acts 6:1-8:4 in relation to the stylistic corpus. The relevant categories are as follows: 1.a verb followed by cognate substantive; 1.c singular/plural; 1.3 negative/positive; 2.c synonymous terms; 2.d substantive followed by apposition; 3.a parallelismus membrorum; 2.c local expressions introducing and concluding episodes; 3.d lists; 3.e sequential patterns; 3.f double clusters. The distribution of these data throughout all sections of the Stephen story testifies to the homogeneity of the writer's creativity. All parts of 6:1-8:4 show a consistent use of the stylistic techniques, patterns, and categories listed in the corpus. From this the conclusion follows that the entire episode, besides its biographic and thematic unity, possesses coherence of structure and composition.

In the list of categories given above, 2.a (cognate expressions) and b (proper names and titles) were purposely omitted. This has been done since these require particular and detailed consideration. The repeated use of terms, phrases, and names throughout the Stephen story is significant as a stylistic and as a structural feature. However, these particular categories are far more crucial in understanding the author's method of composition and purpose (the following chapter), than other elements of the corpus. My intention, then, is to study the Stephen material, with accompanying list of data, in four successive stages: a) the introductory narratives (6:1-7 and 6:8-7:2a); b) the introductory narratives and the speech (7:2b-53); c) the speech and the concluding narrative (7:54-8:4); and d) the three parts of the Stephen story.

a. <u>The Relation between 6:1-7 and 6:8-7:2a</u>

The following data are pertinent to the discussion:

οὗτος	6:1	ἐν δὲ ταῖς ἡμέραις ταύταις
	6:3	ἐπὶ τῆς χρείας ταύτης
	6:13	ὁ ἄνθρωπος οὗτος
	6:13	κατὰ τοῦ τόπου τοῦ ἁγίου τούτου
	6:14	'Ιησοῦς ὁ Ναζωραῖος οὗτος
	6:14	καταλύσει τὸν τόπον τοῦτον
	7:1	εἰ ταῦτα οὕτως ἔχει
θεός	6:2	τὸν λόγον τοῦ θεοῦ
	6:7	ὁ λόγος τοῦ θεοῦ
	6:11	εἰς ... τὸν θεόν
ἀνήρ	6:3	ἄνδρας
	6:5	ἄνδρα
	6:11	ἄνδρας
μαρτυρέω	6:3	ἄνδρας ... μαρτυρουμένους ἑπτά
μάρτυς	6:13	μάρτυρας φευδεῖς
πλήρης	6:3	ἄνδρας ... πλήρεις πνεύματος καὶ σοφίας
	6:5	ἄνδρα πλήρη πίστεως καὶ πνεύματος ἁγίου
	6:8	Στέφανος δὲ πλήρης χάριτος καὶ δυνάμεως
πνεῦμα	6:3	(above)
	6:5	(above)
	6:10	τῇ σοφίᾳ καὶ τῷ πνεύματι ᾧ ἐλάλει
σοφία	6:3	(above)
	6:10	(above)
καθίστημι	6:3	οὓς καταστήσομεν ἐπὶ τῆς χρείας ταύτης
ἵστημι	6:6	οὓς ἔστησαν ἐνώπιον τῶν ἀποστόλων
ἀνίστημι	6:9	ἀνέστησαν δὲ τινες τῶν
ἀνθίστημι	6:10	ἀντιστῆναι τῇ σοφίᾳ καὶ τῷ πνεύματι
ἐφίστημι	6:12	ἐπιστάντες συνήρπασαν αὐτόν

ἵστημι	6:13	ἔστησάν τε μάρτυρας ψευδεῖς
πᾶς	6:5	ἐνώπιον παντὸς τοῦ πλήθους
	6:15	πάντες οἱ καθεζόμενοι
Στέφανος	6:5	ἐξελέξαντο Στέφανον
	6:8	Στέφανος δὲ πλήρης
	6:9	συζητοῦντες τῷ Στεφάνῳ
ἅγιος	6:5	πλήρη πίστεως καὶ πνεύματος ἁγίου
	6:13	κατὰ τοῦ τόπου τοῦ ἁγίου τούτου
ἱερεύς	6:7	πολύς τε ὄχλος τῶν ἱερέων
ἀρχιερεύς	7:1	εἶπεν δὲ ὁ ἀρχιερεύς

From the above list, it is clear that there exist interrelations between the introductory narratives. The author has united these episodes and has not simply joined unrelated sources. The appearance of the roots ἵστημι, μαρτυρέω or of other terms in close succession is consistent with the redactive features observed throughout this study.

The primary relationship between 6:1-7 and 6:8-7:2a is centered on Stephen. In fact, the elements of repetition concern especially his name and qualifications, πλήρης, σοφία and πνεῦμα. These stylistic features show that the main function of 6:1-7 is to serve as a prologue to the Stephen story proper. For that reason, the interconnections between the two narratives are kept to a minimum. This last statement is further indicated by the fact that 6:1-7 has a double function. It introduces both the Stephen and Philip stories and bears stylistic links to both (_infra_, p. 312). The interrelations, then, between Acts 6:1-7 and 6:8-7:2a are governed by the structural role which the former plays vis-à-vis the remainder of the Stephen story.

b. The Relation between the Introductory Narratives (6:1-7; 6:8-7:2a) and the Speech (7:2b-53)

The discussion of the connections between the first part of the Stephen story and the speech will especially consider the following data:

ἡμέρα	6:1	ἐν δὲ ταῖς ἡμέραις ταύταις
	7:8	τῇ ἡμέρᾳ τῇ ὀγδόῃ
	7:26	τῇ τε ἐπιούσῃ ἡμέρᾳ
	7:41	ἐν ταῖς ἡμέραις ἐκείναις
	7:45	ἕως τῶν ἡμερῶν Δαυίδ

οὗτος	6:1,3,13,13,14,14; 7:1	(see list a)
	7:4	εἰς τὴν γῆν ταύτην
	7:7	καὶ μετὰ ταῦτα
	7:7	ἐν τῷ τόπῳ τούτῳ
	7:19	οὗτος κατασοφισάμενος
	7:29	ἐν τῷ λόγῳ τούτῳ
	7:35	τοῦτον τὸν Μωϋσῆν
	7:35	τοῦτον ὁ θεὸς καί
	7:36	οὗτος ἐξήγαγεν αὐτούς
	7:37	οὗτός ἐστιν ὁ Μωϋσῆς
	7:38	οὗτός ἐστιν ὁ γενόμενος
	7:40	ὁ γὰρ Μωϋσῆς οὗτος
	7:50	ἐποίησεν ταῦτα πάντα
πληθύνω	6:1	πληθυνόντων τῶν μαθητῶν
	6:7	ἐπληθύνετο ὁ ἀριθμός
	7:17	ἐπληθύνθη ἐν Αἰγύπτῳ
δώδεκα	6:2	οἱ δώδεκα ... εἶπον
	7:8	τοὺς δώδεκα πατριάρχας
λόγος	6:2	τὸν λόγον τοῦ θεοῦ
	6:4	τῇ διακονίᾳ τοῦ λόγου
	6:5	ἤρεσεν ὁ λόγος
	6:7	ὁ λόγος τοῦ θεοῦ
	7:22	ἐν λόγοις καὶ ἔργοις αὐτοῦ
	7:29	ἐν τῷ λόγῳ τούτῳ
λόγιον	7:38	ἐδέξατο λόγια ζῶντα
θεός	6:2,7,11	(see list a)
	7:2	ὁ θεὸς τῆς δόξης
	7:6	ἐλάλησεν δὲ οὕτως ὁ θεός
	7:9	ἦν ὁ θεὸς μετ' αὐτοῦ
	7:17	ἧς ὡμολόγησεν ὁ θεός
	7:20	ἀστεῖος τῷ θεῷ
	7:25	ὁ θεὸς διὰ χειρὸς αὐτοῦ δίδωσιν
	7:32	ἐγὼ ὁ θεὸς τῶν πατέρων σου
	7:32	ὁ θεὸς 'Αβραάμ
	7:35	τοῦτον ὁ θεός ... ἀπέσταλκεν
	7:37	προφήτην ὑμῖν ἀναστήσει ὁ θεός
	7:40	ποίησον ἡμῖν θεούς
	7:42	ἔστρεψεν δὲ ὁ θεός
	7:43	τὸ ἄστρον τοῦ θεοῦ ὑμῶν

	7:45	ὧν ἐξῶσεν ὁ θεός
	7:46	ὃς εὗρεν χάριν ἐνώπιον τοῦ θεοῦ
	7:46	σκήνωμα τῷ θεῷ 'Ιακώβ
ἐπισκέπτομαι	6:3	ἐπισκέψασθε δέ, ἀδελφοί, ἄνδρας
	7:23	ἐπισκέψασθαι τοὺς ἀδελφοὺς αὐτοῦ
ἀδελφός	6:3	(above)
	7:2	ἄνδρες ἀδελφοὶ καὶ πατέρες
	7:13	ἀνεγνωρίσθη 'Ιωσὴφ τοῖς ἀδελφοῖς αὐτοῦ
	7:23	(above)
	7:25	συνιέναι τοὺς ἀδελφούς
	7:26	ἄνδρες, ἀδελφοί ἐστε
	7:37	ἐκ τῶν ἀδελφῶν ὑμῶν
ἀνήρ	6:3,5,11	(see list a)
	7:2	(above)
	7:26	(above)
μαρτυρέω	6:3	(see list a)
μάρτυς	6:13	(see list a)
μαρτύριον	7:44	ἡ σκηνὴ τοῦ μαρτυρίου
πνεῦμα	6:3,5,10	(see list a)
	7:51	τῷ πνεύματι τῷ ἁγίῳ ἀντιπίπτετε
σοφία	6:3,10	(see list a)
	7:10	ἔδωκεν αὐτῷ χάριν καὶ σοφίαν
κατασοφίζομαι	7:19	οὗτος κατασοφισάμενος
σοφία	7:22	ἐπαιδεύθη Μωϋσῆς πάσῃ σοφίᾳ
καθίστημι	6:3	οὓς καταστήσομεν ἐπὶ τῆς χρείας ταύτης
	7:10	κατέστησεν αὐτὸν ἡγούμενον
	7:27	τίς σε κατέστησεν ἄρχοντα καὶ δικαστήν
	7:35	(above)
ἐνώπιον	6:5	ἤρεσεν ὁ λόγος ἐνώπιον παντός
	6:6	ἔστησαν ἐνώπιον τῶν ἀποστόλων
	7:46	ὃς εὗρεν χάριν ἐνώπιον τοῦ θεοῦ
πᾶς	6:5	(above)
	6:15	πάντες οἱ καθεζόμενοι ἐν τῷ συνεδρίῳ
	7:10	ἐξείλατο αὐτὸν ἐκ πασῶν τῶν θλίψεων αὐτοῦ
	7:14	μετεκαλέσατο ... πᾶσαν τὴν συγγένειαν
	7:22	ἐπαιδεύθη Μωϋσῆς πάσῃ σοφίᾳ Αἰγυπτίων
	7:50	ἐποίησεν ταῦτα πάντα
ἅγιος	6:5	πλήρη ... πνεύματος ἁγίου
	6:13	ῥήματα κατὰ τοῦ τόπου τοῦ ἁγίου τούτου

	7:33	ὁ γὰρ τόπος ἐφ' ᾧ ἕστηκας γῆ ἁγία ἐστίν
	7:51	τῷ πνεύματι τῷ ἁγίῳ ἀντιπίπτετε
ἵστημι	6:6,13	(see list <u>a</u>)
	7:33	(above)
χείρ	6:6	ἐπέθηκαν αὐτοῖς τὰς χεῖρας
	7:25	διὰ χειρὸς αὐτοῦ δίδωσιν
	7:35	ἀπέσταλκεν σὺν χειρὶ ἀγγέλου
	7:41	εὐφραίνοντο ἐν τοῖς ἔργοις τῶν χειρῶν αὐτῶν
	7:50	οὐχὶ ἡ χείρ μου ἐποίησεν
αὐξάνω	6:7	ὁ λόγος τοῦ θεοῦ ηὔξανεν
	7:17	ηὔξησεν ὁ λαός
ὑπακούω	6:7	πολύς τε ὄχλος ... ὑπήκουον τῇ πιστει
ὑπήκοος	7:39	ᾧ οὐκ ἠθέλησαν ὑπήκοοι γενέσθαι
χάρις	6:8	πλήρης χάριτος καὶ δυνάμεως
	7:10	ἔδωκεν αὐτῷ χάριν καὶ σοφίαν ἐναντίον
	7:46	ὃς εὗρεν χάριν ἐνώπιον
δύναμις	6:8	(above)
δυνατός	7:22	ἦν δὲ δυνατὸς ἐν λόγοις καὶ ἔργοις αὐτοῦ
ποιέω	6:8	ἐποίει τέρατα καὶ σημεῖα μεγάλα
	7:19	τοῦ ποιεῖν τὰ βρέφη ἔκθετα
	7:24	ἐποίησεν ἐκδίκησιν
	7:36	ποιήσας τέρατα καὶ σημεῖα
	7:40	ποίησον ἡμῖν θεούς
	7:43	τοὺς τύπους οὓς ἐποιήσατε
	7:44	ποιῆσαι αὐτὴν κατὰ τὸν τύπον
	7:50	οὐχὶ ἡ χείρ μου ἐποίησεν
τέρας	6:8	(above)
	7:36	(above)
σημεῖον	6:8	(above)
	7:36	(above)
μέγας	6:8	(above)
	7:11	ἦλθεν ... θλῖψις μεγάλη
λαός	6:8	τέρατα καὶ σημεῖα μεγάλα ἐν τῷ λαῷ
	6:12	συνεκίνησάν τε τὸν λαὸν καί ...
	7:17	ηὔξησεν ὁ λαός
	7:34	εἶδον τὴν κάκωσιν τοῦ λαοῦ μου
ἀνίστημι	6:9	ἀνέστησαν δέ τινες τῶν ...
	7:18	ἄχρι οὗ ἀνέστη βασιλεὺς ἕτερος
	7:37	προφήτην ὑμῖν ἀναστήσει ὁ θεός

τις	6:9	(above)
	7:24	ἰδών τινα ἀδικούμενον
λέγω	6:9	τῶν ἐκ τῆς συναγωγῆς τῆς λεγομένης
	6:11	ἄνδρας λέγοντας ὅτι
	6:13	μάρτυρας ψειδεῖς λέγοντας
	6:14	αὐτοῦ λέγοντος ὅτι
	7:48	καθὼς ὁ προφήτης λέγει
	7:49	λέγει κύριος
λαλέω	6:10	τῇ σοφίᾳ καὶ τῷ πνεύματι ᾧ ἐλάλει
	6:11	αὐτοῦ λαλοῦντος ῥήματα βλάσφημα εἰς
	6:13	λαλῶν ῥήματα κατά
	7:6	ἐλάλησεν δὲ οὕτως ὁ θεός
	7:38	μετὰ τοῦ ἀγγέλου τοῦ λαλοῦντος αὐτῷ
	7:44	καθὼς διετάξατο ὁ λαλῶν τῷ Μωϋσῇ
ἀκούω	6:11	ἀκηκόαμεν αὐτοῦ λαλοῦντος
	6:14	ἀκηκόαμεν γὰρ αὐτοῦ λέγοντος
	7:2	ἄνδρες ἀδελφοὶ καὶ πατέρες ἀκούσατε
	7:12	ἀκούσας δὲ 'Ιακώβ
	7:34	τοῦ στεναγμοῦ αὐτοῦ ἤκουσα
Μωϋσῆς	6:11	ῥήματα βλάσφημα εἰς Μωϋσῆν
	6:14	τὰ ἔθη ἃ παρέδωκεν ἡμῖν Μωϋσῆς
	7:20	ἐγεννήθη Μωϋσῆς
	7:22	ἐπαιδεύθη Μωϋσῆς
	7:29	ἔφυγεν δὲ Μωϋσῆς
	7:31	ὁ δὲ Μωϋσῆς ἰδών
	7:32	Μωϋσῆς οὐκ ἐτόλμα κατανοῆσαι
	7:35	τοῦτον τὸν Μωϋσῆν ὃν ἠρνήσαντο
	7:37	οὗτός ἐστιν ὁ Μωϋσῆς
	7:40	ὁ γὰρ Μωϋσῆς οὗτος
	7:44	ὁ λαλῶν τῷ Μωϋσῇ
τόπος	6:13	λαλῶν ῥήματα κατὰ τοῦ τόπου τοῦ ἁγίου τούτου
	6:14	καταλύσει τὸν τόπον τοῦτον
	7:7	λατρεύσουσίν μοι ἐν τῷ τόπῳ τούτῳ
	7:33	ὁ γὰρ τόπος ... γῆ ἁγία ἐστίν
	7:49	τίς τόπος τῆς καταπαύσεώς μου
νόμος	6:13	λαλῶν ῥήματα κατά ... τοῦ νόμου
	7:53	οἵτινες ἐλάβετε τὸν νόμον
παραδίδωμι	6:14	τὰ ἔθη ἃ παρέδωκεν
	7:42	παρέδωκεν αὐτοὺς λατρεύειν

πρόσωπον	6:15	εἶδον τὸ πρόσωπον αὐτοῦ
	6:15	ὡσεὶ πρόσωπον ἀγγέλου
	7:45	ὧν ἐξῶσεν ὁ θεὸς ἀπὸ προσώπου τῶν πατέρων
ἄγγελος	6:15	(above)
	7:30	ὤφθη αὐτῷ ... ἄγγελος
	7:35	σὺν χειρὶ ἀγγέλου τοῦ ὀφθέντος αὐτῷ
	7:38	μετὰ τοῦ ἀγγέλου τοῦ λαλοῦντος αὐτῷ
	7:53	τὸν νόμον εἰς διαταγὰς ἀγγέλων

This list of lexical elements is noteworthy first of all because of its length. That a narrative and a speech should bear so many linguistic, thematic, and structural connections speaks against independent sources for these texts. The distribution of these elements throughout is equally damaging to editing theories for the discourse. These parts of the Stephen story have too much in common to be the product of secondary editing.

The important relationships established between Stephen and various personalities of Jewish history are clearly intentional (e.g., the working of wonders and signs, full of grace, etc.). The correlation of themes, particularly those related to the accusations within the narratives and discourse, is equally obvious. The themes of place and customs, the role of God and Moses, as well as Stephen's attitude toward these, are central to speech and narrative.

Stylistically, the relationship between these texts is closer than scholars wish to admit. It suffices to note the peculiar use of οὗτος, the doublet "increase and be multiplied," and the large variety of data presented in the corpus.

It will be a major task of chapter four to investigate the relationship between these texts, and to indicate the significance this fact has for the interpretation of the Stephen story. Presently, it suffices to have listed the stylistic and linguistic evidence at the basis of the principal conclusion of this analysis. The speech, written on the basis of the LXX account of Israel's history, has been composed by the author of Acts as a complementary text to his narrative and bears in relation to it numerous thematic and structural interconnections. The speech is, at least in part, a response to the accusations leveled against Stephen and against early Christianity.

c. The Relation between the Speech and the Concluding Narrative (7:54-8:4)

The following data are pertinent to the discussion:

ἀνήρ	7:2,26	(see list b)
	8:2	συνεκόμισαν ... ἄνδρες εὐλαβεῖς
	8:3	σύρων τε ἄνδρας καὶ γυναῖκας
ἀκούω	7:2,12,34	(see list b)
	7:54	ἀκούοντες δὲ ταῦτα
θεός	7:2,6,7,9,17,20,25,32,32,35,37,40,42,43,45,46,46	(see list b)
	7:55	εἶδεν δόξαν θεοῦ
	7:55	ἑστῶτα ἐκ δεξιῶν τοῦ θεοῦ
	7:56	ἐκ δεξιῶν ἑστῶτα τοῦ θεοῦ
δόξα	7:2	ὁ θεὸς τῆς δόξης ὤφθη
	7:55	(above)
πούς	7:5	οὐδὲ βῆμα ποδός
	7:33	τὸ ὑπόδημα τῶν ποδῶν σου
	7:49	ἡ δὲ γῆ ὑποπόδιον τῶν ποδῶν μου
	7:58	παρὰ τοὺς πόδας νεανίου
ταῦτα	7:7	καὶ μετὰ ταῦτα
	7:50	ἐποίησεν ταῦτα πάντα
	7:54	ἀκούοντες δὲ ταῦτα
πᾶς	7:10,14,22,50	(see list b)
	8:1	πάντες δὲ διεσπάρησαν
μέγας	7:11	καὶ θλῖψις μεγάλη
	7:57	κράξαντες δὲ φωνῇ μεγάλῃ
	7:60	ἔκραξεν φωνῇ μεγάλῃ
	8:1	ἐγένετο ... διωγμὸς μέγας
	8:2	ἐποίησαν κοπετὸν μέγαν ἐπ' αὐτῷ
τίθημι	7:16	ἐτέθησαν ἐν τῷ μνήματι
	7:60	μὴ στήσῃς αὐτοῖς
ποιέω	7:19,24,36,40,43,44,50	(see list b)
	8:2	ἐποίησαν κοπετὸν μέγαν
ἀναιρέω	7:21	ἀνείλατο αὐτὸν ἡ θυγάτηρ Φαραώ
	7:28	μὴ ἀνελεῖν με σὺ θέλεις
	7:28	ὃν τρόπον ἀνεῖλες ἐχθὲς τὸν Αἰγύπτιον
ἀναίρεσις	8:1	συνευδοκῶν τῇ ἀναιρέσει αὐτοῦ
λόγος	7:22,29,38	(see list b)
	8:4	εὐαγγελιζόμενοι τὸν λόγον
καρδία	7:23	ἀνέβη ἐπὶ τὴν καρδίαν αὐτοῦ

	7:39	ἐστράφησαν ἐν ταῖς καρδίαις αὐτῶν
	7:51	ἀπερίτμητοι καρδίαις
	7:54	διεπρίοντο ταῖς καρδίαις αὐτῶν
φωνή	7:31	ἐγένετο φωνὴ κυρίου
	7:57	κράξαντες δὲ φωνῇ μεγάλῃ
	7:60	ἔκραξεν φωνῇ μεγάλῃ
κύριος	7:31	ἐγένετο φωνὴ κυρίου
	7:33	εἶπεν δὲ αὐτῷ ὁ κύριος
	7:49	λέγει κύριος
	7:59	κύριε Ἰησοῦ, δέξαι
	7:60	κύριε, μὴ στήσῃς αὐτοῖς
ἵστημι	7:33	ὁ γὰρ τόπος ἐφ' ᾧ ἕστηκας
	7:55	ἑστῶτα ἐκ δεξιῶν τοῦ θεοῦ
	7:56	ἐκ δεξιῶν ἑστῶτα τοῦ θεοῦ
	7:60	(above)
ἅγιος	7:33,51	(see list b)
	7:55	πλήρης πνεύματος ἁγίου
ἐκκλησία	7:38	ἐν τῇ ἐκκλησίᾳ
	8:1	διωγμὸς μέγας ἐπὶ τὴν ἐκκλησίαν
	8:3	ἐλυμαίνετο τὴν ἐκκλησίαν
δέχομαι	7:38	ὃς ἐδέξατο λόγια ζῶντα
	7:59	δέξαι τὸ πνεῦμά μου
παραδίδωμι	7:42	παρέδωκεν αὐτοὺς λατρεύειν
	8:3	παρεδίδου εἰς φυλακήν
οὐρανός	7:42	λατρεύειν τῇ στρατιᾷ τοῦ οὐρανοῦ
	7:49	ὁ οὐρανός μοι θρόνος
	7:55	ἀτενίσας εἰς τὸν οὐρανόν
	7:56	θεωρῶ τοὺς οὐρανοὺς διηνοιγμένους
μαρτύριον	7:44	ἡ σκηνὴ τοῦ μαρτυρίου
μάρτυς	7:58	οἱ μάρτυρες ἀπέθεντο τὰ ἱμάτια αὐτῶν
λέγω	7:48,49	(see list b)
	7:59	ἐπικαλούμενον καὶ λέγοντα
οὖς	7:51	ἀπερίτμητοι ... τοῖς ὠσίν
	7:57	συνέσχον τὰ ὦτα αὐτῶν
πνεῦμα	7:51	τῷ πνεύματι τῷ ἁγίῳ ἀντιπίπτετε
	7:55	πλήρης πνεύματος ἁγίου
	7:59	δέξαι τὸ πνεῦμά μου
διώκω	7:52	οὐκ ἐδίωξαν οἱ πατέρες ὑμῶν
διωγμός	8:1	ἐγένετο ... διωγμὸς μέγας

The continuity between the speech proper, the invective, and the subsequent narrative is easily demonstrated, especially when the themes of rejection and persecution or the recurrence of the terms δόξα, οὐρανός, καρδία, οὖς, and πνεῦμα are given full consideration. Stephen's vision in vv.55-56 further stresses the role of God in the story and the reintroduction of Jesus (see 6:14).

The relationship between the discourse and the subsequent narrative has already been examined from a structural point of view (*supra*, pp. 224f.). In chapter four the composition and interpretation of these texts will be examined at length. At this point the stylistic data speak for themselves.

d. The Interrelations Between the Three Parts of the Stephen Story

The pertinent data for this part of the study are as follows: λόγος, θεός, μαρτυρέω, πνεῦμα, πᾶς, ἅγιος, ἵστημι, ποιέω, μέγας, λέγω, ἀκούω and παραδίδωμι (see lists *b* and *c* above where all the relevant texts are to be found). In addition to these, terms occurring only in the introductory and concluding narratives are germane to the present analysis.

πλήρης	6:3,5,8	(see list *a*)
	7:55	πλήρης πνεύματος ἁγίου
Στέφανος	6:5,8,9	(see list *a*)
	7:59	ἐλιθοβόλουν τὸν Στέφανον
	8:2	συνεκόμισαν δὲ τὸν Στέφανον
ἀπόστολος	6:6	ἔστησαν ἐνώπιον τῶν ἀποστόλων
	8:1	πλὴν τῶν ἀποστόλων
Ἰερουσαλήμ	6:7	ἐν Ἰερουσαλὴμ σφόδρα
Ἰεροσόλυμα	8:1	ἐπὶ τὴν ἐκκλησίαν τὴν ἐν Ἰεροσολύμοις
ἄνθρωπος	6:13	ὁ ἄνθρωπος οὗτος οὐ παύεται
	7:56	θεωρῶ ... τὸν υἱὸν τοῦ ἀνθρώπου
Ἰησοῦς	6:14	ὅτι Ἰησοῦς ὁ Ναζωραῖος οὗτος
	7:55	εἶδεν ... Ἰησοῦν
	7:59	κύριε Ἰησοῦ, δέξαι
ἀτενίζω	6:15	ἀτενίσαντες εἰς αὐτόν
	7:55	ἀτενίσας εἰς τὸν οὐρανόν

The Stephen story presents remarkable elements of structural unity. The story begins with the theme of λόγος (6:2) and ends on the same note (8:4). God is at the center of this episode: word of God 6:2,7; accusation against God 6:11; history directed by Him 7:2f.; and glory and vision of God 7:55f. Witnesses appear before and after the speech. The role of the Spirit is carefully presented throughout, while the reaction to Him is deliberately stated: Stephen is full of the Spirit; the Hebrews rebel against Him; and once again Stephen is full of the Spirit.

The biography of Stephen gives further unity to the entire story, while the appearance of the apostles, as well as the name "Jerusalem," at the beginning and at the end of the episode, testify to a conscious assembly of narrative elements. The overall unity of the Stephen story when compared to that of most narrative/speech units in Acts is conspicuous.

The stylistic data have been presented and analyzed in terms of their literary and structural function. The following chapter will apply these to an examination of the author's method of composition.

CHAPTER IV

A Redactional Study of Acts 6:1-8:4

In the preceding chapters attention was directed to a variety of data which were considered essential or at least germane to the main concern of this study, namely, an examination of the composition of the Stephen story. After investigating the literary characteristics of the author, particularly his attitude vis-à-vis the LXX text, it was necessary to scrutinize the entire Stephen material from a structural and stylistic point of view. In describing these numerous features, I have been consistently impressed by their nature and distribution. The extensive lists, the variety and quantity of categories, the complexity and peculiarity of the data call for a reevaluation of the composition of the entire episode.

The present chapter, in light of the preceding study will examine the redactive process which produced Acts 6:1-8:4. After a prefatory treatment of theories of redaction, the speech and narratives will be analyzed in relation to the stylistic and structural data. And, finally, a reinterpretation of the Stephen story will be presented in light of the present inquiry.

A. Theories of Redaction

Before setting forth my own observations and conclusions concerning the composition of Acts 6:1-8:4, attention must be given to a few recent studies seriously considering the problem of redaction. The great diversity of scholarly opinion concerning the sources and composition of the Stephen story was noted in chapter one. The statements regarding the origin and nature of the narrative and speech are very numerous; few attempts, however, have been made to analyze the redaction of these texts.

1. The Speech and Its Context

Most studies of the Stephen story treat the problem of redaction at least in a rudimentary way. Inevitably, opinions on this subject depend upon the scholar's conception of the speech, that is, whether it predates Acts totally or in part, or whether it was composed or considerably re-edited by the author. Intimately related to these considerations is the question of the speech's relation to its narrative context.

Since the classic statement by the editors of Beginnings that the discourse was intrusive,[1] and by Dibelius that it interrupted the transfiguration of the martyr,[2] the theory of interpolation has been popular. Authors who propose such a thesis insist upon the following factors: an alleged noncorrespondence between the speech and the narratives, the peculiar character of the former, the self-sufficiency of the latter. While Wilckens has described the process of redaction as the introduction of an independent unit of tradition within the Stephen story,[3] other scholars, recognizing the mixed character of the discourse, lend a more creative role to the author in rewriting the narratives, the speech or both (Dibelius, Simon, Trocmé, Haenchen, Conzelmann). These last-named scholars, while maintaining a theory of interpolation, view the process of redaction as more than just the collation of disparate ele-

---

[1]"If any one will read Acts vi.8-11 and vii.54-viii.1, omitting the intermediate verses, he will not detect any break in the narrative," "Internal Evidence," 2:150.

[2]"It has obviously been inserted by Luke into the story of the martyrdom of Stephen, which he already had at his disposal. This story is told from 6.8 onwards: the trial by witnesses takes place but, to the members of the Sanhedrin, the face of the accused appears like the face of an angel (6.15). The continuation of this verse is found in the heavenly vision (7.55-56): the martyr, who has already been transfigured by heavenly light, now looks up to the open heavens and sees the Son of Man on the right hand of God. In our text, however, the description of the transfigured face of Stephen is followed by the question of the high priest, which gives rise to the long speech (7.1ff.). The speech breaks the sequence between the transfiguration and the looking upward to heaven; obviously Luke contributed it himself when he took the story of the martyrdom into his narrative," "Speeches in Acts," p. 168.

[3]Missionsreden, pp. 208-9 and n. 1, where he refers to the works of Dibelius, Hanechen, and Conzelmann.

ments of tradition.

Finally, following upon the insights of Mundle, scholars such as Bihler[4] and Wilson[5] view the speech as substantially the work of the author; but, contrary to Mundle, they insist that the entire composition, utilizing fragments of tradition, is also the result of that same creative process. Their intended goal, then, is to underscore the interrelations between the speech and narratives and to seek stylistic parallels elsewhere in the writer's work. They conclude that the various sections of the Stephen story complement one another and were so intended by the author.

It is symptomatic of the uncertainty of modern scholarship regarding the Stephen story that such opposed views should be maintained, that is, the total composition of the speech by the author and its complete or partial dependence upon tradition. The analysis of the speech is the key to a proper analysis of the Stephen material. Given the important role the discourse plays in recent studies of the Stephen story, it is surprising how little attention has been paid to its stylistic and structural features.

2. Composition of the Narrative

The narratives have received considerable attention of late, since scholars detect a dual element within the story, both prior to and following the speech, namely, a popular gathering and a judicial assembly as responsible for the accusations and death of Stephen. Although this topic has been dealt with briefly in the first chapter,[6] it is necessary to examine the problem from the point of view of composition.

It is generally agreed that older source critical theories, particularly the compilation of two documents, do not explain the nature of Acts 6:1-7:2 and 7:54-8:4. Instead, scholars defend a more active role on the part of the writer, that is, he has inherited one component from tradition and has contributed the other himself. Thus scholars have attempted to

---

[4]Stephanusgeschichte, p. 86.

[5]"Theologian and Historian," p. 191.

[6]See pp. 20-22 and especially n. 75 for a list of authors and their respective views.

resolve what they consider to be the inconsistencies of the narrative on the one hand and the smooth flow of the story on the other. While the lynching scene theory is by far the more commonly held opinion, a recent scholar such as Bihler opts for an original judgment and death by trial.

In defense of such a view of the writer's redactive activity, Haenchen advances more general considerations concerning the composition of Acts. The "natural climax" of the series of trials (4:17f., 5:33f., and 6:11f.) is the work of the historian as well as the writer who, by introducing a trial (6:12f.), has provided an audience for the subsequent speech.[7] Trocmé also lays great stress upon the latter, since it is his belief that the narrative served primarily as a vehicle for the presentation of the speech inherited from tradition. He further points out that the Sanhedrin has also been introduced by the author into the narrative of Acts 4:5f. and perhaps 22:30f.[8] These and other such considerations are clearly of a stylistic nature. But at the basis of these theories is the overriding preoccupation that what matters most is the quest for the original historical event. This is asserted without proper analysis of the presentation of the event in Acts. Without such a procedure, namely, a detailed stylistic and structural examination of the Stephen story, the investigation of the episode remains a very hypothetical selection of components to defend a particular theory. Special features of the author's method of composition are often enlisted in formulating theological or historical conclusions.

By far the most comprehensive and explicit analysis of the narrative is that of Trocmé. Therefore his views will be presented at length. As a preliminary, however, it must be stated that for him it is the data concerning Paul, and the association of Stephen with the account of the Pauline persecution and conversion, which furnish a solid historical basis. An original document "qui était de servir d'introduction à la conversion de Saul" has been edited, augmented, and applied to a new

---

[7]Acts, pp. 273-74, see also pp. 295-96.

[8]Livre des Actes, p. 186.

situation.[9]

To serve as an appropriate vehicle for the speech, inherited from tradition, the author then constructs a narrative on the basis of the trial of Jesus.

> Il a placé dans la bouche de faux témoins déposant contre Étienne l'accusation qui, selon Mc., avait été lancée à son Maître: ce Jésus détruira le Temple (Mc. 14/56-61). L'intention de notre écrivain est évidente, car il ne reproduit pas ces paroles dans son récit de la Passion et insère ici (6/12-14; 7/1) un texte exactement parallèle: réunion du Sanhédrin (Act. 6/12; Mc. 14/53; Lc. 22/66); déposition de faux témoins (Act. 6/13; Mc. 14/56-57); accusation d'avoir parlé contre le Temple, en annonçant sa destruction par "ce Jésus" (Act. 6/13-14; Mc 14/58); le grand-prêtre demande à l'accusé de répondre (Act. 7/1; Mc. 14/60-61). Au lieu d'allonger inutilement le récit du procès de Jésus, puisque, selon Mc., cette accusation n'avait pas été retenue et que Jésus n'y avait même pas répondu, ce passage sert en Lc.-Act. d'introduction au discours d'Étienne.[10]

The author pursues his analysis of 7:54-60 by insisting upon the following relationships,

Acts 7:55-56	Mk 14:62	Son of Man
57	63-64	violent reaction of hearers (toned down by Lk 22:69-71)
59b	Lk 23:46	(possible)

and the simple creation of 7:2 and 54 as sutures and 7:58 (up to μάρτυρες) as further insistence upon the judiciary nature of the episode.

Trocmé then presents a résumé of his analysis:

> Les données primitives du récit formant la première partie de la relation de la conversion de Paul, devaient donc être les suivantes: des Juifs de la diaspora de langue grecque établis à Jérusalem (6/9) s'acharnent contre ceux d'entre eux qui sont devenus chrétiens; parmi les persécuteurs les plus actifs, figure un jeune homme, Saul de Tarse (8/3; 22/4; 26/10-11); l'épisode le plus dramatique de la persécution est l'exécution

[9] *Ibid.*, p. 187.

[10] *Ibid.*, pp. 186-87.

> sommaire d'un redoutable controversiste chrétien, Étienne (6/11-12 a; 7/57, 59 a, 60); Saul, présent et complice (7/58 b; 8/1; 22/20), a été impressionné par l'attitude de la victime, qui a prié pour ses bourreaux avant d'expirer (7/60).[11]

While it is not my intention to examine in detail the various aspects of this scholar's study, it is necessary to comment upon his methodology and his presuppositions. It is obvious that the above doublets, parallels, and problem texts become infallible signs of the use or abuse of sources and fragments of tradition. At every turn the author of Acts, according to Trocmé, has "maltreated," "forced," misunderstood," "changed the original purpose of" the sources he has utilized,[12] so much so that one can only conclude either that there is little of value remaining in this text, or that the analysis given above is entirely too conjectural. The dissection of the text to conform to the scholar's historical and literary presuppositions fails to do justice to the author's purpose, style, and intelligence. The method of composition will be studied at length below.

3. Redaction of the Speech

It has already been noted that the speech is the key to a proper understanding of the Stephen story. This observation is the basis of the entire study and applies equally to other investigations of Acts 6:1-8:4. For that reason, it is necessary to dwell upon various analyses of the speech. These can be treated in three distinct groups: a) the discourse antedates Acts, b) part of the speech is an old historical summary

---

[11]*Ibid.*, p. 187.

[12]*Ibid.*, pp. 184-87. See Dibelius, "Style Criticism of the Book of Acts," in *Studies*, p. 11, who states: ". . . as he had no other accounts and reconstructed events which took place within the earliest communities after the analogy of a more highly developed condition of the Church, he was quite liable to misinterpret" or Haenchen, *Acts*, who sees the author as making "free with tradition" (p. 111) or "following very bold tactics" (274) to misrepresent his sources and to present his own polemics. Finally, Loisy, *Actes*, p. 293, says of his *rédacteur's* work in the Stephen episode that it "apparait moins maltraitée en cet endroit, après avoir été multilée, découpée, diluée, submergée, dans la partie qui racontait les événements antérieurs à l'organisation du groupe hélléniste."

edited by the writer, and c) the entire composition owes to the author of Acts.

a. Independent Fragments

In the first instance, the presupposition as to the origin of the speech is fundamental, that is, the scholars in question, having judged it an independent fragment of tradition, proceed accordingly in their analysis. Simon for one, concludes: "For my own part I consider it as highly probable that the speech is, in its essentials, pre-Lukan."[13] He then examines the content of the speeches of Peter (3:12f.), Paul (13:16f.), and Stephen, and states:

> Although none of these three speeches was ever delivered exactly in the form in which it is written down in Acts, there are good reasons for thinking that, conventional though they may be in their framing, they none the less express, at least broadly, the thought of the various speakers. Paul's speech is consonant with what we know from his epistles of his attitude towards his own people. Of Peter's views we know very little, but it is most likely that they should in fact have been as described in his speech. As to Stephen's position, it is so exceptional in the early Church that it has every chance of expressing his own personal viewpoint. . . . In fact, Stephen's speech seems rather to conflict with the basic attitude of Acts. It stands, as it were, by itself, which should make us confident of its historical value.[14]

The remainder of the scholar's analysis is then directed to the meaning of the speech and the sources of Stephen's thought. Excluded at the very start, the role of the author of Acts in dealing with or editing the speech is not considered.

b. Edited Historical Document

The theory that Acts 7:2-53 is a revision of a neutral history of Israel from a Hellenistic background has received the adherence of a number of prominent scholars, particularly

---

[13]Stephen, p. 39.

[14]Ibid., p. 43. See also Frederick F. Bruce, Commentary on the Book of the Acts: The English Text with Introduction, Exposition and Notes (Grand Rapids, Mich.: Eerdmans, 1956), pp. 141-44.

Dibelius,[15] Haenchen, Conzelmann,[16] and Wilckens. The views of Haenchen will be presented here, since they are most precise and, therefore, lend themselves to a detailed analysis. Those of Wilckens will then follow, since they offer a new approach to the Stephen speech.

"With few exceptions," Haenchen tells us, "verses 2-46 merely offer a didactic recapitulation of Israel's relations with God."[17] In effect, the Abraham and Joseph stories are free of polemic, while that of Moses (17-44) is only partly so.

> Nevertheless the style and syntax now show that single or grouped verses lending the account a more tendentious significance have been inserted into a "neutral" presentation (Dibelius) of sacred history. It is verse 25 which introduces this new element: "you did not recognize the saviour sent by God", whereas verse 26 continues verse 24 in the old style. With verse 35 the simple narrative is transformed into a rhetorically passionate indictment, taking verse 27 as a "type" of all Jews: it is not individual Jews of a remote past but "they", _the Jews_, who denied and rejected the man appointed by God to be their ἄρχων and λυτρωτής. And now Israel's treatment of Moses and treatment of Jesus appear as parallels: verse 37 explicitly stresses the similarity between Moses and the "prophet like me". Verses 39-43 accuse Israel of idol-worship, _citing a LXX text_. Nobody will maintain that Stephen sought to persuade the High Council with a LXX text which diverges widely from the Hebrew. In sum, then, verses 35, 37, 39-43 and 48-53 appear to be Lucan additions. Verses 44-7 narrate, in themselves without polemic, how the fathers first had the tabernacle, and how the Temple came to be built later. There are visible seams between verses 43 and 44 (Overbeck, 108) and 47 and 48. These testify that Luke has taken over a "history-sermon" _en bloc_ and tailored it for his purposes with additions (and perhaps also abbreviations). So much for the problem of tradition as regards this part. As for verses 51-3, it is plain that they did not form part of the "history-sermon" but come from the hand of Luke--by no means an inexperienced rhetorician.[18]

---

[15]"Speeches in Acts," pp. 167-70.

[16]_Apostelgeschichte_, pp. 57-58.

[17]_Acts_, p. 288.

[18]_Ibid_., pp. 288-89.

From the above it is clear, on the one hand, that the speech is no longer considered as simply borrowed from tradition and, on the other, that the writer is given a more creative role in the redaction process. Both are fully consistent with a growing tendency in recent scholarship to attribute greater freedom and creativity to the author of Acts.

It was necessary to quote extensively from Haenchen to examine the premises for such a theory. First, to the above statement that most of the Stephen speech is a neutral history of Israel, it must be pointed out that, on the contrary, polemical statements are found in every part of the discourse (see below for a detailed treatment of this point). Acts 7 is a very selective history of Israel, whose goal is detected in each choice, omission or alteration of biblical texts and episodes.

Secondly, it is stated that v.25 introduces a new, tendentious element. Once again, a more careful analysis of the quoting process indicates that there are numerous additions to the biblical story, either of extrabiblical elements or of texts from other parts of the OT. V.25 must be viewed in relation to a well-defined tendency of the author throughout the speech, that of supplementing the biblical record to better defend his point of view.

Thirdly, Haenchen notes the parallelism between vv.27 "one Jew" and 35 "all Jews" and in v.37 between Moses and Jesus. From this he concludes that vv.35 and 37 are polemical additions to the neutral history. It has been pointed out in previous chapters, and will be again in this one, that parallelism is an important stylistic, structural, and thematic feature of the Stephen story. Far from indicating an editorial process (i.e., revision of an old document), this characteristic is intrinsic to the author's method of composition. Parallels exist within parts of the so-called neutral history, e.g., between Joseph v.10 ἔδωκεν [God] αὐτῷ χάριν καὶ σοφίαν ἐναντίον . . . and David v.46, εὗρεν χάριν ἐνώπιον τοῦ θεοῦ.

Fourthly, in regard to vv.39-43 it has been stated that the citation of a LXX text diverging from the MT clearly indicates that this part of the discourse is a later addition to the neutral history. I believe that the second chapter demonstrates that the entire Stephen speech depends, in an amazingly detailed fashion at times, upon the LXX translation of the OT. By Haenchen's own logic, it should then be concluded that the complete discourse owes to the author of Acts.

Fifthly, he would have one see vv.44-47 as history without polemics in contrast to the preceding and concluding editorial verses. However, he fails to see the obvious midrashic relationship between vv.42-43 (ἐν τῇ ἐρήμῳ, σκηνὴ τοῦ Μόλοχ, and τύπους οὓς ἐποιήσατε) and v.44 (ἡ σκηνὴ τοῦ μαρτυρίου, ἐν τῇ ἐρήμῳ and ποιῆσαι αὐτὴν κατὰ τὸν τύπον). Furthermore, the structural unity of vv.42-50, centered around the threefold repetition of καθώς, indicates another solution.

Finally, the stylistic unity of vv.35-41 (τοῦτον τὸν Μωϋσῆν, ὃν . . . τοῦτον . . . οὗτος . . . οὗτός ἐστιν ὁ Μωϋσῆς . . . οὗτος . . . ὃς . . . ᾧ . . . ὁ γὰρ Μωϋσῆς οὗτος, ὃς . . .), is sufficient evidence that Haenchen's dissection of this part of the speech (vv. 36 and 38 original and vv.35, 37, and 39f. editorial) is artificial at best.

In this context the position of Wilckens regarding the Stephen speech deserves special attention. After having omitted Acts 7:2-53 in the first two editions of his _Die Missionsreden_, in a third revised edition (1974), in response to scholarly criticism, he has proposed a unique view of this text. According to him: "Die Rede ist zweifellos nicht ein Werk des Lukas."[19] Furthermore it is an independent fragment of tradition, whose content approximates the neutral history of Dibelius, Haenchen, and Conzelmann.[20] This text the author has interpolated within the Stephen account. In light of this presupposition, he proceeds to analyze the speech and its alleged background:

> Doch zeigt eine eingehendere Analyse, dass sie der jüdischen Tradition des deuteronomistischen Geschichtsbildes und der entsprechended Umkehrpredigt zugehört, die sich auch als überlieferungsgeschichtlicher Hintergrund der Apostelpredigten der Acts erwiesen haben.[21]

---

[19]_Missionsreden_, p. 208.

[20]_Ibid_., p. 209, n. 1.

[21]_Ibid_., p. 208.

After an examination of the speech, Wilckens, relying considerably upon the work of O. H. Steck, proceeds to explain the speech as the product of Hellenistic diaspora-Judaeo-Christianity and its Deuteronomic view of history and its preaching tradition.[22]

The influence of the book of Deuteronomy has been noted repeatedly in chapter two. However, it can hardly be said, if the present analysis is reliable, that the speech is Deuteronomic in structure or in inspiration. While vv.36-39 are particularly dependent upon that tradition, the rest of the speech is not. Throughout chapter two it has been demonstrated that the author used the narratives of Genesis and Exodus as his primary sources, and finally the texts of Amos and Isaiah for the composition of vv.42-50.

The main objections, however, to Wilckens' position are the ones leveled against Haenchen's analysis. The Stephen speech betrays from beginning to end the same quoting process, structural techniques, and redactive tendencies. Once again it is the point of departure which is the most vulnerable, that is, the origin of the discourse itself.

c. Creation of the Author

Finally, the view that the entire Stephen speech is a creation of the author of Acts must be given serious consideration. Reference has already been made (see chapter one) to the works of Mundle, Duterme, Wilson, and Bihler, who, by means of a variety of methodologies, arrive at this particular conclusion (the name of Loisy should also be added here). Duterme and Wilson, to a great extent, rely primarily upon lexical and stylistic factors in their attempt to show that the author of Acts is responsible for the composition of the speech, while Bihler adopts a more theological approach to show that the point of view of Acts 7 is consistent with and forms part of the entire book.

Since my conclusions most closely resemble those of Bihler and Wilson, I will not examine the various aspects of their studies at this point (but see p. 38 above for a few methodological observations). Instead, it is necessary to investigate

[22] *Ibid.*, pp. 216-24.

the redaction of Acts 6:1-8:4 and then to conclude this part of the study with general methodological considerations on redaction.

B. Redaction of Acts 6:1-8:4

This section of the study will examine, in light of the analysis of the quoting process and the stylistic data acquired as a result of that investigation, the author's method of composition. A large variety of tendencies, preferences, and peculiarities of the writer throughout the Stephen material, as well as occasional structural parallels in other parts of Acts have been pointed out. At this point, I intend to examine the architectural features of the entire episode and the interrelations between the various components.

1. The Speech

Study of the speeches in Acts has recently attracted the attention of numerous scholars. Ample bibliography and a brief survey of the lines of research regarding the subject was given in the first chapter. However, despite the number of investigations, few consider or even mention the Stephen speech. At most the historical survey and Christological reference of the invective are alluded to in relation to features of the kerygmatic or missionary speeches. It is at this point that the present study begins.

a. Acts 7 and the Other Speeches of Acts

From a structural point of view it is clear that the Stephen speech is to be set apart from the Petrine (2:14f.; 3:12f.; 4:8f.; 5:29f.; 10:34f.) and Pauline (13:16f.; 14:15f.; 17:22f.) discourses. If one follows E. Schweizer's excellent working schema for the eight speeches just mentioned,[23] it becomes clear that Acts 7 bears no more than a rudimentary structural relation to those, namely, "direct address," the "appeal for attention," and a historical sketch (similar to that found in Paul's address, 13:16f.).[24]

---

[23]"Speeches," pp. 208-16, see especially pp. 210f.

[24]The above-mentioned components refer to a, b, and d of Schweizer's "general scheme" pp. 210-11. It is significant in this regard that Wilckens, *Missionsreden*, in the first two editions of his study of the speeches did not include Acts 7 and

The relation of the present text to the other speeches of Acts is not a simple one and, for that reason, this particular subject has received less than satisfactory consideration. There does exist a relationship between Stephen's discourse and "the speeches which contain the missionary proclamation of the apostles to Jews and Gentiles,"[25] on the one hand, and between that same text and later speeches in Acts on the other. However, the similarities to both groups are to be sought in different areas.

Acts 7 bears stylistic and thematic rather than structural relations to the speeches of Peter and the earlier ones of Paul. While the apparent lack of structural similarity between these discourses and that of Stephen has misled scholars in their analysis of this part of Acts, this fact has not prevented a number of commentators from noting important data in this regard. Mundle[26] and Duterme[27] have insisted that the vocabulary of Acts 7 is typical of the author, citing as proof a variety of parallels from the early speeches of Acts. Bihler has consistently pointed out similarities of style and vocabulary between these different sections of the biblical work,[28] while Haenchen has particularly insisted upon correspondences between what he considers polemical additions and other speeches.[29] Recently, Zehnle, in a study of the speeches of Acts 2 and 3, dwells at length upon the parallels between Acts 3 and 7. While I do not subscribe to his theory of a primitive Moses-Jesus typology allegedly borrowed by the author in composing these speeches, I do accept many linguistic and lexical contacts which he notes between these discourses.[30]

---

even when he does address himself to this text in the third edition, concludes that it is entirely taken over from tradition.

[25]Schweizer, "Speeches," p. 208.

[26]"Stephanusrede," p. 135.

[27]"Vocabulaire," p. 28. Note also that Loisy, Actes, pp. 318-47, in maintaining that the entire speech is the work of his rédacteur, consistently indicates stylistic parallels between this chapter and other parts of Acts.

[28]Stephanusgeschichte, pp. 38-81. [29]Acts, pp. 282f.

[30]Pentecost Discourse, pp. 75-89; for the pertinent stylistic data, see in particular pp. 76-78.

It would be possible to draw up an extensive list of contacts of a lexical, stylistic, and thematic nature between Acts 7 (and its narrative context) and the eight "missionary" speeches, but time and space do not permit this. Therefore, a rudimentary survey of the first four discourses will be presented: 2:14f.; 3:12f.; 4:8f.; and 5:29f. In the Pentecost discourse the following relations should be noted: "wonders and signs" (2:19, 22 with ποιέω = 7:36 and 6:8); "Jesus the Nazarean" (2:22 = 6:14); David (2:25, 29, 30, 34 = 7:45); "right hand" (2:25, 33 of God = 7:55, 56); patriarch (2:29 = 7:8, 9); concept of tomb (2:29 = 7:16); prophet(s) (2:30 = 7:37, 42, 48); τοῦτον τὸν Ἰησοῦν ἀνέστησεν ὁ θεός. . . (2:32 and 36) and τοῦτον τὸν Μωϋσῆν. . . τοῦτον ὁ θεός. . . ἀπέσταλκεν (7:35); the "promise" (2:33 = 7:5, 17); οὐρανοί (2:35--Ps 109:1 = 7:49--Is 66:1).

The parallels between Peter's speech in Acts 3 and that of Stephen are even more impressive: θαυμάζω (3:12 = 7:31); ἀτενίζω (3:12 = 6:15; 7:55; see also 3:4); God of Abraham . . . the God of . . . fathers, Ex 3:6 (3:13 = 7:32); "glory/glorify" (3:13 = 7:2, 55); ἀρνέομαι (3:13, 14 = 7:35); "holy one" (3:14 = 7:52); "murderer" (3:14 = 7:52); ἀρχηγός/ἄρχων (3:15 = 7:27, 35); ἀποκτείνω (3:15 = 7:52); καὶ νῦν. . . ἐπράξατε, ὥσπερ καὶ οἱ ἄρχοντες ὑμῖν (3:17) and ὡς οἱ πατέρες ὑμῶν καὶ ὑμεῖς. . . οὗ νῦν ὑμεῖς (7:51-52); προκαταγγέλλω (3:18 = 7:52; see also καταγγέλλω 2:24); prophet(s) (3:18, 21, 22, 23f. = 7:37, 42, 48); ἀποστέλλω (3:20, 26 = 7:34, 35); Moses (3:22 = 7:20f.); quotation of Dt 18:15 (3:22 = 7:37); "covenant" (3:25 = 7:8); "the fathers" (2:25 = 7 throughout); "Abraham and his seed" (3:25 = 7:2-6); ἀποστρέφω/στρέφω (3:36 = 7:39, 42).

Even the short speeches of 4:8f. ("Jesus the Nazarean" 4:10 and 6:14; σωτηρία 4:12 and 7:25; θαυμάζω [4:13] and 7:31; οὗτός ἐστιν ὁ . . . 4:11 and 7:37, 38; κρίνω 4:19 and 7:7) and of 5:29f. ("the God of . . . fathers" 5:30 and 7:32; stylistic and thematic parallels of 5:30-31 and 7:35) are not devoid of striking parallels with the Stephen speech. It should be noted that in this survey I have indicated neither the introductory formulae of the speeches nor the stylistic parallel which were discussed at length in relation to 7:35-41. This last construction, it should be noted, appears in most of the missionary discourses: 2:22-24; 3:13-14; 4:10; 5:30-31; and 10:38-40 (supra, pp. 193-94).

In light of the above discussion, I am led to a conclusion very similar to that drawn by Schweizer, namely: "What has been said so far should suffice to show that one and the same author is decisively involved in the composition of all the speeches here investigated."[31] This observation is true also of the Stephen speech, not in terms of structure, but of style and thematic concern. Drawing further upon this scholar's conclusions, I have been led to consider a new set of data. Schweizer, basing his observation upon the eight speeches mentioned earlier (excluding Acts 7), not only inferred that one author composed all the speeches, but further noted that the variations found in these discourses owed less to the speaker than to the audience.[32] This remark has contributed most to the present analysis.

The Stephen speech is addressed to a law court and, more particularly, to the Sanhedrin (Acts 6:12 and 15). A history of Israel, then, is certainly appropriate in such a context, in the same way that a theological theme (as opposed to a christological one) and a quotation of the Greek poet Aratus are apropos in a discourse addressed to a Gentile audience in 17:22f. It is equally indicative that the one missionary speech which bears the closest affinity to Acts 7, Paul's discourse in 13:16f., should be addressed to synagogue hearers. Both speeches dwell at length, using very similar terminology, upon the history of Israel. The nature of the audience has left its mark upon both the themes and the structures of the two discourses.

Schweizer has noted the similarity between Acts 7 and 13 ("a selective sketch of the history of Israel"), but he has justly added that the former "is composed differently."[33] The reason for this difference, I propose, is to be found both in the audience addressed and in the purpose of the speech. The purpose of Stephen's oration--to be discussed below--and that

---

[31]"Speeches," p. 212.

[32]Ibid., p. 214.

[33]Ibid., p. 211.

of the discourse analyzed by Schweizer are entirely different, and in this resides the fundamental reason for the dissimilarity in structure. Acts 7:2-53 bears considerable similarity to 13:22-41, since a recitation of Jewish history is de rigeur in the first case as a lesson of history (see 7:51), and in the second as an exegesis of that same history (13:15). But at the same time Stephen's discourse is structurally different from the early speeches of Acts,[34] simply because its purpose is not that of missionary proclamation. The same conclusion obtains for the later discourses of Acts, which also differ structurally from the missionary speeches.

As to the later discourses of the book, while no general survey of the structures of these is proposed here, it should be noted that at least one of these bears significant thematic and structural affinity to the Stephen speech. Indeed, the introductory (21:15f.) and concluding (22:22f.) narratives, with their double accusations against Paul (vv.21 and 28), their mixture of mob rule and law-and-order (vv.27f. and 31f.), and their numerous philological, stylistic, and thematic similarities to the narrative of the Stephen story, constitute a fitting context for Paul's discourse to the crowd.

Neither the complexity of the introductory narrative, owing to the constant alternation of narrative and discourse (particularly from 21:36f.), nor the considerable use of doublets (vv.39f.)[35] can obscure the fact that Paul's speech begins like Stephen's,

7:2 ῎Ανδρες ἀδελφοὶ καὶ πατέρες, ἀκούσατε

22:1 ῎Ανδρες ἀλελφοὶ καὶ πατέρες, ἀκούσατέ μου
τῆς πρὸς ὑμᾶς νυνὶ ἀπολογίας,

---

[34]Acts 5:29-32 and its narrative context bear considerable structural similarity to the Stephen story and will be analyzed at length later in the chapter. Nevertheless, Peter's (and the apostles') discourse to the Sanhedrin is not a historical, but a kerygmatic one.

[35]Among others note the following: 21:39 (ἐγὼ ἄνθρωπος μὲν εἰμι Ἰουδαῖος, Ταρσεύς, τῆς Κιλικίας) and 22:3 (ἐγὼ εἰμι ἀνὴρ Ἰουδαῖος, γεγεννημένος ἐν Ταρσῷ τῆς Κιλικίας); 21:39 (οὐκ ἀσήμου πόλεως and 22:3 (ἐν τῇ πόλει ταύτῃ); 21:39 (ἐπιτρεψόν μοι) and 21:40 (ἐπιτρέψαντος δὲ αὐτοῦ); 21:40 (πολλῆς δὲ σιγῆς) and 22:2 (μᾶλλον παρέσχον ἡσυχίαν); 21:40 (προσεφώνσεν τῇ Ἑβραΐδι διαλέκτῳ) and 22:2 (τῇ Ἑβραΐδι διαλέκτῳ προσεφώνει).

uses the history of Paul's conversion (vv.3-21) to make its point, and is abruptly ended in v.22 by the phrase, ἤκουον δὲ αὐτοῦ ἄχρι τούτου τοῦ λόγου. In the two speeches under consideration, the histories of Israel or of Paul's conversion serve similar functions. Both follow upon very similar accusations and present not a point by point refutation of these charges but a history whose length is coextensive with the speech itself, and whose principal point is not essentially apologetic. Even though 22:1f. is called an ἀπολογία (the same is true of Paul's speech in 26:1f. both in terms of apologetics and the role played by the third conversion account within that discourse), the answer given by the speaker is no more pertinent to the charges than that of Stephen to the accusations leveled against him.

While it is not my intention here to deny any relationship between the accusations brought both against Paul and Stephen and the speeches conferred upon them (this will be considered below), it is nevertheless my contention that this factor is not the principal one in determining the purpose of the speeches in question. Instead, it should be noted that the writer had several goals in mind when composing a particular section of his work. This is particularly true of the speeches. The finales of the two discourses under consideration are especially significant in that regard.

Both speeches come to an abrupt ending, since both are followed by a violent reaction on the part of the audience. However, in each case the author has attained his goal. He has terminated the speech at the very point he wished to make. In Paul's discourse the Gentile mission is central: ὅτι ἐγὼ εἰς ἔθνη μακρὰν ἐξαποστελῶ σε (22:21), while in that of Stephen it is the acrimonious invective against Judaism which becomes the focal point. The audience, purpose, and setting of the speech, then, contribute significantly to the understanding of its structure and function.

b. Structure of the Stephen Speech

In the lengthy discussion of the use of OT quotations and the nature and function of the stylistic data of the speech, it has been repeatedly emphasized that the overall structure of this text was that of Israel's history. Beginning with God's appearance to Abraham, the author follows Jewish history to the building of the house of God by Solomon. This outline meets the requirements, at least in part, of the speech's purpose. Just as the personal history of Paul in Acts 22:1f. provides the requisite elements of an ἀπολογία (note the double ἀπολογέομαι introducing Paul's second apologetic discourse in Acts 26), and the historical survey in Acts 13:16f. furnishes the necessary introduction for a παράκλησις, thus the annals of Israel in 7:2f. elucidate the pregnant phrase of 7:51, ὡς οἱ πατέρες ὑμῶν καὶ ὑμεῖς. The story of the fathers--the central structural feature of the speech--provides the outline, the content, and, with considerable assistance from the author of Acts, the constituent elements of Israel's indictment.

At the same time it has become increasingly clear throughout the analysis in chapters two and three that rarely were we dealing with history for its own sake. Repeatedly, there was occasion to note the editorial work of the author, his additions to, modifications of, and, in general, his particular presentation of the OT story.

In light of these observations, then, it is necessary to examine the structure of the speech from a twofold point of view. The first corresponds to an external factor, namely, the source being used, while the second is to be found in more internal, that is, stylistic and thematic considerations. Both elements are intimately related to the author's method of composition.

1) Narrative Structure

The overall unity of the discourse, viewed externally, owes to the historical sequence of the biblical story, beginning with Abraham and ending with Solomon. Indeed, in relation to the OT narrative, the speech consists of 1) a history of the patriarchs (2-16), 2) of Moses (17-34), 3) a historical-thematic section (35-50), and 4) an invective addressed to the audience (51-53).

In the first place vv.2-16 stand out as a unit. The narrative presents Abraham in the land of the Chaldeans, proceeds through the patriarchal story, witnesses the arrival of the Hebrews in Egypt, and terminates with the death and burial of the fathers in Shechem. This section, then, constitutes the history of the patriarchs and, for the most part, the order of events is that of the OT narrative. Clearly the story has been greatly shortened and a choice has been made of episodes presented. Furthermore, a very prominent role has been assigned to Abraham[36] and Joseph in this reconstruction of Jewish history (this is in marked contrast to Jdt 5:6-18 where the historical summary alone is presented). Vv2-7 deal with the former while vv.9-15 treat of the latter. Each section is followed by a summary verse, v.8 regarding circumcision and v. 16 concerning burial.

The observations made above concern content primarily. However, equally important is the order of the events. A list of OT references has been given at the beginning of chapter two. The author's use of his source has been dealt with in relation to the quoting process. The writer begins with the Abraham narrative of Gn 12 and draws both content and quotations from successive chapters of that book. While the detailed examination of this material in chapter two has indicated various combinations of passages and conflation of sources, it was equally evident that the overall sequence was acquired from Genesis. The author selected his data in a very systematic way from his source, borrowing texts, phrases, episodes to construct a mosaic of OT passages. At the same time he supplemented these with seemingly aberrant traditions and thematic elements, but this he did within the framework provided by his source.

Secondly, the story of Moses as retold in vv.17-34 offered by far the best opportunity to examine the intricacies of the author's method of composition. This is particularly true since he follows the OT text so closely. In fact, the entire passage, considered in relation to the biblical source, falls into three parts, each corresponding to one of the first three chapters of Exodus: vv.17-19 consisting of the editing of Ex 1:7-11; vv.20-29 of Ex 2:1-15; and vv.30-34 of Ex 3:1-10.

Again the obvious conclusion follows that the OT text is the direct model upon which the author cast his version of the life of Moses. Each of the first three chapters provided him

---

[36]See Dahl, "Abraham," pp. 142-43.

with the episodes he required; however, into this framework he placed numerous new details and themes. A synoptic study allowed for a more just discernment of the importance of the OT model, the author's editorial work, and his more original contribution in the composition of the Moses episode. He reorganized the time framework, expanded several incidents, and gave Moses the central role within the speech. By comparing the NT text in an overall view to the OT Vorlage, it is clear that the story of Moses is no longer told in an anecdotal fashion. Rather, in making use of numerous terms, phrases, and even extended quotations, the author contrasts the Jews with the Egyptians, the brethren with Moses, the Pharaoh with his daughter, but more particularly he takes great pains to depict the role and vocation of Moses as his central theme. This is cleverly done within the OT framework by editing, expanding, adding, and reorganizing the entire story. In this connection the import of the omission as well as the choice by the author of certain episodes, terms, and expressions is greatly enhanced.

Two episodes in the life of Moses attract the author's attention in a special way. Indeed, he develops these two incidents at great length, making considerable use of the LXX text: the intervention of Moses on behalf of his persecuted brethren vv.23-28, and his encounter with God at Mount Sinai vv.30-34. Both episodes, it will be argued later, owing to their length, structure, situation within the speech, and extended development, are central to the author's theology.

The third section of the discourse, vv.35-50, requires special attention for two major reasons. First of all, scholars, in noting the repetitive use of οὗτος in v.35f., have insisted that this constitutes "an abrupt change of style" as well as author.[37] Secondly, it would seem that the speech no longer follows the OT narrative in a systematic way, but instead indulges in a more thematic and polemical point of view.

These two observations are important in an analysis of the role played by the OT narrative in this part of the speech. Therefore, the following observations are in order. 1) There

---

[37]Haenchen, Acts, p. 282. The views of Dibelius, Haenchen, Holtz, Wilckens, and Conzelmann (see pp. 249-53 above) relie greatly upon this particular observation.

is in fact historical continuity between the first two parts of the discourse and the third. In the analysis of the quoting process both for vv.35-41 and 42-50, it was shown that, in spite of the increasingly thematic concern of the author, the overall structure is intimately related to the narrative sequence of the OT account. The writer pursues his historical survey, borrowing consistently from the book of Exodus for both sections, at the same time generously supplementing his composition with Deuteronomic and prophetic quotations. The narrative framework, then, is discernible throughout the speech.[38]

2) The abrupt transition between vv.34 and 35f. constitutes a problem which is more apparent than real. The occurrence of οὗτος is hardly limited to editorial verses but is found throughout this part of the discourse: 35 (twice), 36, 37, 38, and 40 and again in 7:19 (see also 6:13-14). Furthermore, the writer's use of the OT does not change abruptly with v.35. Instead, as demonstrated in the analysis of the quoting process in vv.17-34, the OT text plays a diminishing part in the author's method of composition. In vv.35f. the writer's attitude vis-à-vis the biblical narrative does not change appreciably, although the polemical tone of the composition continues to increase.

3) The relation of 7:2-34 to 35-50 should be seen in light of the author's method of composition. Since it has already been shown that the extended history of Israel in the discourses of Paul (13:16-41) and Stephen serve similar functions,[39] a further similarity between these texts which will shed light upon the present problem should be indicated. Paul, after dwelling upon the past of the Jewish nation (13:17-22), reaches a turning point, namely, the central concern of the discourse: τούτου ὁ θεὸς ἀπὸ τοῦ σπέρματος κατ' ἐπαγγελίαν ἤγαγεν τῷ 'Ισραὴλ σωτῆρα 'Ιησοῦν (v.23). In a similar manner, and in an equally abrupt way, Stephen, after having reached the central concern of his speech, eulogizes Moses in a very strik-

---

[38] Scholars who defend an editing theory generally insist upon the historical continuity between v.34 and vv.36, 38, 44-47.

[39] See pp. 257-58 above.

ing manner (τοῦτον τὸν Μωϋσῆν . . .). It is also noteworthy that both speakers pursue their historical thrust, Paul concerning John, Jesus, David, and Moses (ending with a bitter invective, 40-41), and Stephen regarding Moses, Aaron, David, and Solomon (terminating with an even more stinging condemnation). The stylistic patterns are abviously related.

Also in relation to the author's method of composition, a further note is needed on a subject treated earlier,[40] that is, the stylistic pattern used in 7:35, τοῦτον τὸν Μωϋσῆν, ὅν . . . τοῦτον . . . . This construction occurs in at least six other passages in Acts. All except one are missionary discourses, where the writer employs the pattern to underscore the role of Jesus. Its use in each case seems to mark a turning point in the speech in a way similar to v.35 in Stephen's discourse.[41] Its occurrence here is an important stylistic indication that v.35 marks the central part of the speech and that the author will direct his attention increasingly to his intended goal.

The third section of the speech (35-50), while marking the focal point of the lengthy discourse, nevertheless acquires its overall structure from the OT narrative and culminates in a paroxysm of condemnation. This invective (51-53), instead of being inspired by the biblical narrative, in the last analysis dictates the form of the Stephen speech: a historical survey of Israel's relation to its God.

2) Architectonic Structure

As has been clearly demonstrated by the discussion of the stylistic data, the discourse possesses a distinct and very cohesive internal structure. The disposition of the structural, stylistic, and thematic data is almost entirely due to the author's creative ability and is rarely related to the OT source.

To underscore the speech's internal cohesiveness, a few

---

[40]Supra, pp. 193-96 and 256-57.

[41]Acts 13:22-23 should probably be classified as an analogous construction: ἤγειρεν τὸν Δαυὶδ αὐτοῖς εἰς βασιλέα, ᾧ καὶ εἶπεν μαρτυρήσας· εὗρον Δαυίδ ... ὃς ποιήσει πάντα τὰ θελήματά μου. τούτου ὁ θεὸς ἀπὸ τοῦ σπέρματος κατ' ἐπαγγελίαν ἤγαγεν τῷ 'Ισραὴλ σωτῆρα 'Ιησοῦν.

structural features could be pointed out.[42] 1) The poignant phrase of 7:51, ὡς οἱ πατέρες ὑμῶν καὶ ὑμεῖς, delineates clearly one aspect of the text's form: vv.2-50 history of the fathers; vv.51-53 address to the audience. 2) The history of the speech follows the well-known pattern of the OT narratives: from the patriarchs, to Moses (personal history and the people under his leadership), and finally the late history of Israel. 3) Throughout this historical sequence the thematic and polemic tone of the discourse increases until it reaches a climax in the invective of vv.51-53. 4) The thematic element of "place" (already announced in 6:13-14) leaves a distinct trace beginning with the departure of Abraham from his land (v.3, note the addition of "this place" in v.7), through the sojourn in Egypt, the desert experience, and terminating with the tabernacle/house theme of vv.42-50. 5) The theme of "descendant" is clearly discernible throughout: Abraham (his seed), Joseph (Jacob), Moses, "the prophet," David (Joshua), the prophets, and the Just One (contrasted to "your" fathers and "you"). 6) The contrasting motif of "the divine versus the human" is discernible in each part of the speech:

vv. 2-8	God commands--a nation will enslave
9-16	Joseph (God) summons his people to Egypt--the brothers sell Joseph into Egypt
17-34	God sends Moses to Egypt--Pharaoh and the Hebrew manifest human concerns
35-41	God acts through Moses his envoy--"god/calf making" is the human answer
42-50	A continuous interweaving of the two (contemporaneity of negative and positive; see below for further discussion)
51-53	Totally negative response of man: persecution, murder, and rejection

---

[42]The themes of the speech will be discussed at greater length later in the chapter. But it should be stated at this point that it is anachronistic to presume that ancient speeches had of necessity to have "one consistent theme" (see Haenchen, *Acts*, pp. 286-87). In this regard, I fully agree with Wilson, *Gentiles*, p. 136, who, after having discussed the variety of unifying themes proposed by scholars for Acts 7, concludes: ". . . it is better to speak of a unified complex of interrelated themes than of a single theme. These are: the faithfulness of God in keeping his promises; the constant disobedience of the Jews, who have rejected his Law, prophets and leaders; and the steady stream of individuals who, over against the mass

The unity of the speech is further enhanced by the great variety of lexical, stylistic, and structural features (discussed in detail in chapter three).

c. Conclusions

Briefly the following conclusions regarding the composition of the speech must be stated. 1) Stephen's discourse is a history of Israel, like other histories found in Jewish works of every period (*supra*, pp. 141-45). Acts 7, like the other historical summaries referred to, presents a peculiar slant which corresponds to its goals. Its didactic and polemic intent is obvious, but it is clearly within the Jewish literary tradition.[43]

2) The speech of Stephen finds its place in Acts along with the great variety of discourses composed by the author. It is in fact his own composition based upon the OT narratives. It has been inserted by him, in what is often considered a manner reminiscent of Herodotus, to mark an important turning point in his narrative. In the words of Cadbury, "the Greek and Roman writers who invent speeches place them, as does Acts, either before some regularly constituted assembly or at some dramatic moment in an exciting narrative."[44] The turning point of the Stephen story is the departure from Jerusalem. However, there is another important factor in the disposition of speeches, usually associated with Thucydides, and that is the use of discourses by the author to explain a course of action. In the present case the judgment of Judaism becomes the principal function of Acts 7. At the same time, fully within the classical tradition the Stephen speech, like those of Paul later in Acts, acquires an added function, namely, defense

---

of Jews, remain righteous--Joseph, Moses, the prophets, Jesus and Stephen."

[43]Historical summaries in the OT invariably betray a general didactic or polemic tendency; see Henrich Schlier's ["θλίβω," in *TDNT* 3:142] statement: "for almost all these real threats to the historical existence of the chosen people come from God as a punishment for its unfaithfulness and serve to fashion an obedient people, 2 Ch. 20:9ff.; Hos. 5:15; Neh. 9:26f.; Is. 26:16; 37:3; 63:9; 65:16; Jer. 10:18 etc." See the excellent analysis of Henry J. Cadbury (and Editors), "Writing History," pp. 16-29.

[44]"Speeches in Acts," p. 417. See also Martin Dibelius,

against accusations.[45]

3) In considering the author's veracity, seriousness, and competence (if one should take either Lk 1:1-4 or Acts 1:1f. seriously), appeal might be made to the famous words of Thucydides (Hist. 1.22) regarding the nature of speeches: ὡς δ' ἂν ἐδόκουν μοι ἕκαστοι περὶ τῶν ἀεὶ παρόντων τὰ δέοντα μάλιστα εἰπεῖν ἐχομένῳ ὅτι ἐγγύτατα τῆς ξυμπάσης γνώμης τῶν ἀληθῶς λεχθέντων οὕτως εἴρηται. What the author thought Stephen did or would have said is no doubt what one finds in Acts 7. His view of Stephen as a man who speaks with wisdom and the Holy Spirit is crucial for an understanding of the purpose and nature of the discourse.

2. Narratives

Attention must now be directed to the composition of the narrative sections of the Stephen story. The goal is to follow the author's process of composition in the light of the stylistic and structural tendencies observed, particularly in the analysis of the speech.

a. Acts 6:1-7

First, it is important to recall the results of the study in the previous chapter concerning the stylistic peculiarities of this text, and call to mind the author's goal (presentation of problem v.1; proposed solution vv.2-4; adoption of solution vv.5-6; and successful resolution v.7). In relation to this, the text's overall structure is: vv.1 and 7--introduction and conclusion forming an inclusio and vv.2-4 and 5-6 comprising a very striking and complex parallel. Clearly the strategic disposition of doublets, cognate terms, and contrasts serve to

---

"Speeches in Acts," pp. 139-40 and again 150f.

[45]See among others P. G. Walsh, Livy: His Historical Aims and Methods (Cambridge: Cambridge University Press, 1961), especially chapter IX: "The Speeches." On p. 220 the author presents an analysis of the variety of discourses employed by historians. It should be noted that the genus iudicale and the genus demonstrativum are particularly illuminating for an understanding of Acts 7. Finally, Philip A. Stadter, ed., The Speeches in Thucydides: A Collection of Original Studies with a Bibliography (Chapel Hill: University of North Carolina Press, 1973), offers several articles of interest to the present analysis.

underscore the author's overriding concerns. As a result, then, of the distribution and frequency of the data as well as the structural disposition of these, one is faced with the inescapable conclusion that vv.1-7 in their present form are substantially the work of the author of Acts.

In light of these observations, the structural features of the parallelism between vv.2-4 and 5-6 ought to be stressed. Not only does the proposal by the Twelve (2-4) find its formal counterpart in the action of the community (5-6), but, as pointed out earlier,[46] most details of these passages form a striking complex of doublets. It is the carefully balanced nature of these two sections--too symmetrical not to be intentional--which leads one to subject Acts 6:1-7 to closer scrutiny.

A recent article ("Acts 6:1-6: A Redactional View") by Joseph T. Lienhard,[47] in which he attempts to distinguish by means of a standard Redacktionsgeschichte method between traditional and redactional elements in this passage, has raised additional questions in my mind regarding the composition of this part of the Stephen story. On the basis of detailed analysis of vocabulary and style, Lienhard concludes that 6:1a and 2-4 are redactional, while 6:1b and 5-6 are taken from tradition and reflect probable historical data.[48] There is one key factor in his analysis which raises serious questions regarding the entire inquiry and calls for closer attention. In his investigation of "the Speech of the Twelve (6:2-4)," he states:

> The first word of the verse [3] again suggests the redactor's hand. Episkeptesthai is a predominantly Lucan word; of eleven NT occurrences, seven are in Lk-Acts. The meaning of the word here is somewhat problematical. In the NT it normally means "to visit." But its sense in Acts 6:3 is different; there is means rather "to select."[49]

Lienhard then proceeds to cite secondary literature to justify

---

[46]See the discussion of the structural features of Acts 6:1-7, pp. 215-19.

[47]CBQ 37 (1975): 228-36.

[48]Ibid., pp. 231, 235, and 236.

[49]Ibid., pp. 232-33.

his interpretation of this verse. This is very assailable methodology. Since it is fundamental to this scholar's approach to establish a particular element as being redactional or, by exclusion, to be traditional, it seems contradictory to label ἐπισκέπτομαι as redactional, that is, typical of the writer, precisely in the one case where lexically it is a NT <u>hapax legomenon</u>.

In light of these several factors, I was led to reinvestigate Acts 6:1-7 and to seek the clue to its composition in a new direction. This evidence is to be found both in the LXX and in the author's method of redaction. In attempting to account for the peculiar combination of ideas in this text, "select . . . appoint over" (v.3) and "choose . . . set before" (vv.5-6), one ought to consider three important OT passages whose ideational structure casts considerable light upon Acts 6:2-6. In order to understand the full implications of these parallels, it will be necessary to present the following textual schema:

2	προσκαλεσάμενοι δὲ οἱ δώδεκα	5	
	τὸ πλῆθος τῶν μαθητῶν εἶπαν		καὶ ἤρεσεν ὁ λόγος
	οὐκ ἀρεστόν ἐστιν ἡμᾶς		ἐνώπιον παντὸς τοῦ πλήθους,
	καταλείψαντας τὸν λόγον τοῦ θεοῦ		
	διακονεῖν τραπέζαις.		
3	ἐπισκέψασθε δέ, ἀδελφοί,		καὶ ἐξελέξαντο
	ἄνδρας ἐξ ὑμῶν		Στέφανον, ἄνδρα
	μαρτυρουμένους		πλήρη πίστεως καὶ πνεύματος ἁγίου,
	ἑπτὰ		καὶ Φίλιππον καὶ Πρόχορον καὶ Νικάνορα καὶ Τίμωνα καὶ Παρμενᾶν
	πλήρεις πνεύματος καὶ σοφίας,		καὶ Νικόλαον προσήλυτον Ἀντιοχέα,
	οὓς καταστήσομεν ἐπὶ τῆς χρείας ταύτης·	6	οὓς ἔστησαν ἐνώπιον τῶν ἀποστόλων,
4	ἡμεῖς δὲ τῇ προσευχῇ		καὶ προσευξάμενοι
	καὶ τῇ διακονίᾳ τοῦ λόγου προσκαρτερήσομεν		ἐπέθηκαν αὐτοῖς τὰς χεῖρας

Gn 41:33 νῦν οὖν σκέψαι ἄνθρωπον φρόνιμον καὶ συνετὸν καὶ κατάστησον αὐτὸν ἐπὶ γῆς Αἰγύπτου· 34 καὶ ποιησάτω Φαρας καὶ καταστησάτω τοπάρχας ἐπὶ τῆς γῆς ...
37 Ἤρεσεν δὲ τὰ ῥήματα ἐναντίον Φαραω καὶ ἐναντίον πάντων τῶν παίδων αὐτοῦ, 38 καὶ εἶπεν Φαραω πᾶσιν τοῖς παισὶν αὐτοῦ Μὴ εὑρήσομεν ἄνθρωπον τοιοῦτον, ὃς ἔχει πνεῦμα θεοῦ ἐν αὐτῷ; 39 εἶπεν δὲ Φαραω τῷ Ιωσηφ Ἐπειδὴ ἔδειξεν ὁ θεός σοι πάντα ταῦτα, οὐκ ἔστιν ἄνθρωπος φρονιμώτερος καὶ συνετώτερός σου·
40 σὺ ἔσῃ ἐπὶ τῷ οἴκῳ μου ... 41 εἶπεν δὲ Φαραω τῷ Ιωσηφ Ἰδοὺ καθίστημί σε σήμερον ἐπὶ πάσης γῆς Αἰγύπτου.
... 43 ... καὶ κατέστησεν αὐτὸν ἐφ' ὅλης γῆς Αἰγύπτου.[50]

Ex 18:19 νῦν οὖν ἄκουσόν μου, καὶ συμβουλεύσω σοι, καὶ ἔσται ὁ θεὸς μετὰ σοῦ ... 21 καὶ σὺ σεαυτῷ σκέψαι ἀπὸ παντὸς τοῦ λαοῦ ἄνδρας δυνατοὺς θεοσεβεῖς, ἄνδρας δικαίους μισοῦντας ὑπερηφανίαν, καὶ καταστήσεις αὐτοὺς ἐπ' αὐτῶν χιλιάρχους ...
24 ἤκουσεν δὲ Μωυσῆς τῆς φωνῆς τοῦ γαμβροῦ καὶ ἐποίησεν ὅσα αὐτῷ εἶπεν. 25 καὶ ἐπέλεξεν Μωυσῆς ἄνδρας δυνατοὺς ἀπὸ παντὸς Ισραηλ καὶ ἐποίησεν αὐτοὺς ἐπ' αὐτῶν χιλιάρχους ...[51]

Dt 1:13 δότε ἑαυτοῖς ἄνδρας σοφοὺς καὶ ἐπιστήμονας καὶ συνετοὺς εἰς τὰς φυλὰς ὑμῶν, καὶ καταστήσω [A αὐτοὺς] ἐφ' ὑμῶν ἡγουμένους ὑμῶν.
14 καὶ ἀπεκρίθητέ μοι καὶ εἴπατε καλὸν τὸ ῥῆμα, ὃ ἐλάλησας ποιῆσαι. 15 καὶ ἔλαβον ἐξ ὑμῶν ἄνδρας σοφοὺς καὶ ἐπιστήμονας καὶ συνετοὺς καὶ κατέστησα αὐτοὺς ἡγεῖσθαι ἐφ' ὑμῶν χιλιάρχους ...[52]

After having considered the above data, it is my opinion that while Gn 41:33f. may be the principal source from which the author of Acts has drawn his inspiration, it is clear that

---

[50] This chapter of Genesis was employed considerably during the composition of the Stephen speech, see the commentary on 7:10-11.

[51] Note that in composing Acts 7:29 the author quotes Ex 2:15b but also conflates Ex 2:22 and 18:3f.

[52] See the references in the analysis of 7:36-37 to the influence of the first chapter of Deuteronomy on the author.

there is a repetition here of a process often encountered in the analysis of the discourse. Similarity of structure and ideas has brought about the conflation of several passages. Furthermore, it is under the combined influence of these LXX texts that the author has formulated the structural unit which comprises Acts 6:1-7. To substantiate these conclusions the six following considerations are proposed.

1) The basic structure of the passage in question consists of four verbal concepts, a Gedankengang occuring in all three OT passages cited above:

Acts 6	ἐπισκέψασθε	...καταστήσομεν	ἐπί	...ἐξελέξαντο	...ἔστησαν ἐνώπιον
Gn 41	σκέψαι	...κατάστησον	...ἐπί	...μὴ εὑπήσομεν...	καθίστημι...ἐπί
Ex 18	σκέψαι	...καταστήσεις	..ἐπί	...ἐπέλεξεν	...ἐποίησεν ...ἐπί
Dt 1	δότε ἑαυτοῖς	..καταστήσω	...ἐπί	...ἔλαβον	...κατέστησα ...ἐπί

In light of this pattern, the striking parallelism of the NT narrative takes on added importance, particularly since it would seem to require that the overall structure owes to the author of Acts. It is around this pattern, borrowed from his OT model, that he has erected one of his many scenes describing the Jerusalem community.

2) The series of verbs employed in Acts are readily understood in view of the author's stylistic preferences and tendencies. His idiosyncratic attitude in the use of verbal roots has often been observed. He adds a prepositional prefix (ἐπί + σκέπτομαι), retains a compound verb unmodified, substitutes one preposition (ἐκ + λέγομαι) for another (ἐπί), and, finally, eliminates a prefix (κατά), retaining the simple root. The first and last verbs of the series need immediate comment. The use of ἵστημι in v.6, apart from meeting the author's lexical demands, also corresponds to a pattern frequently encountered in the study, i.e., the use of cognate terms, particularly of verbal roots.[53] In the case of the first verb, ἐπισκέπτομαι, it is probably the author who transformed the rare verb

---

[53]See the corpus, pp. 165-69.

σκέπτομαι of the LXX[54] to the more frequent compound, which apparently had acquired the meaning of "select"[55] in post-LXX times.[56]

3) The use of ἀνήρ in Acts 6:3 could be explained in terms of the author's preference for this term rather than ἄνθρωπος[57] (if he follows Gn 41:33 closely), or as due to the influence of the other two LXX models which employ that term repeatedly. It will be noted that following his OT paradigm, the writer repeats this element after the verb of "choice" in v.5 making use of a plural/singular contrast to prepare for the subsequent role of Stephen.

4) The following connections should probably be made: ἐξ ὑμῶν (Dt 1:15 with its influence upon ἐξελέξαντο v.5), πνεύματος (Gn 41:38 and its parallel in v.5), σοφίας (Dt 1:13 and 15: σοφός).

5) Acts 6:3, οὓς καταστήσομεν ἐπί + genitive, is identical to all three OT models; however, Acts 7:10, in making use of this construction, employs ἐπί followed by the accusative. These facts argue strongly in favor of LXX sources in both cases (<u>supra</u>, pp. 62-68 for a discussion of 7:10-11).

6) The clause, καὶ ἤρεσεν ὁ λόγος ἐνώπιον παντὸς τοῦ πλήθους, and its relation to Gn 41:37 is most striking and convincing.[58] The use of λόγος in the place of ῥῆμα can be paral-

---

54The verb occurs four times in the LXX: Gn 41:33 (ראה); Ex 18:21 (חזה); Zech 11:13 and Dn LXX Bel 15. Note also Moulton-Milligan, <u>Vocabulary</u>, s.v. "ἐπισκέπτομαι": "The <u>simplex</u> is found P Cairo Preis 48.6 (ii/A.D.) τὸ μὲν πλοῖόν σοι, ὡς ἠθέλησας σκέψομαι."

55"With the use of the verb in Ac 6.3 we may compare P Petr II. 37.2b verso 4 (iii/B.C.) ἐπισκεψάμενος ἐν ἀρχῆι ἃ δεῖ γενέσθαι ἔργα, P Oxy III. 533.20 (ii/iii A.D.) ἐπισκέψασθε ἐκ τοῦ λογιστηρίου τοῦ στρα(τηγοῦ) ἐπιστολ(ὴν) τοῦ διοικητοῦ, 'look out at the office of the strategus a letter of the dioecetes' (Edd.)" <u>ibid</u>.

56At least two occurrences of ἐπισκέπτομαι should probably be rendered "appoint": Nb 27:16 and Neh 7:1, both of which render the Hebrew פקד, also with the meaning "appoint" (see Beyer, "ἐπισκέπτομαι," <u>TDNT</u>, 2:602-3 for additional references). However, nowhere does the verb mean "select," nor does it ever in the LXX represent either ראה or חזה. See below.

57See pp. 82, n. 128; 85, n. 137; and 117.

58See the very different statement of Dt 1:14 and the implied reaction of Moses in Ex 18:24.

leled with the same phenomenon in 7:29, where ἐν τῷ λόγῳ τούτῳ has replaced the τὸ ῥῆμα τοῦτο of Ex 2:15. The change from ἐναντίον to ἐνώπιον is consistent with what was observed in the analysis of the speech[59] (note its repetition in 6:6). Finally the parallel statement of 6:2 οὐκ ἀρεστόν ἐστιν ἡμᾶς renders the above conclusion even more impressive since the technique of composition here is very obvious. One element is borrowed from the OT model (v.5); it is modified for stylistic reasons, then a parallel statement is formulated. This construction at the same time permits the author to indulge in some of his stylistic preferences: a singular/plural as well as a negative/positive contrast.

It is my conclusion, then, in terms of structural unity and architectonic disposition, that Acts 6:1-7 is the work of the author of Acts. That he has inherited various elements of this episode from tradition seems undeniable, e.g., the Hellenist-Hebrew conflict within the early community (v.1b),[60] the list, and probably the tradition of the Seven.[61] However, other factors such as the role of the Twelve/apostles (see also 8:1), of the Seven,[62] of the Spirit (in 1-7 and in relation especially to Stephen 6:10 and 7:55),[63] and the various notions of "service" (and their function within 6:1-7)[64] are so inti-

---

[59]See p. 131, n. 245.

[60]Lienhard, "Acts 6:1-6," pp. 230-1; Wilson, "Theologian and Historian," p. 57; Dibelius, "Speeches in Acts," p. 181; Wilson, *Gentiles*, p. 129.

[61]Dibelius, "Style Criticism," p. 11, n. 20; Schmithals, *Paul and James*, pp. 26-27, 36-37; Borse, "Rahmentext," pp. 188-90; Hengel, "Zwischen Jesus und Paulus," pp. 172-85; Haenchen, *Acts*, pp. 266-67; as well as the authors mentioned in the previous note. See below for further discussion of this subject in relation to the Stephen and Philip stories.

[62]Otto Glombitza, "Zur Charakterisierung des Stephanus in Act 6 und 7," *ZNW* 53 (1962): 238-40; Lienhard, "Acts 6:1-6," p. 236; Hengel, "Zwischen Jesus und Paulus," p. 175.

[63]Bihler, *Stephanusgeschichte*, pp. 25-26; Glombitza, "Zur Charakterisierung," pp. 240-44; Geoffrey W. H. Lampe, "The Holy Spirit in the Writings of St. Luke," in *Studies in the Gospels: Essays in Memory of R. H. Lightfoot*, ed. Dennis E. Nineham (Oxford: Blackwell, 1955), pp. 195-96.

[64]Flender, *Theologian*, p. 128; Wilson, *Gentiles*, pp. 141-42; Haenchen, *Acts*, pp. 265-69.

mately related both to the structural and the thematic character of Acts 6:1-7 that one must consider these in terms principally of the author's purpose and theology. In this regard, a final but crucial argument in favor of such a solution is forthcoming. Earlier in the study an analysis of the parallelism between 6:1 and 7[65] was presented wherein the observation was made that "the twelve" in v.2 and "the apostles" in v.6 formed an inclusio. Structurally and thematically it is very significant that the entire passage dealing with the problem of the community, vv.2-6--artistically situated within 6:1 and 7--should begin and end with the same motif. The initiative (the calling together of the disciples by the Twelve), followed by the proposal of a solution, is clearly attributed to the authorities. The narrative notes that the recommendation is adopted and the entire episode is terminated (ἐπέθηκαν αὐτοῖς τὰς χεῖρας) by an official, institutional act at the hands of the apostles.[66]

b. Acts 6:8-7a; [7:2b-53] and 7:54-8:4

To begin this part of the analysis reference should be made to the pertinent passages in chapter three, where the stylistic data relating to the introductory (6:8-7:2a) and concluding (7:54-8:4) narratives were presented. In both cases it was demonstrated that their distribution and frequency were consistent with the results of the study of the speech. The author's fondness of doublets, lists, cognate terms, and, more telling still, his structural disposition of these features to introduce, to state or to underscore various elements of his

---

[65] Supra, pp. 215-19.

[66] The rite of laying on of hands or of ordination is a subject far beyond the scope of this study; but see the studies of David Daube, The New Testament and Rabbinic Judaism (London: Athlone Press, University of London, 1956), pp. 224-46, and more recently K. Grayston, "The Significance of the Word Hand in the New Testament," in Mélanges bibliques, 479-87. Both arrive at the same conclusion as I have, namely that the author of Acts in composing 6:6 probably utilizes Dt 34:9: "and Joshua the son of Naue was full of the spirit of comprehension (συνέσεως), ἐπέθηκεν γὰρ Μωυσῆς τὰς χεῖρας αὐτου ἐπ' αὐτόν· and the sons of Israel obeyed (εἰσήκουσαν) him." See commentary of 7:38 (Dt 31:30; 32:46-47; 33:2-5); 7:42 (Dt 31:17-18; 32:19) and 7:45 (Dt 34:9).

narrative indicate his redactive activity throughout.

With the results of this analysis in mind, it is clear that old source theories, which attempted to dissect the Stephen story and to allot its parts to dual sources, are clearly invalidated by the data. Indeed, doublets and repetitive elements generally, instead of being indicators of diverse sources have emerged as stylistic characteristics of the author.

Further, in view of the investigation of the narrative, the opportunity arose to scrutinize recent theories of redaction. In defense of an original mob scene transformed into a trial by the author, scholars readily conclude that the latter has been introduced to provide a proper forum for the long speech. On the basis of such an observation, they maintain the historicity of death by lynching.[67] The data amassed in this study lead me to question the presuppositions of such a methodology. If the need for an audience in a given episode of Acts renders various elements of the narrative historically suspect, then by the same logic numerous scenes portrayed in this work should be classified in a similar manner. This approach is particularly troublesome for methodological reasons. The Acts of the Apostles, following the historiographical precepts of its time (both classical and Jewish), makes generous use of speeches in presenting its subject matter. This procedure, recognized by Thucydides (Hist. 1.22) and later historians,[68] is essentially a literary technique whose use by a particular writer is accepted as such. It is methodologically unsound to suppose that discourse, occasion or characters involved acquire their degree of historical verisimilitude according to their relation to literary standards. In the present case, scholars seem to say that since the author of Acts follows the accepted method of historical writing by providing a speech for the occasion, then some element of his text

---

[67]Reference is made particularly to the opinions of Trocmé and Haenchen; but more recently see also Hengel, "Zwischen Jesus und Paulus," p. 198.

[68]Supra, p. 266 for a discussion of this subject. See also Cadbury, "Writing History," pp. 7-15; idem, "Speeches in Acts," pp. 415-22; Dibelius, "Speeches in Acts," pp. 138-45; and Barrett, Luke the Historian, pp. 9-15.

is by that fact suspect. Furthermore, they postulate that since the Stephen speech predates the writing of Acts, in part or totally, and since the accuracy of the author's judicial knowledge can be called into question, it follows ". . . qu'il a modifié le récit que lui apportait la tradition et transformé plus ou moins consciemment une exécution sommaire en procès régulier."[69] It seems to me that the continual mixture of literary and historical considerations without proper regard for their differences methodologically is unacceptable, since evidence of stylistic activity neither rules out nor defends historical reliability.

The method followed in this study is a literary one and, while it does not by that very fact exclude historical factors, it does direct its attention to the study of the structure of the text and the tendencies of the writer. The fact that the author exhibits a fondness for repetitive techniques, stylistic peculiarities, and structural parallels of various kinds may bear upon historical conclusions. However, this is not the primary goal nor the methodological basis of literary analysis.

In light of these considerations, a more thorough structural investigation of the Stephen story is a prerequisite to a proper understanding of its overall function and the nature of its various segments. To that end, the three principal parts of the episode, 6:8-7:2a, 7:2b-53, and 7:54-8:4, will be analyzed since they relate to each other as structural units. Further, its architectural features will be compared to other passages of Acts.

The Stephen story presents the following structure:

6:8-12a	pre-trial confrontation with opponents	
	(v.11) first accusation	
6:12b-15	presentation before the Sanhedrin	
	(v.13-14) second accusation	
7:1-53	interrogation by high priest	
	7:1	question
	7:2-53	response in form of speech
7:54-8:3	post-speech narrative	
	7:54	first reaction
	7:55-56	sequel
		55 narrative
		56 discourse

[69]Trocmé, Livre des Actes, p. 186.

	7:57-8:3	second reaction and resolution
8:4		conclusion

To what extent do the author's literary tendencies or the demands of the narrative determine the structural disposition of the various elements of the Stephen story? By far the most significant parallel to the Stephen story in terms of structure is the trial scene of Acts 5. The similarity between the post-speech narratives of Acts 7:54-8:3 and 5:33-44, as well as between the conclusions of both texts, 8:4 and 5:41-42 has already been noted earlier in this study.[70] This likeness would seem to indicate that the structure owes primarily to the writer's creativity rather than to the needs of the story since very different episodes are cast into the same mould.

For the remainder of the Stephen story Acts 5 would again be the best structural and stylistic analogue. The comparison is as follows:

General/summary statement			
6:8	Στέφανος δέ...ἐποίει τέρατα καὶ σημεῖα μεγάλα ἐν τῷ λαῷ.	5:12	Διὰ δὲ τῶν χειρῶν τῶν ἀποστόλων ἐγίνετο σημεῖα καὶ τέρατα πολλὰ ἐν τῷ λαῷ·
Introduction of main story			
6:9	ἀνέστησαν δέ τινες...	5:17	᾿Αναστὰς δὲ ὁ ἀρχιερεύς...
Dual element before interrogation[71]			
6:9-12a	confrontation & 1st accusation inclusio: λαός vv.8 & 12a	5:17-25	1st arrest & sequel inclusio: λαός vv.12 & 25
6:12b-15	before Sanhedrin & 2nd accusation	5:26-27a	2nd arrest & before Sanhedrin
12b	καὶ ἐπιστάντες συνήρπασαν αὐτὸν καὶ ἤγαγον εἰς τὸ συνέδριον.	27a	ἀγαγόντες δὲ αὐτοὺς ἔστησαν ἐν τῷ συνεδρίῳ.
Interrogation			
7:1	question by high priest	5:27b-28	question by high priest
7:2-53	response: speech	5:29-32	response: speech

---

[70]See pp. 226-27.

[71]The similarity of 5:20 . . . σταθέντες λαλεῖτε ἐν τῷ ἱερῷ τῷ λαῷ πάντα τὰ ῥήματα τῆς ζωῆς ταύτης to the accusation brought against Stephen should not be overlooked, especially

The similarity is remarkable both in details and in organization. The latter, however, must retain our attention. Once again different episodes in the history of the Jerusalem community are related in like fashion. While some contact is expected between these stories--since they both deal with arrests and a subsequent trial--it is all the more interesting that they should bear structural affinity at the very point where they differ most, namely, dual accusations in lieu of two arrests. One can only conclude from the above that the overall schema of the Stephen story is the product of the writer's creative process, rather than the result of an artless combination of disparate sources or the misapprehending and maladroit editing of a hypothetical document.

In relation to the last-mentioned section of the Stephen episode, that is, the accusations, it would be well to refer to another set of accusations found in Acts--those leveled against Paul in chapter 21. It is noteworthy that the author sees fit to introduce these in a twofold formulation: an indirect report (21:21) and a direct accusation (v.28). After an interesting verbal exchange between the participants of the colorful mob scene only then does he allow Paul to discourse upon his personal history. The twofold character of these accusations certainly has some bearing upon the structural considerations made above concerning the Stephen story.

Having made a few general observations concerning the overall composition of the Stephen episode, I will now consider a number of individual problems involving redaction: 1) mob versus trial scene, 2) trial and death of Jesus and its influence upon the Stephen story, 3) Saul tradition.

1) Mob Versus Trial Scene

Ample bibliography and background for a proper understanding of this debate have been given above.[72] Originally the problem was seen exclusively in the light of source criticism; of late the problem of the episode's historicity has come to the fore. Invariably scholars speak of two forces at work before and after the spech which bring about Stephen's death:

6:13.

[72]See pp. 19-22 and n. 75.

a lynch mob and an ordered trial. Authors give as the main reason for such a conclusion a) that from 6:9-12a and generally after the speech the distinct impression is given that the mob is responsible for the death scene, while more particularly in vv.12b-14 and in 7:58b formal trial elements are introduced. In choosing the former as the preferable explanation, scholars have recourse to additional reasons: b) an original mob scene was an unlikely situation for a speech, so an audience is provided for the speech by the addition of a trial setting, and c) the present trial scene betrays the author's incorrect knowledge of Jewish judicial procedures. The above observations will be considered in reverse order.

The judicial knowledge of the author of Acts has often been severely attacked: "He had no idea how judicial stonings were carried out--we know the details from the Mishnah tractate Sanhedrin. . . ."[73] In dealing with this problem, a word should be said about the point made by Haenchen above, rather than to the vast area of first century A.D. Hebrew jurisprudence, for example, the competence of the Sanhedrin at that time, the relation of blasphemy to capital punishment, and a host of other problems.[74] It is too readily accepted that legal statements of the Mishnah were normative for NT times. On the basis of admittedly late traditions, the trial elements of the Stephen episode are called into question, particularly the laying down not of the condemned person's clothes but those of the witnesses in Acts 7:58. That this argument is far less cogent than is usually admitted is illustrated by another example from Acts. In his commentary on Acts 13:16 (ἀναστάς), Haenchen takes the author to task for presenting "Paul as a

---

[73]Haenchen, Acts, p. 296; see also Trocmé, Livre des Actes, p. 186.

[74]Confer pp. 21-22, nn. 76-77 above for bibliographical references to this subject. See also the recent treatment of Doublas R. A. Hare [The Theme of Jewish Persecution of Christians in the Gospel according to St. Matthew (Cambridge: University Press, 1967), pp. 20-30] on the variety of judicial problems involved in a study of Stephen's death. Hare opts for death by lynching not by reason of the author's poor judicial knowledge but because he believes that blasphemy could not be a cause for capital punishment.

Hellenistic orator," whereby the "orator's gesture . . . would [also] be superfluous in a synagogue." But, in a footnote he betrays the uneasiness caused by knowledge of contemporary documents, when he states: "However, Philo, De spec. leg. . . . describes the synagogue service rather as Luke does here: some sit quietly and listen. . . ."[75] In spite of the obvious contradiction involved in the scholar's statements, his example clearly shows that what is really at stake in the analysis of the Stephen story and its judicial verisimiltude is both our knowledge of first century jurisprudence and the proper utilization of our sources. Citing the Mishnah as the ultimate norm of execution by stoning in NT times is unacceptable for scientific reasons.

Turning to the second point, in the words of Trocmé:

> Il était donc strictement impossible de le placer au milieu d'une scène d'émeute comme celle où Étienne avait péri. Le cadre le plus indiqué était un tribunal, devant lequel l'accusé pourrait présenter sa défense à loisir.[76]

In response to this statement one need only refer to Acts 15: 14f. (among several examples), where, rushing into the crowd that wished to worship them, Paul (and Barnabas) has the leisure to give a well-structured, if short, discourse (vv.15-18). The author of Acts, as stage manager, does not need such elaborate procedures to present speeches.[77]

As to the mob and trial elements within the Stephen narrative, clearly both factors are represented in the course of the episode. Their concommitant appearance does not, however, surprise the careful reader of Acts. Indeed, in 16:19f. and 19: 24f. individuals incite the crowds, who in turn drag Paul (and others) before a magistrate where they voice their accusations. Furthermore, the mixture to some degree of mob rule and law-and-order is commonplace in Acts (see 17:5f., 18:12f., 21:18f.). In some cases Jewish officials form part of an unruly crowd

---

[75]Acts, p. 408.

[76]Livre des Actes, p. 186.

[77]Dibelius, "Style Criticism," p. 7: "The raging crowd is silent as soon as Paul wants to speak, but renews its shouting immediately[;] the writer's stagemanaging can use it to emphasize the conclusion (21.40; 22.22)."

(4:1f., 5:17f., 6:12f.).

From this analysis I conclude that the judicial and mob factors, far from artifically combined elements of the Stephen story and, therefore, a basis for unwarranted textual dissection, constitute significant structural features of the author's work. In this regard I would cite a final example to illustrate the obvious mixture of mob and trial elements by the author. In Acts 22:30 the χιλίαρχος formally assembles the chief priests and the entire Sanhedrin. Nevertheless, fully within this trial setting the author has recourse to undeniable mob terminology: as the result of the great στάσεως between the Sadducees and Pharisees (23:10), it is necessary to send in the troops to take Paul by force--ἐκέλευσεν τὸ στράτευμα καταβὰν ἁρπάσαι αὐτόν--lest he be torn to pieces, διασπάω. Clearly one is dealing with literary technique rather than awkward compilation or editing of sources.

2) Trial and Death of Jesus and Its Influence Upon the Stephen Story

Some relationship between Jesus and Stephen has been quite commonly accepted among scholars. At this point I would like to deal at length with this question in terms of redaction. The following eight points of comparison have been noted: 1) meeting of Sanhedrin, 2) deposition by false witnesses, 3) accusation/temple saying, 4) interrogation by high priest, 5) answer/speech, 6) Son of Man saying, 7) violent reaction of hearers, and 8) final words of the dying man.[78] To do justice to this subject it seems best: a) to consider nos. 1, 4, 5, and 7 above in a more general way, and b) to direct our attention to a few alleged and more general contacts between the Synoptic tradition and the Stephen story. Next will be examined in detail: c) the accusations (nos. 2 and 3 above); d) the transfiguration/vision (no. 6 above); and 3) the last words of Stephen (no. 8 above).

---

[78]The list is drawn principally from Trocmé, Livre des Actes, pp. 186-87; but see also Foakes Jackson, "Stephen's Speech," pp. 285-86, who notes particularly parts 2, 3, 5, 6, and 8; confer also Charles H. Talbert, Luke and the Gnostics: An Examination of the Lucan Purpose (Nashville: Abingdon Press, 1966), p. 76 (same treatment in Literary Patterns, p. 97).

a) General Considerations

While it is necessary to note all contacts between Jesus and Stephen to illustrate a theory, it can hardly be maintained that all such factors are persuasive or even illuminating. Since these contacts involve two trials, then certain components are *de rigeur*: a court (the Sanhedrin), witnesses, interrogation by the high priest and consequently question(s) and answer(s). The Sanhedrin and its members are no strangers to the reader of Acts, nor is the high priest as interrogator (see the often referred to trial of Acts 5:17f.). Contacts between the trial of Jesus and the various trials of the apostles, Stephen, and Paul are certainly possible. However, for structural reasons the overall format of the Stephen story finds its best analogies in other episodes found in Acts. Therefore, its structure owes more to the writer's creativity than to imitation of Synoptic texts (see below for further comment). Finally, in regard to the seventh point (the violent reaction of the hearers),[79] I repeat that there are two reactions, one to the speech and one to the vision couplet of 7:55-56. These are structurally motivated.[80]

b) General Contacts Between the Synoptic Tradition and the Stephen Story

In the following study, it will not be possible to examine the broad question of the exact and complete relationship between the Stephen story and the use which the author of Acts makes of Synoptic texts and tradition. Such a goal is entirely too ambitious for the purpose of this study. Instead, I will concentrate upon four important areas (beyond parts c, d, and e which are treated below) where contact with the Synoptic gospels and/or tradition seems possible.

The first text which calls for attention is Lk 4:28-29, where a parallel with Acts 7:54, 57-58 has been noted.[81] The passage in Luke is entirely from L and is appended to the

---

[79]The violent reaction of the hearers is more apparent than real. In Luke the interrogation continues, while in Mark and Matthew only the high priest rips his garments and addresses his fellow jurists to ask for a verdict.

[80]See pp. 224-28 above.

[81]Wilson, "Theologian and Historian," pp. 94-95 and 98.

Synoptic version of Jesus' visit to Nazareth. After the logion concerning the prophet in his own country, Luke adds a double story, one concerning Elijah and another about Elisha. In the case of the former, observe the interesting clause, 4:25 . . . ὅτε ἐκλείσθη ὁ οὐρανὸς ἐπὶ ἔτη τρία καὶ μῆνας ἕξ, ὡς ἐγένετο λιμὸς μέγας ἐπὶ πᾶσαν τὴν γῆν, which could have exerted influence upon Acts 7:11 (supra, p. 65, n.84). However, the principal point of contact concerns Lk 4:

28 καὶ ἐπλήσθησαν πάντες θυμοῦ ἐν τῇ συναγωγῇ ἀκούοντες ταῦτα, 29 καὶ ἀναστάντες ἐξέβαλον αὐτὸν ἔξω τῆς πόλεως, καὶ ἤγαγον αὐτὸν ἕως ὀφρύος τοῦ ὄρους ἐφ' οὗ ἡ πόλις ᾠκοδόμητο αὐτῶν, ὥστε κατακρημνίσαι αὐτόν.

Points of comparison between the post-speech narrative and this Lukan passage are striking. I conclude that the passage in Acts probably represents conscious imitation of this L passage. However, the following points suggest less than a total creation of the Stephen narrative on the basis of this particular episode in the life of Jesus. In Acts 7:47, οἰκοδομέω, in contrast to Lk 4:29 is unaugmented. This point is significant, since in all three instances where the augment is required in Lk (4:29, 7:5, and 17:28), it does in fact occur, while in Acts 7:47 the author modifies the augmented form of 1 K 6:2 or 6:14 and writes: Σολομὼν δὲ οἰκοδόμησεν αὐτῷ οἶκον. In addition, the phrase ἐκβάλλω ἔξω occurs no less than ten times in the gospels (Mt 21:39; Mk 12:8; Lk 4:29; 13:28; 20:15; Jn 9:34, 35; 12:31) and Acts (7:58 and 9:40), while the stoning of Paul outside the city (λιθάσαντες τὸν Παῦλον ἔσυρον ἔξω τῆς πόλεως 14:19) most closely resembles Acts 7:58. I conclude, therefore, that the author probably had Lk 4:28-29 in mind when composing this portion of the Stephen narrative, but that his sources and creative ability far exceeded pure imitation.[82]

The second point of contact with the Synoptic tradition concerns the relation of Acts 6:10 to a saying of Jesus[83] which is found in all three Synoptics (Luke presents a double formulation of it).

---

[82]Contrary to Wilson, ibid., pp. 99-100.

[83]Most commentators refer to this parallel, especially Lk 21:15.

Acts 6:10 καὶ οὐκ ἴσχυον ἀντιστῆναι τῇ σοφίᾳ καὶ τῷ πνεύματι ᾧ ἐλάλει.

Mt 10	Mk 13	Lk 21
19...δοθήσεται γὰρ ὑμῖν	11...ἀλλ' ὃ ἐὰν δοθῇ ὑμῖν	15 ἐγὼ γὰρ δώσω ὑμῖν
ἐν ἐκείνῃ τῇ ὥρᾳ	ἐν ἐκείνῃ τῇ ὥρᾳ	
τί λαλήσητε	τοῦτο λαλεῖτε	στόμα καὶ σοφίαν, ᾗ οὐ δυνήσονται ἀντιστῆναι ἢ ἀντειπεῖν ἅπαντες οἱ ἀντικείμενοι ὑμῖν.
20 οὐ γὰρ ὑμεῖς ἐστε οἱ λαλοῦντες,	οὐ γάρ ἐστε ὑμεῖς οἱ λαλοῦντες	12:12 τὸ γὰρ ἅγιον πνεῦμα διδάξει ὑμᾶς
ἀλλὰ τὸ πνεῦμα τοῦ πατρὸς ὑμῶν	ἀλλὰ τὸ πνεῦμα τὸ ἅγιον.	ἐν αὐτῇ τῇ ὥρᾳ
τὸ λαλοῦν ἐν ὑμῖν		ἃ δεῖ εἰπεῖν.

It is particularly the occurrence of the two terms σοφία and ἀνθίστημι in Lk 21:15 and Acts 6:10 which receives the most attention. While it might be tempting to leave the matter at that, there are serious questions raised by such a solution.[84]

If the author of Acts simply employed the Lukan verse as a model, why the drastic changes? Why would an author who is so fond of double expressions not make better use of his model? Furthermore, it should be noted that Acts 6:10 is closer to the Markan and Matthean versions of the saying than to that of Luke. In the latter the logion is so modified as to place the disciples in Jesus' care, while in the former ". . . it is the help of the Holy Spirit that is promised."[85] It would then seem that the author has rejected the Lukan στόμα and has instead reverted to the original πνεῦμα (even Lk 12:12 uses

---

[84]See among others Haenchen, Acts, p. 271; Bihler, Stephanusgeschichte, p. 10; and Wilson, "Theologian and Historian," p. 82.

[85]Alfred Plummer, A Critical and Exegetical Commentary on the Gospel according to St. Luke (New York: Scribner's, 1896),

τό . . . ἅγιον πνεῦμα--but note that the Spirit teaches rather than speaks). The answer to the above objections should be seen in the use made by Acts of the Synoptic tradition (Luke and Mark combined in this case). The redactor no longer understands the στόμα of Lk 21:15--especially as it relates to ἀντειπεῖν--as an "utterance,"[86] but instead as a "mouthpiece" in the Markan sense. Once this transfer has occurred it is readily understood why the second verb ἀντιλέγω is omitted. Acts 6:10, therefore, is the work of the author who, having borrowed a concept and a few terms from Luke 21:15, has revised these in light of the Markan tradition and has recast the entire verse in his own style.[87] Furthermore, I am led to the conclusion that the author uses very old tradition whereby someone "speaks through the Spirit" (τῷ πνεύματι ᾧ ἐλάλει).[88]

A third point of contact concerns Acts 7:52, 58-59, and the Q sayings of Jesus: concerning the killing of the prophets (Mt 23:29f.; Lk 11:47-48), and the persecution and killing of God's envoys (Mt 23:32f.; Lk 11:49f.), and the lament over Jerusalem (Mt 23:37-39; Lk 13:34-35). The author's dependence upon both versions (note especially 7:52 and Mt 23:35), has already been observed.[89]

---

p. 479.

[86]Liddell-Scott-Jones, Lexicon, s.v. "στόμα." Luke has clearly made use of pairs: στόμα - ἀντειπεῖν and σοφίαν - ἀντιστῆναι.

[87]It should be noted that he writes οὐκ ἴσχυον for the Lukan οὐ δυνήσονται and that he retains the doublet which is most characteristic of his style, see 6:3 πλήρεις πνεύματος καὶ σοφίας and 6:5 πλήρη πίστεως καὶ πνεύματος ἁγίου. Finally, a less important, but nevertheless interesting observation needs to be made concerning the verb λαλέω. Luke in 21:15 has eliminated this verb. In place of the Markan τοῦτο λαλεῖτε or the Matthean τί λαλήσητε he posits an expression involving στόμα. And further still, in his doublet of this Logion, 12:11-12, twice he employs εἶπεν and never λαλέω.

[88]The author of Acts is very familiar with Dt 18:15-21 since he borrows generously from it to compose Acts 7:37-40 and 3:22-23. In this context it is interesting to note that Dt 18:18 (the verse has influenced the author's quotation of Dt 18:15), καὶ δώσω τὸ ῥῆμά μου ἐν τῷ στόματι αὐτοῦ, is passed over in both instances. Further, 4QTest, quoting Dt 18:18-19, does not overlook the passage.

[89]Supra, p. 139. See also Barnabas Lindars, New Testament Apologetic: The Doctrinal Significance of Old Testament Quo-

The fourth and final point concerns special contacts which scholars have observed and which the present research has confirmed between the Stephen story on the one hand and certain parts of Luke on the other, namely, the infancy narratives (1-2), the conclusion of the gospel (24), and, I would add, L materials. This was pointed out by Bacon a long time ago (he cites the work of Soltau as supportive of his position)[90] and revived recently by Bihler.[91] The reference above to Lk 4:28-29 (Acts 7:54, 57-58) and 21:15 (Acts 6:10) is sufficient to illustrate the above statement.

From the previous analysis I conclude that while the author is very familiar with Synoptic tradition, he also had older tradition at his disposal for the composition of both narrative and speech. This conclusion will become even clearer after a detailed study of three important sections of the Stephen story said to be greatly indebted to the Synoptic tradition, or more specifically, to the trial and death of Jesus. It seems best in this case first to state overall conclusions and then to present relevant data for the various passages under consideration. In all three instances (the accusations, the vision, and the last two statements of Stephen) indeed old traditions relating to Jesus are used. However, the situation is more complex than usually admitted. In no individual case is there a simple reproduction of Synoptic tradition; instead these, when compared to their alleged models, reveal considerable variations and, when viewed in their context within Acts, are found to have been incorporated by the author into complex structures: a series of accusations, a transfiguration/vision construct, and a solemn death scene. It is clear that the overall structure owes to the author, who has used a variety of traditional material (Synoptic and other) throughout.

---

tations (London: SCM Press, 1961), pp. 20-21, who states: ". . . it is remarkable that v. 52 is closer to the developed Matthean form of the Q passage than to the Lucan."

[90]"Stephen's Speech," pp. 230-36. See also Mundle, "Stephanusrede," p. 135.

[91]Stephanusgeschichte, pp. 84-85.

c) The Accusations

In attempting to elucidate the charges brought against Stephen, scholars have insisted upon their similarity to those leveled against Paul later in Acts.[92] They have also noted the occurrence both in the trial of Jesus and in that of Stephen of the temple logion.[93] Only through a serious examination of these two factors, along with stylistic and structural considerations, can the redaction of the accusations against Stephen be properly understood.

I would begin this study by referring first to the treatment of this passage in chapter three, where in a detailed fashion the overall structure of the accusation complex was presented. Presently, it is necessary to examine the various parts of this construct, vv.11, 13, and 14. There are three sets of charges and three "accusers." These facts have led commentators, since the time of Loisy, to view the indictments leveled against Stephen as being two in number: concerning Moses/Law/customs and God/This place.[94] While few scholars have gone beyond such general considerations in their presentation of Acts 6:8-15, several have examined and commented further upon the process of redaction. Basically, these authors conclude that the author of Acts--in the words of Haenchen--has "followed very bold tactics"[95] in composing the series of accusations by using the Synoptic temple logion as the basis and, further, has added the "customs saying" of v.14b. Bihler, in an analysis which defends the conclusion presented above, adds the following redactional consideration: "In 6:13-14 werden die Vorwürfe gegen Stephanus in zwei verschiedenen For-

---

[92]Cerfaux and Dupont, Actes, p. 73, refer particularly to Acts 15:1, 5; 21:21, 28; 25:8; 28:17. See also the opinion of Wilson, "Theologian and Historian," p. 100; but see further below for a more detailed assessment of Wilson's treatment of the Pauline traditions in the Stephen story.

[93]See Bruce, Acts, p. 157, who notes both parallels.

[94]Loisy, Actes, p. 309; see p. 222 above.

[95]Acts, p. 274. From his analysis one can only conclude that the total composition is the work of the author, especially in view of his statement: "It would be methodologically wrong to try to deduce something of Stephen's real history from the details of 6.13f." (p. 274).

men angeführt, die aber achlich kaum voneinander abweichen,"[96] thereby implying that the series of charges was composed by the author as further explicitation of the temple saying. This last point is rendered even more explicit by Wilson who maintains that vv.11 (a charge of blasphemy transferred from the trial of Jesus to that of Stephen) through 14 are increasingly explicit statements of the allegations leveled against Stephen.[97] In more general terms, it is readily seen that all three scholars referred to above lend considerable freedom of composition and, I might add, of fabrication to the author in constructing the trial narrative.

Analysis of the three accusation verses, as well as an understanding of the author's method of composition, particularly as seen through the study of the speech in chapter two, has led me to be less radical in my conclusions. A careful examination of the style of v.11 has convincingly shown that the verse owes a considerable debt to tradition. Immediately one is confronted by the unusual expressions, ὑπέβαλον ἄνδρας λέγοντας (ὑποβάλλω is a hapax legomenon in the NT)[98] and λαλοῦντος ῥήματα βλάσφημα εἰς. While there are a number of expressions which bear some resemblance to various aspects of the latter,[99] the combination of the elements found in 6:11 is unique, particularly the adjective βλάσφημος followed by εἰς. In considering v.13, however, the situation is entirely dif-

---

[96]Stephanusgeschichte, p. 12, but see Conzelmann, Apostelgeschichte, p. 51.

[97]"Theologian and Historian," pp. 83 and 86.

[98]Its meaning is clear from epigraphic, contextual, and late LXX evidence. From the context there is no doubt that ὑποβάλλω means "suborn." Besides this sense is attested at least in Stephanus Appian's Bella Civilia (2nd century A.D.: see Liddell-Scott-Jones, Lexicon, s.v. "ὑποβάλλω"). It is important also to note that Moulton-Milligan, Vocabulary, s.v. "ὑποβάλλω," give a number of new occurrences of this verb with a closely related meaning in the papyri. Furthermore the linguistic context of ὑποβάλλω in Dn 3:9 (Theod.): διέβαλον . . . [ὑποβαλόντες] εἶπον followed by accusations, is most instructive as background for Acts 6:11.

[99]While λαλέω βλασφημίας is found in Lk 5:21 and Rev 13:15, the nonoccurrence of the noun in Acts and the use of the adjective only in the present verse and 2 P 2:11 (without εἰς) is important evidence for its unique origin.

ferent. The singular use of οὗτος,[100] a striking rhetorical device--a litotes (οὐ παύεται),[101] and the obvious dependence of λαλῶν ῥήματα κατά upon λαλοῦντος ῥήματα βλάσφημα εἰς of v.11 certainly reveal the literary activity of the author. The last mentioned needs comment. The idiom of 6:11 is related to βλασφημέω εἰς (Mark 3:29 and its Lukan parallel 12:10b)[102] as well as to the λέγω λόγον εἰς of Q (Lk 12:10a). Further, the λαλέω ῥήματα κατά of 6:13 accords with the author's marked prefernece for κατά in a variety of idioms to express the concept "against."[103] It also corresponds to the Matthean (12:32b and a) modification of Mark 3:29 to εἴπῃ κατά and of the Q logion to εἴπῃ λόγον κατά. From this one can conclude that v. 13 is constructed--betraying the author's own style--on the model of v.11, which seems to have been drawn from old tradition that is contemporary somehow to both hypothetical sources (the Markan and Q sources).

The analysis of 6:14 leads immediately in accordance with most commentators, to the topic of sources. The occurrence of the expression μάρτυρας ψευδεῖς in v.13 might have suggested some contact with the Synoptic account of the trial of Jesus,

---

[100]The frequency of this term both in vv.13-14 (four times) and in the Stephen speech (see the discussion of this term in relation to 7:35ff., in chapters two and three) can certainly be regarded as a stylistic characteristic of the author.

[101]In effect the construction concerns the expression οὐ παύω followed by a participle. This verb occurs six times in Acts, four of which involve a litotes: 5:42; 6:13; 13:10; and 20:31 (note the same construction in Eph 1:16 and Col 1:9).

[102]These are the only NT occurrences of the idiom.

[103]In no less than eleven passages κατά with the genitive has been used to express opposition, 4:26; 6:13; 14:2; 16:22; 21:28; 24:1; 25:2, 3, and 27, while εἰς followed by the accusative rarely appears in Acts with this meaning, 6:11; 23:30 (ἐπιβουλὴ εἰς τὸν ἄνδρα) and 25:8. The second case concerns the noun ἐπιβουλή which occurs only in Acts [9:24; 20:3, 19; and 23:30. Note that it is followed by εἰς in Joesphus, Ant 2.197; 16.319 (Arndt-Gingrich, Lexicon, s.v. "ἐπιβουλή") but in the Oxyrhynchus papyri (II.237.vi.31--A.D. 186) it is followed by κατ᾽ ἐμοῦ (see Moulton-Milligan, Vocabulary, s.v. "ἐπιβουλή")] and the third involves an idiom which is well attested in the NT--ἁμαρτάνω εἰς: Mt 18:21 (Q); Luke 15:18, 21; 17:4 (Q); Acts 25:8 and 1 Cor 6:18; 8:12 (twice).

but the appearance of several stylistic features in 6:14a make the dependence upon Mark 14:55f., or upon his source, a virtual certainty. It is obvious that the first part of v.14, ἀκηκόαμεν γὰρ αὐτοῦ λέγοντος ὅτι, is to be related to Mk 14:58, ἡμεῖς ἠκούσαμεν αὐτοῦ λέγοντος ὅτι.[104] This is further enhanced by the fact that both texts introduce the temple logion. An added consideration, of course, is the already mentioned false witnesses who present this testimony. There is also a relationship to be noted between Mk 14:58b ὅτι ἐγὼ καταλύσω τὸν ναὸν τοῦτον τὸν χειροποίητον and Acts 6:14b ὅτι Ἰησοῦς ὁ Ναζωραῖος οὗτος καταλύσει τὸν τόπον τοῦτον. The redactional activity of the author of Acts will account in large measure for the differences between the two versions of the temple saying (note the singular use of οὗτος and the substitution of τόπος for ναός, see Acts 7:7). Furthermore, it should be pointed out that the χειροποίητος/ἀχειροποίητος of Mark will have a decided effect upon the speech (see 7:41, 43, 44, 48, and 50).[105]

The final segment of 6:14, καὶ ἀλλάξει τὰ ἔθη ἃ παρέδωκεν ἡμῖν Μωϋσῆς, presents several difficulties variously explained in relation to Jesus' position vis-à-vis the Law as found in the Synoptic tradition,[106] or in terms of the accusations

---

[104]Only Mark 14:58 and Acts 6:14 present the following pattern: ἀκούω + αὐτοῦ λέγοντος ὅτι. While the verb ἀκούω followed by a genitive construction is common in Acts, 10 occurrences, most of which involve λαλέω in absolute or transitive uses, only 6:14; 11:7; and 22:7 concern λέγω and introduce discourse. The last two speak of a "voice" and should be compared to the similar, but accusative construction of 9:4 and 26:14. In light of these facts the similarity between the Markan text and Acts 6:14 is quite noteworthy. Note, however, the important observation of Cadbury, "Four Features," p. 99: "Acts 6:11, 14 ἀκηκόαμεν. This perfect for ἀκούσαμεν does not occur again in Luke-Acts, even at Acts 22:15 where it might be expected."

[105]See pp. 117f. for a discussion of these verses. It should be noted in passing that the usual argument that, since χειροποίητος ". . . does not appear in par. Matt. 26.61; Mark 15.29 par. Matt. 27.40; John 2.19; Acts 6.14; in Mark 14.58 it may be an addition" [Joachim Jeremias, <u>New Testament Theology: The Proclamation of Jesus</u>, trans. John Bowden (New York: Scribner's, 1971), p. 22, n. 4], does not hold true in regard to the Stephen story. The author of Acts was familiar with the two parts of the Markan and, I believe, pre-Markan form of the temple saying (see n. 104 above).

[106]Haenchen, <u>Acts</u>, p. 272.

leveled against Paul later in Acts.[107] Clearly the actions and words of Jesus form the basis of such a logion. However, the variety of Synoptic texts generally alluded to do not explain the terminology used in the accusation text. The second alternative is more attractive since the author of Acts makes ample and varied use of the term ἔθος: "customs of the fathers" (28:17), "ethnic customs" (16:21; 25:16, 26:3)[108] and "law or custom of Moses" (6:14; 15:1; 21:2;). Only Acts, to my knowledge, offers the last designation.[109] Nevertheless, serious questions remain in adopting such a solution. The verb ἀλλάσσω does not appear in the gospels but only here in Acts. While it occurs in six other NT texts, only in Acts 6:14 does it refer to customs. Furthermore, the uniqueness of Moses "handing on" (παραδίδωμι) these customs leads me to regard this passage as an older piece of tradition, taken over by the author of Acts. As an added reason for choosing the last solution, closer scrutiny of the three passages, allegedly establishing the meaning "customs of Moses," casts doubt upon the interpretation. The first, Acts 15.1, speaks of circumcizing τῷ ἔθει τῷ Μωϋσέως. It is clearly the singular that is used, and because of this, one can conclude that the sense of the term in 15:1 is closer to general Greek usage ("customor habit")[110] than to "customs or Torah." The second passage, 21:21, is even more problematic for such an interpretation. Paul is told of charges being circulated against him, namely, that he teaches apostasy from Moses to the Jews of the Diaspora. He does this by advocating two things: noncircumcision and nonobservance of (not walking according to) τοῖς ἔθεσιν.[111] The more obvious meaning of the

---

[107]Wilson, "Theologian and Historian," p. 145.

[108]The last two usages are well attested in extrabiblical literature, see Liddell-Scott-Jones, <u>Lexicon</u>, s.v. "ἔθος" and Moulton-Milligan, <u>Vocabulary</u>, s.v. "ἔθος," and in the LXX: 2 Mc 11:25; 4 Mc 18:5; Philo, <u>Spec. Laws</u> 2.149 and Josephus, <u>Ant.</u> 20.100.

[109]Ἔθος, in most NT texts, apart from Acts, bears the neutral meaning "custom or habit," (Luke included, whose three uses involve the expression: κατὰ τὸ ἔθος).

[110]See Liddell-Scott-Jones, <u>Lexicon</u>, s.v. "ἔθος" and "ἔθω."

[111]These are clearly two separate charges and yet Haenchen, <u>Acts</u>, p. 274, refers to Acts 21:21 in trying to interpret

latter is "ancestoral customs" and not Torah or Pentateuchal legislation. Acts 6:14 remains unexplained except by the logion itself and the use which the writer makes of it in the Stephen story.

While it has not been a usual procedure in this dissertation to pursue a redaction-critical method, that is, the separation of traditional from redactional elements, it was necessary in this case, because the stylistic data provoked skepticism about the results of recent studies. If the above analysis of the accusations is correct, especially in discovering various fragments of tradition taken from different sources and conscientiously used, then one can conclude that the same process of composition is at work here as throughout the speech. The author borrows from his source--very often two or more sources--a variety of elements: quotations, terms, and ideas. He then combines these to suit his purpose, adds to them, often by imitating the style or theme of the text in question, and, finally, imposes upon this totality his own personal style and structural perspective. The threefold character of the indictment construct with its three accusers and its three accusation doublets (v.11 against Moses and God; v.13 against this holy place and the Law; and v.14 this place and customs) owes to the author's literary activity. Further, using a traditional fragment in v.11, he then constructs a parallel (v.13) by imitating the style and structure of the first. This process is most clearly seen in Acts 7:5, where the writer has restructured an OT quotation (Gn 17:8) to correspond in word order to the preceding quotation (Dt 2:5). The mere fact that the author has left his redactional mark--in the case of 7:5--does not rule out the use of a source. This is an important point often overlooked by redaction criticism.

The accusations in their structure are the work of the author of Acts. The nature of the tradition employed is another matter. The analysis has attempted to show that pre-Synoptic and Synoptic material were used; however, the main objective has been to examine stylistically the composition and structure of the accusations. In light of the study of the

---

the "customs" of 6:14 as ". . . dispensing with circumcision."

speech and the knowledge acquired of the process and techniques employed by the writer in composing that text, it is hoped that a more critical and more discerning understanding of Acts 6:11, 13-14 has resulted.

d) The Transfiguration/Vision

This part of the Stephen story has not been neglected in recent scholarship, particularly 7:55-56. The transfiguration of Stephen's face in Acts 6:15 ("like the face of an angel") has been provided with considerable background and contemporary parallels. The concept of facial transformation occurs in the Old and New Testaments and in late Jewish and early Christian literature.[112] The particular expression used in Acts 6:15 requires closer attention, since it is notably different from other biblical formulations of this particular phenomenon. In Ex 34:29-30, the appearance of the skin of Moses' face is said to be glorified (δεδόξασται ἡ ὄψις τοῦ χρώματος τοῦ προσώπου αὐτοῦ), while that of a man of God is described (Jdg 13:6) in the following way: ἡ ὅρασις αὐτοῦ ὡς ὅρασις [=A; εἶδος αὐτοῦ ὡς εἶδος = B] ἀγγέλου θεοῦ. Even the Synoptic texts of the transfiguration uses very different terminology:

Mk 9:2 καὶ μετεμορφώθη

Mt 17:2 καὶ μετεμορφώθη ... καὶ ἔλαμψεν τὸ πρόσωπον αὐτοῦ ὡς ὁ ἥλιος

Lk 9:29 τὸ εἶδος τοῦ προσώπου αὐτοῦ ἕτερον.

Indeed, the formulation of Stephen's transfigured face finds an interesting parallel in the Greek addition to Est (15:13) εἶδόν σε, κύριε, ὡς ἄγγελον θεοῦ, καὶ εταράχθη ἡ καρδία μου ἀπὸ φόβου τῆς δόξης σου. But, perhaps its closest analogue is in the apocryphal work, Paul and Thecla 3: χάριτος πλήρη, ποτὲ μὲν γὰρ εφαίνετο ὡς ἄνθρωπος, ποτὲ δὲ ἀγγέλου πρόσωπον εἶχεν.[113]

---

[112]Among the important references given by commentators the following OT passages should be noted; Ex 34:29-30; Jdg 13:6; Est 15:13; and NT texts: Mk 9:2 and parallels; Acts 9:3 and parallel accounts, and 2 Cor 3:18. For the Jewish references confer Strack and Billerbeck, Kommentar, 2:665-66. Finally, we note Wilson's list ("Theologian and Historian," p. 91) of late writings: Enoch 104; Martydom of Polycarp 12; 4 Mc 6:2, and Eusebius, Ch. Hist. 5.1.35.

[113]The above work is cited in Jacquier, Actes, p. 200 and Beginnings, 4:69.

Finally, in regard to the transfiguration of Stephen, two important scholars, Loisy and Dibelius,[114] emphasize that the speech is intrusive, since it breaks the continuity of the transfiguration/vision scene.

The literature on the vision of Stephen has been particularly abundant. This has been the case because of the unusual occurrence there of the expression "the Son of Man," and the even more striking ἑστῶτα of 7:55 and 56. It is not the goal of this study even briefly to survey the scholarly works devoted to this subject but instead to submit two recent works which present a convenient appraisal of proposed solutions to the problems raised by Acts 7:55-56. Charles K. Barrett in his 1964 article lists four types of explanations for the unusual character of our text. 1) Ἑστῶτα refers to situation rather than to posture. 2) Jesus, like the angels, stands before God's throne. 3) He stands to welcome Stephen the martyr. 4) Jesus executes his messianic office as witness or as guarantor of the parousia. And lastly, Barrett proposes his own: 5) Jesus welcomes the martyr in an individual parousia.[115] More recently in a short monograph devoted to the vision of Stephen, Rudolf Pesch proposes that Jesus/the Son of Man stands as judge.[116] Neither of the two last-mentioned theories is very convincing, since both overlook the unique character of Ste-

---

[114]For the former see Haenchen, Acts, p. 272, n. 3 and for latter confer "Speeches in Acts," p. 168.

[115]"Stephen and the Son of Man," in Apophoreta: Festschrift für Ernst Haenchen: Zu seinem siebzeten Geburtstag am 10. Dezember 1964, Beiheft zur Zeitschrift fur die neutestamentliche Wissenschaft und die Kunde der älteren Kirche, no. 30 (Berlin: Töpelmann, 1964), pp. 32-34 and 36-37. See, however, Heinz E. Tödt, The Son of Man in the Synoptic Tradition, The New Testament Library, trans. D. M. Barton (London: SCM Press, 1965), who, in "Excursus II: Discussion of the concept of the heavenly Son of Man in Acts 7.56," insists upon the peculiar nature of Acts 7:56 and concludes: "In view of this difference from the synoptic Son of Man sayings we no longer see any possibility of assuming that in Acts 7.56 the parousia theme is already present . . ." p. 305. Confer also the convenient introduction to the history of the problem in Angus J. B. Higgins, Jesus and the Son of Man (Philadelphia: Fortress Press, 1964), pp. 13-25.

[116]Die Vision des Stephanus: Apg 7.55-56 im Rahmen der Apostelgeschichte, Stuttgarter Bibelstudien, no. 12 (Stuttgart: Katholisches Bibelwerk, [1966]), pp. 54-58.

phen's vision.[117]

In beginning an analysis of vv.55-56, the first option mentioned by Barrett deserves more serious consideration, namely that ἵστημι in the present context does not mean "stand." He indicates this possibility but summarily rejects it. His primary objections are:

> If this view is accepted little scope is left for further discussion of the question; yet, even if "standing" could mean "seated," the reader of Acts 7.56 can hardly fail to ask why the explicit καθήμενος of Matt. 26.64; Mark 14.62; Luke 22.69, and of other passages which reflect Ps. 110.1, should here be replaced by ἑστῶς. What point could there be in making the change, unless the author intended to represent the Son of man as standing upright? The versions appear to have understood the Greek in this way.

In a footnote he continues: "Cf. the latin stantem, Syriac qā'ēm. These are not unambiguous, but on the whole suggest an erect posture."[118] Contrary to Barrett's position, I believe this is the correct explanation and intend to pursue the problems involved. First, an examination of the philological backbround of this option is necessary, after which will follow an analysis of 7:55-56 from a redactional point of view, since it is on the basis of these two considerations that this particular solution has been chosen.[119]

In their classification of the various occurrences of ἵστημι, Arndt-Gingrich list 7:55-56, among a considerable number of cases, where "very oft. the emphasis is less on 'standing' than on being, existing."[120] In Acts such a choice is clearly indicated in a variety of passages, among others: 7:33, 55, 56; 9:7; 24:21. The evolution of the term is understandable in light of secular usage where it also means "set

---

[117]See the objections of Tödt, Son of Man, concerning the parousia (n. 115 above) and the standing Son of Man (p. 304); also Norman Perrin, Rediscovering the Teaching of Jesus (New York: Harper and Row, 1967), p. 180.

[118]"Stephen and Son of Man," pp. 32-33.

[119]This position is also defended by Gustaf Dalman, The Words of Jesus trans. D. M. Kay (Edinburgh: Clarke, 1902), p. 311; Charles H. Dodd, According to the Scriptures (London: Nisbet, 1952), p. 35, n. 1; Bruce, Acts, p. 178; Jeremias, NT Theology, p. 273; Lindars, Apologetic, p. 48, n. 2.

[120]Lexicon, s.v. "ἵστημι."

up," "establish," "agree upon," etc.[121] Also to be considered in the examination of the philological data is evidence obtained from the versions. Barrett, in the text quoted above, appeals to these to bolster his position, in spite of the ambiguity of the data. Syriac (ܩܐܡ), Latin (stantem), and Coptic (Bohairic, Sahidic and G67: ⲈϤⲞϨⲒ/Ⲏ) all permit a variety of translations, such as "set," "be," "remain," as well as "stand." Contrary to Barrett, this evidence need not ". . . on the whole suggest an erect posture."

This part of the discussion will be concluded by recalling Barrett's question: Why the change from καθήμενος of Ps 110:1 to ἑστῶς? I concur with Tödt who states:

> The term "standing," however, could be taken over from Dan. 7.13 LXX. Neither in the Aramaic form of this passage nor in the translations of the LXX and of Theodotion is a <u>sitting</u> of the Man mentioned. . . .[122]

His formulation of the problem shows clearly that he does not entertain the possibility that ἑστῶς refers to position rather than posture. The influence of Daniel (ἐθεώρουν . . . ἰδού . . . τοῦ οὐρανοῦ, ὡς υἱὸς ἀνθρώπου ἤρχετο [=LXX; ἐρχόμενος = Theod.]) upon 7:56, therefore, is to be viewed not through the eyes of Mk 14:62 and Mt 26:64, where Ps 110:1 and Dn 7:13 are also combined, but as an independent formulation of early tradition.[123]

Statements by recent scholars defending an independent Son of Man saying in Acts 7:56[124] have led me to consider vv.55 and

---

[121] Liddell-Scott-Jones, <u>Lexicon</u>, s.v. "ἱστάω" and "ἵστημι" (also pointed out by Barrett, "Stephen and the Son of Man," p. 32, n. 4) and Moulton-Milligan, <u>Vocabulary</u>, s.v. "ἵστημι."

[122] <u>Son of Man</u>, p. 301.

[123] See Perrin, <u>Rediscovering</u>, p. 179, for a similar conclusion: ". . . this means that the combination of Ps. 110.1 and Dan. 7.13 found in Mark 14.62 and the same combination found in the pre-Lukan formulation of Acts 7.56 cannot be dependent upon one another, since the one, Mark with the circumlocution, reflects a Jewish way of thinking, and the other, Acts with the direct mention of God, reflects a non-Jewish way of thinking." Perhaps the addition of θεός in 7:56 should also be attributed to the author of Acts.

[124] Perrin, <u>ibid</u>., pp. 179-80; Jeremias, <u>NT Theology</u>, p. 273, n. 5 (who also refers to E. Bammel); and Tödt, <u>Son of Man</u>, p. 305.

56 more closely. The double use of οὐρανός in vv.55 and 56, first in the singular, then in the plural, has often been pointed out in scholarly discussion. The occurrence of οὐρανός in the plural one other time in Acts (2:34), contrary to Pesch's view,[125] confirms the view that the author prefers the Hellenistic form and has retained the plural here, since he is using an old tradition. The unusual occurrence in Acts 7:56 of the term Son of Man also points in the same direction.

To these standard arguments must be added structural considerations. The procedure by which the author in v.55 identifies the one at the Right (Hand) of God as Jesus and in v.56 as the Son of Man resembles the structure of vv.59 and 60, where the name of Jesus is inserted in v.59 to further qualify κύριε (see below). An equally significant structural argument is based on word order.[126] To understand this feature it is necessary to recall the Synoptic Son of Man texts:

Mt 26:64	Mk 14:62	Lk 22:69
...τὸν υἱὸν τοῦ	...τὸν υἱον τοῦ	...ὁ υἱὸς τοῦ
ἀνθρώπου	ἀνθρώπου	ἀνθρώπου
καθήμενον	ἐκ δεξιῶν	καθήμενος
ἐκ δεξιῶν	καθήμενον	ἐκ δεξιῶν
τῆς δυνάμεως	τῆς δυνάμεως	τῆς δυνάμεως τοῦ
		θεοῦ.

Obviously the word order of Acts 7:56 corresponds to that of Mark and that of v.55 to that of Matthew and Luke (see below for the Greek text of Acts 7:55-56). From this I conclude that v.56 is an old piece of tradition whose formulation betrays closer links with the tradition underlying Mk 14:62. A similar redactional phenomenon has already been encountered above in the analysis of Acts 6:11 and 13, where an older piece of tradition (v.11) had been rewritten to formulate a new accusation (v.13). An examination of v.55 reveals the opposite. At every turn the author's redactional activity is evident. The singu-

---

[125]<u>Die Vision</u>, p. 52.

[126]Only Pesch, <u>ibid</u>., p. 53, to my knowledge, has considered this problem. His attempt, however, to explain the difference in word order between vv.55 and 56 by having recourse to an alleged rhythmic schema for these verses is not very convincing.

lar of οὐρανός (note the contrast with v.56), the insertion of the name "Jesus," the word order (compare with that of Mark and Acts 7:56), the occurrence of the phrase ἀτενίσας εἰς ... εἶδεν (identical to that of 6:15; note also the plural/singular contrast), and the reintroduction of the theme of glory, δόξαν θεοῦ (see 7:2 "the God of glory") betray the author of Acts at work. Finally, the intentional use of θεός, as well as its double occurrence in v.55, recalls and further supports the textual conclusion drawn above (supra, 131-32) in the analysis of 7:46: ". . . who found favor before God and asked to found a tabernacle for the God [not house] of Jacob."

The transfiguration/vision of Stephen, then, is a structural unit composed by the author of Acts, who uses elements of old tradition, the idiom of contemporary martyrologies, and the thinking of his time concerning Jesus. The overall pattern of the unit is clearly related to others found throughout the Stephen story, i.e., an extended parallelismus membrorum:[127]

6:15 καὶ ἀτενίσαντες εἰς αὐτὸν πάντες οἱ καθεζόμενοι ἐν τῷ
συνεδρίῳ εἶδον τὸ πρόσωπον αὐτοῦ ὡσεὶ πρόσωπον ἀγγέλου.
7:55 ὑπάρχων δὲ πλήρης πνεύματος ἁγίου
ἀτενίσας εἰς τὸν οὐρανὸν
εἶδεν δόξαν θεοῦ
καὶ Ἰησοῦν ἑστῶτα ἐκ δεξιῶν τοῦ θεοῦ,
56 καὶ εἶπεν·
ἰδοὺ θεωρῶ τοὺς οὐρανοὺς διηνοιγμένους
καὶ τὸν υἱὸν τοῦ ἀνθρώπου ἐκ δεξιῶν ἑστῶτα τοῦ θεοῦ.

Vv.55 and 56 constitute an interesting parallel construction, which structure is further extended by its obvious relation with 6:15. The author has inserted the speech within the

---

[127]Failure to analyze the author's method of composition has led Hay, Glory at the Right Hand, p. 74, to the following unsatisfactory conclusions: ". . . the sheer redundancy of 7.56 coming after 7.55 is striking and is most readily explained if one assumes that Luke took over most or all of 7.56 from a source. Acts 7.55 can then be taken as from Luke's own hand, prefaced to 7.56 for explanatory reasons." He continues in n. 96: "Acts 7.55 explains the vision in terms of a special momentary fullness of the Spirit in Stephen, and tells the reader that the son of man (vs 7.56) is Jesus. The phrase about God's glory may be added to present [sic] the tautology of 7.56 from being too tedious; it has no other obvious function." See Acts 7:2 as a parallel for "the Glory of God."

transfiguration/vision episode, thereby indicating that its interpretation is intimately linked with the entire Stephen story.

e) The Last Words of Stephen

This part of the narrative has received little scholarly attention. Most studies simply point out that Stephen's three post-speech utterances correspond to three of Jesus' "last words:" 7:56 = Lk 22:69; 7:59 = Lk 23:46; and 7:60 = Lk 23:34.[128] The first has been dealt with previously. The last two require further attention in relation to the text of Acts which is as follows:

7:59 καὶ ἐλιθοβόλουν τὸν Στέφανον,
ἐπικαλούμενον καὶ λέγοντα·
κύριε Ἰησοῦ, δέξαι τὸ πνεῦμά μου.
60 θεὶς δὲ τὰ γόνατα
ἔκραξεν φωνῇ μεγάλῃ·
κύριε, μὴ στήσῃς αὐτοῖς ταύτην τὴν ἁμαρτίαν.
καὶ τοῦτο εἰπὼν ἐκοιμήθη.

In regard to the utterances of Stephen, the peculiar formulation of both logia (59 δέχομαι + πνεῦμα and 60 ἵστημι + ἁμαρτίαν) is unique since there is no Old or New Testament analogue for either. Also neither of the Lukan texts is linguistically similar to Acts 7:59 or 60.

Lk 23:34 is problematic since manuscript evidence (P^{75} B D* θ pc a sy^{s} sa) seems to be against its authenticity.

> As the deletion of a saying of such importance is hardly conceivable, v.34a must be an addition to the Third Gospel, but one that derives from an ancient tradition which must have been added very early, as Marcion already bears witness to it.[129]

The saying of the Stephen story, then, would be from an independent tradition rather than a reformulation of an alleged Synoptic logion.

The saying of 7:59 also presents problems when examined in

---

[128]See among others Haenchen, Acts, p. 293, n. 9; Talbert, Literary Patterns, p. 97; and M. C. Goulder, Type and History in Acts (London: S.P.C.K., 1964), pp. 42-43.

[129]Jeremias, NT Theology, p. 298. Note also the statements by Lake and Cadbury, Beginnings, 4:85 and Metzger, Commentary, p. 180.

relation to its presumed source. A comparison of the parallel Synoptic texts is required at this point.

Mt 27:50	Mk 15:37	Lk 23:46
ὁ δὲ Ἰησοῦς πάλιν	ὁ δὲ Ἰησοῦς ἀφεὶς	καὶ φωνήσας φωνῇ μεγάλῃ
κράξας φωνῇ μεγάλῃ	φωνὴν μεγάλην	ὁ Ἰησοῦς εἶπεν πάτερ, εἰς χεῖράς σου παρατίθεμαι τὸ πνεῦμά μου τοῦτο δὲ εἰπὼν
ἀφῆκεν τὸ πνεῦμα	ἐξέπνευσεν	ἐξέπνευσεν.

Several observations cause me to hesitate in seeing Acts 7:59 as a reformulation of Lk 23:46. 1) Acts 7:60 (and 57) follows the Matthean formula (κράξας φωνῇ μεγάλῃ) rather than the Lukan one. 2) Instead of the Lukan expression τοῦτο δὲ εἰπών, the author writes καὶ τοῦτο εἰπών (his preference for the καί-style has been noted repeatedly in chapters two and three). 3) Note the observation of Bauernfeind, reported by Haenchen, that Acts 7:59 is possibly "an older version of Luke 23:46."[130] The formulation of v.59, perhaps using LXX phraseology (see Dt 33:11 κύριε . . . τὰ ἔργα τῶν χειρῶν αὐτοῦ δέξαι), seems to indicate an old tradition, while that of Lk 23:46 is an adaptation employing Ps 30:6.

From the above I conclude that the author of Acts has probably borrowed from the Synoptic accounts of Jesus' death, but that he is drawing primarily upon ancient independent tradition for his formulation of Stephen's final words.[131] These he has situated within a structure similar to the one noted above for the transfiguration/vision. Vv.59-60 form an interesting parallelismus membrorum (note the use of Jesus' name in the first member, the double occurrence of κύριος, and the

[130] Acts, p. 293, n. 6.

[131] A further confirmation of this conclusion is the use of ἐκοιμήθη instead of the Synoptic terms (ἐξέπνευσεν of Mark and Luke, ἀφῆκεν τὸ πνεῦμα of Matthew). Κοιμάω is clearly related to early Christian liturgical formulae (see especially 1 Cor 15:6f.) or the LXX (see Acts 13:36 = a conflation of 1 K 2:10 and Jdg 2:10).

positive/negative contrast). At the same time the structure is related to v.55 where the name of Jesus also appears. By means of this technique the author accentuates the function of the vision.

3) Saul Tradition

In the present narrative of the Stephen story, the activity of Saul is closely linked to the conclusion of the episode. This is his first introduction to the reader of Acts, who will once again meet him on the road to Damascus in chapter nine. Before directing our attention to the primary goal of this analysis--the literary, structural, and thematic role played by the Saul tradition in the Stephen story--it is necessary to treat briefly two preliminary topics.

At the beginning of the present chapter it was necessary, in examining theories of redaction, to present the position of Trocmé, who maintains that the references to Saul in the Stephen episode represents the strongest guarantee of the historicity of the account. He further states that these references once formed part of a document on Paul, where they served as an introduction to his conversion. This hypothesis has not found adherents, no doubt, because of its dependence upon source theories--theories whose major weakness is the too great reliance upon the (clumsy!) editing of documents.

Another suggestion which must be considered briefly is that of Wilson, who maintains that the Stephen episode has been fashioned ". . . by turning to characterizations of other important figures . . . ," of whom Jesus and Paul are the principal ones.[132] To substantiate this conclusion he presents after his analysis of the narrative a list of parallels between Stephen and Paul.[133] My criticism of this scholar's position is directed at his methodology. The parallels between the two early Christians do exist. However, it is not clear why the Pauline texts are deemed of primary "historical" value, and much less, why the Stephen material should be judged as modeled upon them. Both are formulations of the author. The argumentation, then, is circular.

---

[132]"Theologian and Historian," p. 100.

[133]Ibid., pp. 98-99.

Of the host of problems (Paul's role in Acts, the Paul of the epistles versus that of Acts, the chronology of his life, the Saul tradition in Acts, etc.[134]), only issues relating to the stylistic data will be treated. To begin the study I would refer to a recent monograph by Karl Löning on this subject, particularly his literary and structural analysis of this part of the narrative.

> Das Kompositionsverfahren ist durch die Technik mehrfacher Verklammerung gekennzeichnet:
>
> 7,57 Steinigung des Stephanus
> 7,58 Erwahnung des Saulus
>
> 7,59f. Sterbegebet des Stephanus
> 8,1 a Notiz über die zustimmende Haltung des Saulus
> 8,1 b Beginn der "grossen" Verfolgung
>
> 8,2 Bestattung und Totenklage um Stephanus
> 8,3 Verfolgertätigkeit des Saulus
> 8,4 Beginn der ausser-judäischen Mission.[135]

The author pursues the matter no further, since his purpose in presenting this schema was to demonstrate the difficult task of separating tradition from redaction. Löning's analysis is very much to the point. The author of Acts has assembled alternating elements of the Saul tradition with those of the Stephen speech. Clearly he has not simply joined isolated fragments from old documents but instead has carefully integrated the various elements of his narrative.

While 8:1 and 3 do not constitute a parallelismus membrorum, a close literary and thematic relationship exists between

---

[134]See particularly the bibliography on the subject, *supra*, p. 11 n. 40 (especially the work of Vielhauer) and p. 12 n. 45. Confer also Martin Dibelius, "Paul in the Acts of the Apostles," in *Studies*, ed. Greeven, pp. 207-14; S. Dockx, "Chronologie de la vie de Saint Paul, depuis sa conversion jusqu'à son séjour à Rome," *NT* 13 (1971): 261-304; Joseph A. Fitzmyer, "A Life of Paul," in *JBC* 2:215-22; Morton S. Enslin, "Once Again, Luke and Paul," *ZNW* 61 (1970): 253-71. See also Scharlemann, *Stephen*, pp. 109-35 (chapter V: "Stephen and Paul"); Wilson, *Gentiles*, pp. 154-70 (chapter 6: "Paul's Conversion") and 196-218 (chapter 8: "Paul's Speech on the Areopagus"); and Jacob Jervell, *Luke and the People of God: A New Look at Luke-Acts* (Minneapolis: Augsburg Publishing House, 1972), pp. 153-83 ("Paul: The Teacher of Israel").

[135]*Die Saulustradition in der Apostelgeschichte*, Neutestamentliche Abhandlungen, ns, no. 9 (Münster: Aschendorff, [1973]), p. 20.

the two (Σαυλος δέ introduces both verses, double occurrence of ἐκκλησία, a general and particular statement about persecution). As in the case of the parallelismus membrorum, the entire structure is related to a third element within the composition, v.58b, where Saul is also mentioned. In this part of the narrative the author's usual method of redaction is obvious. In relation to the above considerations, note also the previous discussion of this matter (supra, p. 229).

Löning concludes that the joining of the Saul tradition ". . . mit der Uberleitung von der Stephanus--zu den Philippustraditionen (Apg 7,58; 8,la.3) ist redaktionell."[136] However, why is such a conclusion necessary when in Acts 22:19-20 Paul himself is allowed to make the same connection? It is interesting to note, in this regard, that the order of events is reversed. In Acts 7:58f., Paul witnesses and consents to Stephen's death and later persecutes the Christian community, while in 22:19f. he first persecutes then is involved in the killing of Stephen. The order of the first is dictated by the needs of the narrative, since the threefold elements have been linked, from a literary point of view, to the continuous Stephen narrative.

Löning further concludes that since 7:58 and 8:1 are clearly redactional in construction, and since the Wortmaterial of 8:3 recalls later Saul tradition, the latter is from tradition and the former due to the author.[137] Once again I would assail the scholar's methodology. It is agreed that 7:58 and 8:1 betray the author's redactional activity; however, the occurrence in these verses and also in Acts 22:20 of such terms as συνευδοκέω, ἱμάτιον, and ἀναιρέω, when treating the same subject, makes me suspect that the labeling of one passage as redactional and the other as not is at least arbitrary. Furthermore, 8:3 is hardly a good candidate to assign fully to tradition because of the following correlations: Σαῦλος δέ = 8:1; ἐκκλησία = 8:1; εἰσπορεύομαι--four occurrences in Acts; σύρω--three times; "men and women" = 5:14; 8:3, 12; 9:2; 22:4 (see also 17:12); and παραδίδομι εἰς φυλακήν = 8:3; 12:4; and 22:4. Instead it seems more logical to conclude that both the

---

[136]Ibid., p. 25.

[137]Ibid., p. 25.

Stephen story and the Pauline narrative, particularly 21:27-22:23, bear signs of the author's redactive activity.[138]

3. General Conclusions

In this final section on redaction there are two areas to be discussed, namely, a negative and a positive evaluation of methodology and results. First, the study has led me to seriously call into question several approaches to the study of the Stephen story. Secondly, I will summarize the results of my own analysis.

A very general, as well as common, methodological approach to the study of Acts is related to the principle of consistency, whereby one section of the book is employed as a criterion to evaluate another part. As long as such a procedure is used to test an author's thought patterns, style or other internal factors, it is a viable method; however, it becomes a circular approach when particular passages of a work become the basis for the rejection of others. Trocmé, for example, leans heavily upon the passages relating the conversion of Paul, and postulates an old history of Paul which the author of Acts would have dismembered and incorporated into a rudimentary Stephen story.[139] Authenticity, then, is determined by the text which the author chooses as his gauge. Wilson concludes that due to the similarities between the traditions regarding Paul and Stephen, the author of Acts has employed the narratives concerning the former to compose that of the latter.[140] Once again, this is an arbitrary choice, since the Pauline narratives may be as dependent upon the author's creativity as is that of Stephen, as I believe they are. The final example to be noted is a recent study by Udo Borse, who employs this method very systematically. Citing the mention of Philip as one of the Seven in Acts 21:8, and of the death of Stephen in Paul's speech, 22:20 (among other factors and examples), Borse concludes that the author later expanded his earlier narratives, the former relating to 6:1-7 (the election of the

---

138See the similar conclusion of Morgenthaler, Geschichtsschreibung, 1:175-76.

139Supra, pp. 246-48.

140Supra, p. 301. See also the discussion of Loning, supra, pp. 302-3.

Seven)[141] and 8:5-40 (the Philip story),[142] and the latter involving the speech[143] and narrative (the latter being further supplemented by Synoptic parallels).[144]

The principal criticism directed against this method is the arbitrariness of the choices. One passage is judged reliable and another is pitted against it. If there is similarity of style or structure, the latter is dismissed as an imitation or if there is disagreement, the latter is again rejected as being due to a misconception on the part of the author.[145] Analysis has shown that throughout the Stephen story the structural models are the work of the author of Acts. Therefore, when there is similarity of structure and of style between various parts of the book, it is not a sign of fabrication, imitation or unreliability, but simply an indication of the author's literary activity. This is to be seen not in an anachronistic way, that is, creation from nothing, but in the sense of literary formulation and composition.[146]

A second method of criticism often encountered which the data of this study have consistently questioned, is an approach best termed reductionism. By means of a Redaktionsgeschichte procedure scholars have attempted to separate redaction from tradition. This often results in a distillation by which a scholar takes note almost exclusively of vocabulary or themes as they relate to their concept of the author's style or theo-

---

[141]"Rahmentext," p. 189; supra, p. 18 and n. 65 (including Benoit's theory).

[142]Ibid., pp. 190-91.

[143]Ibid., pp. 193-94.

[144]Ibid., pp. 202-3.

[145]Supra, p. 248, n. 12.

[146]It is perhaps unfortunate that for the study of Acts scholars should seek structural and redactional models in the gospels rather than within historiographic works. It is evident that the Synoptics rely heavily upon the preservation of received tradition whereby extensive editing of sources is a major factor. However, Acts like other writings of ancient history concentrates upon the presentation of materials and less on the reproduction of documents. See Cadbury, "Writing History," pp. 8-15 and Dibelius, "Speeches in Acts," pp. 145-50, to a certain extent. Note also Walsh, Historical Aims and Methods, especially chapter two: "The Tradition of Ancient Historiography," pp. 20-45.

logy. The approaches of both Duterme[147] and Wilson[148] are primarily of a lexical nature, whereby particular attention is given to hapax legomena, common words or stylistic features. Lienhard has applied the same method to Acts 1:1-6,[149] while Löning has combined the first procedure mentioned above with this particular approach in his study of Acts 7:58, 8:1, 3.[150] Finally, the work of Bihler follows a similar line, concentrating upon theology rather than lexical or literary factors. His stated goal is to show that the thought patterns and purpose of the Stephen story are compatible with the overall schema of Luke-Acts.[151] The procedure, however, is basically the same as the one described above as lexical. Similarity and dissimilarity become the principal criteria in judging authorship.

It has become clear, particularly in the analysis of the speech, that the author of the Stephen story (in my opinion a similar study would indicate similar results for the entire work) borrows profusely from his source. At the same time, it has been also observed that he restructures his data consistently. He is faithful to his source(s), even in minute details; the structures, however, are his own. On the basis of these facts, I object to a method which on principle labels as redactional, and probably unreliable, expressions and verses which reveal the author's literary activity (vocabulary, theology, style).[152]

Finally, reference should be made to a method described in the introductory chapter (pp. 5-6), a method best described as skepticism. Scholars begin with the presupposition that the author had little or no information to employ, therefore he

---

147"Vocabulaire," pp. 8-27.

148"Theologian and Historian," pp. 80-99 and 165-90; see above, p. 253.

149"Acts 6:1-6," pp. 230-36; see pp. 268-69 above.

150*Saulustradition*, pp. 18-25; *supra*, pp. 302-4.

151*Stephanusgeschichte*, pp. 9-19 and 35-86.

152See J. Julius Scott, "Stephen's Speech: A Possible Method for Luke's Historical Method?" *JETS* 17 (1974): 91-97, who objects to the extremes of redaction criticism (especially p. 97). For similar reservations by Bultmann and Barrett, see chapter one, pp. 6-7.

created or greatly expanded most of his material.[153] S. G. Wilson lists the following as representative of the approach just described: "E. Haenchen, H. Conzelmann, M. Dibelius, J. C. O'Neill, U. Wilckens and Ph. Vielhauer. . ."[154]

The basic objection to the analyses of the scholars just mentioned is their anachronistic view of ancient history. They lend entirely too much freedom to the writer. However, the most discomforting aspect of this particular approach is its presumption that the critic knows more than the author of Acts and, in effect, can call him to task, can go beyond the data given in the biblical text, and finally can reconstruct the original event. While it would be possible to examine further some of these conclusions and reconstructions (pp. 244-54), it suffices to note the extreme diversity among these to realize the degree of subjectivity involved.

The analysis presented in this study has, I believe, provided the basis for a more judicious evaluation of the author's method of composition. The data assembled will have a bearing upon the author's reputation and quality as a "historian." The analysis of the Stephen speech has been the key to my approach. Since for this particular part of the Stephen story we possess the author's sources (amply demonstrated in chapter two), a unique opportunity was afforded to examine in detail the process which occurred during the composition of Acts 7. After a scrutiny of the extensive stylistic data provided by a study of the author's quoting techniques, it was possible to proceed to a similar analysis of the introductory and concluding narratives.

During the course of the present chapter attention was directed more immediately to the question of composition. All the sections of the Stephen story (6:1-7; 6:8-7:2a; 7:2b-53; 7:54-8:4) bear the unmistakable stylistic and structural characteristics of the same author. The constructions, patterns, architectural features, and techniques of these passages lead to the conclusion that the author of Acts composed the entire episode with considerable literary freedom. The framework of

---

153Confer especially Haenchen, "Source-Material," pp. 258-59 and Loisy, <u>Actes</u>, pp. 294f., 305f., and 347f.

154<u>Gentiles</u>, p. 256.

the episodes was clearly delineated on the basis of analogous constructions in other parts of Acts or in relation to OT parallels. The resulting structures invariably were the result of the author's creative process. Clearly the entire Stephen episode is the composition of the writer and not the compilation of a clumsy but well-meaning redactor.

Analysis of the speech has also underscored a remarkable tendency of the writer, namely, his great fidelity to and accuracy in the use of his OT model. In the words of Scott: "Even if one had never seen the OT records he could get some idea, and a reliable idea at that, of the history of Israel from Abraham to Solomon by reading Stephen's speech."[155] The writer follows the biblical narrative rigorously, employs its language with deference, and explores its themes and annals with the precision of the interpreter. It would be fair to say that even Josephus, in his most faithful reproductions of Jewish history, is not as true to the OT narrative as is the author of the Stephen speech.[156]

This attitude led me to investigate the narratives with greater care and to question the assumption of redaction-criticism that signs of an author's redactional activity point to his theological rather than literary achievement. Like classical and Jewish historians, the author of Acts composed a history of Israel (the speech) and the Jerusalem community (the Stephen episode), not by mechanically reproducing archival documents, but by assimilating available traditions (Acts 1:1f.) and restructuring these components into a unified, teleological document (Acts 1:8).

At every turn evidence of old tradition incorporated into familiar structural patterns was forthcoming. I was led repeatedly to the conclusion that within the literary framework of this ancient historical document were trustworthy (μάλιστα) annals of that period. Also I was led seriously to apply the judgment of Thucydides, regarding the trustworthiness of his own <u>Histories</u>, to the quality of the Stephen episode: ἐν δὲ

---

[155]"Stephen's Speech," p. 94.

[156]See Cadbury, "Writing History," pp. 24-29; also Michael Grant, <u>The Ancient Historians</u> (New York: Scribner's, 1970), especially chapter 15: "Josephus," pp. 243-68.

τῶν εἰρημένων τεκμηρίων, ὅμως τοιαῦτα ἄν τις νομίζων μάλιστα ἃ διῆλθον, οὐχ ἁμαρτάνοι (1.21).

It would be possible to pursue the argument indicated above and to analyze the speech of Stephen in light of Thucydidean observations (1.22). However, two considerations dictate otherwise. On the one hand, the literary traditions concerning historiography are well known for the period following the great Athenian historian, especially through Polybius and the Greek and Roman writers of the Roman period. Speeches, character-sketches, prologues, battle-scenes, the role of rhetoric, etc., are well-defined elements of classical historical writing.[157] The Stephen story is fully within that tradition. On the other hand, one should not exaggerate the comparison between Thucydides and the author of Acts nor (through excessive and misguided zeal) to misrepresent the character of the latter's literary work. Instead of comparing the Stephen story, as well as Acts itself, to the great histories whether of Polybius, Livy, Tacitus or Josephus or even to contrast the methodology of Lucian of Samosata to that of Acts,[158] it seems that by far the best analogue for the latter is to be found in the classical historical monograph. For that purpose Sallust's monograph _Bellum Jugurthinum_, whose form, content, and purpose shed considerable light upon Acts (see also his _Bellum Catilinae_) should be particularly noted. Though Jugurtha claims center stage in the work, scholars are hard pressed to properly situate the significant roles of Marius, Metellus, Scaurus, and others (note the problem in Acts concerning the roles of Peter, Paul, James, and others). Furthermore, it is readily admitted that the biographical goal of the work is in fact secondary to that of _avaritia_ . . . _pecunia_ (13.5), _novi atque nobiles_ (8.1), _superbia nobilitatis_ (5.1) and a long series of themes[159] (the

---

[157]For a convenient anthology of Greek texts (in translation) dealing with the art of writing history, see Arnold J. Toynbee, _Greek Historical Thought from Homer to the Age of Heraclius_ (Boston: Beacon Press, 1950), containing prefaces, texts on the philosophy of history, literary techniques, and epilogues.

[158]Cadbury, "Writing History," pp. 8 and 12, see also Barrett, _Luke the Historian_, pp. 9-11.

[159]See Ronald Syme, _Sallust_, Sather Classical Lectures, no. 33 (Los Angeles: University of California Press, 1964), pp.

list of recently proposed themes for Acts is also long).[160] The merits of such a comparison, I believe, lie in the assistance it provides in understanding the biographical/historical and thematic/geographical[161] nature of Acts. All these factors play an important role in the historical monograph. In terminating the present comparison of the author of Acts with Sallust, it should be noted that to classical scholars, the author of the Bellum Jugurthinum is not only a historian but a very reliable one.[162]

In summary then, analysis of the Stephen story has shown first that the discourse is the work of the author and is in the usual style of Jewish historical writing. The material is drawn from the OT and, in the manner of other histories of

---

138f.; 157f.; 176-77 and J. R. Hawthorn, Rome and Jugurtha (London: Macmillan and Co./St Martin's Press, 1969), pp. xxxv-liii.

[160]The following list is adapted from Wilson, Gentiles, p. 266: a defense of Paul (Plooij, Harnack), a degrading of Paul (Klein), a defense of Christianity as a religio licita (Haenchen, Easton), a response to the delay of the parousia (Conzelmann, Grässer), an anti-Gnostic tract (Klein, Talbert), a proclamation of the Spirit's power (Ehrhardt, Luck). Wilson then proceeds to state his own view: "The most convenient is to say that Luke's purpose was a combination of historical and practical elements. He wanted to write history, but history that had a message for his contemporaries."

[161]A major theme of the Bellum Jugurthinum is the constant interplay between Africa and Rome, between the home of the noble, but corruptible savage (6.1f.) and the corrupt, but redeemable Eternal City (114.4). The geographical interest of the author of Acts is well known and the structural significance of the theme much discussed.

[162]A final but interesting parallel between the Bellum Jugurthinum should be pointed out. Syme, Sallust, p. 176, states regarding the conclusion of the work: "Sallust takes leave of Marius at the point and season when Rome looked to him for salvation (114.4). The monograph ends abruptly. There was melancholy and irony if the reader gave a thought to how the great general was to fare in later years: victory over the northern invaders, but eclipse thereafter, rancorous ambition and the seventh consulship achieved in war and murder. Marius had saved the Republic, only to subvert it by all manner of craft and violence." The conclusion of Acts with Paul, the real hero of the book, in jail, free to preach, but facing martyrdom, is a striking parallel. Both authors knew the sequels of their histories but chose an ending appropriate to their goals.

Israel, is composed for a specific goal. The narrative is so structured as to fit into the plan of Acts (as a Jerusalem episode with an introduction 6:1-7), to serve as a fitting context for the long discourse, and to prepare for the persecution and dispersion out of Jerusalem. Careful analysis shows that the author uses his data with thematic perception, with biographical interest, and, if the conclusions concerning the discourse are correct and the analysis of the narratives reliable, with historical trustworthiness.

C. Interpretation

This part of the study will draw tentative conclusions based upon the examination of the entire Stephen material. In light of the structural and stylistic analysis presented, the purpose of the author in composing this section of his work will be investigated. The functional nature of the Stephen story will be dealt with first to examine the use which the author makes of this incident and its various components. Secondly, an attempt will be made to synthesize the thematic data in light of the stylistic and structural study.

1. Structural Function

The Stephen story is hardly an isolated incident within the book of Acts. Too often the dissection of its several parts and the discussion of its underlying problems has tended to obscure that fact. It is to this particular aspect that I now turn.

a. Election of the Seven

At the end of chapter three, through analysis of the stylistic data, it was concluded that the interconnections between Acts 6:1-7 and the rest of the Stephen episode were less numerous and central to the story proper than those interrelating the other parts of Acts 6:1-8:4. These facts call for more consideration.

The election of the Seven, from a structural point of view, serves several purposes. First of all the incident, while it introduces a new era within the early Church, also continues the Jerusalem period of the community. In effect, Acts 6:1-7 is strictly a Jerusalem episode. Its attention is centered upon the Holy City and the concerns of the assembly.

It presents a new problem faced by the brethren--not the first as the Ananias/Sapphira episode testifies--and resolves the difficulty before introducing a new event. 6:1, "in those days," refers back to the early days and conveys a sense of continuity. The author terminates the episode with a summary verse (7), in effect positing another connecting link with Acts 1-5.

Secondly, the election of the Seven forms a self-contained unit (discussed at length above, pp. 215-19 and 267-74). This method of procedure is typical of the author of Acts, who consistently presents episodes as relatively independent units.

Thirdly, Acts 6:1-7 functions as an introduction to the Stephen and Philip stories.[163] This, I believe, is the principal architectonic role of the passage. By means of the list, bearing first the name of Stephen, then that of Philip, the author prepares for two subsequent blocks of material, beginning at 6:8 (Στέφανος δὲ πλήρης) and 8:5 (Φίλιππος δὲ κατελθών). The episodes bear remarkable similarities. Both are introduced by general statements, 6:8 and 8:5-8. In the first one reads: "He performed great wonders and signs"; in the second: "the signs which he performed" (v.6). The stories begin in the following way: 6:9 ἀνέστησαν δέ τινες τῶν ἐκ and 8:9 ἀνὴρ δέ τις ὀνόματι. In concluding this inquiry, I would point out the important contrast which the author draws between these incidents. In Acts 6:9-10 the dispute between Stephen and his opponents leads to disastrous consequences (vv.11f.). In the following incident, on the contrary, the preaching of Philip is accepted, resulting in the evangelization of Samaria.

b. Stephen Story

This part of the book of Acts has rightly been described as "the Hellenistic Breakthrough,"[164] since in Acts 6:8f. forces are set in motion which ultimately bring about the evangelization of the Gentiles. It is within this context that the entire passage must be understood. Like the preceding inci-

---

[163]Wilson, Gentiles, p. 130; see also Dibelius, "Speeches in Acts," p. 181; and Bihler, Stephanusgeschichte, pp. 178-83.

[164]John B. Polhill, "The Hellenistic Breakthrough: Acts 6-12," RE 71 (1974): 475. See also Dibelius, "Speeches in Acts," p. 169.

dent, it is a Jerusalem episode and was so intended by the author. The occurrence of "Jerusalem" in 6:7 and 8:1 is clear evidence of that. Furthermore, the Stephen story presents a distinct climax both in the Jews' treatment of the Christians (warnings, floggings, death--Acts 4-7) and the author's accusations against the Jewish authorities (Acts 2-7).[165]

Further observation indicates that the Stephen story differs from earlier incidents, since it directs the reader's attention away from Jerusalem. In chapter eight the first part of the Philip story leads to Samaria and the second involves a eunuch on the road to Gaza. Further, Paul's conversion in chapter nine announces the Gentile mission, while that of Cornelius in the following chapter records the first Gentile conversion. In this regard the Stephen story must be understood as preliminary to the reception of the Gentiles within the Church. Hanson has stated: "The speech does not so much prepare us for the movement of the Church's mission towards the Gentiles as for its movement away from the Jews."[166] The point is well taken; however, I believe it applies primarily to the narrative. By insisting upon the role of Saul and the persecution that followed Stephen's death, the author clearly prepares for the evangelization of the areas outside of Jerusalem, but he has devoted the speech to Judaism entirely. It is the juxtaposition of the two--intended no doubt by the author--which gives an added dimension to the discourse.

The Stephen story reveals interesting parallels with other sections of Acts: the trial scene of 5:17-42[167] and the Pauline episodes of 13:50-14:28.[168] At the same time, the dis-

---

[165]Haenchen, Acts, pp. 273-74; Wilson, Gentiles, pp. 137-38. Special mention should be made here of Morgenthaler's (Geschichtsschreibung, 1:146-47) suggestion that parallels exist between Acts 1-7 and 21-26, particularly the three trials of 4:1-22; 5:17-42; and 6:8-7:60 as compared to those of 21:27-22:23; 22:30-23:12; and 24:1-21.

[166]Acts, p. 102.

[167]Supra, pp. 223, 225-27; 277-78.

[168]Talbert, Literary Patterns, pp. 23-24, in his ". . . list of parallels which involve both context and sequence" for Acts 1-12 and 13:28, refers to 6:8-8:4 ("Stephen is stoned to death at the instigation of Jews from Asia and elsewhere after a speech. The result of the persecution is the spread of the preaching in a widening circle") and 14:19-23 ("Paul is stoned at the instigation of Jews from Antioch and Iconium after a

course (7:2-53) serves a similar function in Acts as do Paul's speeches in 13:16f.[169] and 17:16f.[170] Furthermore, the accusations leveled against Stephen in 6:11-14 find parallels in those brought later against Paul (see below).

The Stephen story, therefore, directs its attention primarily to Judaism: a final clash (before the exodus out of Jerusalem), and a lengthy indictment of official Judaism. After these elements are properly disposed of, the author directs his narrative away from the Holy City, though not away from the authority of the Christian center.

c. The Speech in Relation to the Narrative

Throughout this study stylistic, thematic, and redactional elements which argued for a close relation between the various parts of the narrative and the speech have been noted at length. Before examining the accusations, the principal source of contact between the two, a few general observations are in order.

1) General Considerations

It has often been pointed out that the Stephen speech forms part of an interrogation scene and is, in fact, a response to the high priest's question. The same procedure is used in 5:27. Similar devices are employed to introduce most speeches. In 4:7 the apostles are asked to account for their action: "By what power or in what name do you do this," yet in 13:15 it is at the invitation of the leaders of the synagogue that Paul gives a homily. Structurally, therefore, the author uses the formula best suited to the context. It is also significant that in the series of trials (chapters four, five, six-seven--progressively more serious), the three speeches are given in response to questions by the Jewish authorities. In this regard the Stephen speech, as well as the martyrdom, is

---

speech so that he is supposed dead. The result of the persecution is further preaching in a wider context")--quotation from p. 23. The present study indicates that the similarity between these two parts of Acts is even more striking when one considers the entire section. Apart from the thematic and structural affinity, the lexical fields of the two episodes greatly resemble one another.

[169] *Supra*, pp. 257-58.

[170] Bihler, *Stephanusgeschichte*, p. 185.

the culminating point, in effect the ultimate condemnation of the motives and the actions of the Jewish leaders. Acts 6:8-7:2a serves as a fitting introduction to Stephen's response.

The concluding narrative, as pointed out earlier (pp. 225-27), follows the same format as 5:33f. The vision of Stephen, already insinuated in 6:15, gives greater structural and thematic unity to the entire episode. The reader knows that the speech, as well as the speaker, is out of the ordinary. The former will be the product of wisdom (6:3 and 10) and the latter, already visibly transformed, will not only speak of "the God of glory" but will see "the glory of God." The concluding narrative, then, addresses itself both to the fate of Stephen (culmination of the trial series ending in death) and to the true interpretation of history, personified in Stephen, who, like the great figures of the past, found favor with God.

Structurally the speech and its narrative context bear numerous interrelations (see pp. 233-38). It is clear that the author wishes to draw a parallel between Stephen and various figures of Hebrew history (see below), or between Jesus and these same persons, particularly Moses. In 6:7 the author notes that "a great group of priests were obedient (ὑπήκουον) to the faith," while their ancestors "did not wish to be obedient (ὑπήκοοι)" to Moses (7:39). The positive/negative contrast is all the more striking owing to the rarity of the terms in Acts.[171] Equally significant is the parallel drawn between the Christian movement (increase of the Word and multiplication of disciples, 6:7) and the people in Egypt (7:17).

2) Accusations

The relationship between the accusations and the response made has long been the subject of controversy. In light of the data of this thesis, a reexamination of the question is possible, but from a new perspective. Both from a structural (pp. 219-24) and a redactional (pp. 287-93) point of view, this subject has been examined. Attention will now be focused on the functional relation which the charges have to the speech.

It is important to insist at the outset that the major obstacle in assessing the data in the past has invariably been

[171]The former twice, 6:7 and 12:13, the latter, once.

a quest for historicity. Scholars either presumed that the accusations and the speech were somehow historically related and then attempted desperately to defend such a view, or rejected this connection and sought to discredit one or the other section of the Stephen story.[172] Further, both approaches presumed, in anachronistic fashion, that the speech must present an appropriate defense against the accusations. Since even the casual observer must admit that the charges are not systematically refuted, the defense of the historicity became less fashionable and its refutation less necessary.

It has already been noted that charges similar to those found in Acts 6:11 and 13-14 are also leveled later against Paul and, more important, that the accused, in his subsequent discourse (22:1f.), is no more concerned about his defense than is Stephen about his own. This is particularly important, since it clearly demonstrates that a forensic goal is not central to the author's purpose. In fact an analysis of the narrative context of most speeches in Acts reveals that the writer is more concerned with the theological message than with an exact correlation between the discourse and its narrative setting.[173] It is unsound methodology to assume that the Stephen speech should address itself primarily to the accusations, since the author does not seem to have this as his principal goal, and since modern literary conventions lead one to expect such a procedure.[174]

The above has been stated in an entirely negative fashion, since the point is a crucial one. However, it is important to note that the accusations did play a role in the formulation of the discourse, even if it was not the central one. The data indicate that the speech does in fact address itself to all the accusations. It is clear from the speech that Stephen does not blaspheme either against Moses or God. On the contrary, he

---

[172]See Haenchen's (Acts, pp. 286-88) treatment of scholarship devoted to this problem.

[173]Dibelius, "Speeches in Acts," pp. 164, 174-75, and 182.

[174]It should be noted that the Synoptic trial scenes, before the Sanhedrin and Pilate, are classic examples of nonresponse to accusations. Jesus responds briefly to questions either of the high priest or Pilate, but says nothing when accused (Mk 14:61 and Mt 26:63; see also Jn 19:9f.).

eulogizes the former and discourses upon the latter's role as the Lord of history. Moses/Law/customs occur in all three accusations. In response to this, the speech largely devotes its attention to the role of Moses, 7:17-41. The themes of "place," "law," and "customs" are variously treated throughout the speech. It is significant that νόμος appears twice in the Stephen story, 6:13 and 7:53 (note also λόγια ζῶντα of 7:38) and that the τόπος of 6:13 and 14 should replace in 7:7 the ὄρος of Ex 3:12 (note likewise the occurrence of τόπος in 7:33, 49 and the contrast with οἶκος of 47 and 49). Finally the "customs" of Moses are presented in a positive historical setting: the promise (7:5), circumcision (8), the "living words" (38), sacrifices (42), the tabernacle (44). The author's negative conclusions are not directed against Moses or God, but rather against the people's response to these throughout history.

On the one hand the accusations leveled against Stephen serve several clear functions. Stephen, like other Christians before and after him, is accused because of his alleged heresy (false witnesses of 6:13, see also v.11) and is thereby condemned.[175] In addition, these charges permit the writer to address himself to more general considerations and present him the proper forum for these. On the other hand, the answer to the accusations constitutes only one objective, albeit a minor one, of the author. The history of Israel and the people's response to God's initiative are far more crucial, though not exclusive, to the writer's point of view.

d. Speech

With the foregoing discussion in mind, it is necessary to inquire about the speech's function within Acts. Since it is not a kerygmatic or missionary discourse either in structure or in content, and since it bears no relation to Paul (as do the later speeches), it has generally been neglected in scholarly studies.

In an earlier section of the present chapter, it was pointed out that numerous thematic connections existed between

---

[175] In a similar fashion charges are leveled against James and others before they are put to death by Ananus the high priest: ὡς παρανομησάντων κατηγορίαν ποιησάμενος παρέδωκε λευσθησομένους (Josephus, Ant. 20.200).

Acts 7 and the other speeches. Further observation has convinced me that Stephen's discourse fits well into the author's overall schema of progressive themes, that is, the Stephen speech repeats, develops further, and supplements many of the motifs of the other discourses. The author's technique of amplifying, differentiating, and reconciling themes from one speech to another is clearly evidenced in Acts 7. The role of David, introduced in the first speech (2:25, 29f.), is often discussed in the speeches, not the least being 7:45-46 and 15:16. The notable theme of the "Just One" (3:14) is taken up again in 7:52 (in a similar way). The importance of Moses (and the "prophet" text of Dt 18:15f.) is only hinted at in 3:22f., but is greatly elaborated in the Stephen story and speech (especially 7:20f.; 35f. and 37f.). Several key themes introduced in the early discourses such as "salvation," "promise," Abraham and his seed, signs and wonders, etc., are taken up once more in Acts 7:2-53. Similarly motifs treated in the Stephen speech receive further elaboration in later discourses: χειροποιέω 7:48 and 17:24 (see also 19:26); the tabernacle of David 7:46 and 15:16; mission 7:34, 35 and 22:21; the "Just One," 7:52 and 22:14; Moses and the prophets 7:20f., 52, and 26:22. Further, the "heart and ears" condemnation of 7:51 is taken up once more at the very end of the book 28:26f. by quoting Is 6:9f. Finally it should be pointed out that the histories of Acts 7 and 13 complement each other, since one emphasizes the early and the other the later history of the Hebrews.[176] The Stephen speech, therefore, is to be understood in light of its function within the author's overall thematic schema.

The function of Stephen's long discourse within the book of Acts is further elucidated when its audience (Sanhedrin and Christian reader), setting (accusations and transfiguration/vision), and purpose (history as condemnation and by implication as vindication) are taken into consideration. The speech is a martyr's witness, the defense of an accused person, a structural element within a trial, a Christian interpretation of Jewish history, a further elaboration of "the things con-

---

[176]Haenchen, Acts, pp. 408 and 415.

cerning God's kingdom" (Acts 1:3). But most important, it is a discourse the author has strategically situated to underscore a critical turning point in the spreading of God's word. This speech is unique, being most in agreement with 13:16f., since it addresses itself to one of the principal concerns of the early community: its historical relation to Judaism. To accomplish this goal, the figure of Moses is given center-stage and the LXX text is transformed into a lesson of history.

2. Thematic Function

As a corollary to the structural analysis presented above, some principal motifs of the Stephen story will be surveyed and commented upon. These observations are based upon the foregoing study of the author's style and method of composition. They will, of necessity, be brief and at the same time constitute a fitting conclusion to the entire investigation.

a. Judaism

The chief concern at this point is an examination of the author's attitude towards Judaism. Even the most cursory reading of the Stephen story conveys the impression that, while it is Stephen who is on trial, official Judaism is irrevocably indicted. In order to better understand the position taken by the writer vis-à-vis Christianity's Hebrew background, it is necessary first to examine the polemical aspect of this episode as well as the techniques used by the author to achieve his purpose.

1) Polemics

Long before Acts 6:8f., the Christian community of Jerusalem, particularly the apostles, had encountered opposition and hostility from the Jewish leaders. They had been warned not to preach in Jesus' name, were thrown into jail, and flogged. In fact, already in 5:17 the high priest and Sadducees take the initiative against the Christian leaders. Throughout these early chapters, however, the attitude of the people remains friendly and only in 6:12 do they show any hostility.

Nevertheless, beginning with the Stephen story proper an increasingly belligerent tone in the narrative is apparent, both in describing the Jewish attitude toward Christianity and, especially within the discourse, in expressing the Christian's view of the Jewish past. The polemical element is particularly evident in this part of Acts.

To express his polemical attitude toward Judaism the author uses a variety of techniques. His use of invective at the end of the speech needs no further comment. Besides, it is paralleled in 13:40-41 and 28:25-28. He also employs a "particular to general" device. This stylistic device has already been noted, so it will suffice to give only a few examples of its use in expressing a polemical point of view. While Moses is on the mountain speaking with God, the Hebrews persuade Aaron to make an idol for them (7:40 = Ex 32:1). Noting several texts in Ex 32 which state that the Jews made a calf, the author generalizes and accuses the Hebrews in 7:41 of calf-making.[177] When Moses visits his brethren (7:23f.), a fellow Hebrew, in pushing him away, retorts: "Who appointed you . . ." (v.27). The author in v.35 again generalizes, when he attributes the same statement to all the Jews. Furthermore, Acts 6:13, "this man never ceases speaking against . . .," seems to be a hyperbolic restatement of the two accusations of 6:14.[178]

---

[177]See the statement by André Pelletier, "Une création de l'apologétique chrétienne: μασχοποιεῖν," RSR 54 (1966): 413-14, concerning this particular example: "Il était de bonne méthode de prendre pour point de départ d'une 'démonstration évangélique' la mauvaise conscience qu'inspirait à ces défenseurs intransigeants du culte sans images la zoolâtrie de leurs ancêtres. Effectivement notre texte résume l'épisode avec les mots mêmes de la Septante. Seulement, il remplace ἐποίησαν ἑαυτοῖς μόσχον par ἐμοσχοποίησαν. Dans la mesure où ce mot attire l'attention sur la forme animal de l'idole, il ne fait que reproduire la nuance péjorative exprimée dans la liturgie juive par 'le boeuf mangeur d'herbe' (Ps. 106) et par la 'vaine fumée égyptienne' de Philon. Mais il y ajoute un élément nouveau. Formé sur le type des verbes de métier: ἀσπιδοποιεῖν, τραπεζοποιεῖν, σκηνοποιεῖν, etc., il évoque une activité habituelle et spécialisée: quelque chose comme 'ces fondeurs de veau en firent un, qu'ils adorèrent, etc.,' mais le tout vigoureusement ramassé en un seul mot. C'était insinuer que la confection de l'idole pour culte zoolâtique n'est pas un simple épisode dans l'histoire d'Israël avec Dieu, malice immédiatement perceptible à des sujets de parler grec."

[178]See Haenchen's statement (Acts, p. 274): "Luke has the accusers maintain that Stephen incessantly speaks against the Temple and the law, and as an instance of this allegedly continual criticism he adduces one isolated logion which they claim to have heard him say. But this logion represents the only concrete material Luke could find on which to base both the accusation and Stephen's defence-speech." Instead of fol-

The author also employs the familiar singular/plural contrast to express his judgment of the Hebrews. The most striking example of this is the parallel he draws between the actions of the one Hebrew, 7:24-28, and those of the Jews, 35f.

Another technique employed to this end is the positive/negative statement of otherwise neutral expressions. In 7:25 the author underscores the judgment of history when he notes that Moses ". . . thought the brothers would understand . . .," but in the same breath concludes ". . . but they did not understand." Likewise in 7:4, after speaking of what was allegedly "the land of promise"--the land where his audience now lives--Stephen launches into a negative statement: ". . . he did not give him an inheritance in it . . ." and concludes with a negative hyperbole: οὐδὲ βῆμα ποδός (7:5). Such declarations hardly fit Dibelius' description of the Stephen speech as "impartial" in tone or a simple "recital of facts."[179]

The writer's repertoire of devices is broader still. Repetition as a stylistic technique is a favorite, and this device he puts to the service of his polemic goal. Leveled against Stephen are not only double charges, but three sets of double accusations. Further, not only is the trial qualified as being trumped up (men are suborned, 6:11) but the official deposition of evidence is appraised as false witnesses (6:13). Another polemical element involving repetition is the double use of ἀνατρέφω 7:20 and 21 to underscore the limited Jewish upbringing of Moses (three months) and his vast Egyptian learning (note that v.22 is an addition to the biblical record: "and Moses was instructed in all the wisdom of the Egyptians"). The use of the verb κατοικέω for Abraham, who is a temporary resident of both Mesopotamia (v.2) and Harran (v.4), is fully acceptable, but the application of the same term to the residents of Jerusalem is clearly polemic (v.4). Besides, the other occurrence of the verb in the Stephen story states that God does not dwell in handmade [places] (v.48). Among the many

---

lowing such a radical conclusion, implying falsification and willful deception on the part of the author, I prefer to see here another technique, a literary one at that, used by the writer in composing his history.

[179]"Speeches in Acts," p. 169.

uses of repetition as a polemic device, a last example, 7:40-41, should be mentioned. Israel's idolatry in fabricating a golden calf is stated by means of a quotation from Ex 32:1 (v.40). Immediately following this, the author repeats and therefore accentuates in three different clauses the perversity of Israel's infidelity. In v.41a he accuses them of calf-making; in 41b he presents them as sacrificing to the idol (εἴδωλον is not employed in Ex 32 but recalls the divine injunction against idols, see Ex 20:4 and Dt 5:8), and 41c, in one of the most bitter statements of the speech, portrays the early Hebrews as "rejoicing in the works of their hands." The expression last mentioned is particularly striking due to its combination of ideas. "The work of human hands," often used in the LXX to refer to the making of idols (Dt 4:28; 27:15; Ps 134:15; Is 44:9ff., etc.) is in clear contrast to 7:50, "Has not my hand made all these things?" (quotation of Is 66:2),[180] while the term "rejoice/take delight in," employed in relation to the works of God and the good deeds of men,[181] is here applied, in an almost perverse way, to the enjoyment of evil.

A last technique deserves particular attention, that of play on words. These are too numerous and obvious to be accidental. At the same time, they are often related to the author's polemical attitude toward Israel. Abraham is said to receive a "covenant of circumcision," and in response performs the rite for his son (7:8); but, in an obvious play on words, the present generation of Jews are accused of being uncircumcised of ear and heart (v.51). The author does not end his diversion at this point, instead he states that the hearers "were cut (διεπρίοντο) to their hearts," (v.54) and later that "they held their ears" (v.57). The opening words of the speech, "Men-brothers . . ." (7:2), are taken up again in v.26 "Men, you are brothers." The latter is significant since it represents a considerable modification of the OT text. The double use of "cry out with a loud voice" in 7:57 and 60 be-

---

[180]The expression "work(s) of hands" is employed of God's handiwork as well as that of men, both in a negative and a positive sense.

[181]Dt 16:15; Ps 91:5; and Ps 103:31. See also Barn 4:11 ἐν τοῖς δικαιώμασιν αὐτοῦ εὐφρανθῶμεν (related partly to Ps 18:9).

trays the author's penchant for repetition, but at the same time illustrates his ability to employ expressions in a favorable (Stephen resembles Jesus, as in Mt 27:50) or an unfavorable (evasion of the truth)[182] manner (note also the plural/singular contrast). In 6:10 Stephen's opponents are "unable to resist (ἀντιστῆναι) the wisdom and Spirit by which he spoke," yet the hearers (v.51) "always resist (ἀντιπίπτετε) the Holy Spirit."[183] Finally, related to the author's play on words is his frequent use of cognate terms but with different nuances or in contrasting and negative/positive contexts.[184] The use of

---

[182]It is very probable that the author was acquainted with Jewish tradition on this matter; see Strack and Billerbeck, *Kommentar*, 2:684; however, the way in which this information is used, note the "holding of the ears" which follows immediately, indicates more than objective reporting.

[183]The occurrence of the term σοφία in the Stephen story (four times--found nowhere else in Acts) could conceivably bear a polemic intent. This aspect is negative and secondary no doubt. In 6:3 the candidates to be chosen must be "full of the Spirit and wisdom." Later it is said that Stephen's opponents (among whom are Cyrenians and Alexandrians, 6:9) are "unable to resist the wisdom and Spirit by which he spoke" (6:10). The other two occurrences of the term are in obvious Egyptian contexts. Joseph is "given grace and wisdom before Pharaoh, king of Egypt" (7:10), while Moses is said to have been "instructed in all the wisdom of the Egyptians" (7:22). The wisdom of Egypt, proverbial in Hellenistic times [see Ulrich Wilckens, "σοφία," *TDNT* 7:514, n. 341] and possessed by Joseph and Moses (7:10, 22), is confounded by a higher wisdom--the wisdom/Spirit of Stephen (6:10). See below for further treatment of Stephen.

[184]The double occurrence of the proper name "Shechem" in 7:16 should be mentioned at this point and discussed briefly. It is clear that v.16 is the result of a conflation of several biblical traditions, Gn 23:16; 33:19; 50:13; Jos 24:32; however, it is doubtful whether the author uses the OT text directly, since there is little or no linguistic relation between his text and the alleged models. This fact leads me to suspect that he is in fact employing an old tradition which presented Shechem as the burial place of the patriarchs. Such a conclusion is rendered more plausible since Josephus can on his part claim Hebron as the locale of their tomb, οἱ ἀπόγονοι ἔθαψαν ἐν Νεβρῶνι (Ant. 2.199). See Haenchen, *Acts*, p. 280, n. 2: "According to Josephus *Ant.* II, 198f., Jubilees 46.8 and the 'Testaments of the Twelve Patriarchs' (see thereon, and on the Rabbinic tradition, Bill. II, 672-8) they were laid to rest with Abraham, Isaac and Jacob in the double cave near Hebron." Such a tradition about Shechem could be related to Gn 48:21 where Israel promises Shechem to Joseph as his portion (MT, LXX Σίκιμα, and *Pseudo-Jonathan*; see also Jn 4:5)

What is its function within the Stephen speech? A number of scholars see in this some type of Samaritan influence:

polemics, therefore, is a characteristic of the entire speech, but it constitutes only one aspect of the author's evaluation of Judaism.

2) Attitude Toward Judaism

It is clear to the reader that the Stephen story, particularly the speech, is severe in its judgment of the Hebrews. Acts 6:8-8:4 is no less than a vicious mock-trial and execution, instigated by Jewish opponents and perpetrated by the leaders and the populace. Nevertheless, careful attention reveals an equally obvious reverence for the Jewish past. This negative/positive attitude toward Israel is the dominant theme of the Stephen story.

While the writer castigates the present generation of Jewish leaders, 7:51-53, he does not fail to note that large numbers of priests joined the community, 6:7. Further, while the accusations indicate very negative relations with the Jewish community, the various statements made in response to these throughout the speech are generally very positive. This conclusion, however, requires considerable elaboration. To the accusations that Stephen speaks against Moses (6:11) or that he preaches the views of Jesus on the abrogation of Mosaic customs (v.14), the writer takes great pains to show the opposite. In fact, Moses is the central figure of the speech, where he is presented in a truly Jewish way. As regards the customs of Moses, one can only state that circumcision (7:8) and the historical role of the Jewish leader are presented in a fully positive way. In an equally favorable manner, he answers the accusation of denigration of the Law (6:13). Moses has been sent (7:34-35) by God and he has received the "living words" (v.38). At the same time the charge that Stephen speaks blasphemous words against God (6:11) is countered by a long dis-

---

Spiro, Scharlemann, Scobie, Gaston, Scroggs among others (see pp. 30-31, nn. 113-15 above). Cadbury, Book of Acts, pp. 105-6, nn. 38-41, for example, proposes that the inclusion of Shechem here is due to anti-Jewish polemic. It is not at all improbable that Cadbury is correct. Nevertheless it should also be noted that the double mention of Shechem in v.16 should be related to Samaria in 8:1 and serves as an added link with the Samaritan mission which occurs in the Philip story.

course on God's role in history. For all the accusations (for those which concern "the place," vv.13 and 14, see below), the author presents a balanced historical account.

However, for each theme suggested by the indictment, a polemical note is forthcoming: Moses is rejected by the fathers (7:35, 39); God turns away from his people (v.42). In the case of the customs and the Law of Moses, the accusations are reversed. The Jews are charged with the rejection of Moses, the nonobservance of the Law (7:53), and of noncircumcision in the real sense (v.51). The polemical element, then, concerns not the history of Israel but the people's response to it.

The accusations concerning "the place" present a more complex situation. This is true since this theme plays such a prominent role in the speech. The charges leveled against Stephen speak of "words against this holy place" (6:13) and destruction of "this place" (v.14). All explicit mention of the temple is avoided (the speech employs the terms "place," "tabernacle," and "house"). The writer has modified the original temple logion by substituting the term τόπος for ναός.[185]

The author responds to this especially edited accusation by developing at length a series of interrelated motifs. After having inhabited two pagan lands--areas of divine choice nevertheless--(appearance of God in Mesopotamia, land of the Chaldeans, 7:2, 4, and command to migrate to Harran, v.3), Abraham is directed to the homeland of the speech's audience (v.4). In v.5 is encountered an important clue to the author's principal motifs. It is explicitly stated that no inheritance is given (see above for the polemic quality of the verse), but only a promise of possession is made to Abraham and his seed. Knowing the author's fondness for doublets, it is significant that

---

[185]Mk 14:58; Mt 26:61; and Jn 2:19. Supra, pp. 287-93 for a discussion of 6:11, 13, and 14. The temple saying also appears in the Gospel of Thomas 71: ⲡⲉϫⲉ ⲓ̅ⲥ̅ ϫⲉ ϯⲛⲁϣⲟⲣ]ϣⲣ ⲙⲡⲉⲉⲓ]ⲏⲉⲓ. The use of ⲏⲉⲓ (= "house," also employed in logion 35 with the same meaning) seems to support the gospel tradition rather than the reading of Acts 6:14. See A. Guillaumont et al., eds., The Gospel according to Thomas: Coptic Text Established and Translated (Leiden: Brill/New York: Harper, 1959), p. 40.

κατάσχεσις is repeated in 7:45 while "inheritance" is not. The latter, by its negative formulation in 7:5, is denied to the Hebrews (the writer casts doubt upon the notion of the "promised land"), while the former remains no more than a promise throughout most of the history recorded by the speech. Only with Joshua will the actual possession, not the inheritance, be a reality. V.5 also introduces the theme of descendants (see below) and relates it to that of place/land.

In v.6 the author pursues further the idea of the pagan setting of Hebrew history, since Abraham's "seed will be a sojourner in a foreign land." In effect the entire Egyptian sojourn, with its numerous references to "Egypt," occurs away from the land in which the audience dwells (7:14). The important modification of "in a land not theirs" to "in a foreign land" should be pointed out, since by this means the writer achieves a double goal. The pagan concept is underscored once more, while nonpossession as well as noninheritance are further emphasized. Egypt is not a land away from home, instead it is paradoxically the land where God's promise will be fulfilled (see vv.7, 17, 25, 34).

A further indication within the Abraham story of the importance of this theme is afforded by the modification of "mountain" to "place" in v.7 where the author conflates Ex 2:22 with Gn 15:13. The use of the term τόπος in the speech (7:7, 33, 49) suggests that he wishes to broaden the concept of "place" so that God's promise is not limited to "this place," i.e., the temple of 6:13, 14. The Egyptian sojourn follows immediately after the Abraham story, where the author's purpose coincides fully with that of the biblical narrative in regard to the theme of "place."

In v.29, during the Egyptian sojourn--ironically it seems --it is stated that Moses must leave Egypt, thereby becoming a sojourner in the land of Midian (note the stylistic relation with 7:6). Egypt is now the Hebrew homeland. During this new sojourn, following the biblical source, the encounter with God occurs. The desert period needs no further elaboration since the author once again follows his OT source in pursuing his theme. In v.45 the author returns to the theme of possession of the land. Also in this part of the speech he directs his attention more particularly to "the house" of God. The responses to the accusations, therefore, are not simple; nor are they irrelevant. On the contrary, the writer expends considerable effort to defend the Christian point of view but on the basis of what he believes to be the true interpretation of the biblical story. Israel and its past are an integral part of this view.

Further indication of the writer's negative/positive attitude toward Judaism is to be found in severe attacks against unworthy descendants of Abraham (see the negative treatment of Joseph's brothers, 7:11; of the quarreling Hebrews, v.25; of the fathers, vv.35f.; of Solomon, v.47; and especially of his Sanhedrin audience, vv.51f.), and in his laudatory presentation of the true seed of Abraham (see below). The author's choice of names for the Hebrews, "our father Abraham," "our/the fathers," "the people," "our race," and "the sons of Israel," certainly exhibits respect for Judaism, while his invective with its list of epithets and its change to "your fathers" reveals his severe condemnation of infidelity, disobedience, and rejection. Equally indicative of the writer's sympathy with Hebrew history is his choice of terms and episodes which illustrate the suffering and ill-treatment of Israel (7:6-7, 19f., 34). It is not without interest that he then describes the fate of Stephen and the persecution (διωγμὸς μέγας, 8:1) of the community, in reality a parallel to the persecution (διώκω, 7:52) of the prophets by the fathers.

Finally, the interpretation of 7:42-50 (also the relation of these verses to the preceding section of the speech) contributes considerably to one's understanding of the author's view of Judaism. Various statements from these verses have been enlisted in favor of opposite opinions concerning the temple and sacrifice. It has also been remarked (p. 127, n. 237) that seemingly contradictory views are expressed by the author, e.g., the references in 42-43 (quoting Am 5:25-27) to true sacrifice and idolatry, the presence of a pagan tabernacle (v.43), the tabernacle of witness (v.44), and the favorable (v.46) and unfavorable (v.47) treatment of David and Solomon, respectively. These facts serve to illustrate both the author's sympathy for Israel and his historical sense. He knows and so presents the contemporaneity of the negative (rebellion, rejection, idolatry, exclusiveness--the house of Solomon) and the positive (the living words, God's presence, fidelity of some, the tabernacle--David) phases of Hebrew history. To describe the desert sojourn he chooses Am 5:25-27 which explicitly states that true sacrifice was offered to God, but at the same time he also dwells upon the people's idolatry. Acts 7:42-43 neither condemns sacrifice as idolatrous[186] nor denies the reality of true sacrifice.[187] Instead the text of Acts simply states the coexistence of the two during the desert period.[188] Further con-

---

[186]Simon, Stephen, p. 49, after discussing what he thinks are the two possible interpretations of the quotation of Amos (sacrifice is forbidden by God or was given to false gods), concludes: "The sacrificial cult first appeared among the Israelites as an act of idolatry and it is fundamentally nothing else; it can be intended only for false gods, and the very fact that the Israelites practice it is the proof that they are given up to worship the host of heaven." See Wilson, Gentiles, p. 133, nn. 2 and 4, for a critique of Simon's position.

[187]Haenchen, Acts, p. 284, states concerning the quotation of Amos as it occurs in Acts: ". . . the following meaning is extracted: 'Israel offered sacrifices in the wilderness not to Yahweh but to graven images--for forty years!'" See also Wilson, Gentiles, p. 133; Bihler, Stephanusgeschichte, pp. 70-71; and Conzelmann, Apostelgeschichte, p. 55 for similar points of view.

[188]Simon, Stephen, p. 49; Haenchen, Acts, p. 284; and also Bihler, Stephanusgeschichte, p. 70, presume that Acts 7:42, in quoting Am 5:25 μὴ σφάγια καὶ θυσίας προσηνέγκατέ μοι, requires a negative answer, thereby denying the historical reality of sacrifice during the desert period (for polemic purposes?). Such an interpretation would certainly enhance a polemical approach and emphasize the author's manipulation of history even to the extent of denying obvious facts (sacrifice during the desert period was a reality which not even Am 5:25 denies: הזבחים ומנחה הגשתם־לי). Such radical negativism is not, according to the data of this study a characteristic of the Stephen speech. For this reason I am led to investigate the grammatical basis of such an interpretation. Arndt-Gingrich, Lexicon, s.v. "Μή," state: "μή is used as an interrogative particle when a negative answer is expected to the question (Bl-D. # 427, 2;4. . . ." They give, among many examples, Acts 7:28 (Ex 2:14) and 7:42 (Am 5:25). Consultation of Blass and Debrunner, Gk Grammar, p. 221 [#427, 2] reveals less than absolute confirmation of the above conclusion. "It [negative use of μή] does not depend of course on the actual answer: Mt 26:25 Judas asks with the others (22) μήτι ἐγώ εἰμι; 'it is not I, is it?' and receives the unexpected answer σὺ εἶπας." [It should be noted that σὺ εἶπας as an answer to a question also appears in Mt 26:64 and Jn 18:37, where it also seems to imply an affirmative response; but see a discussion of this problem in

firmation of this conclusion is the positive statement (immediately following the assertion of Israel's attachment to false gods, v.43) concerning the presence among the fathers (vv.44-45) of the tabernacle of witness, made according to a divine model.[189]

Vv.42-50 present the realities of Israel's history, its fidelity and infidelity, as well as God's good will toward his people and the varied responses of the sons of Israel. The same interpretation, I believe, should be given to the affirmative treatment of David and the tabernacle (vv.47f.). The latter, however, also relates to the author's polemic against "this place." Significantly it is stated that Solomon built a house (it is rejected by God; see vv.49-50), and further that "the Most High" cannot be thus limited. He rejects not God's presence among his people via the tabernacle (it was made according to God's plan) but the temple/house/"this place."[190]

Raymond E. Brown, The Gospel according to John (xiii-xxi): Introduction, Translation, and Notes, The Anchor Bible (Garden City, N.Y.: Doubleday, 1970), pp. 853-54.] The grammarians then present the following examples where ". . . the meaning of μή is slightly modified": Mt 12:23; Lk 17:9; Jn 4:29, 33; 5:28; 7:26; 21:5 (along with several non-NT examples). So many non-applications of a grammatical rule, especially for late Greek, do not foster confidence in such an interpretation. Furthermore, only twice in Acts would we apparently find μή interrogative with an implied negative response. Both of these occur within the Stephen speech and involve explicit OT quotations. Acts 7:28, which is a citation of Ex 2:14, states: "Do you not intend to kill me in the same way you killed the Egyptian yesterday?" The answer in the mind of the speaker is an expected "yes." Moses' reaction (he flees) does not lead one to expect a negative response. Finally, one is left with Acts 7:42-43: "Did you offer slain beasts and sacrifices to me, forty years in the desert, O house of Israel and you took up the tabernacle . . ." The addition of also in the translation, I believe, expresses the author's intended meaning: "you did offer sacrifices to me, but you also whored after other gods." See also Bruce, Acts, p. 173: "They offered sacrifices indeed, but as their hearts were rebellious against God, He could not regard them as offered to Him . . ." and Book of Acts, pp. 154-55.

[189]Bihler, Stephanusgeschichte, p. 72, also insists upon the contemporaneous possession by the fathers of the two tabernacles. Bruce, Book of Acts, pp. 155-56, likewise insists upon this fact.

[190]For similar conclusions, see Haenchen, Acts, p. 285; Wilson, Gentiles, pp. 133-34; and Bihler, Stephanusgeschichte, pp. 72-73. See also Jervell, Luke and the People of God, pp. 133-51 ("The Law in Luke-Acts") for a view of Judaism which

The author's attitude toward Judaism, then, is both positive and negative. Christianity spreads from Jerusalem and cannot be limited to that place. But at the same time it takes its origin and finds its roots in this Jewish center and milieu.

b. God and His People

The writer's treatment of Judaism is invariably related to the role God has played in history and to the actors within that history. These two factors can hardly be overestimated. Therefore, attention is turned now to an analysis of these for a better understanding of the author's purpose.

1) God

In discussing the role which is attributed to God, it is essential to point out that Stephen is accused of "speaking blasphemous words against . . ." Him (6:11), that ὁ θεός is the term preferred rather than κύριος, that God most clearly directs Israel's history, and that the vision of Stephen concerns the "glory of God." These facts are obvious indicators of the author's purpose.

References to God in the introductory and concluding narratives have already been noted; His role in the speech now commands attention. God's presence is carefully noted in each episode of the history: He speaks to and directs Abraham (v. 2f.); He is with Joseph, and, by implication, is not with the brothers (vv.9-11); Moses has a special relation to Him (vv.20, 23, 25), is the recipient of a direct revelation (vv.30f.), and is the mediator of His presence with the people (vv.34, 35f.); in the time of Joshua He drives out the nations before the face of His people; and finally David finds favor before Him.

Not only is He present throughout that history, but it is directed by Him. It is His command (v.3), promise (v.5), threat (v.7), and gift (v.8), which set things in motion. He resettles (μετοικίζω, vv.4 and 43); He is with Joseph, delivers him, gives him favor, and appoints him leader (vv.9-10). He gives salvation (v.25), sends Moses on his mission (ἀποστέλλω, vv.34, 35), turns away in response to the people's turning in

---

confirms many of the conclusions proposed in the present study; see especially pp. 142-47.

their hearts to Egypt (vv.42 and 39). He delivers the people to the worship of the host of heaven (v.42), but He also drives out the nations before their faces (v.45). This notion of God's control of history is further enhanced by the promise/fulfillment/resolution technique, or variations of this, which the writer employs in the discourse. The promises and threats of vv.5-7 (noninheritance, promise of possession, foretelling of wonderings, enslavement, ill-treatment, judgment, deliverance, and worship) are variously alluded to throughout the speech (note that in vv.6-7 the author causes God to address Himself directly to the audience of the speech; see commentary). Inheritance, possession, and sojourn have already been discussed. The stay in Egypt is called the "time of the promise" made to Abraham (v.17); the enslavement and ill-treatment are described in vv.19-21; while the deliverance, ill-treatment, and judgment are resolved in vv.34f.

Finally, a complex but crucial aspect of the author's presentation of God within the history of Israel must be dealt with. Throughout chapter two the writer's preference for the term ὁ θεός has been noted, since he systematically substituted it for κύριος, either by eliminating the latter or adding the former to his OT source.[191] However, it is important to point out that κύριος appears three times in the speech and twice in the concluding narrative. The last mentioned occurs in Stephen's last words and concerns Jesus (see below). Of the three uses of the term within the discourse only the first two require special analysis, since the last (v.49) involves a standard OT speech formula and has already been discussed.

The term κύριος occurs twice (vv.31 and 33) during the passage relating Moses' encounter with God, vv.30-34. In composing this part of his text, the writer has considerably edited and rewritten Ex 3:1-10. It is important to note that in relation to the OT Vorlage the presentation in Acts of the encounter (Moses' role, God's self-revelation, and the divine message) is concise and artistically presented (see p. 191). Presently it is the theme of revelation which demands attention.

---

[191]The double use of the expression ὁ λόγος τοῦ θεοῦ in 6:2 and 7 should be noted. Incidentally only ὁ θεός is employed in the other historical speech of Acts (13:16-41).

The author formulates the theophany of Sinai in the following stages: 1) an angel appears to Moses (v.30), 2) the voice of the Lord speaks to him (v.31), and 3) the Lord Himself addresses Moses. The progressive nature of God's manifestation to Moses is due primarily to the work of the author of Acts. In the first instance he has modified the LXX phrase, ἄγγελος κυρίου, by omitting the term "Lord," while in the second stage he has eliminated the anecdotal character of the OT text and has chosen a very solemn cultic formula, ἐγένετο φωνὴ κυρίου (see p. 90, n. 151), to introduce God's self-declaration: "I am the God of . . ."[192] In formulating the third stage of revelation, the writer has reversed the order of two OT verses, namely, Ex 3:5 ("loosen the sandal . . .") and 6 ("I am the God . . ."), and has placed the element of revelation first. After God has made Himself known to Moses (7:32), He is introduced in v.33 as follows: "and the Lord said to him." Vv.33 and 34 of the speech borrow from the OT text passages dealing with "place," "ill-treatment," "deliverance," and "mission."

The role of God in the Stephen story--especially within the discourse--is presented therefore in view of the author's several themes and objectives. No one hearing Stephen's speech would say he has blasphemed against God. Further, God is fully concerned about his people and its history. God is the God of the Hebrews.

2) <u>Descendants of Abraham</u>

Throughout the speech the history of Israel follows the long list of personalities who played an important part in the events described. Such an approach was standard procedure in writing short chronicles. Beyond that, however, histories of Israel present distinct points of view, as different as the writers who composed them. The Stephen speech, owing to its unique function, assigns special roles to its cast of characters. The people who appear in the discourse are real historical figures whose contributions to history are clearly stated.

---

[192]The elimination of θεός before the names of Isaac and Jacob conforms both to the author's purpose and style. The statement "the God of your fathers" finds a parallel in "the God of Abraham and Isaac and Jacob" as well as a thematic restatement of his attitude toward Israel.

However, they are assigned special qualities and functions in view of the writer's goal.

The role of Abraham (vv.2-8 and 16-17) has been discussed on numerous occasions, so it is not necessary to dwell on his contribution to the history of Acts 7. His special function is surely that of being God's chosen one and father of a long line of descendants. The entire history of Israel finds its origin in "our father Abraham" and the pledges made to him. Through his progeny, he is the connecting link of the entire discourse.[193] This is particularly underscored by the fact that Gn 15 is the focal point of the entire Abraham episode.

The Joseph episode carries the narrative forward at a very accelerated pace, since it immediately introduces the jealousy of the brothers. The author's negative treatment of Joseph's brothers is based upon the data presented by the OT. The selling into Egypt was borrowed from Gn 45:4; the subsequent contrast, though, between Joseph ("God was with him," so all manner of blessings ensued, vv.9c-10) and the brothers ([God is not with them], so tribulation befall them) is clearly his own. The double use of θλῖψις in a positive (v.10) and a negative (v.11) setting, as well as the association of λιμός with the latter, reveals the influence of the OT[194] as well as the author's writing techniques. Furthermore, from his knowledge of OT thought, particularly Gn 42:41,[195] Dt 31:17,[196] and Ps 36:

---

[193]Bihler, <u>Stephanusgeschichte</u>, p. 46 and Dahl, "Abraham," p. 144.

[194]On θλῖψις μεγάλη see Neh 9:37 and 1 Mc 9:27; θλῖψις and λιμός in a speech-history: 2 Chr 20:9 (there are numerous similarities with the Stephen speech).

[195]Gn 42:21 ἐν ἁμαρτίᾳ γάρ ἐσμεν περὶ τοῦ ἀδελφοῦ ἡμῶν, ὅτι ὑπερείδομεν τὴν θλῖψιν τῆς ψυχῆς αὐτοῦ, ὅτε κατεδέετο ἡμῶν, καὶ οὐκ εἰσηκούσαμεν αὐτοῦ· ἕνεκεν τούτου ἐπῆλθεν ἐφ᾽ ἡμᾶς ἡ θλῖψις αὕτη. Note the double use of θλῖψις (as in Acts 7:10-11) as well as the idiomatic use of ἐπέρχομαι ἐπί (as in Acts 7:11). The speech of Reuben then follows (v.22), recalling his attempt to save his brother, Gn 37:21 (this text is used to compose Acts 7:10a--see commentary.

[196]Dt 31:17 καὶ ὀργισθήσομαι θυμῷ εἰς αὐτοὺς ἐν τῇ ἡμέρᾳ ἐκείνῃ καὶ καταλείψω αὐτοὺς καὶ ἀποστρέψω τὸ πρόσωπόν μου ἀπ᾽ αὐτῶν, καὶ ἔσται κατάβρωμα, καὶ εὑρήσουσιν αὐτὸν κακὰ πολλὰ καὶ θλίψεις, καὶ ἐρεῖ ἐν τῇ ἡμέρᾳ ἐκείνῃ Διότι οὐκ ἔστιν κύριος ὁ θεός μου ἐν ἐμοί, εὕροσάν με τὰ κακὰ ταῦτα. Note the "turning away" (Acts 7:42) and God's presence (Acts 7:9). Dt 31:18 then speaks of "turning after strange gods" (see Acts 7:39-40).

16-19,[197] the author presents an interesting portrait of Joseph, but a severe judgment of the other descendants of Abraham. The former possesses χάρις (v.10) like David (v.46) and Stephen (6:8). He is also given σοφία (v.10), see Moses (v.22) and Stephen (6:3 and 10). The appointment (καθίστημι) of Joseph is surely to be related to that of Moses (vv.27 and 35 in terms of rejection) and of the Seven (6:3). The latter, Joseph's brothers, find nothing but tribulation and famine (like the wicked man of OT literature); but at the hands of Joseph (God's envoy), they find satisfaction (vv.11-13).

The remainder of the Joseph episode concerns the history of Israel primarily. One final point deserves particular attention, since it relates to the special function the author lends to the son of Jacob. Like Moses (vv.34, 35) Joseph is intimately connected to the concept of mission. While human perversity was responsible for Joseph's slavery and sojourn in Egypt (v.9) it is God, through Joseph, who summons his people (ἀποστέλλω + μετακαλέω, v.14).[198]

In terms of space the Moses story dominates the entire speech, since vv.17-41 are devoted to his role within the history of his people. The author devotes the majority of the speech to his activities and, at the same time, embellishes this part of his composition with more care than usual. In a way similar to the glorification of Abraham or Noah in late Jewish works,[199] the person of Moses receives special consider-

---

[197]Ps 36:16 κρεῖσσον ὀλίγον τῷ δικαίῳ / ὑπὲρ πλοῦτον ἁμαρτωλῶν πολύν· 17 ὅτι βραχίονες ἁμαρτωλῶν συντριβήσονται, / ὑποστηρίζει δὲ τοὺς δικαίους κύριος. 18 γινώσκει κύριος τὰς ὁδοὺς τῶν ἀμώμων, / καὶ ἡ κληρονομία αὐτῶν εἰς τὸν αἰῶνα ἔσται· 19 οὐ καταισχυνθήσονται ἐν καιρῷ πονηρῷ / καὶ ἐν ἡμέραις λιμοῦ χορτασθήσονται. The following themes are to be noted: "in days of famine" (Acts 7:11), χορτάξω (Acts 7:11 χόρτασμα). See v.12 of the psalm, "The sinner will look for the righteous (δίκαιον) and gnash his teeth at him" (Acts 7:54).

[198]In 7:10a it is stated that "God delivered him from all his tribulations." This is an evident reference to Reuben who tried to save him from his brothers (Gn 37:21), but was unable. The author applies the statement in a positive way to God and borrows the entire structural unit from his source (<u>supra</u>, pp. 61-62). See also n. 195 above.

[199]On Abraham see Jub 11.16f.; on Noah see 1QapGn 11.1f., 1Q19, and Enoch 106-7 (the data concerning Moses is discussed by Joseph A. Fitzmyer, <u>The Genesis Apocryphon of Qumran Cave 1</u>:

ation. Building upon the OT presentation of the birth episode, the author develops and further stresses the "exposure" and "adoption" motifs. His familiarity with secular literature on this subject is well demonstrated by the terminology he employs, βρέφος (v.19), ἐκτίθημι (vv.19, 21), and ἀναιρέω (v.21). The first two are technical terms used in reference to the exposure of children and are well attested in Greek literature,[200] while the last mentioned is borrowed from the LXX ("pick up" Ex 2:5) but is given an entirely different meaning, that of "adopt."[201] The "beauty" of Moses, his education in all the

---

A Commentary, Biblica et Orientalia, no. 18A (Rome: Biblical Institute Press, 1971). For an interesting anaphora glorifying Moses in Samaritan literature, see Selig J. Miller, The Samaritan Molad Mosheh: Samaritan and Arabic Texts Edited and Translated with Introduction and Notes (New York: Philosophical Library, 1949), pp. 128-33.

[200]The verb ἐκτίθημι is employed in the following exposure myths: that of Cyrus the Great (Herodotus 1.112) and of Helios and Selena (Diodorus Siculus 3.56). See also Lucian De Sacrificiis 5 and Aelianus, Varia Historia (who uses the terms βρέφος and ῥίπτω, the latter being the verb found in Ex 1:22). The same verb is used of the Moses episode in Wis 18:5. Philo, Moses, refers to Moses as τὸν παῖδα ἐκτιθέασι (1.10) and to his sister as ἀδελφή . . . τοῦ ἐκτεθέντος βρέφος (1.12). For the above references I am indebted to Duterme, "Vocabulaire," p. 19, n. 3. A text from the papyri should also be noted: "BGU IV.1104.24 (B.C. 8) τὸ βρέφος ἐκτίθεσθαι" Moulton-Milligan, Vocabulary, s.v. "ἐκτίθημι." See also "βρέφος" for papyri evidence supporting the meaning "new-born child."

[201]Both meanings are attested for this verb in the middle voice, the former being the more common. For the latter, however, see Liddell-Scott-Jones, Lexicon, s.v. "ἀναιρέω": "take up in one's arms, Il. 16.8: hence, take up new-born children, own them, Plu. Ant. 36, cf. Ar. Nu. 531; take up an exposed child, Men. Sam. 159, cf. BGU 1110, etc." Note also the interesting examples from the papyri (active and passive): "For the active cf. P Oxy I.37.6 (A.D. 49) . . . ἀνεῖλεν ἀπὸ κοπρίας ἀρρενικὸν σωμάτιον, 'picked up from the dung-heap a male foundling': the corresponding passive is used of the same transaction in ib. 38.6 (A.D. 49-50) . . . ὃ ἀνείρηται ἀπὸ κοπρίας. The recurrent formula δουλικὸν παιδίον ἀναίρετον ὑποτίτθιον (as BGU IV.1107.9--B.C. 13) shows how technical the term had become: cf. Ac 7.21" Moulton-Milligan, Vocabulary, s.v. "ἀναιρέω." The transfer in meaning was no doubt facilitated by the occurrence in all voices of the meaning "adopt" or other related sense. The technical term ἀναιρέω is rendered by the Vulgate and the Latin column of codex Bezae as tollo, the term used in Latin during the Roman ceremony in which the father lifts the newborn child to render him legitimate; see the use which Plautus, Amphitruo 501, makes of this custom.

wisdom of the Egyptians, and his power in words and deeds all serve to make him a worthy central figure of Israel's chronicle. The discourse answers, at least indirectly, the accusations leveled against Stephen (6:11, 13, 14).

The role of Moses is further enhanced by recounting in great detail his first encounter with his brethren. The repeated use of the root ἀδικέω (vv.24 twice, 26, 27 twice) has been previously noted. These terms as well as "defend" (v.24), "peace" (v.26), and the quotation of v.27 must be seen in light of ἐπισκέπτομαι (v.23) and the revealing commentary of v.25. Moses' function in coming to his fellow Hebrews could be seen in terms of brotherly concern, but, when considered in relation to v.25 (salvation from God), it seems clear that the author suggests more, namely, God's visitation of his people through his envoy. The writer no doubt was familiar with Gn 50:24-25, where Joseph speaks to the Sons of Israel of "the visitation with which God will visit" them.[202] Moses, in effect, goes to his brothers and the author comments in v.25: ἐνόμιξεν δὲ συνιέναι τοὺς ἀδελφοὺς ὅτι ὁ θεὸς διὰ χειρὸς αὐτοῦ δίδωσιν σωτηρίαν αὐτοῖς· οἱ δὲ οὐ συνῆκαν. In terms borrowed from the Servant Songs (Is 52:10, 13) the writer expresses his severe judgment of the early Hebrews. In effect, he predisposes his readers for the presentation of one who truly understands God's salvation, one who is granted the vision of God's glory (see below for further development of this theme).

The role of Moses as mediator of salvation is reiterated in 7:35,[203] after his encounter with God at Sinai. Vv.35-38

---

[202]It is significant and perhaps not without bearing upon the Moses episode that *Pseudo-Jonathan* (Gn 50:25) adds: "you will not venture out of Egypt until the time when two Deliverers תרין פרוקין shall come." Moses' two visitations to his brothers, I believe, can be seen as a similar midrashic interpretation of the double פקד / ἐπισκέπτομαι of Gn 50:25.

[203]In 7:25 salvation (σωτηρία) is given by God through Moses and in v.35 the latter is called λυτρωτής. The last-mentioned text is an obvious parallel to the description of Jesus in 5:31 (see pp. 195-96 above). That Moses should be called "Deliverer" is an important indication of the author's attitude toward Judaism. However, it should be observed further that the theme of mediatorship is an important concept of late Jewish thought; see *Assump. Mos.* 3.9 and the note by Charles, *Apocrypha*, 1:417: "The title [Mediator] was commonly assigned to him by the first century A.D. Cf. i.14, iii.12; Gal.

dwell at length upon his second visit to his brothers. By means of an eloquent encomium, the writer presents the central figure of Judaism as God's envoy, the deliverer, the one foreannouncing the prophet, the Law-giver. To further emphasize the primacy of Moses' mission the author uses a long and intricate series of repetitive devices by which he contrasts God's messenger and the fathers, the quarreling Hebrew and the rebellious Jews, the achievements of Moses and those of the people. To that end he employs double clusters, several inclusios, "self-quotations" (27 and 35; 30 and 35; 30 and 38; 34 and 35; 36 and 40), singular/plural, positive/negative contrasts, and numerous cognate doublets. God's visitation and beneficence find their most eloquent expression in the promise of a future prophet, like Moses (v.37). God's messenger then recedes into the background both in the history of Israel and in the speech, as the people turn to idolatry and the writer pursues his polemical thrust.

The next figures of importance in the historical narrative are Joshua, David, and Solomon. The last mentioned is referred to as the personification of Israel's provincialism, since he is the one who built "the house." He is the chosen foil for the writer's attack against "this place" and its connotations in contemporary Jewish thought. Joshua and David, on the contrary, are alluded to in more historical terms. Joshua, an important figure in contemporary Judaism,[204] finds his place in the speech in relation to the tabernacle and the possession of the nations.[205] The role of David, though expressed briefly (7:45c-46), is more complex. He is a historical figure, a true descendant of Abraham. Like Joseph (v.18) he "has found favor before God" (see also Stephen 6:8). Furthermore he is, as is Solomon, the personification of one aspect of Judaism. By

---

iii.18; Philo, Vit. Moys. iii.19; Talmud (see Levy, Neuhebr. und Chald. Lex. iii, 595, 596). It is implied in Heb. viii.6, ix.15, xii.24."

[204]Assump. Mos. 1.6f.; 4QTest 21f. and 4QPssJosh (see Fitzmyer, "4Q Testimonia," pp. 530-31).

[205]The prinicpal influence upon the author of Acts seems to be Dt 34:9. There he encountered a variety of themes which he incorporated within his composition (role of Joshua--7:45, fullness of the spirit of knowledge--6:10, laying on of hands--6:6, and obedience of the sons of Israel--6:7; 7:25, 35, 39).

dwelling upon David, the author insists upon an important criterion of the real descendant of Abraham, the one who finds favor with God, like Moses (7:20; note also the influence of Ex 33:12-17--Moses finds favor--upon 7:45-46) and like Joseph. David's role throughout Acts (eleven occurrences) is significant (note the reference, 15:16, to the rebuilding of his tabernacle, Am 9:11), so much so that his importance in the Stephen speech is greatly enhanced. From the above it is also concluded that, apart from his historical and exemplary role, David represents for the author, as he did for the Qumran community,[206] the personification of true Judaism, a descendant of father Abraham, a man according to God's own heart.

c. Early Christianity

Since the Stephen story is a Jerusalem episode, and since its setting within the book of Acts is transitional in character, its representation of the early Church and its beliefs is significant for the interpretation of the entire passage. The author's view of the various personalities of the story and his presentation of the community require immediate attention.

1) The Community

From the outset one is confronted by a number of problems: the make-up of the community (linguistically and theologically), the role of the Twelve, the Seven, Stephen, Philip, the Hellenists and Paul, and finally the diffusion of Christianity outside of Jerusalem. While it is not my intention to treat at length the host of problems involved, it is possible to consider these in light of the data. 1) Nowhere in the story does the author state that Stephen, or, more generally, the Seven, are Hellenists. Such a conclusion goes beyond the evidence furnished by the text.[207] Acts 6:1 speaks of disciples among whom there are Hellenists and Hebrews. The very next verse states clearly that it is from the assembly of disciples that

---

[206]See in particular 4QFor (representing 2 S 7:11-14 and Am 9:11) and CD 7.16 (=Am 9:11 concerning the fallen tabernacle of David, also quoted in Acts 15:16). Confer de Waard, Comparative Study, pp. 47-48.

[207]See for example, Wilson, Gentiles, pp. 129-30 and Martin Hengel, Judaism and Hellenism: Studies in Their Encounter in Palestine during the Early Hellenistic Period, 2 vol, trans. John Bowden (Philadelphia: Fortress Press, 1974), 1:105.

the Seven are chosen. 2) Ἑλληνιστής (also Ἑλληνιστί, Acts 21:37) refers to linguistic and Ἕλλην to ethnic factors in Acts. The latter in all its occurrences implies a contrast between "Jews and Greeks."[208] The former requires more attention. In all three uses of the term (6:1; 9:29; and 11:20),[209] the people involved are Greek speakers; however, the contexts demand a variety of ethnic and religious backgrounds. 3) In Acts 6:1 both the Hellenists and Hebrews are Christians. The latter are exclusively Jewish in origin, while the former designates both Jewish and Gentile converts (note that Nicolas is explicitly identified as a proselyte, 6:5). That the vast majority of Hellenists would have been Jewish seems logical, but the author does not concern himself with such problems. Instead, after having stated the resolution of the problem through the choice of seven men (all bearing Greek names, but see below), he declares--employing a parallelismus membrorum--that the community of disciples was multiplied and that a large number of priests became members. No further distinction is made concerning the linguistic groups, although the Jewish character of the new converts is emphasized.[210] 4) Acts 9:29 presents Paul as disputing (συζητέω as in 6:9) with Hellenists, who, from the context, are clearly non-Christian Jews (the brethren on hearing of the threat of death at the hands of the Hellenists intervene and send Saul away, v.30). Stephen's opponents probably should be identified in the same way, namely, as Hellenistic Jews living in Jerusalem.[211] The adversaries of both

---

[208]All occurrences of Ἕλλην in Acts, 14:1; 16:1, 3; 17:4; 18:4; 19:10, 17; 20:21; 21:28, involves a contrast between Jews and Greeks/Gentiles, except the last mentioned. However, it is clear from the context that the use of Ἕλλην refers to uncircumcized Greeks, whom Paul is said to have introduced into the temple.

[209]See below, p. 340, for a discussion of the textual problems relating to Acts 11:20; also Ferdinand Hahn, Mission in the New Testament, Studies in Biblical Theology, no. 47 (Naperville, Ill.: Allenson, 1965), pp. 59f.

[210]A variety of scholars have suggested that the priests mentioned in Acts 6:7 were in fact former members of the Qumran community. Apart from being highly speculative, this suggestion has been rejected on other grounds. For a discussion of the problem see Haenchen, Acts, pp. 264 and 269; Schmithals, Paul and James, p. 22, n. 57.

[211]The problem of the Jerusalem synagogues has been much

then are Greek-speaking Jews. 5) The occurrence of the term in 11:20 presents textual problems first of all. I opt for the reading Ἑλληνιστάς with B 𝔎 E pl (note the original εὐαγγελίσ-τας of ℵ) against the Ἕλληνας of P74 A D* pc.[212] Apart from the strong manuscript evidence for this choice, it should be noted that the context also favors such a conclusion since there is no contrasting Ἰουδαῖος. This passage is instructive for an understanding of the author's meaning. The Christian travelers, it is said, preached to no one "except only (εἰ μὴ μόνον) Jews." V.20 then states that they evangelized the Hellenists of Antioch (a great number of whom believed). Once again the context clearly requires that these Hellenists be non-Aramaic speaking Jews. At the same time, since the Christian missionaries themselves are identified as Cypriots and Cyrenians (see 6:9), they should probably also be considered Hellenists.[213]

From the above facts, and in view of the author's method of composition, I conclude that the identification of the Hellenists of 6:1 as Greek-speaking Christians, most of whom would be Jewish, fits into the author's view of the process of evangelization. After the dispersion following Stephen's death,

---

discussed; see among others the older study of Cadbury and Lake, Beginnings, 4:66-68 and the recent exposé by M. Hengel, "Zwischen Jesus und Paulus," pp. 182-85.

[212]It is surprising to read statements such as the following by Hahn, Mission, p. 59: "Then in trustworthy [sic] accounts Acts names in particular Phoenicia, Cyprus, and Antioch in Syria, the latter soon becoming the centre of extensive missionary work, especially as a systematic mission to the Gentiles was undertaken there early." In a note, he continues: "Acts 11.19ff.; 13.1ff. The change to the Gentile mission is reported in Acts 11.20, where the variant Ἕλληνες is certainly to be preferred." The context of Acts clearly speaks of evangelization of Jews, 11:19, and secondly the manuscript evidence is considerably weaker for the reading Ἕλληνες (supra, pp. 150-52 for a discussion of manuscript tendencies) than for Ἑλληνιστάς. The choice of the former by Haenchen, Acts, p. 365, n. 5 indicates his methodological presuppositions (i.e., evidence of a pre-Cornelius Gentile mission), I suspect, rather than an evaluation of the evidence.

[213]While the term "Hellenist" may be applied to a variety of Jewish and Christian groups, whose place of origin is non-Palestinian, it is not to be supposed that language, cultic, and ideological problems are thereby resolved; see below for a discussion of Paul and Barnabas.

they would have been responsible in large measure for the spread of Christianity among non-Aramaic Jews. Beyond this the author says very little concerning linguistic and theological factors. Stephen debated with diaspora Jews living in Jerusalem. From this it would be possible to consider him a Hellenist; however, Paul does the same and is not for that matter considered such. Furthermore, no thought is given in Acts 6:9-15 to language problems since the "Greek" opponents stir up the populace, the elders, and the scribes (v.12--consider the language factors!) and accuse Stephen before an Aramaic Sanhedrin.

The above arguments are brought forth to demonstrate the fallacy of demanding more from the author's narrative than it is capable of communicating. This study of his method of composition has shown that he organizes his data with definable goals in mind. The introduction of the Hellenist/Hebrew factions within the Jerusalem community (a fact for which there is no reason to deny) prepares for the departure, after Stephen's death, of Christianity to Judaea and Samaria, and eventually to synagogues everywhere. The reference to diaspora opponents in 6:9 seems to be warranted by the historical facts since early Christianity found its greatest opponents outside Jerusalem, among the Greek-speaking Jews throughout the Near East.[214] That Hellenistic communities did exist seems obvious, but the Stephen story furnishes very little data for the construction of such theories, since the speech in its present form owes not to Stephen but to the author of Acts, and since it is not proved that Stephen was even himself a Hellenist.

Lastly, the list of seven Greek names (6:5), often cited as evidence for an entirely Hellenistic party as opposed to the Hebrew Twelve, needs attention.[215] Several factors lead one to view this datum as considerably weaker than is usually supposed. While all seven names are Greek, it should be remembered that two of the twelve apostles also bore Greek names, Philip and Andrew. This proportion (two out of twelve) could be viewed as

---

[214]In Acts 20:18f.; 21:27f.; 24:18 the opponents of Paul are Asian Jews or in 14:19f. from Iconium.

[215]Wilson, Gentiles, p. 142; Loisy, Actes, pp. 296 and 302; Bruce, Book of Acts, p. 129; Haenchen, Acts, p. 268; Schmithals, Paul and James, p. 17.

significant. However, if the two lists represent their social classes, mostly fishermen on the one hand, and a group of leaders (Stephen, Philip the Evangelist, a proselyte from Antioch--all men "well-thought-of") on the other,[216] then the outlook is considerably different. Perhaps one should be amazed that, in a group such as were the apostles, two fishermen (see Mk 1:16 and Jn 1:44; Philip is at least from the same city as Peter and Andrew) should have Greek names. The Hellenization of Palestine obviously is easily underestimated.[217] The list of seven then contains a Philip (as does that of the Twelve) and a Nicolas whom one would expect to bear a Greek name. If I am correct in seeing the Hellenists as consisting of Jewish and non-Jewish converts and, more important, if the seven are elected from the two linguistic groups, then the distribution of Greek names is not unusual. Besides the rare occurrence of double names in Acts, almost limited to Simon/Peter and Saul/Paul, shows that tradition was very selective in its choice.

It is necessary, therefore, to return to the question of the role played within the church by the Hellenists. There is considerable data beyond the Stephen story of the part enacted by Greek-speaking Jewish converts to Christianity.[218] This problem is generally viewed in relation to an Antioch source.

---

[216]On the meaning of μαρτυρούμενος see the discussion above, pp. 218 and 268.

[217]See for example the statement by Joseph A. Fitzmyer, "The Languages of Palestine in the First Century A.D.," CBQ 32 (1970): 508: "In all some thirty towns of the area have been counted that were either Greek foundations or transformed poleis. These Hellenistic cities dotted the countryside of Palestine for several centuries prior to the first Christian century and were clearly centers from which the Greek language spread to less formally Hellenistic towns, such as Jerusalem, Jericho, or Nazareth." For a discussion of the numerous problems involved, confer, among others, Nicholas Sherwin-White, Roman Society and Roman Law in the New Testament (Oxford: Clarendon Press, 1963); Sevenster, Do You Know Greek?; Martin Hengel, Judaism and Hellenism, especially chapter two: pp. 58-106 on Greek culture and language in Palestine; Arnold H. M. Jones, The Cities of the Eastern Roman Provinces, 2d. ed. (Oxford: Clarendon Press, 1971), especially chapter ten: pp. 226-94 and 446-69, rev. Michael Avi-Yonah and Henri Seyrig.

[218]See Hahn, Mission, pp. 59-63.

> In my opinion . . . it is beyond question that Acts 6.1-6, 8-15; 7.54-82; 8.4-13, 26-39; 11. 19-30; 12.25; ch. 13f.; 15.1-33 . . . are presented from the point of view of the missionary work of the Hellenists who were driven out of Jerusalem, especially of the Antioch church regarded as a missionary centre; they show a chronological as well as an objective continuity.[219]

It is my belief that scholars too readily dismiss evidence contrary to their theories and proceed to correct the data supplied by the only source available. In the face of Acts 8:1, they maintain that only the Hellenists were persecuted and driven out of Jerusalem.[220] This "solution" already presupposes that Acts 6:1-8:4 deals solely with Hellenists of which group Stephen would be a member. Beyond that, numerous theories are proposed as scenarios of the "real" event and treatises of the theology of the Hellenists are variously elaborated.[221]

The author of Acts, in his presentation of the data, has insisted upon a number of factors. The ones most directly related to the Stephen story will be dealt with. Acts 6:1-7, through the repetition of cognate terms and the structural disposition of themes emphasizes the growth of the community and the relation of this expansion to the "word of God" (vv.2, 7) and "the ministry of the word" (v.4). This activity is placed within the hands of the Jerusalem authorities (see below for the role of Barnabas and Paul among others). However, v.7 underscores, by means of a striking threefold expression of growth, the relationship that exists between the increase of the "word of God," the multiplication of the disciples of Jerusalem, and the "adherence to the faith." The author then returns to the theme of the "spread of the good news" in 8:1 when he clearly states that all (πάντες)--the Jerusalem community--were scattered and proceeded to evangelize the areas of Judaea

---

[219] _Ibid._, p. 61, n. 1. The author refers to the works of Jeremias, Bultmann, Dupont, and Haenchen.

[220] See especially Schmithals, _Paul and James_, pp. 16-37, who presents in great detail a position presupposed by many recent scholars.

[221] Wilson, _Gentiles_, pp. 144f., gives a list of scholarly opinions and a critique of these views.

and Samaria (8:1 and 4). It should be understood that both Hellenists and Hebrews were involved.

In light of these facts it is important to point out that evangelization throughout the so-called Antiochene narratives is not always the work of Hellenists. Philip is one of the Seven, but is he a Hellenist? His labors are supervised and supplemented by Peter and John (8:14f.).[222]

Further in 11:19f. one reads that some of the dispersed brethren, Cypriots and Cyrenians, preach to Hellenistic Jews (11:20). It is probably correct to see the former as Greek-speaking Christians, whether Jewish or Gentile in origin. However, in vv.22f. one is told that the Jerusalem Church sends Barnabas, an official representative of the Christian headquarters. This same disciple in Acts 4:36 is explicitly identified as a Levite from Cyprus.[223] From this one can conclude that the dichotomy between official Church (Hebrews, the Twelve) and Hellenists (the Seven, the dispersed) is not in accord with the data of Acts.

Further, Barnabas is continually associated with Paul. These two disciples (called Apostles in 14:4, 14) are the real missionaries to the Gentiles. Perhaps it would be justifiable to call them both Hellenists as does Wilson.[224] However, nei-

---

[222]The intervention of the Apostles (Hebrew leaders) in Samaria is presumably related to the theme of authority as viewed by the author of Acts. However, the fact should not be overlooked that Aramaic speakers (Peter and John) are appropriate representatives in the Samaritan area for the Jerusalem Church, while Barnabas is an equally well-chosen delegate to be sent to Antioch to supervise the work done by Cypriots and Cyrenians (11:20-22) or as a mediator between the Apostles and the Cilician Paul (9:26-27).

[223]On the background and role of Barnabas, see Hahn, Mission, p. 60. In analyzing the data of Acts, Hahn accepts 4:36f. and later Antiochene references to Barnabas as historical, but 9:27 and 11:22f. as "historically very improbable" (p. 60, n. 1). Schmithals, Paul and James, p. 31, n. 64, on the contrary, dismisses 4:36f. and states: "But it is in the tradition of Antioch alone that [Barnabas] is anchored firmly, and E. Schwartz long ago made the correct conjecture . . . that that first report about Barnabas is derived from the prototype used for 13.1ff. and was transferred to Jerusalem by Luke." Such analyses are more concerned with historical presuppositions than with the received data.

[224]Gentiles, p. 27. See also Loisy's interesting discussion of this problem (Actes, p. 316), where he states of Ste-

ther disciple is ever thus labeled. Besides, Barnabas' relation to the Jerusalem authorities (see also 9:27), and Paul's role in relation to the Jewish authorities before his conversion, seem to point in the opposite direction. No doubt territorial factors (Cyprus for Barnabas and the dispersed missionaries of 11:20, and Cilicia for Paul and the Jews of 6:9) are insufficient data for identifying early Christians and their Jewish contemporaries as Hellenists.

The author of Acts, then, seems to present even the intermediate stage, i.e., the mission outside of Jerusalem but pre-Gentile, as the work of the entire community. Stephen is a representative of the whole community (8:1) as were the Seven (6:3) and the Twelve (6:1-7). The dispersion from Jerusalem is related to persecution (8:1-4; 11:19--threefold occurrence of διασπείρω) and thus facilitates the Gentile mission. Saul is clearly emphasized (7:58, 8:1, 3 and 22:19-20) both as the cause of persecution (therefore of the dispersion) and as the missionary to the Gentiles (9:15). The Stephen story then traces the increase of the "word of God" in Jerusalem (6:7) and in the countryside of Judaea and Samaria (8:4 εὐαγγελιζόμενοι τὸν λόγον). This theme it associates with the growth of the discipleship in the Holy City (6:7) and in the dispersion (8:4, 6, 12f.).

The Jerusalem community, according to the author of Acts, was not free of dissension (see the problems recorded in 5:1f.) nor of external problems (note the series of encounters with the Jewish authorities). Its difficulties, however, were solved in resourceful ways as we note in 6:1-7. The disciples are subject to the leadership of the apostles for it is they who summon, suggest, and finally commission the men chosen for the task (inclusio: twelve and apostles). The author further stresses their stewardship by stating, in a hyperbolic way, that only they were not driven out of Jerusalem by persecution (inclusio once more: twelve, 6:2 and apostles, 8:1). To further underscore this theme, the apostles are made to intervene in the midst of Philip's ministry in Samaria (8:14f.). The

---

phen's Hellenism that he "appartenait à la même famille que Barnabé et que Paul."

role of Jerusalem and its leaders, so important in the development of Acts, finds continuity and evolution during the course of the Stephen story.

The terms for the community are variously given during this episode as "disciples" (6:1) and "number of disciples (v. 7) and as ἐκκλησία (8:1 and 3). It is interesting to note that the last mentioned, employed only in 5:11 before the Stephen story, is now associated with the persecuting activity of Saul and the consequent dispersion throughout the countryside of Judaea and Samaria (8:1). The use of ἐκκλησία in 5:11 and 8:1, 3, specifically of the Jerusalem Church, further emphasizes the centrality and leadership of the founding Church (see also 11: 22; 15:4, etc.).

2) <u>The Role of Stephen</u>

To terminate this treatment of early Christianity as seen in Acts 6:1-8:4, a sketch of the central personality of the episode, Stephen, will be given. It is clear from a reading of 6:5 (and v.3 in retrospect), 8, 10, and 7:55 that the author wishes to draw particular attention to his qualifications. Also the precise references to his gifts, achievements, and recompense (the transfiguration/vision, Acts 6:15 and 7:55-56) show that Stephen is a very exceptional Christian in the mind of the author. The five following considerations illustrate and clarify Stephen's role in Acts 6:1-8:4.

a) <u>Μαρτυρούμενος</u>

After having assembled the disciples, the Twelve recommend the selection of ἄνδρας ἐξ ὑμῶν μαρτυρουμένους ἑπτά (6:3). Stephen, like the rest of the Seven, is identified as a distinguished or reputable member of the community. The same qualification, however, applies to Cornelius (10:22), Timothy (16: 2), and Ananias (22:12). From these facts one can conclude that what follows (the achievements, both act and speech of Stephen and Philip--of the others nothing further is heard), in the mind of the author of Acts, represents not aberrant currents of thought or radical ideas, but rather the considered opinions and acheivements of respected delegates of the community.[225]

---

[225] <u>Contra</u>, Simon, <u>Stephen</u>, pp. 77 and chapter V: "Origin

b) Full of the (Holy) Spirit and Faith

Within the list of qualifications required of the elected members, the Twelve insist that they also be πλήρεις πνεύματος καὶ σοφίας (6:3). Fullness of the Spirit is a striking phrase and even more so since the author applies the phrase to Stephen in 6:5 ("full of faith and the Holy Spirit") and in 7:55 ("being full of the Holy Spirit") and in a modified form to his disputation in 6:10 (see below). The designation is certainly not intended as peculiar to Stephen, even though it is specially emphasized by means of the writer's repetitive and structural techniques. In the first place the same thing is demanded of the other appointees. Furthermore, Barnabas (11:24) and Paul (13:9--πλησθεὶς) are also thus described. Finally, Jesus Himself is annointed by God with the Holy Spirit and with power (10:38). Stephen, then, along with other prominent Christians, shares the promised gift (Acts 1:8) in a special way, but different nevertheless from that of Jesus.[226] The distinctive nature of Stephen's fullness of the Spirit must be seen in relation to σοφία (see point e below).

Stephen is also described as being "full of faith" (6:5). The concept of πίστις is reiterated in 6:7; however, the theme is not applied again to Stephen. But, note the very similar description of Barnabas: . . . ἦν ἀνὴρ ἀγαθὸς καὶ πλήρης πνεύματος ἁγίου καὶ πίστεως (11:24) and Stephen: ἄνδρα πλήρη πίστεως καὶ πνεύματος ἁγίου (6:5). These facts lead one to the conclusion that once again the writer intends to stress his character's orthodoxy. He is very much like Barnabas, the envoy of the Jerusalem Church on the one hand, and on the other he is fully a member of "the faith" (its meaning in 6:7 and often in Acts).

c) Full of Grace and Power (6:8)

The term χάρις should no doubt be explained in terms of

---

and Sources of Stephen's Thought," pp. 78-97, who presents Acts 7 as aberrant Christian thought. See below for a discussion of Stephen (in the view of the author of Acts) as a representative of the whole community, as the "one" Chrisitan interpreter of Jewish history.

226See Conzelmann, Theology, p. 180 and n. 1 (a presentation of C.K. Barrett's position as well as a further elaboration of the problem); Eduard Schweizer, "πνεῦμα," TDNT 6:404-6.

its use in Acts 2:47, where it is said of the believers ἔχοντες χάριν πρὸς ὅλον τὸν λαόν (see also 4:33). This is further indicated since the term is applied to Stephen's activity ἐν τῷ λαῷ (6:8). Added consideration is therefore supplied by its occurrence twice in the discourse: of Joseph (7:10) and David (v.46). The term δύναμις is explained in relation to the following reference to "wonders and signs" being performed and is particularly clarified by its use in relation to Jesus (2:22; 10:38), to the promised Spirit (1:8), to Philip (8:13), and to Paul (19:11). The achievements of Stephen, the author insists, are analogous to those performed both by the representatives of Christianity and by those of Judaism (especially Moses, 7:36).

d) Worker of Wonders and Signs

It has already been pointed out above that the "performing of wonders and signs" (v.8) is related to the concept of δύναμις in Acts. However, the combination "wonders and signs," although not infrequent in the NT (Mt, Mk, and Jn once, Acts nine occurrences, four times in the Pauline corpus--omitted by Luke), appears only in Acts with the verb ποιέω (2:22; 6:8; 7:36; and 15:12), as it does in the author's OT source. Further, only in Acts, to my knowledge, does the word order "wonders and signs" occur (2:19, 43; 6:8; 7:36). I suspect the author is employing old tradition, related nevertheless to the OT.

e) The Wisdom of Stephen

The term σοφία appears in the list of qualifications of 6:3 and is therefore applied to all the Seven. However, it should be noted that in Acts the term appears only four times, 6:3; 6:10 (of Stephen's eloquence); 7:10 (of Joseph); and 7:22 (of Moses), all within the Stephen story. The word occurs several times in the Synoptics, several passages of which furnish interesting background. Mk 6:2[227] speaks of wisdom being given to Jesus and works of power (δύναμις) being performed by him (see Acts 7:10, "he gave [Joseph] grace and wisdom," for the former and Acts 6:8 for the latter). The Q passage concerning the wisdom of Solomon (Mt 12:42 and Lk 11:31) relates to Acts 7:22 ("Moses was instructed in all the wisdom of the

---

[227]See the slightly modified parallel of Mt 13:54. Luke does not record the saying.

Egyptians"), while Luke 2:40 (the child Jesus was "filled with wisdom and the grace of God was upon him," see also 2:52) provides by far the best analogue for Acts 6:3 ("full of the Spirit and wisdom"). Reference has been made to Lk 21:15 and its relation to Acts 6:10 (see pp. 284-85). As mentioned, the best parallels in the Third Gospel are found in the infancy narratives and in Lukan additions (L material).

The key text to an understanding of Stephen's role in Acts is 6:10, where relying upon Mk 13:11 and Lk 21:15, the author presents his main character as possessing the knowledge of God's purpose and the power to understand the mysteries of his counsel (6:10; 7:25, 51-53, 55-56).

The concept of σοφία then requires more attention. Wisdom (interpretation) is a gift from God[228] as Joseph tells Pharaoh (Gn 41:16 and 38--Joseph has the πνεῦμα θεοῦ ἐν αὐτῷ). This wisdom is communicated by the laying on of hands (see Dt 34:9 where Moses lays his hands upon Joshua whereby Ἰησοῦς . . . ἐνεπλήσθη πνεύματος συνέσεως).[229] The influence of this last text upon Acts 6:7 and of Dt 34:10-12 upon the Stephen speech leads one to suspect its influence upon the author's description of Stephen as one filled with wisdom and the Spirit. It is also probable that the connection between those gifts and the laying on of hands by the Twelve is not lost upon the author of Acts.

Contemporary thought, however, has doubtless played an important role in the characterization of Stephen. As Wilckens has pointed out, for Josephus ". . . as for the Rabb . . . , wisdom is the content of the Torah."[230] This concept is important for an understanding of Stephen's role within Acts 6:1-8:4. In addition, the apocalyptic text Eth En 63.2 speaks of God as "the Lord of glory and the Lord of wisdom" and further (51.3) associates this gift to the Son of Man: "In those days the chosen one will sit on my throne and all the secrets of wisdom

---

[228]See Georg Fohrer, "σοφία" *TDNT*, 7:493.

[229]Note that while the LXX uses σύνεσις for Dt 34:9, representing חכמה, Origen's Alios column employs σοφία, a common term in the LXX for חכמה.

[230]"Σοφία," *TDNT*, 7:502. Wilckens refers to *Ant*. 18.82 and 20.264.

will come from the thoughts of his mouth, for the Lord of spirits has granted it to him and glorified him."[231] The association in this text of wisdom and glory, as well as the Son of Man and glorification, can hardly be less striking than the similar association of themes in Acts 6:1-8:4.

The concept of Stephen speaking with wisdom and the Spirit (6:10) finds a close analogue to that of the teachers and interpreters of the Qumran community (see 1QS 9.16-19; CD 6.11; 4QFlor 2.3; 1QpHab 7.4-5; etc.), who through God's Spirit have achieved an inner vision, heard God's secrets, and witnessed the splendor of His glory (see especially 1 QH 11.27-12.13). The communication of the Spirit and wisdom/knowledge gives understanding of the Law. In like manner, the author of Acts not only presents Stephen as an irresistible debator but more especially as the principal interpreter of Jewish history (note that he also makes Philip, one of the Seven, an unparalleled expositor of scripture, 8:32-35).[232] Acts 7 is in essence the revelation of God's purpose by the one who possessed the wisdom and Spirit of God.

Finally, it is hardly accidental that *Pseudo-Jonathan* in its presentation of both Joseph (Gn 41:43) and Moses (Ex 2:12) should characterize them, as does the Stephen speech, as having wisdom (חכמתא).[233] Contemporary Jewish thought then played a significant part in the particular formulation of Stephen's role vis-à-vis the historical figures of Hebrew history.

The author, therefore, uses a variety of epithets to describe the different functions Stephen is made to fulfill in the episode. His eloquence, power, faith, grace, and Spirit permeate the episode entirely. It is the speech and Stephen's role as interpreter, however, which is the pivotal point of Acts 6:1-8:4. He possesses the gift of interpretation, like

---

[231]Both references and quotations are taken from Wilckens, *ibid*., p. 504 and n. 267.

[232]On the interpretation of Pseudo-Jonathan, Gn 41:43, see John Bowker, *The Targums and Rabbinic Literature: An Introduction to Jewish Interpretations of Scripture* (Cambridge: Cambridge University Press, 1969), pp. 254-55.

[233]On Stephen and the Seven as expositors of the Scriptures, see Glombitza, "Zur Characterisierung," pp. 243-44.

Joseph (7:10),[234] and like Moses himself he has received the "living words" (v.38) and the wisdom from God to understand. Contrary to the Hebrew(s) of old (vv.25 and 35f.), Stephen has understood (συνίημι--see the negative contrast of v.25) the salvation from God. The speech itself is proof of wisdom par excellence.

Since various aspects of the speech and its interpretation have been dealt with at length in chapters two, three, and four, it should now be sufficiently clear that the discourse is the central part of the entire Stephen episode. The speaker has been presented to the audience and readers of Acts as the one best qualified to speak of God's plan and its interpretation.

In conclusion it should be noted that the author of Acts pursues still further the characterization of the central actor of the episode. Stephen, like the Servant Jesus (Acts 3:13 = Is 52:13), understands and so is permitted to see the Glory of God and Jesus Himself.[235] Drawing further upon Is 52:14, the author describes Stephen's transfigured face (6:15) and the

---

[234]Not only has the author made generous use of the Joseph episode (Gn 41-42) for the composition of 7:10-12 but has probably modeled the structure of Acts 6:3-6 upon that of Gn 41:33. It should also be noted that Josephus (Ant. 2.87) in reporting the reaction of Pharaoh to the interpretation given by Joseph (Gn 41:24-33) states: θαυμάσαντος δὲ τοῦ βασιλέως τὴν φρόνησιν καὶ τὴν σοφίαν τοῦ Ἰωσήπου. . . . The wisdom of Joseph, then, is not an invention or addition unique to the author of Acts.

[235]In Acts 3:13, ὁ θεὸς Ἀβραὰμ καὶ ὁ θεὸς Ἰσαὰκ καὶ ὁ θεὸς Ἰακώβ, ὁ θεὸς τῶν πατέρων ἡμῶν, ἐδόξασεν τὸν παῖδα αὐτοῦ Ἰησοῦν, ὃν ὑμεῖς μὲν παρεδώκατε καὶ ἠρνήσασθε . . . , the author cites freely from Is 52:13, Ἰδοὺ συνήσει ὁ παῖς μου καὶ ὑψωθήσεται καὶ δοξασθήσεται σφόδρα. Stephen is not glorified but allowed to see the Glory of God. In fact the author makes this connection even clearer when he says: "The God of glory appeared . . ." (7:2). A further indication of the writer's intention is the "intrusive" verse which he has added to the biblical story of Moses' visit with his brethren, v.25: "he thought the brothers would understand (συνίεναι) . . . salvation . . . but they did not understand (οἱ δὲ οὐ συνῆκαν)." The double use of συνίημι in a positive/negative contrast is significant. At the same time the nonunderstanding of the Hebrews (the author uses the plural even in the episode dealing with the one malfactor) is in clear contrast to the wisdom of Stephen, who understands the design of God. The author consistent with his own view that Jesus is the Servant (παῖς 3:13; 4:27, 30), reserves for the disciple a vision of the glorified

subsequent vision of the Son of Man (7:55-56).[236] Like his master, he is led to death because of the ἀνομία[237] of the people (Is 53:8 and Acts 7:57-58).[238] Stephen's role in presenting the true meaning of Jewish history is further emphasized by his having introduced, as did Moses (Acts 7:37), the Prophet to come (Dt 18:15), the one called Δίκαιος (see Pseudo-Jonathan: Dt 18:14 and Is 53:11).[239]

The Stephen story, narrative and discourse, finds its place in Acts at an important juncture of the Church's growth. In the midst of debate and threats, the author allows the action of his narrative to pause for an instant. He permits himself a serious definitive review of Israel's history. The wisdom and Spirit of God, Stephen concludes, finds Judaism wanting and so the mission is launched beyond Jerusalem, only to end in Rome, the goal of the initial command: λήμψεσθε δύναμιν ἐπελθόντος τοῦ ἁγίου πνεύματος ἐφ' ὑμᾶς, καὶ ἔσεσθέ μου μάρτυρες ἔν τε Ἰερουσαλὴμ καὶ ἐν πάσῃ τῇ Ἰουδαίᾳ καὶ Σαμαρείᾳ καὶ ἕως ἐσχάτου τῆς γῆς (Acts 1:8).

Servant.

236Is 52:14 . . . οὕτως ἀδοξήσει ἀπὸ ἀνθρώπων τὸ εἶδός σου καὶ ἡ δόξα σου ἀπὸ τῶν ἀνθρώπων is clearly problematic since it diverges markedly from the MT (including 1QIsa[b]): כן-משחת מאיש מראהו ותארו מבני אדם. Nevertheless, the text seems to grant scope, especially in relation to Is 52:13, for transfiguration imagery in relation to a heavenly vision of the Son of Man (note the איש in the first Hebrew colon as a parallel to the בני אדם of the second.

237Knowing the author's detailed fidelity to his OT model, I do not exclude the influence of ἀπὸ τῶν ἀνομιῶν τοῦ λαοῦ μου upon 7:53: ἐλάβετε τὸν νόμον ... καὶ οὐκ ἐφυλάξατε.

238Is 53:9 states that "he did no evil nor deceit with his mouth" (see 6:10).

239The striking combination of themes (prophet like Moses involving Dt 18:15, 18 and the Just One) in Pseudo-Jonathan and Acts (3:14, 22 and 7:37, 52) is another indication of the strong influence which Jewish thought had upon the author of Acts. Further, the reference to the Just One in Is 53:11 is often recognized by scholars as being the source of that title for Jesus in Acts (see among others Lindars, Apologetics, pp. 20 and 79).

CHAPTER V

Concluding Summary

Having presented in considerable detail the data available for an analysis of the Stephen story, Acts 6:1-8:4, I would now like to summarize the overall conclusions of this study. To this end, a chapter by chapter review seems most appropriate.

Chapter 1

The survey of the literature pertinent to this study consisted of an examination of three areas: a general, brief history of Acts research; a review of scholarship devoted to the speeches of Acts; and, finally, a presentation of the broad spectrum of opinions regarding various aspects of Acts 6:1-8:4 and related topics.

1) Beginning with "the awakening historical criticism" of the eighteenth century (p. 2), the quest for a better understanding of the author's source-material and personal contribution continues to the present. While the preoccupation with sources was predominant at the end of the nineteenth and beginning of the twentieth century (pp. 4-5), the inquiry into the author's "tendency" or theology has been most noticeable in recent scholarship (pp. 5-6). The latter clearly represents the prevalent attitude of contemporary research in its approach to Acts, although greater attention lately has been directed to the author's source-material (pp. 6-8).

2) The scholarship devoted to the Stephen material has been greatly conditioned by the history of Acts research. On the one hand, the overriding concern for historicity dominated early investigations (pp. 14-16), only to decrease in the wake of source and form studies (pp. 16-17). In recent research a similar historical concern has emerged once more as a central issue in the study of Acts and, more particularly, of the

Stephen episode. This preoccupation is especially manifest in the attitudes adopted by scholars, that is, whether they believe the author or his sources are reliable or whether they consider the biblical narrative as factually tendentious or untrustworthy, at best. In light of this, studies devoted to the many problems encountered in the Stephen story show considerable diversity (pp. 27-31). On the other hand, research has intensified its investigation of the author's method of composition, both in the examination of source-materials (pp. 17-19) and techniques of compilation, editing or redaction (pp. 19-26). In this regard, scholars tend to lend an increasing amount of freedom to the author in the production of Acts 6:1-8:4.

Chapter 2

Owing to the great diversity of opinion regarding all aspects of the Stephen story, it was necessary to investigate the data from a new point of view. Since the speech is, in effect, a history of Israel, a detailed analysis of its episodes and their relation to the OT narrative was presented. The obvious methodology for such an investigation was a synoptic comparison between the LXX text and that of Acts 7:2-53. This approach allowed for a philological as well as a thematic study of the discourse and its alleged sources.

There are several purposes to this research. Since a scholarly consensus regarding the composition and origin (pp. 20-26; 248-54), as well as the meaning and purpose (pp. 27-28), of the speech is conspicuously lacking, I thought that I should investigate the degree of originality which belonged to the author of the text. To that end considerable attention was given to the exact relation between the historical narrative of the OT and that of Acts. It was necessary, on many occasions, to examine at length a number of biblical passages to determine as closely as possible the author's real source. On other occasions the influence of LXX idiom required attention. The goal was to observe the writer's attitude, approach, and use of OT materials, whether quotations or themes. Both his fidelity to his model and his originality were described by this investigation.

This particular method also allowed for an analysis of the

author's quoting process. For each section of the speech, it was possible to trace this process with considerable probability. His choice of quotations, themes, and episodes was closely linked to his OT model.

The results of this study have emphasized the fidelity of the writer to his sources, his concern for detail and accuracy, his preservation and imitation of LXX idiom, and his considerable familiarity with the OT narrative. These characteristics, amply illustrated in the sections of the study titled "Quoting Process," served as the basis for a reevaluation of the author's method of composition in chapter four.

As the investigation progressed, a large variety of stylistic data emerged which suggested additional research. Clearly the occurrence throughout the speech of repetitive techniques, contrasting episodes and terms, structural patterns, and a diversity of redactional tendencies required further study. These considerations led to the insights of chapter three.

In light of the conclusions stated above, it became clear that the Stephen speech, like other histories of Israel, was the product of a conscious literary process whereby a given writer, with a very specific goal in mind, set out to present the Jewish past to his audience. Beyond that, however, it was concluded that Acts 7 was an independent composition whose purpose was to be sought in the editing and quoting process which occurred in the course of redaction.

Chapter 3

A systematic investigation of the stylistic data was the logical consequence of the examination of the quoting process. Throughout chapter two it became increasingly evident that the stylistic and structural factors were germane to the study of the author's method of composition. These elements were particularly accentuated by the obvious modifications which he imposed upon the OT narrative.

The result of this research was a lengthy stylistic corpus (pp. 158-80), presented under descriptive headings: grammatical, lexical, and pattern-related categories. The distribution and frequency of these further suggested the examination of their nature and function. This was done in relation to the various sections of the speech. The use of cognate expressions, structural and thematic contrasts, inclusio, parallelismus membrorum, etc., betrayed serious literary activity on the part of the author. This conclusion was particularly underscored by an examination of the stylistic data and their relation to the OT model (pp. 206-14). In very few cases can it be said that the structural or stylistic features of the speech owe to the quoting process. Numerous elements are borrowed from the OT model, but, invariably, the ordering of these features into some architectonic framework owes to the activity of the writer of the speech (p. 214). Furthermore, the organization of the discourse and its purpose are intimately related to the functional nature of the stylistic data. The large variety of themes, the episodes, and personalities presented in 7:2-53 are adroitly presented with a didactic survey of Israelite history by means of sophisticated literary techniques and stylistic patterns.

By extension, the same method of analysis was applied to the introductory (pp. 215-23) and concluding (pp. 224-31) narratives. The distribution and nature of the data pointed to common authorship, since similar organizational patterns and stylistic features played in these narratives a role analogous to that observed in the discourse. The overriding conclusion drawn from the analysis of both speech and narrative is that the structural composition and literary features of Acts 6:1-8:4 owe to a common author.

Finally, an examination of the relation between the narratives and the speech (pp. 231-42), as viewed in light of the stylistic corpus, disclosed a variety of interconnections between the different parts of the Stephen episode. The manifest use of familiar patterns and techniques to express these interrelations leads to the same conclusion, namely, that a single author has composed these units for a structural purpose and has not simply combined disparate sources. Whether relations or contrasts posited between Stephen and prominent figures of Jewish history or between various themes within the episode, they are clearly composed in view of their structural disposition. Lastly, the figure of Stephen gives to Acts 6:1-8:4 its overall cohesiveness.

Chapter 4

This part of the study was devoted to the question of redaction. To that end the first section of the chapter examined briefly the major theories regarding the composition of Acts 6:1-8:4. Characteristic of the uncertainty of contemporary scholarship regarding the Stephen story is its contradictory views of the speech: total composition by the author, editing of a neutral history, or total dependence upon tradition (pp. 249-54). Analyses of the narrative agree in only one aspect, i.e., granting considerable freedom to the author in composing the trial and death scenes (pp. 245-48).

A second part of the chapter directed its attention to a reinvestigation of redaction, first of the speech, then of the narratives. In light of the data furnished by chapters two and three, it was necessary to compare Acts 7 to other speeches of the work. The results of this examination were most revealing. From structural, stylistic, and thematic points of view, the relation between the various discourses indicated common authorship. Further comparison with the Pauline speeches (13 and 22) manifest similarity of audience, purpose, and setting. Analysis of Acts 7 (its structure, setting, and purpose) has led to several important conclusions: 1) It is an original history of Israel written on the basis of the LXX narrative, but within the Jewish literary tradition of "histories of Israel." 2) The discourse is a creation of the author of Acts, as are the other speeches, and is strategically situated to underscore, introduce, and interprete the variety of aims envisaged by its writer. 3) Acts 7, as in the classical and Jewish historical tradition, represents the speech "most apropos" for the central character of the episode, Stephen (p. 267).

Investigation of the narratives exhibited the same combination of factors noted in the speech, namely, considerable dependence upon tradition for the data of the text, but notable structural and stylistic restatement. An examination of the trial and death (accusations, transfiguration/vision, and final words of Stephen), as well as the Saul tradition, indicated the use of older material within a new architectural setting (pp. 306-09).

The final section investigated the purpose of the author

in composing the Stephen story. The principal concern of the inquiry was the functional role which the episode and its various parts played within the book of Acts. Both speech and narrative components revealed significant structural relations to one another and to the surrounding episodes of the Jerusalem and dispersion/missionary period of the first part of Acts. The trial, speech, and death of 6-8 represent the first of a double block of material introduced by Acts 6:1-7 (the second being the Philip story 8:5-41). At the same time, the Stephen episode constitutes the first turning away from Judaism (on an ideational level), while the Philip episode represents the actual departure from the Holy City.

The structural analysis of Acts 6:1-8:4 and the correlation of the data amassed in chapters two and three have suggested considerable reinterpretation of the principal motifs of the Stephen episode. The author's positive/negative evaluation of Judaism (pp. 319-30), his presentation of God's plan in terms of divine and human participation within history (pp. 330-38), and his estimation of the early Christian community's role in the spreading of God's word (pp. 338-46) are to be viewed in relation to the characterization, activity, and function of Stephen. Among the various personalities presented throughout Acts, Stephen represents for the author--and surely for the early Church--the interpreter par excellence of God's promise to man, beginning with Abraham, proceeding through Hebrew history to the coming of the Just One. The dynamic nature of salvation and its renunciation by the Fathers lead to persecution and dispersion, and, therefore, usher in a new historical period. The nonunderstanding of the Hebrews (7:25) inevitably announces the new wisdom and understanding of the real descendants of Abraham. Stephen exemplifies, therefore, the true heir of the promise, the genuine interpreter of the law, the one who has found favor with God and has seen his Glory (pp. 346-52).

The Stephen story is an integral part of the book of Acts, providing scope for the author's vision of early Christianity and its relation to its cultural milieu. Judaism is not a negative past that Christianity has discarded but rather its source and inspiration. Through the figure of Stephen the early community reviews its Jewish background. Through his wisdom and the Spirit it understands that the salvation given by God cannot be hindered, and eventually realizes that it cannot be limited to any "place."

BIBLIOGRAPHY

Books

Aland, Kurt; Black, Matthew; Metzger, Bruce M. and Wikgren, Allen, eds. *The Greek New Testament*. New York: American Bible Society, 1966.

Apophoreta: Festschrift für Ernst Haenchen: Zu seinem siebzeten Geburtstag am 10. Dezember 1964. Beiheft zur Zeitschrift für die neutestamentliche Wissenschaft und die Kunde der älteren Kirche, no. 30. Berlin: Töpelmann, 1964.

Arndt, William F. and Gingrich, F. Wilbur, eds. *A Greek-English Lexicon of the New Testament and Other Early Christian Literature*. 4th rev. and aug. ed., 1952. Chicago: University of Chicago Press, 1974.

Aspects du Judéo-Christianisme. Colloque de Strasbourg, 23-25 avril 1964. Paris: P.U.F., 1965.

Bammel, Ernst, ed. *The Trial of Jesus: Cambridge Studies in Honour of C.F.D. Moule*. London: SCM Press, 1970.

Barrett, Charles K. *Luke the Historian in Recent Study*. Facet Books. Philadelphia: Fortress Press, 1970.

_______. *New Testament Essays*. London: S.P.C.K., 1972.

Betz, Otto; Hengel, Martin; and Schmidt, Peter, eds. *Abraham unser Vater: Juden und Christen in Gespräch über die Bibel: Festschrift für Otto Michel zum 60. Geburtstag*. Leiden: Brill, 1963.

Biblical and Semitic Studies: Critical and Historical Essays by the Members of the Semitic and Biblical Faculty of Yale University. New York: Scribner's, 1901.

Bieder, Werner. *Die Apostelgeschicte in der Historie: Ein Beitrag zur Auslegungsgeschichte des Missionsbuches des Kirche*. Zurich: EVZ-Verlag, 1960.

Bihler, Johannes. *Die Stephanusgeschichte im zusammenhang der Apostelgeschichte*. Münchener theologische Studien, 1. Historische Abteilhung, no. 30. Munich: M. Hueber, 1963.

Black, Matthew. *An Aramaic Approach to the Gospels and Acts*. 3d ed. Oxford: Clarendon Press, 1967.

Black, Matthew and Smalley, W.A., eds. On Language, Culture, and Religion: In Honor of Eugene A. Nida. The Hague/Paris: Mouton, 1974.

Black, Matthew and Rowley, Harold H., eds. Peake's Commentary on the Bible. London: Nelson and Sons, 1963.

Blass, Friedrich W. and Debrunner, Albert. A Greek Grammar of the New Testament and Other Early Christian Literature. Translated and revised by Robert W. Funk. Chicago: University of Chicago Press, 1961.

Blinzler, Joseph. Der Prozess Jesu. 3d ed. Regensburg: Verlag Friedrich Pustet, 1960.

Bornhäuser, Karl B. Studien zur Apostelgeschichte. Gütersloh: Bertelsmann, 1934.

Borsch, Frederick H. The Son of Man in Myth and History. Philadelphia: Westminster Press, 1967.

Bowker, John. The Targums and Rabbinic Literature: An Introduction to Jewish Interpretations of Scripture. Cambridge: Cambridge University Press, 1969.

Brock, S.P.; Fritsch, C.T.; and Jellicoe, Sidney. A Classified Bibliography of the Septaugint. Leiden: Brill, 1973.

Brooke, Alan E. and McLean, Norman, eds. The Old Testament in Greek according to the Text of Codex Vaticanus, Supplemented from Other Uncial Manuscripts, with a Critical Apparatus Containing the Variants of the Chief Ancient Authorities for the Text of the Septaugint. Vol. 1: The Octateuch. Cambridge: Cambridge University Press, 1906.

Brown, Francis; Driver, Samuel R.; and Briggs, Charles A., eds. A Hebrew and English Lexicon of the Old Testament. Oxford: Clarendon Press, 1968.

Brown, Raymond E. The Gospel according to John: Introduction, Translation, and Notes. The Anchor Bible. 2 vols. Garden City, New York: Doubleday, 1966-70.

Brown, Raymond E.; Fitzmyer, Joseph A.; and Murphy, Roland E., eds. 2 vols. The Jerome Biblical Commentary. Englewood Cliffs, New Jersey: Prentice-Hall, 1968.

Brown, Schuyler. Apostasy and Perseverance in the Theology of Luke. Analecta Biblica, no. 36. Rome: Pontifical Institute, 1969.

Bruce, Frederick F. The Acts of the Apostles. London: Tyndale Press, 1953.

_____. Commentary on the Book of the Acts: The English Text with Introduction, Exposition and Notes. Grand Rapids, Mich.: Eerdmans, 1956.

______. The Speeches in the Acts of the Apostles. London: Tyndale Press, [1943].

Cadbury, Henry J. The Book of Acts in History. New York: Harper/London: Adam and Charles Black, 1955.

______. The Making of Luke-Acts. New York: Macmillan Co., 1927; reprint, London: S.P.C.K., 1961.

Cerfaux, Lucien and Dupont, Jacques. Les Actes des Apôtres. La Sainte Bible, traduite en français sous la direction de l'Ecole biblique de Jérusalem. Paris: Editions du Cerf, 1953.

Charles, Robert H. The Apocrypha and Pseudepigrapha of the Old Testament. 2 vols. Oxford: Clarendon Press, 1913.

Clark, Albert C. The Acts of the Apostles: A Critical Edition with Introduction and Notes on Selected Passages. Oxford: Clarendon Press, 1933; reprint, 1970.

Conzelmann, Hans. Die Apostelgeschichte. Handbuch zum Neuen Testament, no. 7. 2d ed. Tübingen: Mohr, 1972.

______. The Theology of St. Luke. Translated by Geoffrey Buswell. New York: Harper and Row, 1961.

Cross, Frank M. The Ancient Library of Qumran and Modern Biblical Studies. The Haskell Lectures, 1956-57. Garden City, N.Y.: Doubleday, 1958.

Dalman, Gustaf. The Words of Jesus. Translated by D.M. Kay. Edinburgh: Clarke, 1902.

Daube, David. The New Testament and Rabbinic Judaism. London: Athlone Press, University of London, 1956.

Davies, William D. and Daube, David, eds. The Background of the New Testament and Its Eschatology: In Honour of C.H. Dodd. Cambridge: Cambridge University Press, 1956.

Descamps, Albert and de Halleux, André, eds. Mélanges bibliques en hommage au R.P. Béda Rigaux. [Gembloux]: Duculot, 1970.

Dibelius, Martin. Studies in the Acts of the Apostles. Edited by Heinrich Greeven. Translated by Mary Ling. New York: Scribner's, 1956 and London: SCM Press, 1966.

Dodd, Charles H. According to the Scriptures. London: Nisbet, 1952.

______. The Apostolic Preaching and Its Developments: Three Lectures with an Appendix on Eschatology and History. London: Hodder and Stoughton, 1936; reprint ed., New York: Harper, [1960].

Dupont, Jacques. Les sources du Livre des Actes: état de la question. [Bruges]: Desclée de Brouwer, [1960]. [English translation: The Sources of the Acts. Translated by Kathleen Pond. New York: Herder and Herder, (1964).]

Duterme, Georges. "Le Vocabulaire du Discours d'Etienne AA. VII.2-53." Licence en Théologie thesis, University of Louvain, [1950].

Easton, Burton S. Early Christianity: The Purpose of Acts and Other Papers. Edited by Frederick C. Grant. London: S.P.C.K., 1955.

Ehrhardt, Arnold. The Acts of the Apostles: Ten Lectures. Manchester: Manchester University Press, 1969.

Ellis, E. Earle and Wilcox, Max, eds. Neotestamentica et Semitica: Studies in Honour of Matthew Black. Edinburgh: Clarke, 1969.

Epp, Eldon J. The Theological Tendency of Codex Bezae Cantabrigiensis in Acts. Society for New Testament Studies, Monograph Series, no. 3. Cambridge: Cambridge University Press, 1966.

Feine, Paul. Eine vorkanonische Uberlieferung des Lukas. Gotha: Friedrich Andreas Perthes, 1891.

Field, Frederick. Origenis hexaplorum quae supersunt: sive veterum interpretum graecorun in totum vetus testamentum fragmente. 2 vols. Oxford: Clarendon Press, 1875.

Fitzmyer, Joseph A. Essays on the Semitic Background of the New Testament. London: Geoffrey Chapman, 1971.

________. The Genesis Apocryphon of Qumran Cave 1: A Commentary. Biblica et Orientalia, no. 18A. 2d rev. ed. Rome: Biblical Institute Press, 1971.

Flender, Helmut. St. Luke: Theologian of Redemptive History. Translated by Reginald H. and Ilse Fuller. Philadelphia: Fortress Press, 1967.

Foakes Jackson, Frederick J. The Acts of the Apostles. The Moffatt New Testament Commentary. London: Hodder and Stoughton, 1931.

Foakes Jackson, Frederick J., and Lake, Kirsopp, gen. eds. The Acts of the Apostles. The Beginnings of Christianity, part 1. 5 vols. London: Macmillan & Co., 1920-33. Vol. 1: Prolegomena I: The Jewish, Gentile Background, gen. eds. (1920). Vol. 2: Prolegomena II: Criticism, gen. eds. (1922). Vol. 3: The Text of Acts, by James H. Ropes (1926). Vol. 4: English Translation and Commentary, by Kirsopp Lake and Henry J. Cadbury (1933). Vol. 5: Additional Notes to the Commentary. eds. Kirsopp Lake and Henry J. Cadbury (1933).

Fuller, Reginald H. The New Testament in Current Study. London: SCM Press, 1962; New York: Scribner's, 1962.

Gärtner, Bertil. The Areopagus Speech and Natural Revelation. Acta Seminarii Neotestamentici Upsaliensis, no. 21. Uppsala: C.W.K. Gleerup, 1955.

Gasque, W. Ward and Martin, Ralph P., eds. Apostolic History and the Gospel: Biblical and Historical Essays Presented to F.F. Bruce on His 60th Birthday. Exeter Devon: Paternoster Press, 1970.

Gaston, Lloyd. No Stone on Another: Studies in the Significance of the Fall of Jerusalem in the Synoptic Gospels. Supplements to Novum Testamentum, no. 23. Leiden: Brill, 1970.

Ginsburger, Moses. Pseudo-Jonathan (Thargum Jonathan ben Usiel zum Pentateuch) nach der Londoner Handschrift. Berlin: Calvary, 1903; reprinted ed., Jerusalem: Makor, 1974.

Goguel, Maurice. The Birth of Christianity. Translated by H.C. Snape. London: Allen and Unwin, 1933 and New York: Macmillan Co., 1954.

Goulder, M. D. Type and History in Acts. London: S.P.C.K., 1964.

Grant, Michael. The Ancient Historians. New York: Scribner's, 1970.

Grossouw, William. The Coptic Versions of the Minor Prophets: A Contribution to the Study of the Septaugint. Monumenta biblica et ecclesiastica, no. 3. Rome: Pontifical Biblical Institute, 1938.

Guignebert, Charles. Le Christ: l'évolution de l'humanité. Synthèse collective, no. 29. Paris: Albin Michel, 1943.

Guillaumont, A.; Puech, H.-Ch.; Quispel, G.; Till, W.; and Yassah 'Abd al Masīḥ, eds. The Gospel according to Thomas: Coptic Text Established and Translated. Leiden: Brill/New York: Harper, 1959.

Haenchen, Ernst. The Acts of the Apostles: A Commentary. Translated by Robert McL. Wilson. Philadelphia: Westminster Press, 1971.

Hahn, Ferdinand. Mission in the New Testament. Studies in the New Testament, no. 47. Naperville, Ill.: Allenson, 1965.

Hanson, Richard P. C. The Acts in the Revised Standard Version with Introduction and Commentary. Oxford: Clarendon Press, 1967.

Hare, Douglas R. A. The Theme of Jewish Persecution of Christians in the Gospel according to St. Matthew. Cambridge: Cambridge University Press, 1967.

Harnack, Adolf von. New Testament Studies. Part 3: The Acts of the Apostles. London: Williams and Norgate, 1909.

Harrop, Clayton K. "The Influence of the Thought of Stephen upon the Epistle to the Hebrews." Ph.D. dissertation, Southern Baptist Seminary, Louisville, Kentucky, 1955.

Hawthorn, J. R. Rome and Jugurtha. London: Macmillan & Co./ St. Martin's Press, 1969.

Hay, David M. Glory at the Right Hand: Psalm 110 in Early Christianity. Society of Biblical Literature, Monograph Series, no. 18. Nashville: Published for the Society of Biblical Literature by Abingdon Press, [1973].

Hengel, Martin. Judaism and Hellenism: Studies in Their Encounter in Palestine during the Early Hellenistic Period. 2 vols. Translated by John Bowden. Philadelphia: Fortress Press, 1974.

Higgins, Angus J. B. Jesus and the Son of Man. Philadelphia: Fortress Press, 1964.

_______, ed. New Testament Essays: Studies in Memory of T.W. Manson 1893-1938. [Manchester]: Manchester University Press, [1959].

Holtz, Traugott. Untersuchungen über die alttestamentlichen Zitate bei Lukas. Texte und Untersuchungen zur Geschichte der altchristlichen Literature, no. 104. Berlin: Akademie -Verlag, 1968.

Jacquier, Eugène. Les Actes des Apôtres. Etudes bibliques. Paris: J. Gabalda, 1926.

Jeremias, Joachim. New Testament Theology: The Proclamation of Jesus. Translated by John Bowden. New York: Scribner's, 1971.

Jervell, Jacob. Luke and the People of God: A New Look at Luke-Acts. Minneapolis: Augsburg Publishing House, 1972.

Jones, Arnold H. M. The Cities of the Eastern Roman Provinces. 2d ed. Oxford: Clarendon Press, 1971.

Kahle, Paul. The Cairo Geniza. Schweich Lectures. London: Oxford University Press, 1947.

Käsemann, Ernst. Essays on New Testament Themes. Studies in Biblical Theology, no. 41. Translated by W.J. Montague. Naperville, Ill.: Allenson, [1964].

Kasser, Rudolf, ed. Papyrus Bodmer XVII: Actes des Apôtres, Epitres de Jacques, Pierre, Jean et Jude. Cologny-Genève: Bibliotheca Bodmeriane, 1961.

Keck, Leander E. and Martyn, J. Louis, eds. Studies in Luke-Acts: Essays in Honor of Paul Schubert. Nashville: Abingdon Press, [1966].

Kittel, Gerhard and Friedrich, Gerhard, gen. eds. Theological Dictionary of the New Testament. 9 vols. Translated and edited by Geoffrey W. Bromiley. Grand Rapids, Mich.: Eerdmans, 1964-74.

Kittel, Rudolf, gen. ed. Biblia hebraica. Stuttgart: Württemborgische Bibelanstalt, 1966.

Knox, Wilfred L. The Acts of the Apostles. Cambridge: Cambridge University Press, 1948.

Kümmel, Werner G. Introduction to the New Testament. Revised Edition. Translated by Howard C. Kee. Nashville: Abingdon Press, 1975.

______. The New Testament: The History of the Investigation of Its Problems. Translated by Samuel McL. Gilmour and Howard C. Kee. Nashville: Abingdon Press, 1972.

Liddell, Henry G. and Scott, Robert, eds. A Greek-English Lexicon. Revised and Augmented by Henry S. Jones and Roderick McKenzie. Oxford: Clarendon Press, 1940; reprint ed., 1966.

Lindars, Barnabas. New Testament Apologetic: The Doctrinal Significance of Old Testament Quotations. London: SCM Press, 1961.

Loisy, Alfred. Les Actes des Apôtres. Paris: Emile Nourry, 1920.

Löning, Karl. Die Saulustradition in der Apostelgeschichte. Neutestamentliche Abhandlungen, ns, no. 9. Münster: Aschendorff, [1973].

McCullough, W. S., ed. The Seed of Wisdom: Essays in Honour of T.J. Meek. Toronto: University of Toronto Press, 1964.

Manson, William. The Epistle to the Hebrews: An Historical and Theological Reconsideration. The Baird Lecture, 1949. London: Hodder and Stoughton, 1951.

Marshall, I. Howard. Luke: Historian and Theologian. [Exeter Devon]: Paternoster Press, [1970].

Mattill, Andrew J. and Mattill, Mary B. A Classified Bibliography of Literature on the Acts of the Apostles. New Testament Tools and Studies, no. 7. Leiden: Brill, 1966.

Merk, Augustin, ed. Novum Testamentum Graece et Latine. 7th ed. Rome: Biblical Pontifical Institute, 1951.

Metzger, Bruce M. A Textual Commentary on the Greek New Testament. A Companion Volume to the United Bible Societies' Greek New Testament. London: United Bible Societies, 1971.

Milik, Jósef T. Ten Years of Discovery in the Wilderness of Judaea. Studies in Biblical Theology, no. 26. Translated by John Strugnell. Naperville, Ill.: Allenson, 1959; London: SCM Press, 1959.

Miller, Selig J. The Samaritan Molad Mosheh: Samaritan and Arabic Text Edited and Translated with Introduction and Notes. New York: Philosophical Library, 1949.

Morgenthaler, Robert. Das Zweiheitsgesetz im lukanischen Worke: Eine stilkritische Untersuchung. Zurich: Zwingli-Verlag, 1949.

__________. Die lukanische Geschichtsschreibung als Zeugnis: Gestalt und Gehalt der Kunst des Lukas. 2 vols. Zurich: Zwingli-Verlag, 1949.

Moulton, James H. and Milligan, George. The Vocabulary of the Greek Testament Illustrated from the Papyri and Other Non-literary Sources. Grand Rapids, Mich.: Eerdmans, 1930; reprint ed., 1974.

Moulton, James H., gen. ed. A Grammar of New Testament Greek. 3 vols. Edinburgh: Clark, 1908-63. Vol. 1: Prolegomena, by James H. Moulton (1908, reprint ed., 1957); Vol. 2: Accidence and Word-Formation, idem (1925). Vol. 3: Syntax by Nigel Turner (1963).

Munck, Johannes. The Acts of the Apostles: Introduction, Translation, and Notes. The Anchor Bible. Revised by William F. Albright and Charles S. Mann. Garden City, N.Y.: Doubleday, 1967.

Nestle, Erwin and Aland, Kurt, eds. Novum Testamentum Graece. 25th ed. Stuttgart: Württembergische Bibelanstalt for the American Bible Society, 1963.

Neusner, Jacob, ed. Religions in Antiquity: Essays in Memory of Erwin Ramsdall Goodenough. Leiden: Brill, 1968.

Nineham, Dennis E., ed. Studies in the Gospels: Essays in Memory of R.H. Lightfoot. Oxford: Blackwell, 1955.

Norden, Eduard. Agnostos Theos: Untersuchungen zur Formengeschichte religlöser Rede. 4th ed. Stuttgart: Teubner, 1956.

O'Neill, J. C. The Theology of Acts in Its Historical Setting. 2d rev. ed. London: S.P.C.K., 1970.

Packer, J. W. The Acts of the Apostles: Commentary. The Cambridge Bible Commentary on the New English Bible. Cambridge: Cambridge University Press, 1966.

Perrin, Norman. Rediscovering the Teaching of Jesus. New York: Harper and Row, 1967.

Pesch, Rudolf. Die Vision des Stephanus: Apg 7, 55-56 im Rahmen der Apostelgeschichte. Stuttgarter Bibelstudien, no. 12. Stuttgart: Katholisches Bibelwerk, [1966].

Plummer, Alfred. A Critical and Exegetical Commentary on the Gospel according to St. Luke. New York: Scribner's, 1896.

Preuschen, Erwin. Die Apostelgeschichte. Handbuch zum neuen Testament. Tübingen: Mohr, 1912.

Rackham, Richard B. The Acts of the Apostles: An Exposition. London: Methuen, 1957.

Rahlfs, Alfred, ed. Septauginta, id est Vetus Testamentum Graece iuxta LXX Interpretes. 3d ed. 2 vols. Stuttgart: Privilegierte Württembergische Bibelanstatt, 1949.

Reicke, Bo I. Glaube und Leben der Urgemeinde: Bemerkungen zu Apg. 1-7. Abhandlungen zur Theologie des Alten und Neuen Testaments, no. 32. Zurich: Zwingli-Verlag, 1957.

______. The New Testament Era: The World of the Bible from 500 B.C. to A.D. 100. Translated by David E. Green. Philadelphia: Fortress Press, 1968.

Renié, J. Actes des Apôtres traduits et commentés. La Sainte Bible, 11/1. Paris: Letouzey et Ané, 1951.

Rese, Martin. Alttestamentliche Motive in des Christologie des Lukas. Studien zum Neuen Testament, no. 1. [1. Aufl.]. [Gütersloh]: Gütersloher Verlagshaus G. Mohn, [1969].

Rosenthal, Franz, ed. An Aramaic Handbook. Porta Linguarum Orientalium. 2 vols. Wiesbaden: Horrassowitz, 1967.

Sahlin, Harold. Der Messias und das Gottesvolk: Studien zur protolukanischen Theologie. Acta seminarii neotestamentici upsaliensis, no. 12. Uppsala: Almquist & Wiksells, 1945.

Scharlemann, Martin H. Stephen: A Singular Saint. Analecta Biblica, no. 34. Rome: Pontifical Institute, 1968.

Schmithals, Walter. Paul and James. Studies in Biblical Theology, no. 46. Translated by Dorothea M. Barton. Naperville, Ill.: Allenson, 1965.

Schoeps, Hans-Joachim. Das Judenchristentum. Bern: A. Francke, 1964.

______. Theologie und Geschichte des Judenchristentums. Tübingen: Mohr, 1949.

______. Urgemeinde Judenschristentum Gnosis. Tübingen: Mohr, 1956.

Schumacher, Rudolf. Der Diakon Stephanus. Münster: Verlag der Aschendorffschen Buchbanlung, 1910.

Sevenster, Jan N. Do You Know Greek? How Much Greek Could the First Jewish Christians Have Known? Supplements to Novum Testamentum, no. 19. Leiden: Brill, 1969.

Sherwin-White, Nicholas. Roman Society and Roman Law in the New Testament. Oxford: Clarendon Press, 1963.

Simon, Marcel. St. Stephen and the Hellenists in the Primitive Church. The Haskell Lectures, 1956. London: Longmans, Green, [1958].

Strack, Hermann L. and Billerbeck, Paul. Kommenter zum Neuen Testament aus Talmud und Midrash. 5 vols. Munich: Beck, 1922-28. Vol. 1: Das Evangelium nach Matthaus erläutert aus Talmud und Midrash (1922). Vol. 2: Das Evangelium nach Markus, Lukas und Johannes und die Apostelgeschichte erläutert aus Talmud and Midrash (1924).

Stadter, Philip A., ed. The Speeches in Thucydides: A Collection of Original Studies with a Bibliography. Chapel Hill: University of North Carolina Press, 1973.

Surkau, Hans W. Martyrien in jüdischer und frühchristlicher Zeit. Forschungen zur Religion und Literatur des Alten und Neuen Testaments, Neue Folge, no. 36. Göttingen: Vandenhoeck & Ruprecht, 1938.

Syme, Ronald. Sallust. Sather Classical Lectures, no. 33. Los Angeles: University of California, 1969.

Talbert, Charles H. Literary Patterns, Theological Themes and the Genre of Luke-Acts. Society of Biblical Literature Monograph Series, no. 20 [Missoula, Montana]: Society of Biblical Literature and Scholars Press, 1974.

______. Luke and the Gnostics: An Examination of the Lucan Purpose. Nashville: Abingdon Press, 1966.

Tödt, Heinz E. The Son of Man in the Synoptic Tradition. The New Testament Library. Translated by D.M. Barton. London: SCM Press, 1965.

Torrey, Charles C. The Composition and Date of Acts. Harvard Theological Studies, no. 1. Cambridge: Harvard University Press, 1961; New York: Kraus Reprint, 1969.

Toynbee, Arnold J. Greek Historical Thought from Homer to the Age of Heraclius. Boston: Beacon Press, 1950.

Trocmé, Etienne. Le "Livre des Actes" et l'histoire. Etudes d'histoire et de philosophie religieuses, no. 45. Paris: P.U.F., 1957.

Vööbus, Arthur. Peschitta und Targumim des Pentateuchs, neues Licht zur Frage des Herkunft des Peschitta aus dem alt-palästinischen Targum, Handschriftstudien. Papers of the Estonian Theological Society in Exile, no. 9. Stockholm: ETSE, 1958.

Waard, Jan de. A Comparative Study of the Old Testament Text in the Dead Sea Scrolls and in the New Testament. Studies on the Texts of the Desert of Judah, no. 4. Leiden: Brill, 1965; Grand Rapids, Mich.: Eerdmans, 1966.

Walsh, P. G. Livy: His Historical Aims and Methods. Cambridge: Cambridge University Press, 1961.

Wendt, Hans H. Die Apostelgeschichte. Kritisch-exegetischer Kommentar. Part 3. Göttingen: Vandenhoeck & Ruprecht, 1899.

Wevers, John W., ed. Genesis. Vol. 1 of Septuaginta Vetus Testamentum Graecum Auctoritate Academiae Scientiarum Gottingensis Editum. Göttingen: Vandenhoeck & Ruprecht, 1974.

Wilckens, Ulrich. Die Missionsreden der Apostelgeschichte form-und traditionsgeschichliche Untersuchungen. Wissenschaftliche Monographien zum Alten und Neuen Testament, no. 5. 3d rev. ed. Neukirchen-Vluyn: Neukirchener Verlag des Erziehungsvereins GMBH, 1974.

Wilcox, Max. The Semitisms of Acts. Oxford: Clarendon Press, 1965.

Williams, Charles S. C. A Commentary on the Acts of the Apostles. Black's New Testament Commentaries. London: Adam & Charles Black, 1957.

Wilson, Jack H. "Luke's Role as a Theologian and Historian in Acts 6:1-8:3." Ph.D. dissertation, Emory University, 1962.

Wilson, Stephen G. The Gentiles and the Gentile Mission in Luke-Acts. Society for New Testament Studies Monograph Series, no. 23. Cambridge: Cambridge University Press, 1973.

Winter, Paul. On the Trial of Jesus. Studia Judaica, no. 1. Berlin: Walter de Gruyter, 1961.

Zahn, Theodor von. Die Apostelgeschichte des Lucas. Kommentar zum Neuen Testament, no. 5. Leipzig: A. Deichert, 1919.

Zehnle, Richard F. Peter's Pentecost Discourse: Tradition and Lukan Reinterpretation in Peter's Speeches of Acts 2 and 3. Society of Biblical Literature Monograph Series, no. 15. Nashville: Abingdon Press, 1971.

Zeller, Edward. The Contents and Origin of the Acts of the Apostles Critically Investigated. 2 vols. Translated by Joseph Dare. London: Williams and Norgate, 1875-76.

Ziegler, Joseph, ed. Duodecim prophetae. Vol. 13 of Septuaginta Vetus Testamentum Graecum Auctoritate Societatis Litterarum Gottingensis. Göttingen: Vanderhoeck & Ruprecht, 1943.

_______. Isaias. Vol. 14 of Septauginta Vetus Testamentum Graecum Auctoritate Societatis Litterarum Gottingensis. Göttingen: Vandenhoeck & Ruprecht, 1939.

Articles

Albright, William F. "New Light on Early Recensions of the Hebrew Bible." BASOR 140 (1955):27-33.

Argyle, Aubrey W. "The Greek of Luke and Acts." NTS 20 (1974): 441-45.

Bacon, Benjamin W. "Stephen's Speech: Its Argument and Doctrinal Content." In Biblical and Semitic Studies (see under Biblical and Semitic Studies), pp. 213-76.

Barnard, Leslie W. "Saint Stephen and Early Alexandrian Christianity." NTS 7 (1960-61):31-45.

Barrett, Charles K. "The Acts and the Origins of Christianity." In New Testament Essays (see under Barrett, Charles K.), pp. 101-15.

_______. "Stephen and the Son of Man." In Apophoreta (see under Apophoreta), pp. 32-38.

Barthélemy, Dominique. "Pourquoi la Torah a-t-elle été traduite en grec?" In On Language (see under Black, Matthew), pp. 23-41.

Benoit, Pierre. "La deuxième visite de saint Paul à Jérusalem." Bib 40 (1959):778-92.

Bertram, Georg. "στρέφω." TDNT 7:714-29.

Betz, Hans D. Review of Stephen: A Singular Saint, by Martin H. Scharlemann. Int 23 (1969):252.

Betz, Otto. "φωνή." TDNT 9:278-309.

Bayer, Hermann W. "διακονέω." TDNT 2:81-93.

Bihler, Johannes. "Der Stephanusbericht (Apg. 6.8-15 und 7.54-8.2)." BZ 31 (1959):252-70.

Borgen, Peder. "Von Paulus zu Lukas." ST 20 (1966):140-57.

Borse, Udo. "Der Rahmentext in Umkreis der Stephanusgeschichte (Apg 6,6-11, 26)." BL 14 (1973):187-204.

Bowker, John W. "Speeches in Acts: A Study in Proem and Yallammedenu Form." NTS 14 (1967-68):96-111.

Bultmann, Rudolf. "Zur Frage nach den Quellen der Apostelgeschichte." In New Testament Essays (see under Higgins, Angus J. B.), pp. 68-80.

Cadbury, Henry J. "Four Features of Lucan Style." In Studies (see under Keck, Leander E.), pp. 87-102.

______. "Lexical Notes on Luke-Acts IV. On Direct Quotation, with Some Uses of ὅτι and εἰ." JBL 48 (1929):412-25.

______. "The Relative Pronouns in Acts and Elsewhere." JBL 42 (1923):150-57.

______. "The Speeches in Acts." In Beginnings (see under Foakes Jackson, Frederick J.), 5:402-27.

Cadbury, Henry J. and the Editors [Foakes Jackson, Frederick J. and Lake, Kirsopp]. "The Greek and Jewish Traditions of Writing History." In Beginnings (see under Foakes Jackson, Frederick J.), 2:7-29.

Cerfaux, Lucien. "Citations scripturaires et tradition textuelle dans le Livre des Actes." In Recueil Lucien Cerfaux: études d'exégèse et d'histoire religieuse, 2:93-103. Edited by Lucien Cerfaux. 2 vols. Gembloux: Duculot, 1954.

Charlier, Célestin. "Le manifeste d'Etienne (Actes 7)." BVC 3 (1953):83-93.

Clarke, William K. L. "The Use of the Septuagint in Acts." In Beginnings (see under Foakes Jackson, Frederick J.), 2:66-105.

Clifton, James P. "Shaping the Kerygma: A Study of Acts." LL 10 (1973):522-30.

Colmenero Atienza, Javier. "Hechos 7,17-43 y las corrientes cristológices dentro de la primitiva comunidad cristiana." EstBib 33 (1974):31-62.

Colpe, Carsten. "υἱὸς τοῦ ἀνθρώπου." TDNT 8:400-77.

Conzelmann, Hans. "συνίημι." TDNT 7:888-96.

Cross, Frank M. "The History of the Biblical Text in the Light of Discoveries in the Judaean Desert." HTR 57 (1964): 281-99.

_____. "A New Qumran Biblical Fragment Related to the Original Hebrew Underlying the Septaugint." BASOR 132 (1953):15-26.

Cullmann, Oscar. "A New Approach to the Interpretation of the Fourth Gospel." ExpT 71 (1959-60):8-12; 39-43.

________. "L'opposition contre le temple de Jérusalem, motif commun de la théologie johannique et du monde ambiant." NTS 5 (1959):157-73.

Dahl, Nils A. "The Story of Abraham in Luke-Acts." In Studies (see under Keck, Leander E.), pp. 139-58.

Daniélou, Jean. "L'Etoile de Jacob et la mission chrétienne à Damas." VC 11 (1957):121-38.

Dibelius, Martin. "Paul in the Acts of the Apostles." In Studies (see under Dibelius, Martin), pp. 207-14.

________. "The Speeches in Acts and Ancient Historiography." In Studies (see under Dibelius, Martin), pp. 138-85.

Dillon, Richard J. and Fitzmyer, Joseph A. "Acts of the Apostles." In JBC (see under Brown, Raymond E.), 2:165-214.

Dockx, S. "Chronologie de la vie de Saint Paul, depuis sa conversion jusqu'à son séjour à Rome." NT 13 (1971):261-304.

______. "Date de la mort d'Etienne la Protomartyr." Bib 55 (1974):65-73.

Dupont, Jacques. "Les Discours missionaires des Actes d'après un ouvrage récent." RB 69 (1962):36-60.

______. "L'utilisation apologétique de l'ancien testament dans les discours des Actes." ETL 29 (1953):288-327.

Ellis, E. Earle. "Midrash, Targum and New Testament Quotations." In Neotestamentica et Semitica (see under Ellis, E. Earle), pp. 61-69.

______. "Midrashic Features in the Speeches of Acts." In Mélanges bibliques (see under Descamps, Albert), pp. 303-12.

______. "The Role of the Christian Prophet in Acts." In Apostolic History and the Gospel (see under Gasque, W. Ward), pp. 55-67.

Enslin, Morton S. "Once Again, Luke and Paul." ZNW 61 (1970):253-71.

Evans, Charles F. "The Kerygma." JTS 7 (1956):25-41.

______. "'Speeches' in Acts." In Mélanges bibliques (see under Descamps, Albert), pp. 287-302.

Filson, Floyd V. "The Septaugint and the New Testament." BA 9 (1946):34-42.

Fitzmyer, Joseph A. "The Contribution of Qumran Aramaic to the Study of the New Testament." NTS 20 (1974):382-407.

________. "'4Q Testimonia' and the New Testament." TS 18 (1958):513-37.

________. "Jewish Christianity in Acts in Light of the Qumran Scrolls." In Studies (see under Keck, Leander E.), pp. 233-57.

________. "The Languages of Palestine in the First Century A.D." CBQ 32 (1970):501-31.

________. "A Life of Paul." In JBC (see under Brown, Raymond E.), 2:215-22.

________. "The Use of Explicit Old Testament Quotations in Qumran Literature and in the New Testament." NTS 7 (1960-61):489-507.

Foakes Jackson, Frederick J. "Stephen's Speech in Acts." JBL 49 (1930):283-86.

Foerster, Werner. "Stephanus und die Urgemeinde." In Dienst unter dem Wort: Festgabe für H. Schreiner, pp. 9-30. Edited by Werner Foerster. Güttersloh: Bertelsmann, 1953.

Friedrich, Gerhard. "Die Gegner des Paulus im 2. Korintherbrief." In Abraham unser Vater (see under Betz, Otto), pp. 181-215.

Géoltrain, Pierre. "Esséniens et Hellénistes." TZ 16 (1959): 241-54.

Giblin, Charles H. "A Prophetic Vision of History and Things (Acts 6:8-8:3)." BT 63 (1972):994-1001.

Glombitza, Otto. "Zur Charakterisierung des Stephanus in Act 6 und 7." ZNW 53 (1962):238-44.

Goppelt, Leonhard. "τύπος." TDNT 8:246-59.

Grayston, K. "The Significance of the Word Hand in the New Testament." In Mélanges bibliques (see under Descamps, Albert), pp. 479-87.

Grundmann, Walter; Rad, Gerhard von; and Kittel, Gerhard. "ἄγγελος." TDNT 1:74-87.

Haenchen, Ernst. "The Book of Acts as Source-Material for the History of Early Christianity." In Studies (see under Keck, Leander E.), pp. 258-78.

Hanson, Richard P. C. "Studies in Texts (Acts 6.12-14)." Theology 50 (1947):142-45.

Hengel, Martin. "Zwischen Jesus und Paulus: Die 'Hellenisten,' die 'Sieben' und Stephanus (Apg 6,1-15; 7,58-8,3)." ZTK 72 (1975):157-72.

Hunkin, Joseph W. "British Work on the Acts." In *Beginnings* (see under Foakes Jackson, Frederick J.), 2:396-433.

Jeremias, Joachim. "Μωυσῆς." *TDNT* 4:848-73.

________. "Untersuchungen zum Quellenproblem der Apostelgeschichte." *ZNW* 36 (1937):205-21.

________. "Zur Geschichlichkeit des Verhörs Jesu vor dem Hohen Rat." *ZNW* 43 (1950-53):145-50.

Johnson, Sherman E. "The Septuagint and the New Testament." *JBL* 56 (1937):331-45.

Jones, C. P. M. "The Epistle to the Hebrews and the Lucan Writings." In *Studies in the Gospels* (see under Nineham, Dennis E.), pp. 113-43.

Käsemann, Ernst. "Paul and Early Catholicism." In *Essays on New Testament Themes* (see under Kasemann, Ernst), pp. 236-51.

Katz, Peter, "Septuagint Studies in the Mid-century: Their Links with the Past and Their Present Tendencies." In *New Testament and Its Eschatology* (see under Davies, William D.), pp. 176-208.

Kilpatrick, G. D. "Acts VII.52 ΕΛΕΥΣΙΣ." *JTS* 46 (1945):136-45.

Kleinknecht, Hermann; Baumgärtel, Friedrich; Bieder, Werner; Sjöberg, Erik; and Schweizer, Eduard. "πνεῦμα." *TDNT* 6:332-455.

Klijn, Albertus F. J. "Stephen's Speech-Acts VII.2-53." *NTS* 4 (1957-58):25-31.

Lampe, Geoffrey W. H. "The Holy Spirit in the Writings of St. Luke." In *Studies in the Gospels* (see under Nineham, Dennis E.), pp. 159-200.

Le Déaut, Roger. "The Current State of Targumic Studies." *BIB* 4 (1974):3-32.

Lienhard, Joseph T. "Acts 6:1-6: A Redactional View." *CBQ* 37 (1975):228-36.

Linton, Olof. "Le *Parallelismus Membrorum* dans le nouveau testament, simple remarques." In *Mélanges bibliques* (see under Descamps, Albert), pp. 489-507.

Lohse, Eduard. "Σινᾶ." *TDNT* 7:282-86.

McGiffert, Arthur C. "The Historical Criticism of Acts in Germany." In *Beginnings* (see under Foakes Jackson, Frederick J.), 2:363-95.

Marshall, I. Howard. "Recent Study of the Acts of the Apostles." *ExpT* 80 (1969):292-96.

Metzger, Bruce M. "The Early Versions of the New Testament." In Peake's Commentary (see under Black, Matthew), pp. 671-75.

_______. "The Formulas Introducing Quotations of Scripture in the NT and the Mishnah." JBL 70 (1971):297-307.

Michel, Otto. "οἶκος." TDNT 5:115-59.

Moule, Charles F. D. "The Christology of Acts." In Studies (see under Keck, Leander E.), pp. 159-85.

Mundle, Wilhelm. "Die Stephanusrede Apg. 7: eine Märtyrerapologie." ZNW 20 (1921):133-47.

Neirynck, F. "Duality in Mark." ETL 47 (1971):394-463.

_______. "Duplicate Expressions in the Gospel of Mark." ETL 48 (1972):150-209.

_______. "Mark in Greek." ETL 47 (1971):144-98.

Nestle, Eberhard. "'Sirs, ye are Brethren.'" ExpT 23 (1911-12):528.

Owen, H. P. "Stephen's Vision in Acts VII.55-6." NTS 1 (1954-55):224-26.

Payne, D. F. "Semitisms in the Book of Acts." In Apostolic History and the Gospel (see under Gasque, W. Ward), pp. 134-50.

Pelletier, André. "Une création de l'apologétique Chrétienne: μασχοποιεῖν." RSR 54 (1966):411-16.

Pohhill, John B. "The Hellenistic Breakthrough: Acts 6-12." RE 71 (1974):475-86.

Preisker, Herbert. "ἔθος." TDNT 2:372-73.

Purvis, James D. "The Fourth Gospel and the Samaritans." NT 17 (1975):161-98.

Rengstorf, Karl H. "ἀποστέλλω." TDNT 1:398-447.

[Richard, Earl. "Acts 7: An Investigation of the Samaritan Evidence." CBQ 39 (1977):190-208.]

Robinson, John A. T. "The Most Primitive Christology of All?" JTS (1956):177-89. [Also in Twelve New Testament Studies. Studies in Biblical Theology, no. 34, pp. 139-53. London: SCM Press, 1962.]

Schlier, Heinrich. "θλίβω." TDNT 3:139-48.

Schoeps, Hans-Joachim. "Die ebionitioche Wahrheit des Christentums." In The Background of the New Testament (see under Davies, William D.), pp. 115-23.

________. "Das Judenchristentum in den Parteienkämpfen der alten Kirche." In Aspects du Judéo-Christianism (see under Aspects), pp. 53-75.

Schmidt, Karl L. "ἀπωθέω." TDNT 1:448.

________. "διασπορά." TDNT 2:98-104.

Schmidt, Karl L; Schmidt, Martin A.; and Meyer, Rudolf. "πάροικος." TDNT 5:84-54.

Schultz, Joseph P. "Angelic Opposition to the Ascension of Moses and the Revelation of the Law." JQR 61 (1970-71): 282-307.

Schweizer, Eduard. "Concerning the Speeches." In Studies (see under Keck, Leander E.), pp. 186-93.

________. "The Son of Man." JBL 79 (1960):119-29.

Scobie, C. H. H. "The Origins and Development of Samaritan Christianity." NTS 19 (1972-73):390-400.

Scott, J. Julius. "Stephen's Speech: A Possible Method for Luke's Historical Method?" JETS 17 (1974):91-97.

Scroggs, Robin. "The Earliest Hellenistic Christianity." In Religions in Antiquity (see under Neusner, Jacob), pp. 176-206.

Skehan, Patrick W. "Exodus in the Samaritan Recension from Qumran." JBL 74 (1955):182-87.

Skehan, Patrick W.; MacRae, George W.; and Brown, Raymond E. "Texts and Versions." In JBC (see under Brown, Raymond E.), 2:561-89.

Smith, T. C. "The Significance of the Stephen Episode in Acts." In Society of Biblical Literature: 1975 Seminar Papers, 2:15-26. Edited by George MacRae. Missoula, Montana: Scholars Press, 1975.

Soltau, Wilhelm. "Die Herkunft der Reden in der Apostelgeschichte." ZNW 4 (1903):128-54.

Sparks, Hedley F. D. "The Semitisms of the Acts." JTS 1 (1950):16-28.

Spiro, Abraham. "Stephen's Samaritan Background." In The Acts of the Apostles (see under Munck, Johannes), pp. 285-300.

Unnik, Willem C. van. "Luke-Acts, A Storm Center in Contemporary Scholarship." In Studies (see under Keck, Leander E.), pp. 15-32.

Vielhauer, Philipp. "On the 'Paulinism' of Acts." In Studies (see under Keck, Leander E.), pp. 35-50.

Wendt, Hans H. "Die Hauptquelle der Apostelgeschichte." ZNW 24 (1925):293-305.

Wevers, John W. "Proto-Septuagint Studies." In The Seed of Wisdom (see under McCullough, W. S.), pp. 58-77.

Wilckens, Ulrich and Fohrer, Georg. "σοφία." TDNT 7:465-528.

Windisch, Hans. "Ἕλλην." In TDNT 2:504-16.